Stata Programming Manual
Release 7

Stata Press
College Station, Texas

Stata Press, 4905 Lakeway Drive, College Station, Texas 77845

The suggested citation for this software is

StataCorp. 2001. *Stata Statistical Software: Release 7.0*. College Station, TX: Stata Corporation.

Contents of Programming Manual

Subject Table of Contents

This is a subset of the Subject Table of Contents of the *Reference Manual* and the complete contents for this manual.

Data manipulation and management

Functions and expressions

Utilities

Basic utilities

Error messages

Saved results

Internet

Data types and memory

Advanced utilities

Matrix commands

Basics

Programming

Other

Programming

Basics

Program control

Parsing and program arguments

Console output

Title

intro — Introduction to programming manual

Description

This entry describes the *Stata Programming Manual*.

Remarks

Some commands are documented in this manual, and some are documented in the *Stata Reference Manual*. In this manual, you will find

1. Stata's matrix-manipulation commands,

2. commands for programming Stata,

3. commands and discussions of interest to programmers,

4. commands that are of such a technical nature that you would nearly have to be a programmer to use them, even if they have nothing to do with programming (e.g., **hexdump**).

This manual is arranged alphabetically, like the *Reference Manual*.

The *User's Guide* also contains a chapter on programming Stata; see [U] **21 Programming Stata**. To learn about writing your own maximum-likelihood estimation commands, we recommend the book *Maximum-likelihood Estimation with Stata*. For an up-to-date list of books about Stata, visit the Stata bookstore at http://www.stata.com/bookstore.

We also recommend the Stata NetCourses^{TM}. At the time that this introduction was written, our current offering of Stata programming NetCourses included

NC-151 An introduction to Stata programming
NC-152 Advanced Stata programming
NC-200 Maximum-likelihood estimation with Stata

To learn more about NetCourses and to view the current offerings of NetCourses, visit http://www.stata.com/info/products/netcourse.

What's new, programming-wise, in Stata 7

1. The first thing you will notice is that names are now allowed to be 32 characters long (local macro names are allowed to be 31 characters). The new limit applies to variable names, label names, program names, saved results, macros, matrices, and everything else. The longer variable names are especially useful for program and subroutine names.

A side effect of this is that you do not want casually to change an old, working program from being declared **version 6** to **version 7**; it may very well stop working. Old programs can use long variable names (and program names, etc.) just as can new programs, so there is no reason to change the **version** statement. The reason for not changing the **version** statement has to do with macros. Pretend that you have an option **generate()** to your old command. Then previously, **syntax** would put the contents of the option, when specified, in the macro `generat´, `generat´ because local macro names could be only 7 characters long in Stata 6. In **version 7** programs, the contents would go into the macro named `generate´. So, if you changed your working program from **version 6** to **version 7**, you would have to change all your references of `generat´ to `generate´.

Moreover, in your old version 6 program, you could refer to the macro `generate´, and that was the same as referring to `generat´ because the macro expander paid attention to only the first 7 characters. Under version 7, `generate´ and `generat´ are different macros.

It is easier simply not to change the **version**. Stata handles everything under version control, so you do not have to worry about any of this. There is no speed penalty for running a **version 6** program, and you can use long variable names with both **version 6** and **version 7** programs.

2. You should learn about the new **abbrev()** function. In writing programs, you do not want to leave 32 characters for displaying names, and **abbrev()** supplies the solution. **abbrev(**s,n**)** returns an n-character abbreviation of name s. In our output, we try to leave 12 characters for names, and so use **abbrev(**s**,12)**.

Concerning your old programs, while they will work with long variable names, if they format for themselves any output incorporating variable names, that output will probably be misaligned when long variable names are used. Results will still be readable, but if you want to fix the problem, we recommend finding the places where variable names are displayed and then displaying **abbrev("**`varname´**",8)**, since your old program probably left eight spaces for names. **abbrev()** can be used in **version 6** (and earlier) programs.

As an aside, it is no longer an error to have '**display** ... **_skip(**_negative number_**)** ...' or '**display** ... **_col(**_negative number_**)** ...'. This change was made so that old ado-files will at least work with long variable names. Ado-files often calculate how many spaces to display in front of or after names in order to align results and, with long variable names, these programs sometimes calculate negative skip amounts.

3. '`~`' is the new abbreviate character. For instance, say that **rep~1978** refers to a variable named **repair_record_in_1978**. The new '`~`' is very much like '`*`'—it says that 0 or more characters go here. Unlike '`*`', it also asserts that only one variable name will match the abbreviated form.

4. Stata's wildcard expansion for varlists now allows '`*`' to be used anywhere: **rep***, **rep***1978, ***1978**, and even ***, the last of which means **_all**.

5. SMCL is Stata's new output processor. All output goes through SMCL, and SMCL can create some wonderful special effects including solid lines in and around tables. One of its more interesting capabilities is the ability to create clickable links in your output. You can even program things so that you display some output and, should the user click on a certain part of the output, some other Stata command executes. SMCL is very important to programmers; see [P] **smcl**.

SMCL has so many useful capabilities that you may want to go back and modify your old programs. You will quickly discover that **display**, running under version control, bypasses SMCL. **display** does this so that old programs continue to work in the anticipated way. Do _not_ change the version number at the top of old programs, for the reason explained in (1) above. Instead, code **display in smcl** for your old **display** statements. That will give you all the new features without having to translate the rest of your program.

6. Going along with SMCL, you are no longer supposed to code **in green**, **in yellow**, etc., on your **display** statements. You can continue to code that, even in modern programs, but you should code **as text** (for green), **as result** (for yellow), **as error** (for red), and **as input** (for white). The color blue is now gone; in your old programs, **in blue** will display in green (which is to say, **as text**). Blue is now reserved for links; see (5) above. See [P] **display** for more information.

7. Programs no longer need to leave datasets in a different sort order from which they started just because the program needs to change the sort order in the midst of calculation. The jargon for this is "sort stable". A program is sort stable if it does not change the sort order of the data. All current Stata commands have been made sort stable except, of course, for the obvious ones,

such as `sort`. You can easily change your programs to be sort stable, too, by adding the option `sortpreserve` to their `program define` statements; see [P] **sortpreserve**.

`egen` is now sort stable. We mention that because we have seen a few programs that depend on the changed order in which `egen` used to leave the data, and this behavior is not mimicked under version control. `egen` now leaves the data in the order in which it found them. If, when running an old program, you get an unexpected "not sorted" error message, check whether you are using `egen` and then add the necessary `sort` command after the `egen`. Also, think about adding `sortpreserve` to the top so that your program will now be sort stable.

8. Ado-files (programs) can be made to work with `by` *varlist*:. The jargon for this is "byable"; a program is byable if it works with the `by` prefix. We have modified all our ado-files to be byable, and you can modify your programs, too. In most cases, it's as easy as adding `byable(recall)` to the `program define` line. See [P] **byable**.

There is a new `noby` option on `mark` and `marksample`. This has to do with how `byable()` works. In a `byable(recall)` program, `mark` and `marksample` know to restrict themselves to the current by-group. `noby` prevents this. We have not yet seen a program that needed `noby`. See [P] **mark**.

9. `by` *varlist*: has a new syntax of special interest to programmers:

$$\text{by } \textit{varlist}_1 \ (\textit{varlist}_2): \ \ldots$$

The above verifies that the data are sorted by *varlist*$_1$ *varlist*$_2$ and then performs the same action that `by` *varlist*$_1$: would perform. The idea is this: You are about to make a calculation `by` `id` but, in making that calculation, you are assuming that, within `id`, the data are sorted by `time`. Now you can code

```
by `id' (`time'): generate ...
```

The advantage is that, if you are wrong about the data being sorted by `time` within `id`, Stata will issue a "not sorted" error message and stop your program, rather than letting it continue to calculate an incorrect result. `by` also has a new `sort` option, so you can type

```
by `id' (`time'), sort: generate ...
```

which would sort the data by `id` `time` and then perform the action `by` `id`. The `sort` option is cute, but it only saves a step:

```
sort `id' `time'
by `id' (`time'): generate ...
```

`by`'s new parentheses notation can save you from making an error.

10. The new `confirm names` (`names` is new, not `confirm`) verifies that what follows, follows Stata's naming syntax—which is to say, starts with a letter or underscore and thereafter contains letters, underscores, or digits—and is not too long.

In our own ado-files, we found instances where a new variable name was obtained from the user, say, by a user-specified option and, being thorough, we checked that the length of the name was not greater than 8. Stata now allows longer names, so we wanted to change those lines. In the process, we found it easier and more thorough to use `confirm name`.

11. The new `foreach` command is an alternative to `while`, and is a command well worth learning. It is not only more readable, but is faster for doing things such as stepping through a varlist. Using `foreach`, rather than code

```
tokenize `varlist'
while "`1'"~="" {
        ... `1' ...
        mac shift
}
```

you code

```
foreach x in local varlist {
        ... `1´ ...
}
```

See [P] **foreach**.

12. The new `forvalues` is another alternative to `while` that is useful for stepping through numeric values. Using `forvalues`, rather than code

```
local i = 1
while `i´ <= `n´ {
        ... `i´ ...
local i = `i´ + 1
}
```

you code

```
foreach i = 1(1)`n´ {
        ... `i´ ...
}
```

See [P] **forvalues**.

13. The new `continue` (and `continue, break`) command allows you to continue out of, or break out of, `while`, `forvalues`, and `foreach` loops; see [P] **continue**.

14. `version` has picked up an additional syntax which is sometimes useful:

version #:   *anycommand* ...

executes *anycommand* under the specified version. See [P] **version**.

15. The new `hexdump` command will give you a hexadecimal dump of files. Even more useful is its `analyze` option, which will analyze the dump for you and just report the summary. This can be useful for diagnosing problems with raw datasets. See [P] **hexdump**.

16. Stata's density and distribution functions have been renamed. First, all the old names continue to work, even when not documented in the manual, at least under version control. The new standard, however, is, if X is the name of a distribution, then

Xden()	is its density
X()	is its cumulative distribution
inv$X$()	is its inverse cumulative
Xtail()	is its reverse cumulative
inv$X$tail()	is its inverse reverse cumulative

Not all functions necessarily exist and, if they do not, that is not solely due to laziness on our part. In particular, concerning the choice between X() and inv$X$(), the functions exist that we have accurately implemented. In theory, you only need one because Xtail() $= 1 - X$(), but in practice, the one-minus subtraction wipes out lots of accuracy. If one really wants an accurate right-tail or left-tail probability, one needs a separately written Xtail() or X() routine, written from the ground up.

Anyway, forget everything you ever knew about Stata's distribution functions. Here is the new set:

`normden()`	same as old `normd()`
`norm()`	same as old `normprob()`
`invnorm()`	same as old `invnorm()`
`chi2()`	related to old `chiprob()`; see below
`invchi2()`	related to old `invchi()`; see below
`chi2tail()`	related to old `chiprob()`
`invchi2tail()`	related to old `invchi()`
`F()`	related to old `fprob()`
`invF()`	related to old `invfprob()`
`Ftail()`	same as old `fprob()`
`invFtail()`	equal to old `invfprob()`
`ttail()`	related to old `tprob()`; see below
`invttail()`	related to old `invt()`; see below
`nchi2()`	equal to old `nchi()`
`invnchi2()`	equal to old `invnchi()`
`npnchi2()`	equal to old `npnchi()`

We want to emphasize that if a function exists, it is calculated accurately. To wit, `F()` accurately calculates left tails, and `Ftail()` accurately calculates right tails; `Ftail()` is far more accurate than $1 - \mathtt{F}()$.

There is no `normtail()` function. The accurate way to calculate left-tail probabilities ($z < 0$) is `norm(z)`. The accurate way to calculate right-tail probabilities ($z > 0$) is `norm(-z)`.

Nothing has been done about renaming `Binomial()` and `invbinomial()`. Those two names remain unchanged.

All the old functions still exist, but in two cases, they work only under version control: The old `invt()`, under the new naming logic, ought to be the inverse of the cumulative, but is not, so `invt()` goes into forced retirement for a release or two. It works if `version` is set to 6 or before, but otherwise you get the error "unknown function invt()". Similarly, the old `invchi()` goes into forced retirement because it is too close to the new name `invchi2()`.

Concerning translating old code, should you wish to undertake that (it is not necessary), here are the ones where changes other than to the name are required:

old code:	new code
`chiprob(`a`, `b`)`	`1-chi2(`a`, `b`)`
`invchi(`a`, `b`)`	`invchi2(`a`, 1-`b`)`
`tprob(`a`, `b`)`	`2*ttail(`a`, abs(`b`))`
`invt(`a`, `b`)`	`invttail(`a`, (1-`b`)/2)`

17. There are new string functions: `match()`, `subinstr()`, `subinword()`, and `reverse()`.

`match(`s_1`,`s_2`)` returns 1 if string s_1 "matches" s_2. In the match, `*` in s_2 is understood to mean zero or more characters go here, and `?` is understood to mean one character goes here. `match("this","*hi*")` is true. In s_2, `\\`, `\?`, and `\*` can be used if you really want a `\`, `?`, or `*` character.

`subinstr(`s_1`,`s_2`,`s_3`,`n`)` and `subinword(`s_1`,`s_2`,`s_3`,`n`)` substitute the first n occurrences of s_2 in s_1 with s_3. `subinword()` restricts "occurrences" to be occurrences of words. In either, n may be coded as missing value, meaning to substitute all occurrences. For instance, `subinword("measure me","me","you",.)` returns "measure you", and `subinstr("measure me","me","you",.)` returns "youasure you".

`reverse(`s`)` returns s turned around. `reverse("string")` returns "gnirts".

18. The new `inrange()` function handles missing values elegantly for selecting subsamples such as $a \leq x \leq b$. `inrange(x,a,b)` answers the question, "Is a known to be in the range a to b?" Obviously, `inrange(.,1000,2000)` is false. a or b may be missing. `inrange(x,a,.)` answers whether it is known that $x \geq a$, and `inrange(x,.,b)` answers whether it is known that $x \leq b$. `inrange(.,.,.)` returns 0 which, if you think about it, is inconsistent but is probably what you want.

19. The new `inlist(x,a,b,...)` function elegantly handles selecting samples if $x = a$, or $x = b$, or ....

20. `estimates hold` has two new options and one new behavior.

    The new behavior is that if estimates are held under a temporary name, they are now automatically discarded when the program terminates.

    The new `restore` option schedules the held estimates for automatic restoration on program termination. The new `not` option to `estimates unhold` cancels the previously scheduled restoration.

    The new `copy` option to `estimates hold` copies the current estimates rather than moving them. `estimates hold, copy` leaves the current estimates in place and makes a copy for later restoration. `copy` may be used with or without `restore`.

21. The new macro extended function : $\{r|e|s\}(\{scalars|macros|matrices|functions\})$ returns the names of all the saved results of the indicated type. For instance, `local x : e(scalars)` returns the names of all the scalars currently stored in `e()`.

22. *numlist* now allows the syntax $a[b]c$ as well as $a(b)c$, because too many users wanted to type ranges using square brackets.

23. `display` has the new directive `_char(#)` for $1 \leq \# \leq 255$. For instance, 'display `_char(12)`' would display a control-L (followed by a newline character). This is unimportant since that feature is also duplicated in SMCL. `display "{c 12}"` would do the same thing.

24. Stata has a new `cluster` command for performing cluster analysis, and that command can be extended by user-written routines. See [P] **cluster subroutines** and [P] **cluster utilities**.

25. The new commands `_rmcoll` and `_rmdcoll` assist in removing collinear variables from varlists; see [P] **_rmcoll**.

26. Stata's numeric formats `%g`, `%f`, and `%e` will now display ',' for decimal points. For instance, `%9,2f` is the same as `%9.2f`, except that one and one-half would display as 1,50.

27. Stata's `.dta` dataset format has changed to accommodate the new, longer names. Specify `save`'s `old` option if you need to create datasets in Stata 6 format.

28. The default value of `adosize` is now 128, meaning that more memory is now allocated to Stata's ado-files.

29. Ado-files execute between 8.8% and 11.8% faster. Some programs, we have observed, execute 13% faster.

For a complete list of all new features in Stata 7, see [U] **1.3 What's new**.

Also See

Complementary:	[U] **21 Programming Stata**, *Maximum Likelihood Estimation with Stata*
Background:	[R] **intro**

Title

| assert — Verify truth of claim |

Syntax

assert *exp* [if *exp*] [in *range*] [, rc0]

by ... : may be used with assert; see [R] **by**.

Description

assert verifies that *exp* is true. If it is, the command produces no output. If it is not, assert informs you that the "assertion is false" and issues a return code of 9; see [U] **11 Error messages and return codes**.

Options

rc0 forces a return code of 0 even if the assertion is false.

Remarks

assert is seldom used interactively since it is easier to use inspect, summarize or tabulate to look for evidence of errors in the dataset. These commands, however, require that you review the output to spot the error. assert is useful because it tells Stata not only what to do, but what you can expect to find. Groups of assertions are often combined in a do-file to certify data. If the do-file runs all the way through without complaining, every assertion in the file is true.

```
. do myassert
. use trans, clear
(xplant data)
. assert sex=="m" | sex=="f"
. assert packs==0 if ~smoker
. assert packs>0 if smoker
. sort patient date
. by patient: assert sex==sex[_n-1] if _n>1
. by patient: assert abs(bp-bp[_n-1]) < 20 if bp~=. & bp[_n-1]~=.
. by patient: assert died==0 if _n~=_N
. by patient: assert died==0 | died==1 if _n==_N
. by patient: assert n_xplant==0 | n_xplant==1 if _n==_N
. assert inval==int(inval)
.
.
end of do-file
```

▷ Example

You receive data from Bob, a co-worker. He has been working on this data for some time and it has now been delivered to you for analysis. Before analyzing the data, you (smartly) verify that the data are as Bob claims. In Bob's memo, he claims that (1) the dataset reflects the earnings of 522 employees, (2) the earnings are only for full-time employees, (3) the variable `female` is coded 1 for female and 0 otherwise, and (4) the variable `exp` contains the number of years, or fraction thereof, on the job. You assemble the following do-file:

```
use frombob, clear
assert _N==522
assert sal>=6000 & sal<=125000
assert female==1 | female==0
gen work=sum(female==1)
assert work[_N]>0
replace work=sum(female==0)
assert work[_N]>0
drop work
assert exp>=0 & exp<=40
```

Let's go through these assertions one by one. After using the data, you assert that _N equals 522. Remember, _N reflects the total number of observations in the dataset; see [U] **16.4 System variables (_variables)**. Bob said it was 522, so you check it. Bob's second claim was that the data are for only full-time employees. You know that everybody in your company makes a salary between $6,000 and $125,000, so you check that the salary figures are within this range. Bob's third assertion was that the `female` variable was coded zero or one.

You add something more. You know your company employs both males and females, so you check that there are some of each. You create a variable called `work` equal to the running sum of female observations and then verify that the last observation of this variable is greater than zero. You then repeat the process for males and discard the `work` variable. Finally, you verify that the `exp` variable is never negative and never larger than 40.

You save the above file as `check.do` and here is what happens when you run it:

```
. do check
. use frombob, clear
(5/21 data)
. assert _N==522
. assert sal>6000 & sal<=125000
14 contradictions in 522 observations
assertion is false
r(9);
end of do-file
r(9);
```

Everything went fine until you checked the salary variable, and then Stata told you that there were 14 contradictions to your assertion and stopped the do-file. Seeing this, you now interactively `summarize` the `sal` variable and discover that 14 people have missing salaries. You dash off a memo to Bob asking him why these data are missing.
◁

▷ Example

Bob responds quickly. There was a mistake in reading the salaries for the consumer relations division. He says it's fixed. You believe him, but check with your do-file again. This time you type `run` instead of `do`, suppressing all the output:

```
. run check
. _
```

Even though you suppressed the output, if there had been any contradictions, the messages would have printed. check.do ran fine, so all its assertions are true.

◁

❑ Technical Note

assert is especially useful when you are processing large amounts of data in a do-file and wish to verify that all is going as expected. The error in this case may not be in the data but in the do-file itself. For instance, your do-file is rolling along and it has just merged two datasets that it created by subsetting some other data. If everything has gone right so far, then every observation should have merged. When you are performing merge interactively, we recommend that you tabulate _merge to verify that the expected happened. In a do-file, we recommend you include the line

        assert _merge==3

to verify the correctness of the merge. If all the observations did not merge, the assertion will be false and your do-file will stop.

As another example, you are combining data from numerous sources and you know that after the first two datasets are combined, every individual's sex should be defined. So you include the line

        assert sex~=.

in your do-file. Experienced Stata users include lots of assertions in their do-files when they process data.

❑

❑ Technical Note

assert is smart in how it evaluates expressions. When you say something like assert _N==522 or assert work[_N]>0, assert knows that the expression need be evaluated only once. When you say assert female==1 | female==0, assert knows that the expression needs to be evaluated once for each observation in the dataset.

Here are some more examples demonstrating assert's intelligence.

        by female: assert _N==100

asserts that there should be 100 observations for every unique value of female. The expression is evaluated once per by-group.

        by female: assert work[_N]>0

asserts that the last observation on work in every by-group should be greater than zero. It is evaluated once per by-group.

        by female: assert work>0

is evaluated once for each observation in the dataset and, in that sense, is formally equivalent to assert work>0. It is different in that, if there are any contradictions, it will tell you in which by-group the contradiction occurs.

❑

Also See

Complementary:	[P] **capture**, [P] **confirm**
Background:	[U] **19 Do-files**

Title

> **break** — Suppress Break key

Syntax

> nobreak *stata_command*
>
> break *stata_command*

Typical usage is

> nobreak {
>
>   ...
>
>   capture noisily break ...
>
>   ...
>
> }

Description

nobreak temporarily turns off recognition of the *Break* key. It is seldom used. break temporarily reestablishes recognition of the *Break* key within a nobreak block. It is even more seldom used.

Remarks

Stata commands honor the *Break* key. This honoring is automatic and, for the most part, requires no special code as long as you follow these guidelines:

1. Obtain names for new variables from tempvar; see [U] **21.7.1 Temporary variables**.

2. Obtain names for other memory aggregates such as scalars and matrices from tempname; see [U] **21.7.2 Temporary scalars and matrices**.

3. If you need to temporarily change the user's data, use preserve to save it first; see [U] **21.6 Temporarily destroying the data in memory**.

4. Obtain names for temporary files from tempfile; see [U] **21.7.3 Temporary files**.

If you follow these guidelines, your program will be robust to the user pressing *Break* because Stata itself will be able to put things back as they were.

Still, there are instances when a program must commit to executing a group of commands that, were *Break* honored in the midst of the group, the user's data would be left in an intermediate, undefined state. nobreak is for those instances.

▷ Example

You are writing a program and following all the guidelines listed above. In particular, you are using temporary variables. There is a point in your program, however, where you wish to list the first five values of the temporary variable and you would like, temporarily, to give the variable a pretty name, so you temporarily rename it. If the user were to press *Break* during the period the variable is renamed, however, Stata would not know to drop it and it would be left behind in the user's data. You wish to avoid this. In the code fragment below, `myv´ is the temporary variable:

```
nobreak {
        rename `myv´ Result
        list Result in 1/5
        rename Result `myv´
}
```

It would not be appropriate to code the fragment as

```
nobreak rename `myv´ Result
nobreak list Result in 1/5
nobreak rename Result `myv´
```

because the user might press *Break* during the periods between the commands.

◁

❏ Technical Note

It is unlikely that you will ever use **break** since it is only of use to those writing replacement command interpreters for Stata. Nevertheless, here is an example of how **nobreak** might be used.

There is a version of Stata for undergraduate teaching called StataQuest, which is, by comparison with Stata, limited but it does have a fancy menu system. StataQuest was written as a set of ado-files. These ado-files amount to a front-end interpreter for Stata. Early on in the initialization process, the *Break* key is turned off so that, should the student press *Break*, it does not abort the StataQuest system itself. Basically, the main driver of StataQuest is

```
program define Quest
        ( initialization code )
        nobreak {
                SQ_sys
        }
        ( closeout code )
end
```

SQ_sys.ado contains the guts of the StataQuest system and, while it is running, the *Break* key is ignored. Now, deep within **SQ_sys** it periodically executes a command on behalf of the student. Perhaps the student has asked to list the data. We want to honor the *Break* key during these periods so that, if the student presses *Break*, the listing is aborted. This code fragment reads

```
...
capture noisily break `cmd´
if _rc {
        ( process error or break condition )
}
...
```

When we execute the command `cmd´ on the student's behalf, we must anticipate that something could go wrong; thus, we capture the return code. **capture** turns off command output, so we use **noisily** to restore it. Finally, we turn the *Break* key back on for the duration of this command.

❏

Also See

Complementary: [P] **capture**

Background: [U] **12 The Break key**

Title

> **byable** — Make programs byable

Description

This entry discusses the writing of programs so that they will allow the use of Stata's **by** *varlist*: prefix. If you take no special actions and write the program myprog, then **by** *varlist*: cannot be used with it:

```
. by foreign:  myprog
myprog may not be combined with by
r(190);
```

By reading this section, you will learn how to modify your program so that **by** does work with it:

```
. by foreign:  myprog
```

```
-> foreign = Domestic
```
(*output for first by-group appears*)

```
-> foreign = Foreign
```
output for first by-group appears)

```
. _
```

Remarks

Remarks are presented under the headings

> *byable(recall) programs*
> *The use of sort in byable(recall) programs*
> *Byable estimation commands*
> *byable(onecall) programs*
> *The use of sort by byable(onecall) programs*
> *Combining byable(onecall) with byable(recall)*
> *The by-group header*

If you have not read [P] **sortpreserve**, please do so soon; it is relevant.

Programs that are written to be used with **by** *varlist*: are said to be "byable". Byable programs do not require the use of **by** *varlist*:; they merely allow it. There are two ways that programs can be made to be byable, known as **byable(recall)** and **byable(onecall)**.

byable(recall) is easy to use and is sufficient for programs that report the results of calculation (class-1 programs as defined in [P] **sortpreserve**). **byable(recall)** is the method most commonly used to make programs byable.

byable(onecall) is more work to program and is intended for use in all other cases (class-2 and class-3 programs as defined in [P] **sortpreserve**).

byable(recall) programs

Pretend that you already have written a program (ado-file) and that it works; it merely does not allow `by`. If your program reports the results of calculations (think `summarize`, `regress`, and most of the oher statistical commands), then probably all you have to do to make your program byable is add the option `byable(recall)` to its `program define` statement. For instance, if your program's `program define` statement currently reads

```
program define myprog, rclass sortpreserve
       ...
end
```

change it to read

```
program define myprog, rclass sortpreserve byable(recall)
       ...
end
```

The only change you should need to make is to add `byable(recall)` to the `program define` statement. Adding `byable(recall)` will be the only change required if

1. Your program leaves behind no newly created variables. Your program might create temporary variables in the midst of calculation, but it must not leave behind new variables for the user. If your program has a `generate()` option, for instance, some extra effort will be required.

2. Your program uses `marksample` or `mark` to restrict itself to the relevant subsample of the data. If your program does not use `marksample` or `mark`, some extra effort will be required.

Here is how `byable(recall)` works: If your program is invoked with a `by` *varlist*: prefix, your program will be executed K times, where K is the number of by-groups formed by the by-variables. Each time your program is executed, `marksample` will know to mark out the observations that are not being used in the current by-group.

Therein is the reason for the two guidelines on when you only need to include `byable(recall)` to make `by` *varlist*: work:

1. If your program creates permanent, new variables, then it will create those variables when it is executed for the first by-group, meaning that those variables will already exist when it is executed for the second by-group, causing your program to issue an error message.

2. If your program does not use `marksample` to identify the relevant subsample of the data, then each time it is executed, it will use too many observations—it will not honor the by-group—and so will produce what are incorrect results.

There are ways around both problems, and here is more than you need:

(Continued on next page)

function `_by()`	takes no arguments returns 0 when program is not being by'd returns 1 when program is being by'd
function `_bylastcall()`	takes no arguments returns 1 when program is not being by'd returns 1 when program is being by'd and is being called with the last by-group returns 0 otherwise
function `_byindex()`	takes no arguments returns 1 when program is not being by'd returns 1, 2, ... when by'd and 1st call, 2nd call, ...

macro `` `_byindex´ ``	contains nothing when program is not being by'd
	contains name of temporary variable when program is being by'd
	    variable contains 1, 2, ..., for each observation in data
	    recorded value indicates to which by-group
	    each observation belongs

macro `` `_byvars´ ``	contains nothing when program is not being by'd contains names of the actual by-variables otherwise

So let's consider the problems one at a time, beginning with the second problem. Your program does not use `marksample` and we will assume that your program has good reason for not doing so, because the easy fix would be to use `marksample`. Still, your program must somehow be determining which observations to use, and we will assume that you are creating a `` `touse´ `` temporary variable containing 0 if the observation is to be omitted from the analysis and 1 if it is to be used. Somewhere, early in your program, you are setting the `` `touse´ `` variable. Right after that, make the following addition (shown in bold):

```
program define ..., ... byable(recall)
        ...
        if _by() {
                quietly replace `touse´ = 0 if `_byindex´ ~= _byindex()
        }
        ...
end
```

The fix is easy: you ask if you are being by'd and, if so, you set `` `touse´ `` to 0 in all observations for which the value of `` `byindex´ `` is not equal to the by-group you are currently considering, namely `_byindex()`.

The first problem is also easy to fix. Pretend that your program has a `generate`(*newvar*) option. Ergo, your code must contain

```
program define ..., ...
        ...
        if "`generate´" != "" {
                ...
        }
        ...
end
```

Change the program to read

```
program define ..., ... byable(recall)
        ...
        if "`generate'" != "" & _bylastcall() {
                ...
        }
        ...
end
```

Note that `_bylastcall()` will be 1 (meaning true) whenever your program is not being by'd and, when it is being by'd, when the program is being executed for the last by-group. The result is that the new variable will be created containing only the values for the last by-group, but, with a few exceptions, that is how all of Stata works. Alternatives are discussed under `byable(onecall)`.

All the other macros and functions that are available are for creating special effects and are rarely used in `byable(recall)` programs.

The use of sort in byable(recall) programs

You may use `sort` freely within `byable(recall)` programs and, in fact, you can use any other Stata command you wish; there are simply no issues. You may even use `sortpreserve` to restore the sort order at the conclusion of your program; see [P] **sortpreserve**.

We will discuss the issue of `sort` in depth just to convince you that there is nothing with which you must be concerned.

When a `byable(recall)` program receives control and is being by'd, the data are guaranteed to be sorted by `` `_byvars' `` only when `_byindex()` $= 1$—only on the first call. If the program re-sorts the data, the data will remain resorted on the second and subsequent calls even if `sortpreserve` is specified. This may sound like a problem, but it is not. `sortpreserve` is not being ignored; the data will be restored to their original order after the final call to your program. Let's go through the two cases: either your program uses `sort` or it does not.

1. If your program finds it necessary to use `sort`, it will probably need a different sort order for each by-group. For instance, a typical program that uses `sort` will include lines such as

   ```
   sort `touse' `id' ...
   ```

   and so move the relevant sample to the top of the dataset. Note that this `byable(recall)` program makes no reference to the `` `_byvars' `` themselves, nor does it do anything differently when the by prefix is specified and when it is not. That is typical; it is a rare `byable(recall)` program that finds it necessary to refer to the `` `_byvars' `` directly.

   In any case, since this program is sorting the data explicitly every time it is called (and we know it must be because `byable(recall)` programs are executed once for each by-group), there is no reason for Stata to waste its time restoring a sort order that will just be undone anyway. The original sort order only needs to be reestablished after the final call.

2. The other alternative is that the program does not use `sort`. In that case, it is free to exploit that the data are sorted on `` `_byvars' ``. Because the data will be sorted on the first call, the program does no `sort`s, so the data will be sorted on the second call, and so on. It is a rare `byable(recall)` program that would exploit the sort order, but the program is free to do so.

Byable estimation commands

Estimation commands are natural candidates for the `byable(recall)` approach. There is, however, one issue that requires special attention. Estimation commands really have two syntaxes: One at the time of estimation

[by *varlist*:] *estcmd varlist* ... [, *estimation_options replay_options*]

and another for redisplaying results:

estcmd [, *replay_options*]

With estimation commands, `by` is not allowed when results are redisplayed. This is what we must arrange for in our program and that is easy enough. The general outline for an estimation command is

```
program define estcmd, ...
        if replay() {
                if "`e(cmd)´"~="estcmd" { error 301 }
                syntax [, replay_options ]
        }
        else {
                syntax ... [, estimation_options replay_options ]
                ... estimation logic. . .
        }
        . . . display logic. . .
```

and to this, we make the changes shown in bold:

```
program define estcmd, ... byable(recall)
        if replay() {
                if "`e(cmd)´"~="estcmd" { error 301 }
                if _by() { error 190 }
                syntax [, replay options ]
        }
        else {
                syntax ... [, estimation options replay options ]
                . . . estimation logic. . .
        }
        . . . display logic. . .
```

In addition to adding `byable(recall)`, we add the line

```
                if _by() { error 190 }
```

in the case where we have been asked to redisplay results. If we are being by'd (if _by() is true), then we issue error 190 (request may not be combined with by).

byable(onecall) programs

`byable(onecall)` is more work to use. We strongly recommend using `byable(recall)` whenever possible.

The main use of `byable(onecall)` is to create programs such as **generate** and **egen**, which allow the `by` prefix, but which operate on all the data and create a new variable containing results for all the different by-groups.

`byable(onecall)` programs are, as the name implies, executed only once. The `byable(onecall)` program is responsible for handling all the issues concerning the `by`, and it is expected to do that using

function `_by()`	takes no arguments
	returns 0 when program is not being by'd
	returns 1 when program is being by'd
macro `` `_byvars' ``	contains nothing when program is not being by'd
	contains names of the actual by-variables otherwise
macro `` `_byrc0' ``	contains nothing or "rc0"
	contains "rc0" if by's rc0 option was specified

In `byable(onecall)` programs, you are responsible for everything, including the output of by-group headers, if you want them.

The typical candidates for `byable(onecall)` are programs that do something special and odd with the by-variables. We offer the following guidelines:

1. Ignore that you are going to make your program byable when you first write it. Instead, include a `by()` option on your program. Since your program cannot be coded using `byable(recall)`, you already know that the by-variables are intertangled with the logic of your routine. Make your program work.

2. Now go back and modify your program. Include `byable(onecall)` on the `program define` line. Remove the `by(varlist)` from your `syntax` statement and, immediately after the `syntax` statement, add the line

   `local by "`_byvars'"`

3. Test your program. If it worked before, it will still work now. To use what was the `by()` option, you put the `by` *varlist*: prefix out front.

4. Ignore the macro `` `_byrc0' ``. It is a rare byable program that does anything different when the user specifies by's `rc0` option.

The use of sort by byable(onecall) programs

You may use `sort` freely within `byable(onecall)` programs. You may even use `sortpreserve` to restore the sort order at the conclusion of your program.

When a `byable(onecall)` program receives control and is being by'd, the data are guaranteed to be sorted by `` `_byvars' ``.

Combining byable(onecall) with byable(recall)

One use of `byable(onecall)` is as an interface to other byable programs. Let's pretend that you are writing a command—we will call it `switcher`—that calls one of two other commands based perhaps on some aspect of what the user typed or, perhaps, based on what was previously estimated. The rule by which `switcher` decides to call one or the other does not matter for this discussion; what is important is that `switcher` switches between what we will call `prog1` and `prog2`. `prog1` and `prog2` might be actual Stata commands, or Stata commands that you have written, or even subroutines of `switcher`.

We will further imagine that `prog1` and `prog2` have been implemented using the `byable(recall)` method and we now want `switcher` to allow the `by` prefix, too. The easy way to do that is

```
program define switcher, byable(onecall)
        if _by() {
                local by "by `_byvars´, `_byrc0´:"
        }
        if (whatever makes us decide in favor of prog1) {
                `by´ prog1 `0´
        }
        else    `by´ prog2 `0´
end
```

`switcher` works by recreating the `by` *varlist*: prefix in front of **prog1** or **prog2** if by was specified. `switcher` will be executed only once even if by was specified. **prog1** and **prog2** will be executed repeatedly.

In the above outline, it is not important that **prog1** and **prog2** were implemented using the `byable(recall)` method. They could just as well be implemented using `byable(onecall)`, and `switcher` would change not at all.

The by-group header

Usually, when you use a command with `by`, a header is produced above each by-group:

```
. by foreign:  summarize mpg weight
```

```
-> foreign = Domestic
( output for first by-group appears)
```

```
-> foreign = Foreign
( output for first by-group appears)

. _
```

The by-group header does not always appear:

```
. by foreign:  generate new = sum(mpg)

. _
```

When you write your own programs, the header will appear by default if you use `byable(recall)`, and will not appear if you use `byable(onecall)`.

If you want the header and use `byable(onecall)`, you will have to write the code to output it.

If you do not want the header and use `byable(recall)`, you can specify `byable(recall, noheader)`:

```
program define ..., ... byable(recall, noheader)
        ...
end
```

Also See

Complementary: [P] **program**, [P] **sortpreserve**

Background: [R] **by**

Title

> **capture** — Capture return code

Syntax

> capture *command*

Description

capture executes *command*, suppressing all its output (including error messages, if any) and issues a return code of zero. The actual return code generated by *command* is stored in the built-in scalar _rc.

Remarks

capture is useful in do-files and programs since their execution terminates when a command issues a nonzero return code. Preceding sensitive commands with the word capture allows the do-file or program to continue in spite of errors. In addition, do-files and programs can be made to respond appropriately to any situation by conditioning their remaining actions on the contents of the scalar _rc.

▷ Example

You will never have cause to use capture interactively, but a few interactive experiments will demonstrate what capture does:

```
. drop _all
. list myvar
no variables defined
r(111);
. capture list myvar
. display _rc
111
```

When we said list myvar, we were told that we had no variables defined and got a return code of 111. When we said capture list myvar, we got no output and a zero return code. First, you should wonder what happened to the message "no variables defined". capture suppressed that message. It suppresses (eats) all output produced by the command it is capturing. Next, we see no return code message, so the return code was zero. We already know that typing list myvar generates a return code of 111, so capture ate that, too.

capture places the return code in the built-in scalar _rc. When we display the value of this scalar, we see that it is 111.

◁

▷ Example

Now that we know what `capture` does, let's put it to use. `capture` is used in programs and do-files. In some cases, you will write programs that do not care about the outcome of a Stata command. You may want to ensure, for instance, that some variable does not exist in the dataset. You could do so by including `capture drop result`.

If `result` exists, it is now gone. If it did not exist, `drop` did nothing and its nonzero return code and the error message have been intercepted. The program (or do-file) continues in any case. If you have written a program that creates a variable named `result`, it would be good practice to begin such a program with `capture drop result`. This way you could use the program repeatedly without having to worry whether the variable `result` already exists.

◁

❏ Technical Note

When combining `capture` and `drop`, never say something like `capture drop var1 var2 var3`. Remember that Stata commands do either exactly what you say or nothing at all. We might think our command would be guaranteed to eliminate `var1`, `var2`, and `var3` from the data if they exist. It is not. Imagine that `var3` did not exist in the data. `drop` would then do nothing. It would *not* drop `var1` and `var2`. To achieve the desired result, we must give three commands:

```
capture drop var1
capture drop var2
capture drop var3
```

❏

▷ Example

Here is another example of using `capture` to dispose of nonzero return codes: When using do-files to define programs, it is quite common to begin the definition with `capture program drop` *progname* and then put `program define` *progname*. This way you can rerun the do-file to load or reload the program.

◁

▷ Example

Let's consider programs whose behavior is contingent upon the outcome of some command. You write a program and want to ensure that the first argument (the macro ``1´`) has the interpretation of a new variable. If it does not, you want to issue an error message:

```
capture confirm new variable `1´
if _rc~=0 {
        display "`1´ already exists"
        exit _rc
}
( program continues... )
```

You use the `confirm` command to determine if the variable already exists and then condition your error message on whether `confirm` thinks ``1´` can be a new variable. We did not have to go to the trouble in this case. `confirm` would have automatically issued the appropriate error message and its nonzero return code would have stopped the program anyway.

◁

▷ Example

As before, you write a program and want to ensure that the first argument has the interpretation of a new variable. This time, however, if it does not, you want to use the name _answer in place of the name specified by the user:

```
capture confirm new variable `1´
if _rc~=0 {
        local 1 _answer
        confirm new variable `1´
}
( program continues. . . )
```

◁

▷ Example

There may be instances where you want to capture the return code but not the output. You do that by combining `capture` with `noisily`. For instance, we might change our program to read

```
capture noisily confirm new variable `1´
if _rc~=0 {
        local 1 _answer
        display "I´ll use _answer"
}
( program continues. . . )
```

`confirm` will generate some message such as ". . . already exists" and then we will follow that message with "I'll use _answer".

◁

❑ Technical Note

`capture` can be combined with {} to produce *capture blocks*. Consider the following:

```
capture {
        confirm var `1´
        confirm integer number `2´
        confirm number `3´
}
if _rc~=0 {
        display "Syntax is variable integer number"
        exit 198
}
( program continues. . . )
```

If any of the commands in the capture block fail, the subsequent commands in the block are aborted but the program continues with the `if` statement.

Capture blocks can be used to intercept the *Break* key, as in

```
capture {
        stata_commands
}
if _rc==1 {
        Break key cleanup code
        exit 1
}
( program continues. . . )
```

Remember that *Break* always generates a return code of 1. There is no reason, however, to restrict the execution of the cleanup code to *Break* only. Our program might fail for some other reason, such as insufficient room to add a new variable, and we would still want to engage in the cleanup operations. A better version would read

```
capture {
        stata_commands
}
if _rc~=0 {
        local oldrc = _rc
        Break key and error cleanup code
        exit `oldrc'
}
( program continues. . . )
```

❏

❏ Technical Note

The treatment of `exit` inside capture blocks is also worth noting. If, in our program above, the *stata_commands* included an `exit` or an `exit 0`, the program would terminate and return 0. Neither the *cleanup* nor *program continues* code would be executed. If *stata_commands* included an `exit` 198, or any other `exit` that sets a nonzero return code, however, the program would not exit. `capture` would catch the nonzero return code and execution would continue with the *cleanup code*.

❏

Also See

Complementary: [P] **break**, [P] **confirm**

Background: [U] **21.2 Relationship between a program and a do-file**

Title

char — Characteristics

Syntax

char [define] *evarname*[*charname*] [["]*text*["]]

char list [*evarname*[[*charname*]]]

char rename *varname*₁ *varname*₂

where *evarname* is a variable name or _dta and *charname* is a characteristic name. In the syntax diagrams, distinguish carefully between [], which you type, and [], which indicates the element is optional.

Description

See [U] **15.8 Characteristics** for a description of characteristics. These commands allow manipulating characteristics.

Remarks

We begin by showing how the commands work mechanically and then continue to demonstrate the commands in more realistic situations.

char define sets and clears characteristics, although there is no reason to type the define:

```
. char _dta[one] this is char named one of _dta
. char _dta[two] this is char named two of _dta
. char mpg[one]  this is char named   one   of mpg
. char mpg[two] "this is char named   two   of mpg"
. char mpg[three] "this is char named three of mpg"
```

Whether we include the double quotes does not matter. You clear a characteristic by defining it to be nothing:

```
. char mpg[three]
```

char list is used to list existing characteristics; it is typically used for debugging purposes:

```
. char list
    _dta[two]      :  this is char named two of _dta
    _dta[one]      :  this is char named one of _dta
    mpg[two]       :  this is char named   two   of mpg
    mpg[one]       :  this is char named   one   of mpg
. char list _dta[]
    _dta[two]      :  this is char named two of _dta
    _dta[one]      :  this is char named one of _dta
. char list mpg[]
    mpg[two]       :  this is char named   two   of mpg
    mpg[one]       :  this is char named   one   of mpg
. char list mpg[one]
    mpg[one]       :  this is char named   one   of mpg
```

23

The order may surprise you—it is the way it is because of how Stata's memory-management routines work—but it does not matter.

`char rename` moves all the characteristics associated with *varname*₁ to *varname*₂:

```
. char rename mpg weight
. char list
       _dta[two]        :  this is char named two of _dta
       _dta[one]        :  this is char named one of _dta
     weight[two]        :  this is char named   two    of mpg
     weight[one]        :  this is char named   one    of mpg
. char rename weight mpg                        /* put it back */
```

The contents of specific characteristics may be obtained in the same way as local macros by referencing the characteristic name between left and right single quotes; see [U] **15.8 Characteristics**.

```
. display "`mpg[one]´"
this is char named   one     of mpg
. display "`_dta[]´"
two one
```

Referring to a nonexisting characteristic returns null string:

```
. display "the value is |`mpg[three]´|"
the value is ||
```

How to program with characteristics

▷ Example

You are writing a program that needs the value of the variable recording "instance" (first time, second time, etc.). You want your command to have an option ins(*varname*) but, after the user has specified the variable once, you want your program to remember it in the future, even across sessions. An outline of your program is

```
program define ...
        version 7.0
        syntax ... [, ... ins(varname) ... ]
        ...
        if "`ins´"=="" {
                local ins "`_dta[Instance]´"
        }
        confirm variable `ins´
        char _dta[Instance] : `ins´
        ...
end
```

◁

▷ Example

You write a program and, among other things, it changes the contents of one of the variables in the user's data. You worry about the user pressing *Break* while the program is in the midst of the change and so properly decide to construct the replaced values in a temporary variable and, only at the conclusion, dropping the user's original variable and replacing it with the new one. In this example, macro `uservar´ contains the name of the user's original variable. Macro `newvar´ contains the name of the temporary variable that will ultimately replace it.

There are the following issues in duplicating the original variable: You want the new variable to have the same variable label, the same value label, the same format, and the same characteristics.

```
program define ...
        version 7.0
        ...
        tempvar newvar
        ...
        ( code creating `newvar´)
        ...
        local varlab : variable label `uservar´
        local vallab : value label `uservar´
        local format : format `uservar´
        label var `newvar´ "`varlab´"
        label values `newvar´ `vallab´
        format `newvar´ `format´
        char rename `uservar´ `newvar´
        drop `uservar´
        rename `newvar´ `uservar´
end
```

You are supposed to notice the **char rename** to move the characteristics originally attached to `uservar´ to `newvar´. See [P] **macro**, [R] **label**, and [R] **format** for information on the commands preceding the **char rename** command.

This code is almost perfect, but if you are really concerned about the user pressing *Break*, there is a potential problem. What happens if the user presses *Break* between the **char rename** and the final **rename**? The last three lines would be better written as

```
nobreak {
        char rename `uservar´ `newvar´
        drop `uservar´
        rename `newvar´ `uservar´
}
```

Now, even if the user presses *Break* during these last three lines, it will be ignored; see [P] **break**.

◁

Also See

Background: [U] **15.8 Characteristics**,
                     [U] **21.3.6 Extended macro functions**,
                     [U] **21.3.11 Referencing characteristics**

Title

> **cluster subroutines** — Add cluster analysis routines

Description

This entry describes how to extend Stata's `cluster` command; see [R] **cluster**. Programmers can add subcommands to `cluster`; add functions to `cluster generate` (see [R] **cluster generate**); and set up an alternate command to be executed when `cluster dendrogram` is called (see [R] **cluster dendrogram**).

The `cluster` command also provides utilities for programmers; see [P] **cluster utilities** to learn more.

Remarks

Remarks are presented under the headings

Adding a cluster subroutine
Adding a cluster generate function
Applying an alternate cluster dendrogram routine

Adding a cluster subroutine

You add a `cluster` subroutine by creating a Stata program with the name `cluster_subcmdname`. For example, to add the subcommand `xyz` to `cluster`, create `cluster_xyz.ado`. Users could then execute the `xyz` subcommand with

```
cluster xyz ...
```

Everything entered on the command line following `cluster xyz` is passed to the `cluster_xyz` command.

You can add new clustering methods, new cluster management tools, and new post clustering programs. The `cluster` command has subcommands available that are helpful to cluster analysis programmers; see [P] **cluster utilities**.

▷ Example

We demonstrate the addition of a `cluster` subroutine by writing a simple post cluster-analysis routine that provides a cross tabulation of two cluster analysis grouping variables. The syntax of the new command will be

```
cluster mycrosstab clname1 clname2 [, tabulate_options ]
```

Here is the program:

```
program define cluster_mycrosstab
        gettoken clname1 0 : 0 , parse(" ,")
        gettoken clname2 rest : 0 , parse(" ,")
        cluster query `clname1'
        local groupvar1 `r(groupvar)'
        cluster query `clname2'
        local groupvar2 `r(groupvar)'
        tabulate `groupvar1' `groupvar2' `rest'
end
```

See [P] **gettoken** for information on the `gettoken` command, and see [R] **tabulate** for information on the `tabulate` command. The `cluster query` command is one of the cluster programming utilities that is documented in [P] **cluster utilities**.

We can demonstrate `cluster mycrosstab` in action. This example starts with two cluster analyses, named `cl1` and `cl2`, having already been performed. The dissimilarity measure and the variables included in the two cluster analyses differ. We want to see how closely the two cluster analyses match.

```
. cluster list, type method dissim var
cl2  (type: partition,  method: kmeans,  dissimilarity: L(1.5))
        vars: gvar2 (group variable)

cl1  (type: partition,  method: kmeans,  dissimilarity: L1)
        vars: cl1gvar (group variable)

. cluster mycrosstab cl1 cl2, chi2
```

			gvar2			
cl1gvar	1	2	3	4	5	Total
1	0	0	10	0	0	10
2	1	4	0	5	6	16
3	8	0	0	4	1	13
4	9	0	8	4	0	21
5	0	8	0	0	6	14
Total	18	12	18	13	13	74

```
          Pearson chi2(16) =  98.4708   Pr = 0.000
```

The `chi2` option was included to demonstrate that we were able to exploit the existing options of `tabulate` with very little programming effort. We just pass along to `tabulate` any of the extra arguments received by `cluster_mycrosstab`.

◁

Adding a cluster generate function

Programmers can add functions to the `cluster generate` command; see [R] **cluster generate**. This is accomplished by creating a command called `clusgen_name`. For example, if I wanted to add a function called `abc()` to `cluster generate`, I would create `clusgen_abc.ado`. Users could then execute

```
cluster generate newvarname = abc( ... ) ...
```

Everything entered on the command line following `cluster generate` is passed to `clusgen_abc`.

▷ Example

Here is the beginning of a `clusgen_abc` program that expects an integer argument and that has one option called **name**(*clname*) that gives the name of the cluster. If **name()** is not specified, it defaults to the most recently performed cluster analysis. We will assume, for illustration purposes, that the cluster analysis must be `hierarchical` and will check for this in the `clusgen_abc` program.

```
program define clusgen_abc
      /* we use gettoken to work our way through the parsing */
      gettoken newvar 0 : 0 , parse(" =")
      gettoken temp 0 : 0 , parse(" =")
      if `"`temp'"' ~= "=" {
            error 198
      }
      gettoken temp 0 : 0 , parse(" (")
      if `"`temp'"' ~= "abc" {
            error 198
      }
      gettoken funcarg 0 : 0 , parse(" (") match(temp)
      if `"`temp'"' ~= "(" {
            error 198
      }
      /* funcarg holds the integer argument to abc() */
      confirm integer number `funcarg'

      /* we can now use syntax to parse the option */
      syntax [, Name(str) ]
      /* cluster query will give us the list of cluster names */
      if `"`name'"' == "" {
            cluster query
            local clnames `r(names)'
            if "`clnames'" == "" {
                  di "{err}no cluster solutions defined"
                  exit 198
            }
            /* first name in the list is the latest clustering */
            local name : word 1 of `clnames'
      }
      /* cluster query followed by name will tell us the type */
      cluster query `name'
      if "`r(type)'" ~= "hierarchical" {
            di "{err}only allowed with hierarchical clustering"
            exit 198
      }
      /*
         you would now pull more information from the call of
                  cluster query `name'
         and do your computations and generate `newvar'
      */
      ...
end
```

See [P] **cluster utilities** for details on the cluster query command.

◁

Applying an alternate cluster dendrogram routine

Programmers can change the behavior of the cluster dendrogram command (alias cluster tree); see [R] **cluster dendrogram**. This is accomplished by using the other() option of the cluster set command (see [P] **cluster utilities**), with a *tag* of treeprogram and with *text* giving the name of the command to be used in place of the standard Stata program for cluster dendrogram. For example, if I had created a new hierarchical cluster analysis method for Stata that needed a different algorithm for producing dendrograms, I would use the command cluster set *clname* , other(treeprogram *progname*)

to set *progname* as the program to be executed when cluster dendrogram is called.

▷ Example

If I am creating a new hierarchical cluster analysis method called myclus, I would create a program called cluster_myclus (see the discussion at the beginning of the Remarks section). If myclus needed a different dendrogram routine from the standard one used within Stata, I would include the following line inside cluster_myclus.ado at the point where I set the cluster attributes.

cluster set `clname´ , other(treeprogram myclustree)

I would then also create a program called myclustree in a file called myclustree.ado that implements the particular dendrogram program needed by myclus.

◁

Also See

Background: [R] **cluster**,
                       [P] **cluster utilities**

Title

cluster utilities — Cluster analysis programming utilities

Syntax

cluster query [*clname*]

cluster set [*clname*] [, <u>add</u>name <u>type</u>(*type*) <u>method</u>(*method*)

{ <u>s</u>imilarity(*measure*) | <u>dis</u>similarity(*measure*) } <u>var</u>(*tag varname*)

<u>char</u>(*tag charname*) <u>o</u>ther(*tag text*) <u>note</u>(*text*)]

cluster <u>del</u>ete *clname* [, zap <u>del</u>name <u>type</u> <u>method</u> <u>dis</u>similarity <u>s</u>imilarity

<u>note</u>s(*numlist*) <u>alln</u>otes <u>var</u>(*tag*) <u>allv</u>ars <u>varzap</u>(*tag*) <u>allvarzap</u> <u>char</u>(*tag*)

<u>allc</u>hars <u>charzap</u>(*tag*) <u>allcharzap</u> <u>o</u>ther(*tag*) <u>allo</u>thers]

cluster <u>parsedist</u>ance *measure*

cluster measures *varlist* [if *exp*] [in *range*] , <u>compare</u>(*numlist*)

<u>g</u>enerate(*newvarlist*) [*measure* <u>propvars</u> <u>propc</u>ompares]

Description

The cluster query, cluster set, cluster delete, cluster parsedistance, and cluster measures commands provide tools for programmers to add their own cluster analysis subroutines to Stata's cluster command; see [R] **cluster** and [P] **cluster subroutines**. These commands make it possible for the new command to take advantage of Stata's cluster management facilities.

cluster query provides a way to obtain the various attributes of a cluster analysis in Stata. If *clname* is omitted, cluster query returns in r(names) a list of the names of all currently defined cluster analyses. If *clname* is provided, then the various attributes of the named cluster analyses are returned in r(). These attributes include the type, method, (dis)similarity used, created variable names, notes, and any other information attached to the cluster analysis.

cluster set allows you to set the various attributes that define a cluster analysis in Stata. This includes giving a name to your cluster results and adding that name to the master list of currently defined cluster results. With cluster set, you can provide information on the type, method, and (dis)similarity measure of your cluster analysis results. You can associate variables and Stata characteristics (see [P] **char**) with your cluster analysis. cluster set also allows you to add notes and other named fields to your cluster analysis result. These items become part of the dataset and are saved with the data.

cluster delete allows you to delete attributes from a cluster analysis in Stata. This command is the inverse of cluster set.

cluster parsedistance takes the similarity or dissimilarity *measure* name and checks it against the list of those provided within Stata, taking account of allowed minimal abbreviations and aliases. Aliases are resolved (for instance, Euclidean is changed into the equivalent L2).

cluster measures computes the similarity or dissimilarity *measure* between the observations listed in the compare() option and the observations included based on the if and in conditions, and places the results in the variables specified by the generate() option.

Stata also provides a method for programmers to extend the cluster command by providing subcommands. This is discussed in [P] **cluster subroutines**.

Options

Options for cluster set

addname adds *clname* to the master list of currently defined cluster analyses. When *clname* is not specified, the addname option is mandatory, and in this case, cluster set automatically finds a cluster name that is not currently in use and uses this as the cluster name. cluster set returns the name of the cluster in r(name). If addname is not specified, the *clname* must have previously been added to the master list (for instance, through a previous call to cluster set).

type(*type*) sets the cluster type for *clname*. type(hierarchical) indicates that the cluster analysis is some kind of hierarchical clustering, and type(partition) indicates that it is a partition style of clustering. You are not restricted to these types. For instance, you might program some kind of fuzzy partition clustering analysis and could, in that case, use type(fuzzy).

method(*method*) sets the name of the clustering method for the cluster analysis. For instance, Stata uses method(kmeans) to indicate a kmeans cluster analysis, and uses method(single) to indicate single linkage cluster analysis. You are not restricted to the names currently employed within Stata.

dissimilarity(*measure*) and similarity(*measure*) set the name of the dissimilarity or similarity measure used for the cluster analysis. For example, Stata uses dissimilarity(L2) to indicate the L2 or Euclidean distance. You are not restricted to the names currently employed within Stata. See [R] **cluster** for a listing and discussion of (dis)similarity measures.

var(*tag varname*) sets a marker called *tag* in the cluster analysis that points to the variable *varname*. For instance, Stata uses var(group *varname*) to set a grouping variable from a kmeans cluster analysis. With single linkage clustering, Stata uses var(id *idvarname*), var(order *ordervarname*), and var(height *hgtvarname*) to set the id, order, and height variables that define the cluster analysis result. You are not restricted to the names currently employed within Stata. Up to ten var() options may be specified with a single cluster set command.

char(*tag charname*) sets a marker called *tag* in the cluster analysis that points to the Stata characteristic named *charname*; see [P] **char**. This can be either an _dta[] dataset characteristic or a variable characteristic. Up to ten char() options may be specified with a single cluster set command.

other(*tag text*) sets a marker called *tag* in the cluster analysis with *text* attached to the tag marker. Stata uses other(k #) to indicate that k (the number of groups) was # in a kmeans cluster analysis. You are not restricted to the names currently employed within Stata. Up to ten other() options may be specified with a single cluster set command.

note(*text*) adds a note to the *clname* cluster analysis. The cluster notes command (see [R] **cluster notes**) is the command for users to add, delete, or view cluster notes. The cluster notes command uses the note() option of cluster set to actually add a note to a cluster analysis. Up to ten note() options may be specified with a single cluster set command.

Options for cluster delete

zap deletes everything possible for cluster analysis *clname*. It is the same as specifying the delname, type, method, dissimilarity, similarity, allnotes, allcharzap, allothers, and allvarzap options.

delname removes *clname* from the master list of current cluster analyses. This option does not touch the various pieces that make up the cluster analysis. To remove them, use the other options of cluster delete.

type deletes the cluster type entry from *clname*.

method deletes the cluster method entry from *clname*.

dissimilarity and similarity delete the dissimilarity and similarity entries, respectively, from *clname*.

notes(*numlist*) deletes the specified numbered notes from *clname*. The numbering corresponds to the returned results from the cluster query *clname* command. The cluster notes drop command (see [R] **cluster notes**) is the command for users to drop a cluster note. It, in turn, calls cluster delete, using the notes() option to drop the notes.

allnotes removes all notes from the *clname* cluster analysis.

var(*tag*) removes from *clname* the entry labeled *tag* that points to a variable. This option does not delete the variable.

allvars removes all the entries pointing to variables for *clname*. This option does not delete the corresponding variables.

varzap(*tag*) is the same as var(), with the addition of actually deleting the referenced variable.

allvarzap is the same as allvars, with the addition of actually deleting the variables.

char(*tag*) removes from *clname* the entry labeled *tag* that points to a Stata characteristic (see [P] **char**). This option does not delete the characteristic.

allchars removes all the entries pointing to Stata characteristics for *clname*. This option does not delete the characteristics.

charzap(*tag*) is the same as char(), with the addition of actually deleting the characteristic.

allcharzap is the same as allchars, with the addition of actually deleting the characteristics.

other(*tag*) deletes from *clname* the *tag* entry and its associated text, which were set using the other() option of the cluster set command.

allothers deletes all entries from *clname* that have been set using the other() option of the cluster set command.

Options for cluster measures

compare(*numlist*) is required and specifies the observations to use as the comparison observations. Each of these observations will be compared to the observations implied by the if and in conditions using the specified (dis)similarity *measure*. The results are stored in the corresponding new variable from the generate() option. There must be the same number of elements in *numlist* as variable names in the generate() option.

generate(*newvarlist*) is required and specifies the names of the variables to be created. There must be as many elements in *newvarlist* as numbers specified in the compare() option.

measure is one of the similarity or dissimilarity measures allowed by Stata. The default is L2 (meaning Euclidean distance). A list of allowed *measures* and their minimal abbreviations can be found in [R] **cluster**.

propvars is for use with binary measures. It indicates that the observations implied by the if and in conditions are to be interpreted as proportions of binary observations. The default action with binary measures treats all nonzero values as one (excluding missing values). With propvars, the values are confirmed to be between zero and one inclusive. See [R] **cluster** for a discussion of the use of proportions with binary measures.

propcompares is for use with binary measures. It indicates that the comparison observations (those specified in the compare() option) are to be interpreted as proportions of binary observations. The default action with binary measures treats all nonzero values as one (excluding missing values). With propcompares, the values are confirmed to be between zero and one inclusive. See [R] **cluster** for a discussion of the use of proportions with binary measures.

Remarks

▷ Example

Programmers can determine which cluster solutions currently exist by using the cluster query command without specifying a cluster name. It returns the names of all currently defined clusters.

```
. cluster dir
grpk7L1
grpk6L1
grpk7L2
grpk6L2
. cluster query
. return list
macros:
            r(names) : "grpk7L1 grpk6L1 grpk7L2 grpk6L2"
```

In this case, there are four cluster solutions. A programmer can further process the r(names) returned macro. For example, if we want to determine which current cluster solutions used kmeans clustering, we would loop through these four cluster solution names, and for each one call cluster query to determine its properties.

```
. local clusnames `r(names)´
. foreach cname of local clusnames {
  2.         cluster query `cname´
  3.         if "`r(method)´" == "kmeans" {
  4.                 local kmeancls `kmeancls´ `cname´
  5.         }
  6. }
. di "{tab}Cluster analyses using kmeans: `kmeancls´"
        Cluster analyses using kmeans: grpk7L2 grpk6L2
```

In this case, we examined r(method), which records the name of the cluster analysis method. Two of the four cluster solutions used kmeans.

◁

▷ Example

We interactively demonstrate `cluster set`, `cluster delete`, and `cluster query`, though in practice these would be used within a program.

First, we add the name `myclus` to the master list of cluster analyses, and at the same time set the type, method, and similarity.

```
. cluster set myclus, addname type(madeup) method(fake) similarity(who knows)
. cluster query
. return list

macros:
            r(names) : "myclus grpk7L1 grpk6L1 grpk7L2 grpk6L2"
. cluster query myclus
. return list

macros:
             r(name) : "myclus"
       r(similarity) : "who knows"
           r(method) : "fake"
             r(type) : "madeup"
```

`cluster query` shows that `myclus` was successfully added to the master list of cluster analyses, and that the attributes that were `cluster set` can also be obtained.

Now we add a reference to a variable. We will use the word **group** as the *tag* for a variable `mygrpvar`. Additionally, we add another item called **xyz** and associate some text with the **xyz** item.

```
. cluster set myclus, var(group mygrpvar) other(xyz some important info)
. cluster query myclus
. return list

macros:
             r(name) : "myclus"
          r(o1_val) : "some important info"
          r(o1_tag) : "xyz"
        r(groupvar) : "mygrpvar"
         r(v1_name) : "mygrpvar"
          r(v1_tag) : "group"
       r(similarity) : "who knows"
           r(method) : "fake"
             r(type) : "madeup"
```

The `cluster query` command returned the `mygrpvar` information in two ways. The first way is with $r(v\#\_tag)$ and $r(v\#\_name)$. In this case, there is only one variable associated with `myclus`, so we have `r(v1_tag)` and `r(v1_name)`. This allows the programmer to loop over all the saved variable names without knowing beforehand what the *tag*s might be or how many there are. You could loop as follows:

```
local i 1
while "`r(v`i´_tag)´" ~= "" {
        ...
        local i = `i´ + 1
}
```

The second way the variable information is returned is in a `r()` result with the *tag* name appended by var, `r(tagvar)`. In our example, this is `r(groupvar)`. This second method is convenient when, as the programmer, you know exactly which *varname* information you are seeking.

The same logic applies with regards to characteristic attributes that are `cluster set`.

Now we continue with our interactive example:

```
. cluster delete myclus, method var(group)
. cluster set myclus, note(a note) note(another note) note(a third note)
. cluster query myclus
. return list

macros:
              r(name) :  "myclus"
             r(note3) :  "a third note"
             r(note2) :  "another note"
             r(note1) :  "a note"
            r(o1_val) :  "some important info"
            r(o1_tag) :  "xyz"
        r(similarity) :  "who knows"
              r(type) :  "madeup"
```

We used `cluster delete` to remove the method and the `group` variable we had associated with `myclus`. Three notes were then simultaneously added using the `note()` option of `cluster set`. In practice, users will use the `cluster notes` command (see [R] **cluster notes**) to add and delete cluster notes. The `cluster notes` command is implemented using the `cluster set` and `cluster delete` programming commands.

We finish our interactive demonstration of these commands by deleting some more attributes from `myclus` and then completely eliminating `myclus`. In practice, users would remove a cluster analysis with the `cluster drop` command (see [R] **cluster utility**), which is implemented using the `zap` option of the `cluster delete` command.

```
. cluster delete myclus, allnotes similarity
. cluster query myclus
. return list

macros:
              r(name) :  "myclus"
            r(o1_val) :  "some important info"
            r(o1_tag) :  "xyz"
              r(type) :  "madeup"
. cluster delete myclus, zap
. cluster query
. return list

macros:
             r(names) :  "grpk7L1 grpk6L1 grpk7L2 grpk6L2"
```

The cluster attributes that are `cluster set` become a part of the dataset. They are saved with the dataset when it is `save`d, and are available again when the dataset is `use`d; see [R] **save**.

◁

❏ Technical Note

You may wonder how Stata's cluster analysis data structures are implemented. Stata data characteristics (see [P] **char**) hold the information. The details of the implementation are not important, and in fact, we encourage you to use the `set`, `delete`, and `query` subcommands to access the cluster attributes. This way, if we ever decide to change the underlying implementation, you will be protected through Stata's version control feature.

❏

▷ Example

The `cluster parsedistance` programming command takes as an argument the name of a similarity or dissimilarity measure. Stata then checks this name against those implemented within Stata (and available to you through the `cluster measures` command). Upper or lower case letters are allowed, and minimal abbreviations are checked. Some of the measures have aliases. These are resolved so that a standard measure name is returned. We demonstrate the `cluster parsedistance` command interactively:

```
. cluster parsedistance max
. sreturn list

macros:
            s(drange) : "0 ."
            s(dtype) : "dissimilarity"
             s(dist) : "Linfinity"
. cluster parsedistance Eucl
. sreturn list

macros:
            s(drange) : "0 ."
            s(dtype) : "dissimilarity"
             s(dist) : "L2"
. cluster parsedistance correl
. sreturn list

macros:
            s(drange) : "1 -1"
            s(dtype) : "similarity"
             s(dist) : "correlation"
. cluster parsedistance jacc
. sreturn list

macros:
            s(drange) : "1 0"
            s(binary) : "binary"
            s(dtype) : "similarity"
             s(dist) : "Jaccard"
```

`cluster parsedistance` returns `s(dtype)` as either `similarity` or `dissimilarity`, and returns `s(dist)` as the standard Stata name for the (dis)similarity. `s(drange)` gives the range of the measure (most similar to most dissimilar). If the measure is designed for binary variables, then `s(binary)` is returned with the word `binary`, as seen above.

See [R] **cluster** for a listing of the similarity and dissimilarity measures and their properties.

◁

▷ Example

`cluster measures` computes the similarity or dissimilarity measure between each comparison observation and the observations implied by the `if` and `in` conditions (or all the data if no `if` or `in` conditions are specified).

We demonstrate using the auto dataset:

```
. cluster measures turn trunk gear_ratio in 1/10, compare(3 11) gen(z3 z11) L1
. format z* %8.2f
```

```
. list turn trunk gear_ratio z3 z11 in 1/11
           turn     trunk   gear~o        z3       z11
    1.       40        11     3.58      6.50     14.30
    2.       40        11     2.53      6.55     13.25
    3.       35        12     3.08      0.00     17.80
    4.       40        16     2.93      9.15      8.65
    5.       43        20     2.41     16.67      1.13
    6.       43        21     2.73     17.35      2.45
    7.       34        10     2.87      3.21     20.59
    8.       42        16     2.93     11.15      6.65
    9.       43        17     2.93     13.15      4.65
   10.       42        13     3.08      8.00      9.80
   11.       44        20     2.28         .         .
```

Using the three variables `turn`, `trunk`, and `gear_ratio`, we computed the L1 (or absolute value) distance between the third observation and the first ten observations and placed the results in the variable `z3`. The distance between the eleventh observation and the first ten was placed in variable `z11`.

There are many measures designed for binary data. Below we illustrate `cluster measures` with the matching coefficient binary similarity measure. We have eight observations on ten binary variables, and we will compute the matching similarity measure between the last three observations and all eight observations.

```
. cluster measures x1-x10, compare(6/8) gen(z6 z7 z8) matching
. format z* %4.2f
. list, nodisplay
        x1   x2   x3   x4   x5   x6   x7   x8   x9  x10     z6     z7     z8
   1.    1    0    0    0    1    1    0    0    1    1   0.60   0.80   0.40
   2.    1    1    1    0    0    1    0    1    1    0   0.70   0.30   0.70
   3.    0    0    1    0    0    0    1    0    0    1   0.60   0.40   0.20
   4.    1    1    1    1    0    0    0    1    1    1   0.40   0.40   0.60
   5.    0    1    0    1    1    0    1    0    0    1   0.20   0.60   0.40
   6.    1    0    1    0    0    1    0    0    0    0   1.00   0.40   0.60
   7.    0    0    0    1    1    1    0    0    1    1   0.40   1.00   0.40
   8.    1    1    0    1    0    1    0    1    0    0   0.60   0.40   1.00
```

Stata will treat all nonzero observations as being one (except missing values, which are treated as missing values) when computing these binary measures.

When the similarity measure between binary observations and the means of groups of binary observations is needed, the `propvars` and `propcompares` options of `cluster measures` provide the solution. The mean of binary observations is a proportion. The value 0.2 would indicate that 20 percent of the values were one and 80 percent were zero for the group. See [R] **cluster** for a discussion of binary measures. The `propvars` option indicates that the main body of observations should be interpreted as proportions. The `propcompares` option indicates that the comparison observations should be treated as proportions.

We compare ten binary observations on five variables to two observations holding proportions by using the `propcompares` option:

```
. cluster measures a* in 1/10, compare(11 12) gen(c1 c2) matching propcompare
. list, nodisplay
        a1   a2   a3   a4   a5       c1       c2
   1.    1    1    1    0    1       .6      .56
   2.    0    0    1    1    1      .36       .8
   3.    1    0    1    0    0      .76      .56
   4.    1    1    0    1    1      .36      .44
   5.    1    0    0    0    0      .68       .4
```

```
 6.    0    0    1    1    1        .36        .8
 7.    1    0    1    0    1        .64        .76
 8.    1    0    0    0    1        .56        .6
 9.    0    1    1    1    1        .32        .6
10.    1    1    1    1    1        .44        .6
11.   .8   .4   .7   .1   .2         .          .
12.   .5    0   .9   .6    1         .          .
```

◁

Saved Results

cluster query with no arguments saves in r():

Macros
r(names) cluster solution names

cluster query with an argument saves in r():

Macros
r(name)	cluster name
r(type)	type of cluster analysis
r(method)	cluster analysis method
r(similarity)	similarity measure name
r(dissimilarity)	dissimilarity measure name
r(note#)	cluster note number #
r(v#_tag)	variable tag number #
r(v#_name)	varname associated with r(v#_tag)
r(*tag*var)	varname associated with *tag*
r(c#_tag)	characteristic tag number #
r(c#_name)	characteristic name associated with r(c#_tag)
r(c#_val)	characteristic value associated with r(c#_tag)
r(*tag*char)	characteristic name associated with *tag*
r(o#_tag)	other tag number #
r(o#_val)	other value associated with r(o#_tag)

cluster set saves in r():

Macros
r(name) cluster name

cluster parsedistance saves in s():

Macros
s(dist)	(dis)similarity measure name
s(darg)	argument of (dis)similarities that take them, such as L(#)
s(dtype)	the word similarity or dissimilarity
s(binary)	the word binary if the measure is for binary observations

`cluster measures` saves in `r()`:

Macros
`r(generate)`	variable names from the `generate()` option
`r(compare)`	observation numbers from the `compare()` option
`r(dtype)`	the word `similarity` or `dissimilarity`
`r(distance)`	the name of the (dis)similarity measure
`r(binary)`	the word `binary` if the measure is for binary observations

Also See

Background: [R] **cluster**,
                    [P] **cluster subroutines**

Title

confirm — Argument verification

Syntax

<u>conf</u>irm <u>e</u>xistence [*string*]

<u>conf</u>irm [<u>new</u>] <u>f</u>ile *filename*

<u>conf</u>irm <u>name</u>s *names*

<u>conf</u>irm [<u>integer</u>] <u>n</u>umber [*string*]

<u>conf</u>irm [new | numeric | <u>str</u>ing | *type*] <u>v</u>ariable [*varlist*]

where *type is* {byte | int | long | float | double | str#}

Description

confirm verifies that the arguments following confirm ... are of the claimed type and issues the appropriate error message and nonzero return code if they are not.

Remarks

confirm is useful in *do-files* and *programs* when you do not want to bother issuing your own error message. confirm can also be combined with capture to detect and handle error conditions before they arise; also see [P] **capture**.

confirm existence

confirm existence displays the message " ´´ found where something expected" and returns 6 if text does not exist.

confirm file

confirm file verifies that *filename* exists and is readable and issues the appropriate error message and return code if not.

confirm new file verifies that *filename* does not exist and that *filename* could be opened for writing and issues the appropriate error message and return code if not.

The possible error messages and return codes are

Message	Return Code
´´ found where filename expected	7
file ___ not found	601
file ___ already exists	602
file ___ could not be opened	603

Messages 7 and 603 are possible for both `confirm file` and `confirm new file`. In the case of `confirm new file`, message 603 indicates that the filename is invalid or the specified directory does not exist. For instance, `confirm new file newdir\newfile` generates an error because, while the file would be new, it could not be opened because `newdir` does not exist and so is not a valid file for writing.

confirm names

`confirm names` verifies that the argument or arguments are valid names according to Stata's naming conventions. It produces the message

<code>'text' invalid name</code>

with return code 7 if the name(s) are not valid.

confirm number

`confirm number` verifies that the argument can be interpreted as a number, such as `1`, `5.2`, `-5.2`, or `2.5e+10`. It produces the message

$\{$ 'text' $|$ nothing $\}$ <code>found where number expected</code>

with return code 7 if not.

`confirm integer number` adds the restriction that the argument must be an integer, such as 1 or 2.5e+10, but not 5.2 or −5.2. If not, it produces a return code of 7 and a slight variation on the message above:

$\{$ 'text' $|$ nothing $\}$ <code>found where integer expected</code>

confirm variable

`confirm variable` verifies that the *varlist* can be interpreted as an existing *varlist* of any types of variables. If not, the appropriate error message and nonzero return code are returned:

Message	Return Code
`'' found where numeric variable expected`	7
`'' found where string variable expected`	7
`no variables defined`	111
`____ not found`	111
`____ invalid name`	198

`confirm numeric variable` adds the restriction that all the variables are numeric. If the variable exists but is not numeric, the message " `''` found where numeric variable expected" is displayed and return code 7 is issued.

`confirm string variable` adds the restriction that all the variables are strings. If the variable exists but is not a string variable, then the message " `''` found where string variable expected" is displayed and return code 7 is issued.

`confirm` *type* `variable` verifies that all variables are of the indicated storage type. For instance, `confirm int variable myvar` or `confirm float variable myvar thatvar`. As with `confirm string variable`, the additional appropriate message and return code 7 are possible.

`confirm new variable` verifies that the *varlist* can be interpreted as a new *varlist*. The possible messages and return codes are

Message	Return Code
´´ found where varname expected	7
____ already defined	110
____ invalid name	198

▷ Example

`confirm` is a cheap way to include minimal syntax checking in your programs. For instance, you have written a program that is supposed to take a single, integer argument. Although you do not have to include any syntax checking at all—the program will probably blow up with some error if the argument is incorrect—it is safer to add one line at the top of the program:

```
confirm integer number `1´
```

Now if the first argument is not an integer, you will get a reasonable error message and the program will stop automatically.

◁

▷ Example

More sophisticated programs often combine the `confirm` and `capture` commands. For instance, `ttest` has a complex syntax: If the user types `ttest var=5`, it tests that the mean of `var` is 5 using one set of formulas, and if the user types `ttest var=var2`, it tests equality of means using another set of formulas. Which it does is determined by whether there is a number or a variable to the right of the equal sign. This was done by

```
capture confirm number `exp´
if _rc==0 {
        ( code for test against a constant )
        exit
}
( code for test of two variables )
```

◁

Also See

Complementary: [P] **capture**

Title

continue — Break out of loops

Syntax

continue $\left[\, ,\, \underline{\text{br}}\text{eak}\right]$

Description

The `continue` command within a `foreach`, `forvalues`, or `while` loop breaks execution of the current loop iteration and skips the remaining commands within the loop. Execution resumes at the top of the loop unless the `break` option is specified, in which case, execution resumes with the command following the looping command. See [P] **foreach**, [P] **forvalues**, and [P] **while** for a discussion of the looping commands.

Options

`break` indicates that the loop is to be exited. The default is to skip the remaining steps of the current iteration and to resume loop execution again at the top of the loop.

Remarks

We illustrate `continue` with the `forvalues` command, but it can be used in the same way with the `foreach` and `while` commands.

▷ Example

The following `forvalues` loop lists the odd and even numbers from one to four.

```
. forvalues x = 1(1)4 {
  2.         if mod(`x´,2) {
  3.                 display "`x´ is odd"
  4.         }
  5.         else {
  6.                 display "`x´ is even"
  7.         }
  8. }
1 is odd
2 is even
3 is odd
4 is even
```

It could be coded using the `continue` command instead of `else`.

```
. forvalues x = 1(1)4 {
  2.          if mod(`x´,2) {
  3.                  display "`x´ is odd"
  4.                  continue
  5.          }
  6.          display "`x´ is even"
  7. }
1 is odd
2 is even
3 is odd
4 is even
```

When `continue` is executed, any remaining statements that exist in the loop are ignored. Execution continues at the top of the loop where, in this case, `forvalues` sets the next value of `` `x´ ``, compares that with 4, and then perhaps begins the loop again.

◁

▷ Example

`continue, break` causes execution of the loop to stop; it prematurely exits the loop.

```
. forvalues x = 6/1000 {
  2.          if mod(`x´,2)==0 & mod(`x´,3)==0 & mod(`x´,5)==0 {
  3.                  display "The least common multiple of 2, 3, and 5 is `x´"
  4.                  continue, break
  5.          }
  6. }
The least common multiple of 2, 3, and 5 is 30
```

Although the `forvalues` loop was scheduled to go over the values 6 to 1,000, the `continue, break` statement forced it to stop after 30.

◁

Also See

Complementary: [P] **foreach**, [P] **forvalues**, [P] **while**

Related: [P] **if**

Background: [U] **21 Programming Stata**

Title

> **#delimit** — Change delimiter

Syntax

#delimit { cr | ; }

Description

The **#delimit** command resets the character that marks the end of a command. It may be used only in do-files or ado-files.

Remarks

#delimit (pronounced *pound-delimit*) is a Stata preprocessor command. *#commands* do not generate a return code, nor do they generate ordinary Stata errors. The only error message associated with *#commands* is "unrecognized #command".

Commands given from the console are always executed when you press carriage return, also called the *Enter* key. **#delimit** cannot be used interactively, so you cannot change Stata's interactive behavior.

Commands in a do-file, however, may be delimited with a carriage return or a semicolon. When a do-file begins, the delimiter is carriage return. The command '**#delimit ;**' changes the delimiter to a semicolon. To restore the carriage return delimiter inside a file, use **#delimit cr**.

When a do-file begins execution, the delimiter is automatically set to carriage return even if it was called from another do-file that set the delimiter to semicolon. Also, the current do-file need not worry about restoring the delimiter to what it was because Stata will do that automatically.

▷ Example

```
/*
      When the do-file begins, the delimiter is carriage return:
*/
use basedata, clear
/*
      The last command loaded our data.
      Let's now change the delimiter:
*/
```

```
#delimit ;
summarize sex
           salary ;
/*
     Since the delimiter is semicolon, it doesn't matter that our
     command took two lines.
     We can change the delimiter back:
*/
#delimit cr
summarize sex salary
/*
     Now our lines once again end on return.  The semicolon delimiter
     is often used when loading programs:
*/
capture program drop fix
program define fix
     confirm var `1´
     #delimit ;
     replace `1´ = .  if salary==. | salary==0 |
                         hours==.  | hours==0 ;
     #delimit cr
end
fix var1
fix var2
```

◁

Also See

Background: [U] **19.1.3 Long lines in do-files**,
                    [U] **21.11.2 Comments and long lines in ado-files**

Title

discard — Drop automatically loaded programs

Syntax

```
discard
```

Description

discard drops all automatically loaded programs (see [U] **20.2 What is an ado-file?**); clears e(), r(), and s() saved results (see [P] **return**); and eliminates information stored by the most recent estimation command (see [P] **estimates**).

discard may not be abbreviated.

Remarks

Use discard to debug ado-files. Making a change to an ado-file will not cause Stata to update its internal copy of the changed program. discard clears all automatically loaded programs from memory, forcing Stata to refresh its internal copies with the versions residing on disk.

In addition, all of Stata's estimation commands have the ability to reshow their previous output when the command is typed without arguments. They achieve this by storing information on the problem in memory. predict calculates various statistics (predictions, residuals, influence statistics, etc.), vce shows the covariance matrix, lincom calculates linear combinations of estimated coefficients, and test and testnl perform hypotheses tests, all using that stored information. discard eliminates that information, making it appear as if you never estimated the model.

Also See

Background: [U] **20 Ado-files**

Title

display — Display strings and values of scalar expressions

Syntax

display [*subcommand* [*subcommand* [...]]]

where *subcommand* is

"*double quoted string*"

`"*compound double quoted string*"´

[*%fmt*] [=] *exp*

as {text | txt | result | error | input}

in smcl

_asis

_skip(*#*)

_column(*#*)

_newline[(*#*)]

_continue

_dup(*#*)

_request(*macname*)

_char(*#*)

,

,,

Description

display displays strings and values of scalar expressions. display is the way you produce output from the programs you write.

Remarks

Interactively, display can be used as a substitute for a hand calculator; see [R] **display**. You can type things such as 'display 2+2'.

display's *subcommands* are used in do-files and programs to produce formatted output. The subcommands are

"*double quoted string*"	displays the string without the quotes
`"*compound double quoted string*"´	displays the string without the outer quotes; allows embedded quotes
$\left[\%\mathit{fmt}\right]$ $\left[=\right]$ exp	allows results to be formatted; see [U] **15.5 Formats: controlling how data are displayed**
as *style*	sets the style ("color") for the subcommands that follow; there may be more than one as *style* per display
in smcl	switches from _asis mode to smcl mode in smcl is the default mode if version is $\geq$ 7
_asis	switches you from smcl mode to _asis mode _asis is the default mode if version is $<$ 7
_skip(#)	skips # columns
_column(#)	skips to the #th column
_newline	goes to a new line
_newline(#)	skips # lines
_continue	suppresses automatic newline at end of display command
_dup(#)	repeats the next subcommand # times
_request(*macname*)	accepts input from the console and places it into the macro *macname*
_char(#)	displays the character for ASCII code #
,	displays a single blank between two subcommands
,,	places no blanks between two subcommands

▷ Example

Here is a nonsense program called silly that illustrates the subcommands:

```
. program list silly
silly:
  1.       set obs 10
  2.       gen myvar=uniform()
  3.       di as text _dup(59) "-"
  4.       di "hello, world"
  5.       di %~59s "This is centered"
  6.       di "myvar[1] = " as result myvar[1]
  7.       di _col(10) "myvar[1] = " myvar[1] _skip(10) "myvar[2] = " myvar[2]
  8.       di "myvar[1]/myvar[2] = " %5.4f myvar[1]/myvar[2]
  9.       di "This" _newline _col(5) "That" _newline _col(10) "What"
 10.       di `"She said, "Hello""´
 11.       di substr("abcI can do string expressionsXYZ",4,27)
 12.       di _char(65) _char(83) _char(67) _char(73) _char(73)
 13.       di _dup(59) "-" " (good-bye)"
```

and here is the result of running it:

```
. silly
obs was 0, now 10
-----------------------------------------------------------
hello, world
                        This is centered
myvar[1] = .13698408
        myvar[1] = .13698408            myvar[2] = .64322066
myvar[1]/myvar[2] = 0.2130
This
    That
        What
She said, "Hello"
I can do string expressions
ASCII
--------------------------------------------------------- (good-bye)
```

◁

Styles

Stata has four styles, called `text`, `result`, `error`, and `input`. Typically these styles are rendered in terms of color,

$$text = green$$

$$result = yellow$$

$$error = red$$

$$input = white$$

or, at least, that is the default in the Results window when the window has a black background. On a white background, the defaults are

$$text = black$$

$$result = black \text{ and bold}$$

$$error = red \text{ and bold}$$

$$input = black$$

and, in any case, the user can reset the styles to be whatever they want them to be by pulling down **Prefs** and choosing **General Preferences**.

The `display` directives `as text`, `as result`, `as error`, and `as input` allow you the programmer to specify in which rendition subsequent items in the `display` statement are to be displayed, so if a piece of your program reads

```
quietly summarize mpg
display as text "mean of mpg = " as result r(mean)
```

what might be displayed is

```
mean of mpg = 21.432432
```

where, above, our use of boldface for the 21.432432 is to emphasize that it would be displayed differently than the "mean of mpg =" part. In the Results window, if we had a black background, the "mean of mpg =" part would be in green and the 21.432432 would be in yellow.

You can switch back and forth among styles within a `display` statement and between `display` statements. Here is how we recommend using the styles:

`as result` should be used to display things that depend on the data being used. For statistical output, think of what would happen if the names of the dataset remained the same but all the data changed. Clearly, calculated results would change. That is what should be displayed `as result`.

`as text` should be used to display the text around the results. Again, think of the experiment where you change the data but not the names. Anything that would not change should be displayed `as text`. This will include not just the names, but table lines and borders, variable labels, etc.

`as error` should be reserved for displaying error messages. `as error` is special in that it not only displays the message as an error (probably meaning that the message is displayed in red), but in that it also forces the message to display even if output is being suppressed. (There are two commands for suppressing output: `quietly` and `capture`. `quietly` will not suppress `as error` messages but `capture` will, the idea being that `capture`, since it captures the return code, is anticipating errors and will take the appropriate action.)

`as input` should never be used unless you are creating a special effect. `as input` (white on a black background) is reserved for what the user types, and the output your program is producing is definitionally not being typed by the user. Stata uses `as input` when it displays what the user types.

❑ Technical Note

Prior to Stata 7, `display` had a syntax that allowed the directives `in green`, `in yellow`, `in blue`, `in red`, and `in white`. Stata still allows this, so that old programs continue to work. The mapping is

$$\text{in green} = \text{as text}$$

$$\text{in yellow} = \text{as result}$$

$$\text{in blue} = \text{as text } (sic)$$

$$\text{in red} = \text{as error}$$

$$\text{in white} = \text{as input}$$

You can use the old or the new syntax in both old and new programs; it does not matter. Notice that the color blue has disappeared; you can specify `in blue`, but it means `as text`, which is to say, `in green`. Blue is no longer available as a color because that color is now reserved for displaying links.

❑

display used with quietly and noisily

`display`'s output will be suppressed by `quietly` at the appropriate times. Consider the following:

```
. program list example1
example1:
  1. di "hello there"
. example1
hello there
. quietly example1
. _
```

The output was suppressed because the program was run `quietly`. Messages displayed `as error`, however, are considered error messages and are always displayed:

```
. program list example2
example2:
  1.      di as error "hello there"
. example2
hello there
. quietly example2
hello there
```

Even though the program was run `quietly`, the message `as error` was displayed. Error messages should always be displayed `as error` so that they will always be displayed at the terminal.

Programs often have parts of their code buried in `capture` or `quietly` blocks. `display`s inside such blocks produce no output:

```
. program list example3
example3:
  1. quietly {
  2.     display "hello there"
  3. }
. example3

.
```

Had the `display` included `as error`, the text would have been displayed, but only error output should be displayed that way. For regular output, the solution is to precede the `display` with `noisily`:

```
. program list example4
example4:
  1. quietly {
  2.     noisily display "hello there"
  3. }
. example4
hello there
```

This method also allows Stata to correctly treat a `quietly` specified by the caller:

```
. quietly example4

.
```

Despite its name, `noisily` does not really guarantee that the output will be shown—it restores the output only if output would have been allowed at the instant the program was called.

For more information on `noisily` and `quietly`, see [P] **quietly**.

Columns

display can only move forward and downward. The subcommands that take a numeric argument allow only nonnegative integer arguments. It is not possible to back up to make an insertion in the output.

```
. program list cont
cont:
  1.        di "Stuff" _column(9) "More Stuff"
  2.        di "Stuff" _continue
  3.        di _column(9) "More Stuff"
. cont
Stuff    More Stuff
Stuff    More Stuff
```

display and SMCL

SMCL is Stata's output formatter, and all Stata output passes through SMCL. See [P] **smcl** for a complete description. Here we just want to emphasize that all the features of SMCL are available to `display` and so motivate you to turn to the SMCL section of this manual.

In our opening silly example, we included the line

```
di as text _dup(59) "-"
```

That line would have better read

```
di as text "{hline 59}"
```

The first `display` produces this:

```
-----------------------------------------------------------
```

and the second produces this:

```
_____
```

It was not `display` that produced that solid line—`display` just displayed the characters {hline 59}. Output of Stata, however, passes through something called SMCL, and SMCL interprets what it hears. When SMCL heard {hline 59}, SMCL drew a horizontal line 59 characters wide.

SMCL has lots of other capabilities, including the ability to create clickable links in your output that, when you click on them, can even cause other Stata commands to execute.

If you carefully review the SMCL documentation, you will discover lots of overlap in the capabilities of SMCL and `display` that will lead you to wonder whether you should use `display`'s capabilities or SMCL's. For instance, in the section above we demonstrated the use of `display`'s _column() feature to skip forward to a column. If you read the SMCL documentation, you will discover that SMCL has a similar feature, {col}. You can type

```
display "Stuff" _column(9) "More Stuff"
```

or you can type

```
display "Stuff{col 9}More Stuff"
```

So which should you type? The answer is that it makes no difference, and that when you use `display`'s _column() directive, `display` just outputs the corresponding SMCL {col} directive for you. This rule generalizes beyond _column(). For instance,

```
display as text "hello"
```

and

```
display "{text}hello"
```

are equivalent. There is, however, one important place where `display` and SMCL are different:

```
display as error "error message"
```

is not quite the same as

```
display "{error}error message"
```

Use `display as error`. The SMCL `{error}` directive sets the rendition to that of errors, but it does not tell Stata that the message is to be displayed even if output is otherwise being suppressed. `display`'s `as error` both sets the rendition and tells Stata to override output suppression if that is relevant.

❏ Technical Note

All Stata output passes through SMCL, and one side effect of that is that open and close brace characters { and } are treated oddly by `display`. Try the following:

```
display as text "{1, 2, 3}"
{1, 2, 3}
```

The result is just as you expect. Now try

```
display as text "{result}"
```

The result will be to display nothing because `{result}` is a SMCL directive. The first displayed something even though it contained braces because `{1, 2, 3}` is not a SMCL directive.

You want to be careful when displaying something that might itself contain braces. You can do that by using `display`'s `_asis` directive. Once you specify `_asis`, whatever follows in the display will be displayed exactly as it is, without SMCL interpretation:

```
display as text _asis "{result}"
{result}
```

You can switch back to allowing SMCL interpretation within the line using the `in smcl` directive:

```
display as text _asis "{result}" in smcl "is a {bf:smcl} directive"
{result} is a **smcl** directive
```

Each and every `display` command in your program starts off in SMCL mode unless the program is running with `version` set to 6 or before, in which case each and every `display` starts off in `_asis` mode. If you want to use SMCL in old programs without otherwise updating them, you can include `display`'s `in smcl` directive.

❏

Displaying variable names

Let us assume that a program we are writing is to produce a table that looks like this:

```
    Variable |    Obs        Mean    Std. Dev.       Min        Max
-------------+-------------------------------------------------------
         mpg |     74     21.2973     5.785503        12         41
      weight |     74     3019.459    777.1936      1760       4840
       displ |     74     197.2973    91.83722        79        425
```

Putting out the header in our program is easy enough:

```
        di in text "    Variable {c |}      Obs" /*
            */ _col(37) "Mean    Std. Dev.       Min       Max"
        di in text "{hline 13}{c +}{hline 53}"
```

We use the SMCL directive {hline} to draw the horizontal line, and we use the SMCL characters {c |} and {c +} to output the vertical bar and the "plus" sign where the lines cross.

Now let's turn to putting out the rest of the table. Let us remember that variable names can be of unequal length and can even be very long. If we are not careful, we might end up putting out something that looks like this:

```
    Variable |     Obs        Mean    Std. Dev.       Min       Max
    ---------+
miles_per_gallon |     74     21.2973   5.785503          12        41
    weight |     74    3019.459   777.1936        1760      4840
displacement |     74    197.2973   91.83722          79       425
```

If it were not for the too-long variable name, we could avoid the problem by displaying our lines with something like this:

```
    display in text %12s "`vname'" " {c |}" /*
        */ as result /*
        */ %8.0g `n' "    " /*
        */ %9.0g `mean' "  " %9.0g `sd'   "  " /*
        */ %9.0g `min'  "  " %9.0g `max'
```

What we are imagining here is that we write a subroutine to display a line of output and that the display line above appears in that subroutine:

```
    program define output_line
        args n mean sd min max
        display in text %12s "`vname'" " {c |}" /*
            */ as result /*
            */ %8.0g `n' "    " /*
            */ %9.0g `mean' "  " %9.0g `sd'   "  " /*
            */ %9.0g `min'  "  " %9.0g `max'
    end
```

In our main routine, we would calculate results and then just call output_line with the variable name and results to be displayed. This subroutine would be sufficient to produce the following output:

```
    Variable |     Obs        Mean    Std. Dev.       Min       Max
    ---------+
miles_per_gallon |     74     21.2973   5.785503          12        41
      weight |     74    3019.459   777.1936        1760      4840
displacement |     74    197.2973   91.83722          79       425
```

The short variable name weight would be spaced over because we specified the %12s format. The right way to handle the miles_per_gallon variable is to display its abbreviation using Stata's abbrev() function:

```
    program define output_line
        args n mean sd min max
        display in text %12s abbrev("`vname'",12) " {c |}" /*
            */ as result /*
            */ %8.0g `n' "    " /*
            */ %9.0g `mean' "  " %9.0g `sd'   "  " /*
            */ %9.0g `min'  "  " %9.0g `max'
    end
```

With this improved subroutine, we would get the following output:

Variable	Obs	Mean	Std. Dev.	Min	Max
miles_per_~n	74	21.2973	5.785503	12	41
weight	74	3019.459	777.1936	1760	4840
displacement	74	197.2973	91.83722	79	425

The point of this is to convince you to learn about and use Stata's `abbrev()` function. `abbrev("`vname'",12)` returns `vname` abbreviated to 12 characters.

If we now wanted to modify our program to produce the following output,

Variable	Obs	Mean	Std. Dev.	Min	Max
miles_per_~n	74	21.2973	5.785503	12	41
weight	74	3019.459	777.1936	1760	4840
displacement	74	197.2973	91.83722	79	425

all we would need do is add a `display` at the end of the main routine that reads

```
di in text "{hline 13}{c BT}{hline 53}"
```

Note the use of `{c BT}`. The characters that we use to draw lines in and around tables are summarized in [P] **smcl**.

❏ Technical Note

Let us now consider outputting the table in the following form:

Variable	Obs	Mean	Std. Dev.	Min	Max
miles_per_~n	74	21.2973	5.785503	12	41
weight	74	3019.459	777.1936	1760	4840
displacement	74	197.2973	91.83722	79	425

where the boldfaced entries are clickable and, if you click on them, the result is to execute `summarize` followed by the variable name. We assume you have already read [P] **smcl** and so know that the relevant SMCL directive to create the link is `{stata}`, but continue reading even if you have not read [P] **smcl**.

The obvious fix to our subroutine would be simply to add the `{stata}` directive, although to do that we will have to store `abbrev("`vname'",12)` in a macro so that we can refer to it:

```
program define output_line
        args n mean sd min max
        local abname = abbrev("`vname'",12)
        display in text %12s "{stata summarize `vname':`abname'}" /*
            */ " {c |}" /*
            */ as result /*
            */ %8.0g `n' "    " /*
            */ %9.0g `mean' "  " %9.0g `sd'    "  " /*
            */ %9.0g `min'  "  " %9.0g `max'
end
```

The SMCL directive `{stata summarize `vname':`abname'}` says to display `abname` as clickable and, if the user clicks on it, to execute `summarize `vname'`. Notice that we used the abbreviated name to display and the unabbreviated name in the command.

The single problem with this fix is that our table will not align correctly because `display` does not know that "`{stata summarize `vname´:`abname´}`" displays only `abname´. To `display`, the string looks very long and is not going to fit into a `%12s` field. The solution to that problem is

```
program define output_line
        args n mean sd min max
        local abname = abbrev("`vname´,12)
        display in text "{ralign 12:{stata summarize `vname´:`abname´}}" /*
            */ " {c |}" /*
            */ as result /*
            */ %8.0g `n´ "    " /*
            */ %9.0g `mean´ "  " %9.0g `sd´    "    " /*
            */ %9.0g `min´ "  " %9.0g `max´
end
```

The SMCL `{ralign #:text}` macro right aligns *text* in a field 12 wide, and so is equivalent to `%12s`. The *text* we are asking be aligned is "`{stata summarize `vname´:`abname´}`", but SMCL understands that the only displayable part of the string is `abname´ and so will align it correctly.

If we wanted to duplicate the effect of a `%-12s` format using SMCL, we would use `{lalign 12:text}`.

❑

Obtaining input from the terminal

`display`'s `_request(`*macname*`)` option accepts input from the console and places it into the macro *macname*. For example,

```
. display "What is Y? " _request(yval)
What is Y? i don´t know
. display "$yval"
i don´t know
```

If `yval` had to be a number, the code fragment to obtain it might be

```
global yval "junk"
capture confirm number $yval
while _rc~=0 {
        display "What is Y? " _request(yval)
        capture confirm number $yval
}
```

One will typically want to store such input into a local macro. Remember that local macros have names that really begin with a '_':

```
local yval "junk"
capture confirm number `yval´
while _rc~=0 {
        display "What is Y? " _request(_yval)
        capture confirm number `yval´
}
```

Also See

Complementary:	[P] **capture**, [P] **quietly**
Related:	[P] **smcl**; [P] **return**, [R] **list**, [R] **outfile**
Background:	[U] **15.5 Formats: controlling how data are displayed**, [U] **21 Programming Stata**

Title

error — Display generic error message and exit

Syntax

error *exp*

Description

error displays the most generic form of the error message associated with expression and sets the return code to the evaluation of the expression. If expression evaluates to 0, error does nothing. Otherwise, the nonzero return code will force an exit from the program or capture block in which it occurs. error sets the return code to 197 if there is an error in using error itself.

Remarks

error is used two ways inside programs. In the first case, you want to display a standard error message so that users can look up your message using search:

```
if `nvals´>100 {
        error 134
}
```

According to [R] **search**, return code 134 is associated with the message "too many values". During program development, you can verify that by typing the error command interactively:

```
. error 134
too many values
r(134);
```

Below, we list the individual return codes so that you can select the appropriate one for use with error in your programs.

error is also used when you have processed a block of code in a capture block, suppressing all output. If anything has gone wrong, you want to display the error message associated with whatever the problem was

```
capture {
        code continues
}
local rc=_rc                    preserve return code from capture
cleanup code
error `rc´                      present error message and exit if necessary
code could continue
```

One hopes that in the majority of cases the return code will be zero so that error does nothing.

You can interrogate the built-in variable _rc to determine the type of error that occurred and then take the appropriate action. Also see [U] **19.1.4 Error handling in do-files**.

The return codes are numerically grouped, which is a feature that you may find useful when you are writing programs. The groups are

Return Codes	Meaning
1–99	sundry "minor" errors
100–199	syntax errors
300–399	failure to find previously stored result
400–499	statistical problems
500–599	matrix-manipulation errors
600–699	file errors
700–799	operating-system errors
800–899	gph errors
900–999	insufficient-memory errors
1000–1999	system-limit-exceeded errors
2000–2999	non-errors (continuation of 400–499)
3000–3999	programmer use in the dialog manager
8000–8999	pd error messages
9000–9999	system-failure errors

Summary

1. You pressed *Break*. This is not considered an error.

2. `connection timed out`
   An Internet connection has timed out. This can happen when the initial attempt to make a connection over the Internet has not succeeded within a certain time limit. You can change the time limit that Stata uses under this condition by typing `set timeout1` *#seconds*. Or, the initial connection was successful, but a subsequent attempt to send or receive data over the Internet has timed out. You can also change this time limit by typing `set timeout2` *#seconds*.

3. `no dataset in use`
   You attempted to perform a command requiring data and have no data in memory.

4. `no; data in memory would be lost`
   You attempted to perform a command that would substantively alter or destroy the data and the data has not been saved, at least since it was last changed. If you wish to continue anyway, add the `clear` option to the end of the command. Otherwise, `save` the data first.

5. `not sorted`
   `master data not sorted`
   `using data not sorted`
   In the case of the first message, you typed `by` *varlist*: *command* but the data in memory is not sorted by *varlist*. Type `sort` *varlist* first; see [R] **sort**.

   In the second and third cases, both the dataset in memory and the dataset on disk must be sorted by the variables specified in the *varlist* of `merge` before they can be merged. If the *master* dataset is not sorted, `sort` it. If the *using* dataset is not sorted, `use` it, `sort` it, and then `save` it. See [R] **sort** and [R] **save**.

6. Return code from `confirm existence` when *string* does not exist.

7. `` `_____' found where _____ expected ``
   You are using a program which in turn is using the `confirm` command to verify that what you typed makes sense. The messages indicate what you typed and what the program expected to find instead of what you typed.

9. `assertion is false`
   `no action taken`
   Return code and message from `assert` when the assertion is false; see [P] **assert**.
   Or, you were using `mvencode` and requested Stata change '.' to # in the specified *varlist*, but # already existed in the *varlist*, so Stata refused; see [R] **mvencode**.

18. `you must start with an empty dataset`
   The command (e.g., `infile`) requires that no data be in memory—you must `drop _all` first. You are probably using `infile` to append additional data to the data in memory. Instead, `save` the data in memory, `drop _all`, `infile` the new data, and then `append` the previously saved data; see [R] **append**.

100. `varlist required`
     `= exp required`
     `using required`
     `by() option required`
     Certain commands require a *varlist* or another element of the language. The message specifies the required item that was missing from the command you gave. See the command's syntax diagram. For example, `merge` requires `using` be specified; perhaps, you meant to type `append`. Or, `ranksum` requires a `by()` option; see [R] **signrank**.

101. `varlist not allowed`
     `weights not allowed`
     `in range not allowed`
     `if not allowed`
     `= exp not allowed`
     `using not allowed`
     Certain commands do not allow an `if` *exp* or other elements of the language. The message specifies which item in the command is not allowed. See the command's syntax diagram. For example, `append` does not allow a *varlist*; perhaps you meant to type `merge`.

102. `too few variables specified`
     The command requires more variables than you specified. For instance, `stack` requires at least two variables. See the syntax diagram for the command.

103. `too many variables specified`
     The command does not allow as many variables as you specified. For example, `tabulate` takes only one or two variables. See the syntax diagram for the command.

104. `nothing to input`
     You gave the `input` command with no *varlist*. Stata will input onto the end of the dataset, but there is no existing dataset in this case. You must specify the variable names on the `input` command.

106. `_____ is _____ in using data`
     You have attempted to match-merge two datasets and yet one of the key variables is a string in one dataset and a numeric in the other. The first blank is filled in with the variable name and the second blank with the storage type. It is logically impossible to fulfill your request. Perhaps you meant another variable.

107. `not possible with numeric variable`
     You have requested something that is logically impossible with a numeric variable, such as `encoding` it. Perhaps you meant another variable or typed `encode` when you meant `decode`.

108. `not possible with string variable`
     You have requested something that is logically impossible with a string variable, such as `decoding` it. Perhaps you meant another variable or typed `decode` when you meant `encode`.

109. `type mismatch`
     You probably attempted to `generate` a new string variable and forgot to specify its type, so Stata assumed the new variable was to be numeric. Include a `str#` before the name of the new variable in your `generate` statement. More generally, in an expression you attempted to combine a string and numeric subexpression in a logically impossible way. For instance, you attempted to subtract a string from a number or you attempted to take the substring of a number.

110. `_____ already defined`
     A variable or a value label has already been defined, and you attempted to redefine it. This occurs most often with `generate`. If you really intend to replace the values, use `replace`. If you intend to replace a value label, first give the `label drop` command. If you are attempting to alter an existing label, specify the `add` or `modify` option with the `label define` command.

111. `_____ not found`
     `no variables defined`
     The variable does not exist. You may have mistyped the variable's name.

     `variables out of order`
     You specified a *varlist* containing *varname1-varname2*, yet *varname1* occurs *after* *varname2*. Reverse the order of the variables if you did not make some other typographical error. Remember, *varname1-varname2* is taken by Stata to mean *varname1*, *varname2*, and all the variables in *dataset order* in between. Type `describe` to see the order of the variables in your dataset.

_____ not found in using data
You specified a *varlist* with **merge**, yet the variables on which you wish to merge are not found in the using dataset, so the **merge** is not possible.

_____ ambiguous abbreviation
You typed an ambiguous abbreviation for a variable in your data. The abbreviation could refer to more than one variable. Use a nonambiguous abbreviation or, if you intend all the variables implied by the ambiguous abbreviation, append a '*' to the end of the abbreviation.

119. statement out of context
This is the generic form of this message; more likely, you will see messages such as "may not streset after . . . ". You have attempted to do something that, in this context, is not allowed or does not make sense.

120. invalid %format
You specified an invalid *%fmt*; see [U] **15.5 Formats: controlling how data are displayed**.

Return codes 121–127 are errors that might occur when you specify a *numlist*. For details about *numlist*, see [U] **14.1.8 numlist**.

121. invalid numlist

122. invalid numlist has too few elements

123. invalid numlist has too many elements

124. invalid numlist has elements out of order

125. invalid numlist has elements outside of allowed range

126. invalid numlist has noninteger elements

127. invalid numlist has missing values

130. expression too long
     too many SUMs
In the first case, you specified an expression that is too long for Stata to process—the expression contains more than 255 pairs of nested parentheses or more than 66 dyadic operators. Break the expression into smaller parts. In the second case, the expression contains more than five **sum()** functions. This expression, too, will have to be broken into smaller parts.

131. not possible with test
You requested a **test** of a hypothesis that is nonlinear in the variables. **test** tests only linear hypotheses. Use **testnl**.

132. too many '(' or '['
     too many ')' or ']'
You specified an expression with unbalanced parentheses or brackets.

133. unknown function _____()
You specified a function that is unknown to Stata; see [U] **16.3 Functions**. Alternatively, you may have meant to subscript a variable and accidentally used parentheses rather than square brackets; see [U] **16.7 Explicit subscripting**.

134. too many values
(1) You attempted to **encode** a string variable that takes on more than 65,536 unique values. (2) You attempted to **tabulate** a variable or pair of variables that take on too many values. If you specified two variables, try interchanging the two variables. (3) You issued a **graph** command using the **by** option. The by-variable takes on too many different values to construct a readable chart.

135. not possible with weighted data
You attempted to **predict** something other than the prediction or residual, yet the underlying model was weighted. Stata cannot calculate the statistic you requested using weighted data.

140. repeated categorical variable in term
At least one of the terms in your **anova** model or **test** statement has a repeated categorical variable, such as **reg*div*reg**. Either you forgot to specify that the variable is continuous or the second occurrence of the variable is unnecessary.

141. repeated term
In the list of terms in your **anova** model or **test** statement is a duplicate of another term, although perhaps ordered differently. For instance, **X*A*X** and **A*X*X**. Remove the repeated term.

142. `attempt to classify extraneous variable`
    You have specified a variable as continuous or categorical that is not contained in your `anova` model. Perhaps you inadvertently left the variable out of your model. On the other hand, if the variable does not belong in your model, then it should not appear in the `continuous()` or `category()` options.

143. `variable left unclassified`
    You can get this error only if you specify *both* the `continuous()` *and* the `category()` options. It is not necessary to do this since specifying one or the other is sufficient—Stata assumes that the remaining variables fall into the omitted class. If you do specify both, you must account for every variable in your model. You left one or more variables unclassified.

144. `variable classified inconsistently`
    Please see the explanation for return code 143. In this case, you placed the same variable in both the `continuous()` and the `category()` lists.

145. `term contains more than 8 variables`
    One of the terms in your `anova` model `test` statement contains more than 8 variables. Stata cannot estimate such models.

146. `too many variables or values  (matsize too small)`
    Your `anova` model resulted in a specification containing more than `matsize` − 2 explanatory variables; see [R] **matsize**.

147. `term not in model`
    Your `test` command refers to a term that was not contained in your `anova` model.

148. `too few categories`
    You attempted to estimate a model such as `mlogit`, `ologit`, or `oprobit` when the number of outcomes is smaller than 3. Check that the dependent variable is the variable you intend. If it takes on exactly two values, use `logit` or `probit`.

149. `too many categories`
    You attempted to estimate a model such as `mlogit`, `ologit`, or `oprobit` with a dependent variable that takes on more than 50 outcomes (Intercooled Stata) or 20 outcomes (Small Stata).

151. `non r-class program may not set r()`
    Perhaps you specified `return local` in your program, but forgot to declare the program `rclass` in the `program define` statement.

152. `non e-class program may not set e()`
    Perhaps you specified `estimates local` in your program, but forgot to declare the program `eclass` in the `program define` statement.

153. `non s-class program may not set s()`
    Perhaps you specified `sreturn local` in your program, but forgot to declare the program `sclass` in the `program define` statement.

170. `unable to chdir`
    (*Unix and Macintosh.*) `cd` was unable to change to the directory you typed because it does not exist, it is protected, or it is not a directory.

180. `invalid attempt to modify label`
    You are attempting to modify the contents of an existing *value label* using the `label define` command. If you mean to completely replace the existing label, first `label drop` it and then `label define` it. If you wish to modify the existing label, be sure to specify either the `add` option or the `modify` option on the `label define` command. `add` lets you add new entries but not change existing ones, and `modify` lets you do both. You will get this error if you specify `add` and then attempt to modify an existing entry. In that case, edit the command and substitute `modify` for the `add` option.

181. `may not label strings`
    You attempted to assign a value label to a string variable, which makes no sense.

182. `_____ not labeled`
    The indicated variable has no value label, yet your request requires a labeled variable. You may, for instance, be attempting to `decode` a numeric variable.

190. `request may not be combined with by`
    Certain commands may not be combined with `by`, and you constructed such a combination. See the syntax diagram for the command.

in may not be combined with by
in may never be combined with by. Use if instead; see [U] **14.5 by varlist: construct**.

196. nl_____ refused query, rc=_____
error #_____ occurred in program nl_____
Your nl*func* program did not work properly with the nl command.

197. invalid syntax
This error is produced by syntax and other parsing commands when there is a syntax error in the use of the command itself rather than in what is being parsed.

198. invalid syntax
_____ invalid
range invalid
_____ invalid obs no
invalid filename
_____ invalid varname
_____ invalid name
multiple by's not allowed
_____ found where number expected
on or off required
All items in this list indicate invalid syntax. These errors are often, but not always, due to typographical errors. Stata attempts to provide you with as much information as it can. Review the syntax diagram for the designated command.

In giving the message "invalid syntax", Stata is not very helpful. Errors in specifying expressions often result in this message.

199. unrecognized command
Stata failed to recognize the command, program, or ado-file name, probably because of a typographical or abbreviation error.

301. last estimates not found
You typed an estimation command such as regress without arguments or attempted to perform a test or typed predict, but there were no previous estimation results.

302. last test not found
You have requested the redisplay of a previous test, yet you have not run a test previously.

303. equation not found
You referred to a coefficient or stored result corresponding to an equation or outcome that cannot be found. For instance, you estimated a mlogit model and the outcome variable took on the values 1, 3, and 4. You referred to [2]_b[var] when perhaps you meant [#2]_b[var] or [3]_b[var].

304. ml model not found
You have used mleval, mlsum, or mlmatsum without having first used the other ml commands to define the model.

305. ml model not found
Same as 304.

399. may not drop constant
You issued a logistic or logit command and the constant was dropped. Your model may be underidentified; try removing one or more of the independent variables.

401. may not use noninteger frequency weights
You specified an fweight frequency weight with noninteger weights, telling Stata your weights are to be treated as replication counts. Stata encountered a weight that was not an integer, so your request made no sense. You probably meant to specify aweight analytic weights; see [U] **14.1.6 weight**.

402. negative weights encountered
negative weights not allowed
You specified a variable that contains negative values as the weighting variable, so your request made no sense. Perhaps you meant to specify another variable.

403. may not specify norobust with pweights
You specified one of Stata's estimation commands with both the norobust and the pweight options. You cannot do this since robust is a request that pweight be used. See [U] **23.11 Obtaining robust variance estimates**.

404. `not possible with pweighted data`
    You requested a statistic which Stata cannot calculate with `pweighted` data either because of a shortcoming in Stata or because the statistics of the problem have not been worked out. For example, perhaps you requested the standard error of the survival curve, and you had previously specified `pweight` when you `stset` your data (a case where no one has worked out the statistics).

406. `not possible with analytic weights`
    You specified a command that does not allow analytic weights. See the syntax diagram for the command to see which types of weights are allowed.

407. `weights must be the same for all observations in a group`
    `weights not constant for same observation across repeated variables`
    For some commands, weights must be the same for all observations in a group for statistical or computational reasons. For the `anova` command with the `repeated()` option, weights must be constant for an observation across the repeated variables.

409. `no variance`
    You were using `lnskew0` or `bcskew0`, for instance, but the *exp* that you specified has no variance.

411. `nonpositive values encountered`
    `_____ has negative values`
    `time variable has negative values`
    For instance, you have used `graph` with the `xlog` or `ylog` options, requesting log scales, and yet some of the data or the labeling you specified is negative or zero.
    Or, perhaps you were using `ltable` and specified a time variable that has negative values.

412. `redundant or inconsistent constraints`
    For instance, you are estimating a constrained model with `mlogit`. Among the constraints specified is at least one that is redundant or inconsistent. A redundant constraint might constrain a coefficient to be zero that some other constraint also constrains to be zero. An inconsistent constraint might constrain a coefficient to be 1 that some other constraint constrains to be zero. List the constraints, find the offender, and then reissue the `mlogit` command omitting it.

416. `missing values encountered`
    You were using a command which requires that no values be missing.

420. `_____ groups found, 2 required`
    You used a command (such as `ttest`) and the grouping variable you specified does not take on 2 unique values.

421. `could not determine between-subject error term; use bse() option`
    You specified the `repeated()` option to `anova`, but Stata could not automatically determine certain terms that are needed in the calculation; see [R] **anova**.

422. `could not determine between-subject basic unit; use bseunit() option`
    You specified the `repeated()` option to `anova`, but Stata could not automatically determine certain terms that are needed in the calculation; see [R] **anova**.

430. `convergence not achieved`
    You have estimated a maximum-likelihood model and Stata's maximization procedure failed to converge to a solution; see [R] **maximize**. Check if the model is identified.

450. `_____ is not a 0/1 variable`
    `number of successes invalid`
    `p invalid`
    `_____ takes on _____ values, not 2`
    You have used a command, such as `bitest`, that requires the variable take on only the values 0, 1, or missing, but the variable you specified does not meet that restriction. (You can also get this message from, for example, `bitesti`, when you specify a number of successes greater than the number of observations or a probability not between 0 and 1.)

451. `invalid values for time variable`
    For instance, you specified `mytime` as a time variable and `mytime` contains noninteger values.

459. `something that should be true of your data is not`
    This is the generic form of this message; more likely, you will see messages such as "y must be between 0 and 1" or "x not positive". You have attempted to do something that, given your data, does not make sense.

460. `only one cluster detected`
`only one PSU detected`
`stratum with only one PSU detected`
`stratum with only one observation detected`
You were using the `cluster()` option and you had only one cluster; you must have at least two clusters—preferably much more than two. Or, you were using an `svy` command, and you had only one PSU in one stratum; the `svydes` command will determine which stratum and the [R] **svydes** entry shows how to deal with the situation.

461. `number of obs must be greater than # for robust variance computation`
`number of obs in subpopulation must be greater than #`
`no observations in subpopulation`
You had insufficient observations for the robust variance estimator. Or, you were trying to produce estimates for a subpopulation and had insufficient observations in the subpopulation.

462. `fpc must be >= 0`
`fpc for all observations within a stratum must be the same`
`fpc must be <= 1 if a rate, or >= no. sampled PSUs per stratum if PSU totals`
There is a problem with your `fpc` variable; see [R] **svymean**.

463. `sum of weights equals zero`
`sum of weights for subpopulation equals zero`
When weights sum to zero, the requested statistic cannot be computed.

471. `esample() invalid`
This concerns `estimates post`. The variable *varname* specified by the `esample(`*varname*`)` option must contain exclusively 0 and 1 values (never, for instance, 2 or missing). *varname* contains invalid values.

480. `starting values invalid or some RHS variables have missing values`
You were using `nl` and specified starting values that were infeasible, or you have missing values for some of your independent variables.

481. `equation/system not identified`
`cannot calculate derivatives`
You were using `reg3`, for instance, and the system that you have specified is not identified.

You specified an `nl` *fcn* for which derivatives cannot be calculated.

482. `nonpositive value(s) among _____, cannot log transform`
You specified an `lnlsq` option in `nl` that attempts to take the log of a nonpositive value.

491. `could not find feasible values`
You are using `ml` and it could not find starting values for which the likelihood function could be evaluated. You could try using `ml search` with the `repeat()` option to randomly try more values or you could use `ml init` to specify valid starting values.

498. *various messages*
The statistical problem described in the message has occurred. The code 498 is not helpful, but the message is supposed to be. Return code 498 is reserved for messages that are unique to a particular situation.

499. *various messages*
The statistical problem described in the message has occurred. The code 499 is not helpful, but the message is supposed to be. Return code 499 is reserved for messages that are unique to a particular situation.

501. `matrix operation not found`
You have issued an unknown `matrix` subcommand or used `matrix define` with a function or operator that is unknown to Stata.

503. `conformability error`
You have issued a `matrix` command attempting to combine two matrices that are not conformable, for example, multiplying a 3×2 matrix by a 3×3 matrix. You will also get this message if you attempt an operation that requires a square matrix and the matrix is not square.

504. `matrix has missing values`
You have issued a `matrix` command attempting a matrix operation that, were it carried out, would result in a matrix with missing values; dividing by zero is a good example.

505. `matrix not symmetric`
You have issued a `matrix` command that can only be performed on a symmetric matrix and your matrix is not symmetric. While fixing their code, programmers are requested to admire our choice of the "symmetric" number 505—it is symmetric about the zero—for this error.

506. `matrix not positive definite`

You have issued a `matrix` command that can only be performed on a positive definite matrix and your matrix is not positive definite.

507. `name conflict`

You have issued a `matrix post` command and the variance–covariance matrix of the estimators does not have the same row and column names or, if it does, those names are not the same as for the coefficient vector.

509. `matrix operators that return matrices not allowed in this context`

Expressions returning nonmatrices, such as those in `generate` and `replace`, may use matrix functions returning scalars, such as `trace(A)`, but may not include subexpressions evaluating to matrices, such as `trace(A+B)`, which requires evaluating the matrix expression $A + B$. (Such subexpressions are allowed in the context of expressions returning matrices, such as those in `matrix`.)

601. `file _____ not found`

The filename you specified cannot be found. Perhaps you mistyped the name, or it may be on another diskette or directory. If you are a Macintosh user, perhaps you had an unintentional blank at the beginning or ending of your filename when it was created. In Finder, click on the file to blacken the name. If you see anything other than a thin, even space on each side of the name, rename the file to eliminate the leading and trailing space characters.

602. `file _____ already exists`

You attempted to write over a file that already exists. Stata will never let you do this accidentally. If you really intend to overwrite the previous file, reissue the last command specifying the `replace` option.

603. `file _____ could not be opened`

This file, although found, failed to open properly. This error is unlikely to occur. You will have to review your operating system's manual to determine why it occurred.

604. `log file already open`

You attempted to open a `log` file when one is already open. Perhaps you forgot you have the file open or forgot to close it.

606. `no log file open`

You have attempted to `close`, turn `on`, or turn `off` logging when no log file was open. Perhaps you forgot to open the log file.

607. `no cmdlog file open`

You have attempted to `close`, turn `on`, or turn `off` logging when no cmdlog file was open. Perhaps you forgot to open the cmdlog file.

609. `file xp format`

The designated file is stored in an unsupported cross-product format.

610. `file _____ not Stata format`

The designated file is not a Stata-format file. This occurs most frequently with `use`, `append`, and `merge`. You probably typed the wrong filename.

611. `record too long`

You have attempted to process a record that exceeds 7,998 (18,998 for Unix) characters in length using formatted-`infile` (i.e., `infile` with a dictionary). When reading formatted data, records may not exceed this maximum. If the records are not formatted, you can read this data using the standard `infile` command (i.e., without a dictionary). There is no maximum record length for unformatted data.

612. `unexpected end of file`

You used `infile` with a dictionary, and the file containing the dictionary ended before the '`}`' character. Perhaps you forgot to type the closing brace, or perhaps you are missing a hard return at the end of your file. You may also get this message if you issued the command `#delimit ;` in a do-file and then subsequently forgot to use '`;`' before the '`end`' statement.

613. `file does not contain dictionary`

You used `infile` with a dictionary, yet the file you specified does not begin with the word '`dictionary`'. Perhaps you are attempting to `infile` data without using a dictionary and forgot to specify the *varlist* on the `infile` command. Alternatively, you forgot to include the word `dictionary` at the top of the dictionary file or typed `DICTIONARY` in uppercase.

614. `dictionary invalid`

You used `infile` with a dictionary and the file appears to contain a dictionary. Nevertheless, you have made some error in specifying the dictionary and Stata does not understand your intentions. The contents of the dictionary are listed on the screen and the last line is the line that gave rise to the problem.

615. `cannot determine separator -- use tab or comma option`
You used the `insheet` command to read a file, but Stata is having trouble determining whether the file is tab- or comma-separated. Reissue the `insheet` command and specify the `comma` or `tab` option.

616. `wrong number of values in checksum file`
The checksum file being used to verify integrity of another file does not contain values in the expected checksum format.

621. `already preserved`
You specified `preserve`, but you have already `preserved` the data.

622. `nothing to restore`
You issued the `restore` command, but you have not previously specified `preserve`.

Return codes 630–696 are all messages that you might receive when executing any command with a file over the network.

631. `host not found`

632. `web filename not supported in this context`

633. `saving to web files not supported in this version of Stata`

639. `file transmission error (checksums do not match)`

640. `package file too long`

660. `proxy host not found`
The host name specified as a proxy server cannot be mapped to an IP address. Type `query` to determine the host you have set.

662. `proxy server refused request to send`
Stata was able to contact the proxy server, but the proxy server refused to send data back to Stata. The proxy host or port specified may be incorrect. Type `query` to determine your settings.

663. `remote connection to proxy failed`
Although you have set a proxy server, it is not responding to Stata. The likely problems are you specified the wrong port; you specified the wrong host; the proxy server is down. Type `query` to determine the host and port that you have set.

665. `could not set socket non-blocking`

667. `wrong version winsock.dll`

668. `could not find a valid winsock.dll`

669. `invalid URL`

670. `invalid network port number`

671. `unknown network protocol`

672. `server refused to send file`

673. `authorization required by server`

674. `unexpected response from server`

675. `server reported server error`

676. `server refused request to send`

677. `remote connection failed`
You requested that something be done over the web, but Stata could not contact the specified host. Perhaps, the host is down; try again later.

If all of your web access results in this message, perhaps your network connection is via a proxy server. If it is, then you must tell Stata. Contact your system administrator and ask for the name and port of the "http proxy server". See *Using the Internet* in the *Getting Started* manual for details on how to inform Stata.

678. `could not open local network socket`

681. `too many open files`

691. `I/O error`

A filesystem error occurred during input or output. This typically indicates a hardware or operating system failure, although it is possible that the disk was merely full and this state was misinterpreted as an I/O error.

692. `file I/O error on read`

693. `file I/O error on write`

696. `_____ is temporarily unavailable`

699. `insufficient disk space`

You ran out of disk space while writing a file to disk. The file is now closed and probably erased. Review your operating system documentation to determine how to proceed.

702. `op. sys. refused to start new process`

703. `op. sys. refused to open pipe`

900. `no room to add more variables`

The maximum number of variables allowed by Small Stata is 99. The maximum number of variables allowed by Intercooled Stata is 2,047. If you are using Intercooled Stata and have less than 2,047 variables, you are short on memory; see [U] **7 Setting the size of memory**.

901. `no room to add more observations`

The maximum number of observations allowed by Small Stata is *approximately* 1,000. The maximum number of observations allowed by Intercooled Stata is 2,147,483,647. If you are using Intercooled Stata, you are short on memory; see [U] **7 Setting the size of memory**.

902. `no room to add more variables`

Try typing `compress`; see [R] **compress**.

903. `no room to add more variables`

See 902.

908. `matsize too small; type -help matsize-`

You have attempted to estimate a model requiring a larger `matsize`; see [R] **matsize**.

909. `op. sys. refuses to provide memory`

You have attempted to `set memory` or `set matsize` and, although the request seems reasonable to Stata, the operating system has refused to provide the extra memory.

910. `value too small`

You attempted to change the size of memory, but specified values for memory, maximum observations, maximum width, or maximum variables that are too small. Stata wants to allocate a minimum of 300K.

912. `value too large`

You attempted to change the size of memory, but specified values for memory, maximum observations, maximum width, or maximum variables that are too large.

913. `op. sys. refuses to provide sufficient memory`
`op. sys. provided base request, but then refused to provide`
`sufficient memory for matsize`

You attempted to `set memory` or `set matsize` and, although the request seems reasonable to Stata, the operating system refused to provide the memory for matsize (although the operating system would provide memory for the data).

This return code has the same implications as `r(909)`. Stata allocates memory separately for the data and for matsize. `r(913)` merely indicates that it was the second rather than the first request that failed. Typically the first request fails because it is the request for additional memory.

914. `op. sys. refused to allow Stata to open a temporary file`

To honor your request for memory, Stata needed to open a temporary disk file and the operating system said it could not do so. This most often occurs under Unix and, in that case, the text of the error message provided additional information on how to repair the problem.

920. `too many macros`

You specified a line containing too many macros, so that after expansion of the macros the line exceeds 67,784 (Intercooled Stata) or 3,400 (Small Stata) characters. The line was ignored.

950. `insufficient memory`

There is insufficient memory to fulfill the request. Type `discard`, press return, and try the command again. If that fails, consider dropping value labels, variable labels, or macros.

1000. `system limit exceeded`
See [R] **limits**.

1001. `too many values`
You have attempted to create a table that has too many rows or columns. For a one-way table, the maximum number of rows is 500 for Small Stata and 3,000 for Intercooled. For a two-way table in Small Stata, the maximum number of rows is 160 and columns is 20; For a two-way table in Intercooled Stata, the maximum number of rows is 300 and columns is 20. Thus, `tabulate y x` may not result in too many values even if `tabulate x y` does.

1002. `too many by variables`
The number of `by` variables exceeded 2,047 (Intercooled Stata) or 99 (Small Stata). You cannot exceed these maximums.

1003. `too many options`
The number of options specified exceeded 50. You cannot exceed that maximum.

1004. `command too long`
You attempted to issue a Stata command in a do-file, ado-file, or program, and the command exceeded 67,800 characters (3,500 for Small Stata).

1400. `numerical overflow`
You have attempted something that, in the midst of the necessary calculations, has resulted in something too large for Stata to deal with accurately. Most commonly, this is an attempt to estimate a model (say with `regress`) with more than 2,147,483,647 effective observations. This effective number could be reached with far fewer observations if you were running a frequency-weighted model.

2000. `no observations`
You have requested some statistical calculation and there are no observations on which to perform it. Perhaps you specified `if` *exp* or `in` *range* and inadvertently filtered all the data.

2001. `insufficient observations`
You have requested some statistical calculation and, while there are some observations, the number is not sufficient to carry out your request.

9xxx. Various messages, all indicating a catastrophic system failure. You should never see such a message. If one occurs, `save` your data and `exit` Stata immediately. Please call us and report the problem.

Other messages

`no observations`
`insufficient observations`
You have requested something when there are either no observations or insufficient observations in memory to carry forth your request.

`(_____ not found)`
You referred to the indicated value name in an expression and no such value label existed. A missing value was substituted.

`(eof before end of obs)`
`infile` was reading your data and encountered the end-of-file marker before it had completed reading the current observation. Missing values are filled in for the remaining variables. This message indicates that the dataset may contain more or fewer variables than you expected.

`(_____ missing values generated)`
The command resulted in the creation of the indicated number of missing values. Missing values occur when a mathematical operation is performed on a missing value or when a mathematical operation is infeasible.

`(note: file _____ not found)`
You specified the `replace` option on a command, yet no such file was found. The file was saved anyway.

`(note: ____ is ____ in using data but will be ____ now)`
Occurs during `append` or `merge`. The first blank is filled in with a variable name and the second and third blanks with a storage type (`byte`, `int`, `long`, `float`, `double`, or `str#`). For instance, you might receive the message "myvar is str5 in using data but will be float now". This means `myvar` is of type `float` in the *master dataset*, but that a variable of the same name was found in the *using dataset* with type `str5`. You will receive this message when one variable is a string and the other is numeric.

(label _____ already defined)
Occurs during `append` or `merge`. The *using* data has a label definition for one of its variables. A label with the same name exists in the *master* dataset. Thus, you are warned that the label already exists, and the previous definition (the one from the *master* dataset) is retained.

(note: hascons false)
You specified the `hascons` option on `regress`, yet an examination of the data revealed that there is no effective constant in your *varlist*. Stata added a constant to your regression.

_____ real changes made
You used `replace`. This is the actual number of changes made to your data, not counting observations that already contained the replaced value.

_____ was _____ now _____
Occurs during `replace`, `append`, or `merge`. The first blank is filled in with a variable name and the second and third blanks are filled in with a numeric storage type (`byte`, `int`, `long`, `float`, or `double`). For instance, you might receive the message, "myvar was byte now float". Stata automatically promoted `myvar` to a `float` to prevent truncation.

Also See

Complementary:	[P] **break**, [P] **capture**, [R] **search**
Related:	[P] **exit**
Background:	[U] **19.1.4 Error handling in do-files**

Title

> **estimates** — Post and redisplay estimation results

Syntax

estimates <u>loc</u>al *name* ...   (see [P] **macro**)

estimates <u>sca</u>lar *name* = *exp*

estimates <u>mat</u>rix *name matname*

estimates clear

estimates <u>l</u>ist

estimates <u>est</u>imates post **b V** $\begin{bmatrix} \mathbf{C} \end{bmatrix}$ $\begin{bmatrix} , & \underline{\text{dep}}\text{name}(\textit{string}) & \underline{\text{o}}\text{bs}(\#) & \underline{\text{d}}\text{of}(\#) & \underline{\text{e}}\text{sample}(\textit{varname}) \end{bmatrix}$

estimates <u>rep</u>ost $\begin{bmatrix} \text{b} = \text{b} \end{bmatrix}$ $\begin{bmatrix} \text{V} = \text{V} \end{bmatrix}$ $\begin{bmatrix} , & \underline{\text{e}}\text{sample}(\textit{varname}) & \underline{\text{ren}}\text{ame} \end{bmatrix}$

estimates <u>di</u>splay $\begin{bmatrix} , & \underline{\text{ef}}\text{orm}(\textit{string}) & \underline{\text{f}}\text{irst} & \text{neq}(\#) & \underline{\text{p}}\text{lus} & \underline{\text{l}}\text{evel}(\#) \end{bmatrix}$

estimates <u>h</u>old *holdname* $\begin{bmatrix} , & \underline{\text{c}}\text{opy} & \underline{\text{r}}\text{estore} \end{bmatrix}$

estimates <u>u</u>nhold *holdname* $\begin{bmatrix} , & \text{not} \end{bmatrix}$

estimates dir

estimates drop $\left\{ \textit{holdname(s)} \mid \_\text{all} \right\}$

where *name* is the name of the macro, scalar, or matrix that will be returned in **e**(*name*) by the estimation program, *matname* is the name of an existing matrix, *holdname* is the name under which estimation results will be held, **b** is a $1 \times p$ coefficient vector (matrix), **V** is a $p \times p$ covariance matrix, and **C** is a $c \times (p+1)$ constraint matrix.

Description

estimates local, estimates scalar, and estimates matrix set the e() macros, scalars, and matrices returned by estimation commands. estimates clear clears the e() saved results. See [P] **return** for more discussion on returning results. estimates list lists the names and values of the e() returned macros and scalars and the names and sizes of the e() returned matrices from the last estimation command.

estimates post saves the coefficient vector (b) and variance–covariance (V) matrices in Stata's system areas, making all the post-estimation features described in [U] **23 Estimation and post-estimation commands** available. estimates repost changes the b or V matrix (allowed only after estimation commands that posted their results using estimates post) or changes the declared estimation sample. The specified matrices cease to exist after post or repost; they are literally moved into Stata's system areas. The resulting b and V matrices in Stata's system areas can be reobtained by reference to e(b) and e(V). estimates post and repost deal with only the coefficient and variance–covariance matrices while estimates matrix is used to save other matrices associated with the estimation command. estimates display displays or redisplays the coefficient table corresponding to results that have been previously posted using estimates post or repost. For a discussion of posting results with constraint matrices (**C** in the syntax diagram above), see [P] **matrix constraint**, but only after reading this entry.

estimates hold, unhold, dir, and drop provide a mechanism for saving and later restoring up to 10 estimation results. estimates hold moves or copies—which depending on whether the copy option is specified—all information associated with the last estimation command into *holdname*. If *holdname* is a temporary name, it will automatically be deleted when you exit from the current program. estimates unhold restores the information from the estimation command previously moved into *holdname* and eliminates *holdname*. estimates dir lists the *holdname(s)* under which estimation results are currently held. estimates drop eliminates the estimation results stored under the specified *holdname(s)*. In addition, if the restore option is specified when the estimates are held, those estimates will be automatically restored when the program concludes; it is not necessary to perform an estimates unhold in that case.

Options

Options for estimates post, repost, and display

depname(*string*) specified with estimates post supplies a name which should be that of the dependent variable but can be anything; that name is saved and added to the appropriate place on the output whenever estimates display is executed.

obs(*#*) specified with estimates post supplies the number of observations on which the estimation was performed; that number is saved and stored in e(N).

dof(*#*) specified with estimates post supplies the number of (denominator) degrees of freedom that is to be used with t and F statistics and is saved and stored in e(df_r). This number is used in calculating significance levels and confidence intervals by estimates display and by subsequent test commands performed on the posted results. If the option is not specified, normal (Z) and χ^2 statistics are used.

esample(*varname*) specified with estimates post or repost gives the name of the 0/1 variable indicating the observations involved in the estimation. The variable is removed from the dataset, but is available for use as e(sample); see [U] **23.4 Specifying the estimation subsample**. If the esample() option is not specified with estimates post, it is set to all zeros (meaning no estimation sample). See [P] **mark** for details of the marksample command that can help create *varname*.

rename is allowed only with the b = b syntax of estimates repost and tells Stata to use the names obtained from the specified **b** matrix as the labels for both the b and V estimation matrices. These labels are subsequently used in the output produced by estimates display.

eform(*string*) specified with `estimates display` indicates that the exponentiated form of the coefficients is to be output and that reporting of the constant is to be suppressed. *string* is used to label the exponentiated coefficients; see [R] **maximize**.

first requests that Stata display only the first equation and make it appear as if only one equation were estimated.

neq(*#*) requests that Stata display only the first *#* equations and make it appear as if only *#* equations were estimated.

plus changes the bottom separation line produced by `estimates display` to have a + symbol at the position of the dividing line between variable names and results. This is useful if you plan on adding more output to the table.

level(*#*), an option of `estimates display`, supplies the significance level for the confidence intervals of the coefficients; see [U] **23 Estimation and post-estimation commands**.

Options for estimates hold, unhold

copy, an option of `estimates hold`, requests that all information associated with the last estimation command be copied into *holdname*. By default, it is moved, meaning that the estimation results temporarily disappear. The default action is faster and uses less memory.

restore, an option of `estimates hold`, requests that the information in *holdname* be automatically restored when the program ends regardless of whether that occurred because the program exited normally, the user pressed *Break*, or there was an error.

not, an option of `estimates unhold`, is used after `estimates hold, restore`. It specifies that the previous request for automatic restoration be canceled. The previously held estimation results are discarded from memory without restoration, now or later.

Remarks

Remarks are presented under the headings

Estimation class programs
Setting individual estimation results
Posting estimation coefficient and variance–covariance matrices
Holding multiple estimation results

Estimation class programs

An important feature of Stata is that, after any estimation command, you can obtain individual coefficients and standard errors using _b[] and _se[] (see [U] **16.5 Accessing coefficients and standard errors**), list the coefficients using `matrix list e(b)`, list the variance–covariance matrix of the estimators using `matrix list e(V)` or in a table using vce (see [R] **vce**), obtain the linear prediction and its standard error using predict (see [R] **predict**), and test linear hypotheses about the coefficients using test (see [R] **test**). Other important information from an estimation command can be obtained from the returned e() results. (For example: The estimation command name is returned in e(cmd). The dependent variable name is returned in e(depvar).) The e() results from an estimation command can be listed using the `estimates list` command. All these features are summarized in [U] **23 Estimation and post-estimation commands**.

If you decide to write your own estimation command, your command can share all these features as well. This is accomplished by posting the results you calculate to Stata. The basic outline of an estimation command is

```
program define myest, eclass
        version 7.0
        if ~replay() {
                syntax whatever [, whatever Level(integer $S_level)]
                marksample touse       /* see [P] mark */
                perform any other parsing of the user's estimation request;
                local depn "dependent variable name"
                local nobs = number of observations in estimation
                tempname b V
                produce coefficient vector `b´ and variance–covariance matrix `V´
                est post `b´ `V´, obs(`nobs´) depname(`depn´) esample(`touse´)
                est local depvar "`depn´"
                store whatever else you want in e()
                est local cmd "myest"      /* set e(cmd) last */
        }
        else {    /* replay */
                if "`e(cmd)´"~="myest" { error 301 }
                syntax [, Level(integer $S_level)]
        }
        if `level´<10 | `level´>99 {
                di as err "level() must be between 10 and 99 inclusive"
                exit 198
        }
        output any header above the coefficient table;
        est display, level(`level´)
end
```

We will not discuss here how the estimates are formed, but see [P] **matrix** for an example of programming linear regression and see [R] **ml** for examples of programming maximum likelihood estimators. However the estimates are formed, our interest is in the posting of those results to Stata.

When programming estimation commands, remember to declare them as estimation commands. This is accomplished with the `eclass` option to `program define`; see [U] **21 Programming Stata**. If you do not specify your program to be `eclass`, Stata will produce an error if you use `estimates local`, `estimates scalar`, or `estimates matrix` in your program. For more information on the general topic of saving program results, see [P] **return**.

❏ Technical Note

Notice the use of the `replay()` function in our estimation program example. This function is not like other Stata functions; see [R] **functions**. `replay()` simply returns 1 if the command line is empty or begins with a comma and 0 otherwise. Said more simply, `replay()` indicates whether the command is an initial call to the estimation program (`replay()` returns 0) or a call to redisplay past estimation results (`replay()` returns 1).

In fact,

```
if ~replay() {
```

is equivalent to

```
if trim(`"`0´"´) == "" | substr((trim(`"`0´"´),1,1) == "," {
```

but is easier to read.

❏

The `estimates local`, `scalar`, `matrix`, `clear`, and `list` commands are discussed in the *Setting individual estimation results* section. The `estimates post`, `repost`, and `display` commands are discussed in the *Posting estimation coefficient and variance–covariance matrices* section. The `estimates hold`, `unhold`, `dir`, and `drop` commands are discussed in the *Holding multiple estimation results* section.

Setting individual estimation results

Stata's estimation commands save the command name in the returned macro `e(cmd)` and the name of the dependent variable in `e(depvar)`. Other macros and scalars are also saved. For example, the estimation sample size is saved in the returned scalar `e(N)`. The model and residual degrees of freedom are saved in `e(df_m)` and `e(df_r)`.

These `e()` macro and scalar results are saved using the `estimates local` and `estimates scalar` commands. Matrices may be saved using the `estimates matrix` command. The coefficient vector `e(b)` and variance–covariance matrix `e(V)`, however, are handled differently and are only saved using the `estimates post` and `repost` commands discussed in the next section.

▷ Example

Assume that we are programming an estimation command called `xyz` and that we have the dependent variable in `` `depname' ``, the estimation sample size in `` `nobs' ``, and other important information stored in other local macros and scalars. Additionally, we wish to save an auxiliary estimation matrix that our program has created called `lam` into the saved matrix `e(lambda)`. We would save these results using commands such as the following in our estimation program:

```
...
est local depvar "`depname'"
est scalar N = `nobs'
est matrix lambda lam
...
est local cmd "xyz"
```
◁

The matrix given to the `estimates matrix` command is removed and the new `e()` matrix is then made available. For instance, in the last example we had the line

```
est matrix lambda lam
```

After this line has executed, the matrix `lam` is no longer available for use but you can instead refer to the newly created `e(lambda)` matrix.

The `e()` results from an estimation command can be viewed using the `estimates list` command.

▷ Example

We demonstrate the use of `estimates list` after regressing automobile weight on length and engine displacement using the auto dataset.

```
. use auto
(1978 Automobile Data)
. regress weight length displ
```

Source	SS	df	MS
Model	41063449.8	2	20531724.9
Residual	3030728.55	71	42686.3176
Total	44094178.4	73	604029.841

Number of obs =	74
F(2, 71) =	480.99
Prob > F =	0.0000
R-squared =	0.9313
Adj R-squared =	0.9293
Root MSE =	206.61

weight	Coef.	Std. Err.	t	P>|t|	[95% Conf. Interval]	
length	22.91788	1.974431	11.61	0.000	18.98097	26.85478
displacement	2.932772	.4787094	6.13	0.000	1.978252	3.887291
_cons	-1866.181	297.7349	-6.27	0.000	-2459.847	-1272.514

```
. estimates list
scalars:
                e(N) =  74
             e(df_m) =  2
             e(df_r) =  71
               e(F) =  480.9907735088096
              e(r2) =  .9312669232040125
            e(rmse) =  206.6066736285298
             e(mss) =  41063449.82964133
             e(rss) =  3030728.548737053
            e(r2_a) =  .9293307801956748
              e(ll) =  -497.9506459758983
            e(ll_0) =  -597.0190609278627
macros:
          e(depvar) : "weight"
             e(cmd) : "regress"
         e(predict) : "regres_p"
           e(model) : "ols"
matrices:
               e(b) :  1 x 3
               e(V) :  3 x 3
functions:
          e(sample)
```

In addition to listing all the e() results after an estimation command, you can access individual e() results.

```
. display "The command is: `e(cmd)'"
The command is: regress
. display "The adjusted R-squared is: `e(r2_a)'"
The adjusted R-squared is: .9293307801956748
. display "The residual sums-of-squares is: `e(rss)'"
The residual sums-of-squares is: 3030728.548737053
. matrix list e(V)
symmetric e(V)[3,3]
                    length   displacement          _cons
      length     3.8983761
displacement    -.78935643      .22916272
       _cons    -576.89342      103.13249      88646.064
. matrix list e(b)
e(b)[1,3]
          length   displacement          _cons
y1     22.917876      2.9327718     -1866.1807
```

For more information on referencing e() results, see [P] **return**.

◁

The *Reference Manual* entries for Stata's estimation commands have a section describing the e() results that are returned by the command. If you are writing an estimation command, we recommend that you save the same kind of estimation results using the same naming convention as Stata's estimation commands. This is important if you want post-estimation commands to work after your estimation command. See [U] **23 Estimation and post-estimation commands** and [P] **return** for details.

When programming your estimation command, you will want to issue either an `estimates clear` command or an `estimates post` command before you save any estimation results. The `estimates clear` command clears all e() results. The `estimates post` command, which is discussed in the next section, also first clears all previous e() results and then performs the post.

We recommend that the clearing of past estimation results and the setting of new e() results be postponed until late in your program. If an error occurs early in your program, the last successful estimation results will remain intact. The best place in your estimation program to set the e() results is after all other calculations have been completed and before displaying the estimation results.

Our next recommendation is that you save the command name in `e(cmd)` as your very last act of saving results. This ensures that if `e(cmd)` is present, then all the other estimation results have also been successfully saved. Post-estimation commands assume that if `e(cmd)` is present then the estimation command completed successfully and all expected results were saved. If you saved `e(cmd)` early in your estimation command and the user presses *Break* before the remaining e() results are saved, then post-estimation commands operating on the partial results would likely produce an error.

Posting estimation coefficient and variance–covariance matrices

The most important estimation results are the coefficient vector **b** and the variance–covariance matrix **V**. Since these two matrices are at the heart of an estimation command, for increased command execution speed Stata handles these matrices in a special way. The `estimates post`, `repost`, and `display` commands work on these matrices. The `estimates matrix` command discussed in the last section cannot be used to save or post the **b** and **V** matrices.

The discussion of the `estimates post`, `repost`, and `display` commands is divided under the following subheadings:

> *Single-equation models*
> *Multiple-equation models*
> *Single-equation models masquerading as multiple-equation models*
> *Setting the estimation sample*
> *Reposting results*
> *Minor details: the depname() and dof() options*

Single-equation models

Before posting, the coefficient vector is stored as a $1 \times p$ matrix and the corresponding variance–covariance matrix as a $p \times p$ matrix. The names bordering the coefficient matrix and the variance–covariance matrix play an important role. First, they must be the same. Second, it is these names that tell Stata how the results link to Stata's other features.

User estimation results come in two flavors: single-equation models and multiple-equation models. The absence or presence of equation names in the names bordering the matrix (see [P] **matrix rowname**) tells Stata which it is.

▷ Example

For instance, consider

```
. matrix list b
b[1,3]
        weight        mpg        _cons
y1    1.7465592   -49.512221   1946.0687
. matrix list V
symmetric V[3,3]
            weight        mpg        _cons
weight    .41133468
   mpg    44.601659    7422.863
 _cons   -2191.9032  -292759.82    12938766
```

If these were your estimation results, they would correspond to a single-equation model because the names bordering the matrices have no equation names. Here we post these results:

```
. estimates post b V
. estimates display
```

	Coef.	Std. Err.	z	P>|z|	[95% Conf. Interval]	
weight	1.746559	.6413538	2.72	0.006	.4895288	3.003589
mpg	-49.51222	86.15604	-0.57	0.566	-218.375	119.3505
_cons	1946.069	3597.05	0.54	0.588	-5104.019	8996.156

Once the results have been posted, anytime the estimates display command is executed, Stata will redisplay the coefficient table. Moreover, all of Stata's other post-estimation features work. For instance,

```
. correlate, _coef
           weight        mpg        _cons
weight     1.0000
   mpg     0.8072     1.0000
 _cons    -0.9501    -0.9447     1.0000
. test weight
 ( 1)  weight = 0.0
            chi2(  1) =      7.42
          Prob > chi2 =    0.0065
. test weight=mpg/50
 ( 1)  weight -  .02 mpg = 0.0
            chi2(  1) =      4.69
          Prob > chi2 =    0.0303
```

If the user were to type predict pred, predict would create a new variable based on

$$1.746559\,\text{weight} - 49.51222\,\text{mpg} + 1946.069$$

except that it would carry out the calculation using the full, double-precision values of the coefficients. All determinations were made by Stata based on the names bordering the posted matrices.

◁

Multiple-equation models

If the matrices posted using the estimates post or repost commands have more than one equation name, then the estimation command is treated as a multiple-equation model.

▷ Example

Consider the following two matrices before posting:

```
. mat list b
b[1,6]
           price:      price:      price:      displ:      displ:      displ:
           weight         mpg       _cons      weight     foreign       _cons
y1       1.7417059   -50.31993   1977.9249   .09341608  -35.124241  -74.326413
. mat list V
symmetric V[6,6]
                       price:      price:      price:      displ:      displ:
                       weight         mpg       _cons      weight     foreign
price:weight         .38775906
  price:mpg          41.645165   6930.8263
  price:_cons       -2057.7522  -273353.75   12116943
  displ:weight       .00030351  -.01074361  -.68762197   .00005432
  displ:foreign     -.18390487    -30.6065    1207.129   .05342871   152.20821
  displ:_cons       -.86175743   41.539129   1936.6875   -.1798972  -206.57691
                       displ:
                       _cons
  displ:_cons        625.79842
```

Notice that the row and column names of the matrices include equation names. Here we post these matrices to Stata and then use the posted results:

```
. estimates post b V
. estimates display
```

	Coef.	Std. Err.	z	P>|z|	[95% Conf. Interval]	
price						
weight	1.741706	.622703	2.80	0.005	.5212304	2.962181
mpg	-50.31993	83.25158	-0.60	0.546	-213.49	112.8502
_cons	1977.925	3480.94	0.57	0.570	-4844.592	8800.442
displ						
weight	.0934161	.0073701	12.67	0.000	.0789709	.1078612
foreign	-35.12424	12.33727	-2.85	0.004	-59.30484	-10.94364
_cons	-74.32641	25.01596	-2.97	0.003	-123.3568	-25.29603

```
. test [price]weight
 ( 1)   [price]weight = 0.0
            chi2( 1) =     7.82
          Prob > chi2 =    0.0052
. test weight
 ( 1)   [price]weight = 0.0
 ( 2)   [displ]weight = 0.0
            chi2( 2) =   164.51
          Prob > chi2 =    0.0000
```

Stata determined that this was a multiple-equation model because of the presence of the equation names. All of Stata's equation name features (such as those available with the test command) are then made available. The user could type predict pred to obtain linear predictions of the [price] equation (because predict defaults to the first equation), or the user could type predict pred, equation(displ) to obtain predictions of the [displ] equation:

$$.0934161\,weight - 35.12424\,foreign - 74.32641$$

◁

Single-equation models masquerading as multiple-equation models

Sometimes, it may be convenient to program a single-equation model as if it were a multiple-equation model. This occurs when there are ancillary parameters. Think of linear regression: in addition to the parameter estimates, there is s, an estimate of σ, the standard error of the residual. This can be calculated on the side in that one can calculate $\mathbf{b} = (\mathbf{X'X})^{-1}\mathbf{X'y}$ independently of s and then calculate s given $\mathbf{b}$. Pretend that were not the case—think of a straightforward maximum likelihood calculation where s is just one more parameter (in most models, ancillary parameters and the coefficients must be solved for jointly). The right thing to do would be to give s its own equation:

▷ Example

```
. mat list b

b[1,4]
           price:        price:        price:        _anc:
          weight           mpg         _cons         sigma
y1     1.7465592    -49.512221     1946.0687          2514
. matrix list V
(output omitted)

. estimates post b V

. estimates display
```

	Coef.	Std. Err.	z	P>|z|	[95% Conf. Interval]	
price						
weight	1.746559	.6413538	2.72	0.006	.4895288	3.003589
mpg	-49.51222	86.15604	-0.57	0.566	-218.375	119.3505
_cons	1946.069	3597.05	0.54	0.588	-5104.019	8996.156
_anc						
sigma	2514	900	2.79	0.005	750.0324	4277.968

Now consider the alternative, which would be simply to add s to the estimated parameters without equation names:

```
. matrix list b

b[1,4]
          weight           mpg         _cons         sigma
y1     1.7465592    -49.512221     1946.0687          2514
. matrix list V
(output omitted)

. estimates post b V

. estimates display
```

	Coef.	Std. Err.	z	P>|z|	[95% Conf. Interval]	
weight	1.746559	.6413538	2.72	0.006	.4895288	3.003589
mpg	-49.51222	86.15604	-0.57	0.566	-218.375	119.3505
_cons	1946.069	3597.05	0.54	0.588	-5104.019	8996.156
sigma	2514	900	2.79	0.005	750.0324	4277.968

This second solution is inferior because, were the user to type `predict pred`, `predict` would attempt to form the linear combination:

$$1.746559\,\texttt{weight} - 49.51222\,\texttt{mpg} + 1946.069 + 2514\,\texttt{sigma}$$

There are only two possibilities and neither is good; either `sigma` does not exist in the dataset—which is to be hoped—and `predict` produces the error message "variable sigma not found", or something called `sigma` does exist and `predict` goes on to form this meaningless combination.

◁

On the other hand, if the parameter estimates are separated from the ancillary parameter (which could be parameters) by the equation names, the user can type `predict pred, equation(price)` to obtain a meaningful result. Moreover, the user can omit the `equation(price)` part because `predict` (and Stata's other post-estimation commands) default to the first equation.

We recommend that ancillary parameters be collected together and given their own equation and that the equation be called `_anc`.

Setting the estimation sample

In our previous examples, we did not indicate the estimation sample as specified with the `esample(varname)` option. In general, you provide this either with your initial `estimates post` command or with a subsequent `estimates repost` command. Some post-estimation commands automatically restrict themselves to the estimation sample and if you do not provide this information they will complain that there are no observations; see [U] **23.4 Specifying the estimation subsample**. Also, users of your estimation command expect to successfully use `if e(sample)` in commands they execute after your estimation command.

▷ Example

Returning to our first example,

```
. estimates post b V
. estimates display
  (output omitted )
. summarize price if e(sample)
```

Variable	Obs	Mean	Std. Dev.	Min	Max
price	0				

does not produce what the user expects. Specifying the estimation sample with the `esample()` option of `estimates post` produces

```
. estimates post b V, esample(estsamp)
. estimates display
  (output omitted )
. summarize price if e(sample)
```

Variable	Obs	Mean	Std. Dev.	Min	Max
price	74	6165.257	2949.496	3291	15906

◁

The `marksample` command (see [P] **mark**) is a useful programming command that aids in creating and setting up an estimation sample indicator variable.

Reposting results

There are certain programming situations where only a small part of a previous estimation result needs to be altered. `estimates repost` allows us to change four parts of a previously posted (using `estimates post`) estimation result. We can change the coefficient vector, variance–covariance matrix, declared estimation sample (using the `esample()` option), and variable names for the coefficients (using the `rename` option). A programmer might, for instance, simply replace the variance–covariance matrix provided by a previous `estimates post` with a robust covariance matrix to create a new estimation result.

In some cases, a programmer might `preserve` the data, make major alterations to the data (using `drop`, `reshape`, etc.) in order to perform needed computations, post the estimation results, and then finally `restore` the data. In this case, when `estimates post` is called, the correct estimation sample indicator variable is unavailable. `estimates repost` with the `esample()` option allows us to set the estimation sample without changing the rest of our posted estimation results.

▷ Example

For example, inside an estimation command program we might have

```
...
estimates post b V
...
estimates repost, esample(estsamp)
...
```

◁

❑ Technical Note

`estimates repost` may only be called from within a program that has been declared as an estimation class program (using the `eclass` option of the `program define` statement). The same is not true of `estimates post`. We believe that the only legitimate uses of `estimates repost` are in a programming context. `estimates post`, on the other hand, may be important for some non e-class programming situations.

❑

Minor details: the depname() and dof() options

Single-equation models may have a single dependent variable; in those that do, you should specify the identity of this single dependent variable in the `depname()` option with `estimates post`. The result is simply to add a little more labeling to the output.

At the time of posting, if you do not specify the `dof(#)` option, normal (Z) statistics will be used to calculate significance levels and confidence intervals on subsequent `estimates display` output. If you do specify `dof(#)`, t statistics with $#$ degrees of freedom will be used. Similarly, if `dof()` is not specified, any subsequent `test` commands will present a χ^2 statistic; if `dof(#)` is specified, subsequent `test` commands will use the F statistic with $#$ denominator degrees of freedom.

▷ Example

We illustrate the `depname()` and `dof()` options by adding the dependent variable name and degrees of freedom to our first example.

```
. estimates post b V, depname(price) dof(71)
. estimates display
```

price	Coef.	Std. Err.	t	P>|t|	[95% Conf. Interval]	
weight	1.746559	.6413538	2.72	0.008	.467736	3.025382
mpg	-49.51222	86.15604	-0.57	0.567	-221.3025	122.278
_cons	1946.069	3597.05	0.54	0.590	-5226.244	9118.382

Note the addition of the word `price` at the top of the table. This was produced because of the `depname(price)` option specification. Also note that t statistics were used instead of normal (Z) statistics because of the `dof(71)` option specification.

◁

Holding multiple estimation results

`estimates hold` and `unhold` are typically used in programs and ado-files, although they can be used interactively. After estimating, say, a regression using `regress`, you should be aware that you can replay the regression by typing `regress` without arguments, that you can obtain predicted values using `predict`, and the like; see [U] **23 Estimation and post-estimation commands**. This is because Stata stored information associated with the regression in what we will call the "last estimation results". The "last estimation results" include the coefficient vector and variance–covariance matrix as well as the other `e()` saved results.

When you type `estimates hold myreg`, Stata moves the last estimation results to a holding area with the name `myreg`. After giving this command, you can no longer replay the regression, calculate predicted values, etc. From Stata's point of view, the estimates are gone. When you type `estimates unhold myreg`, however, Stata moves the estimates back. You can once again type `regress` without arguments, calculate predicted values, and everything else just as if the last estimation results were never disturbed.

If you instead type `estimates hold myreg, copy`, Stata copies, rather than moves, the results, meaning that you can still redisplay results. Obviously, the reason to hold estimates is because you want to estimate some other model and then get these estimates back, so generally holding-by-moving works as well as holding-by-copying. Sometimes, however, you may want to hold-by-copy so that you can modify the estimates in memory and still retrieve the original.

▷ Example

Thus, you could run a regression, `hold` the results, run another regression, and then `unhold` the original results. One way you could use this is

```
regress y x1 x2 x3          ( estimate first model )
estimates hold model1       ( and save it )
regress y x1 x2 x3 x4       ( estimate the second model )
estimates hold model2       ( and save it, too )
use newdata                 ( use another dataset )
estimates unhold model1
predict yhat1               ( predict using first regression )
estimates unhold model2
predict yhat2               ( predict using second regression )
```

Understand that you are not limited to doing this with regression. You can do this with any estimation command.

◁

❏ Technical Note

Warning: Holding estimation results can tie up considerable amounts of memory, the amount depending on the kind of model and the number of variables in it. This is why there is a limit of 10 held estimation results.

❏

`estimates dir` and `drop` are utilities associated with `estimates hold` and `unhold`. `estimates dir` lists the name(s) of held estimation results. `estimates drop` drops held estimation results.

❏ Technical Note

Despite our interactive example, `estimates hold` and `unhold` are typically used inside programs. For instance, `linktest` estimates a model of the dependent variable, the prediction, and the prediction squared and shows the result. Yet when it is over, the user's original model remains as the last estimation result just as if no intervening model had been estimated. `linktest` does this by holding the original model, performing its task, and then restoring the original model.

In addition to moving Stata's last estimation result matrices, `e(b)` and `e(V)`, `estimates hold` and `unhold` also move the other `e()` results. When you `hold` the current estimates, `e(b)`, `e(V)`, `e(cmd)`, `e(depvar)`, and the other `e()` results disappear. When you `unhold` them, they are restored.

In order to avoid naming conflicts, we recommend that estimates be held under a name created by `tempvar` or `tempname`; see [P] **macro**. Thus, the code fragment is

```
tempvar est
estimates hold `est´
( code including new estimation )
estimates unhold `est´
```

❏

Estimates held under a temporary name will automatically be discarded when the program ends. You can also specify `estimates hold`'s `restore` option when you hold the estimates and then the held estimates will be restored when the program ends, too.

Saved Results

`estimates post` saves the number of observations in `e(N)` and the number of degrees of freedom, if specified, in `e(df_r)`. With `estimates post` all previously stored estimation results—`e()` items—are removed. `estimates repost`, however, does not remove previously stored estimation results. `estimates hold` removes the estimation results—`e()` items. `estimates unhold` restores the previously held `e()` results. `estimates clear` permanently removes the current `e()` results.

Also See

Complementary: [P] **macro**, [P] **mark**, [P] **matrix**, [P] **matrix constraint**, [P] **matrix rowname**, [R] **maximize**, [R] **ml**, [R] **predict**, [R] **test**, [R] **vce**

Related: [P] **return**,
[R] **saved results**

Background: [U] **16.5 Accessing coefficients and standard errors**,
[U] **21 Programming Stata**,
[U] **23 Estimation and post-estimation commands**

Title

> **exit** — Exit from a program or do-file

Syntax

$\underline{e}xit \ \big[\ [=]exp\big]\ \big[\ , \ \texttt{clear STATA}\ \big]$

Description

exit, when typed from the keyboard, causes Stata to terminate processing and returns control to the operating system. If the dataset in memory has changed since the last **save** command, you must specify the **clear** option before Stata will let you leave. Use of the command in this way is discussed in [R] **exit**.

More generally, **exit** causes Stata to terminate the current process and returns control to the calling process. The return code is set to the value of the expression or 0 if no expression is specified. Thus, **exit** can be used to exit a program or do-file and return control to Stata. With an option, **exit** can even be used to exit Stata from a program or do-file. Such use of **exit** is the subject of this entry.

Options

clear permits you to **exit** even if the current dataset has not been **saved**.

STATA exits Stata and returns control to the operating system even when given from a do-file or program. The **STATA** option is implied when **exit** is issued from the keyboard.

Remarks

exit can be used at the terminal, from do-files, or from programs. From the terminal, it allows you to leave Stata. Given from a do-file or program without the **STATA** option, it causes the do-file or program to terminate and return control to the calling process, which might be the keyboard or another do-file or program.

▷ Example

Here is a useless program that will tell you whether a variable exists:

```
. program define check
  1. capture confirm variable `1´
  2. if _rc~=0 {
  3.     display "`1´ not found"
  4.     exit
  5. }
  6. display "The variable `1´ exists."
  7. end
. check median_age
The variable median_age exists.
. check age
age not found
```

Notice that `exit` did not close Stata and cause a return to the operating system. It instead terminated the program.

◁

▷ Example

You type `exit` from the keyboard to leave Stata and return to the operating system. If the dataset in memory has changed since the last time it was saved, however, Stata will refuse. At that point, you can either `save` the data and then `exit` or type `exit, clear`:

```
. exit
no; data in memory would be lost
r(4);
. exit, clear
```
(*Operating system prompts you for next command*)

◁

❏ Technical Note

You can also exit Stata and return to the operating system from a do-file or program by including the line `exit, STATA` in your do-file or program. If you wish to return to the operating system regardless of whether the dataset in memory has changed, you include the line `exit, STATA clear`.

❏

❏ Technical Note

When using `exit` to force termination of a program or do-file, you may specify an expression following the `exit` and the resulting value of that expression will be used to set the return code. Not specifying an expression is equivalent to specifying `exit 0`.

❏

Also See

Complementary:	[P] **capture**, [P] **error**,
	[R] **error messages**
Related:	[R] **exit**

Title

file formats .dta — Description of .dta file format

Description

The information contained in this highly technical entry probably does not interest you. We describe in detail the format of Stata datasets for those interested in writing programs in C or other languages that read and write our datasets.

Stata-format datasets record data in a way generalized to work across computers that do not agree on how data are recorded. Given a computer, datasets are divided into two categories: native-format and foreign-format datasets. Stata uses the following two rules:

R1. On any computer, Stata knows how to write only native-format datasets.

R2. On all computers, Stata can read foreign-format as well as native-format datasets.

Rules R1 and R2 ensure that Stata users need not be concerned with dataset formats. If you are writing a program to read and write Stata datasets, you will have to determine whether you want to follow the same rules or instead restrict your program to operate on only native-format datasets. Since Stata follows rules R1 and R2, such a restriction would not be too limiting. If the user had a foreign-format dataset, he or she could enter Stata, **use** the data, and then **save** it again.

Representation of strings

1. Strings in Stata may be from 1 to 80 bytes long. The file format is general for strings from 1 to 128 bytes long. Stata does not currently support strings with lengths in excess of 80 characters.

2. Stata records a string with a trailing binary 0 (\0) delimiter if the length of the string is less than the maximum declared length. The string is recorded without the delimiter if the string is of the maximum length.

3. Leading and trailing blanks are significant.

4. Strings use ASCII encoding.

Representation of numbers

1. Numbers are represented as 1-, 2-, and 4-byte integers and 4- and 8-byte floats. In the case of floats, IEEE format is used.

2. Byte ordering varies across machines for all numeric types. Bytes are ordered either least-significant to most-significant, dubbed LOHI, or most-significant to least-significant, dubbed HILO. Pentiums, for instance, use LOHI encoding. The HP-RISC and Sun SPARC-based computers use HILO encoding.

3. For purposes of written documentation, numbers are written with the most significant byte listed first. Thus, x´0001´ refers to an **int** taking on the logical value 1 on all machines.

4. When reading a HILO number on a LOHI machine or a LOHI number on a HILO machine, perform the following before interpreting the number:

byte	no translation necessary
2-byte int	swap bytes 0 and 1
4-byte int	swap bytes 0 and 3, 1 and 2
4-byte float	swap bytes 0 and 3, 1 and 2
8-byte float	swap bytes 0 and 7, 1 and 6, 2 and 5, 3 and 4

5. Stata has five numeric data types. They, along with their missing value codes, are

			missing value	
type	encoding	value	HILO	LOHI
byte	1-byte signed int	127	7f	7f
int	2-byte signed int	32,767	7f ff	ff 7f
long	4-byte signed int	2,147,483,647	7f ff ff ff	ff ff ff 7f
float	4-byte IEEE float	2^127	7f 00 00 00	00 00 00 7f
double	8-byte IEEE float	2^1023	7f e0 00 00 00 00 00 00	00 00 00 00 00 00 e0 7f

Final cautions

1. The number of observations in a dataset is stored in a 4-byte integer. Nevertheless, Small Stata cannot process more than about 1,000 observations. This limit does not apply to Intercooled Stata.

2. All variable numbers are recorded as 2-byte integers. Nevertheless, Small Stata will not allow more than 99 variables in a dataset. Intercooled Stata allows up to 2,047 variables. These constraints may be relaxed in future versions.

Description

Stata-format datasets contain five components, which are, in order,
1. Header
2. Descriptors
3. Variable Labels
4. Expansion Fields
5. Data
6. Value Labels

The Header is defined as

Contents	Length	Format	Comments
release	1	byte	Contains 110 = x´6e´
byteorder	1	byte	x´01´→HILO, x´02´→LOHI
filetype	1	byte	x´01´
unused	1	byte	x´00´
nvar (number of vars)	2	int	encoded per byteorder
nobs (number of obs)	4	int	encoded per byteorder
data_label	81	char	dataset label, \0 terminated
time_stamp	18	char	date and time saved, \0 terminated
Total	109		

time_stamp[17] must be set to binary zero. When writing a dataset, you may record the time stamp as blank (time_stamp[0] = binary zero), but you must still set time_stamp[17] to binary zero as well. If you choose to write a time stamp, its format is "dd Mon yyyy hh:mm"; dd and hh may be written with or without leading zeros, but if leading zeros are suppressed, a blank must be substituted in their place.

The Descriptor is defined as

Contents	Length	Format	Comments
typlist	nvar	byte array	
varlist	33*nvar	char array	
srtlist	2*(nvar+1)	int array	encoded per byteorder
fmtlist	12*nvar	char array	
lbllist	33*nvar	char array	

typlist stores the type of each variable, $1, \ldots, $ nvar. Stata stores five numeric types: double, float, long, int, and byte, encoded 'd', 'f', 'l', 'i', and 'b'. If nvar $= 4$, a typlist of 'idlf' indicates that variable 1 is an int, variable 2 a double, variable 3 a long, and variable 4 a float. Types above 0x80 are used to represent strings, encoded as *length* $+ $ 0x7f. For example, a string with maximum length 8 would have type 0x87. If typlist is read into the C-array char typlist[], then typlist[i-1] indicates the type of variable i.

varlist contains the names of the Stata variables $1 \ldots $ nvar, each up to 32 characters in length, and each terminated by a binary zero (hereafter denoted as \0). For instance, if nvar $= 4$,

```
0        33        66        99
|        |         |         |
vbl1\0...myvar\0...thisvar\0...lstvar\0...
```

would indicate that variable 1 is named vbl1, variable 2 myvar, variable 3 thisvar, and variable 4 lstvar. The byte positions indicated by periods will contain random numbers (and note that we have omitted some of the periods). If varlist is read into the C-array char varlist[], then &varlist[(i-1)*33] points to the name of the ith variable.

srtlist specifies the sort-order of the dataset and is terminated by an (int) 0. Each 2 bytes is a single int and contains either a variable number or zero. The zero marks the end of the srtlist, and the array positions after the zero contain random junk. For instance, if the data are not sorted, the first int will contain a zero and the ints thereafter will contain junk. If nvar $= 4$, the record will appear as

'0000...............'

If the dataset is sorted by a single variable myvar and if that variable is the second variable in the varlist, the record will appear as

'02000000............' (if byteorder $=$ LOHI)
'00020000............' (if byteorder $=$ HILO)

If the dataset is sorted by myvar and within myvar by vbl1, and if vbl1 is the first variable in the data, the record will appear as

'020001000000........' (if byteorder $=$ LOHI)
'000200010000........' (if byteorder $=$ HILO)

If srtlist were read into the C-array int srtlist[], then srtlist[0] would be the number of the first sort variable or, if the data were not sorted, 0. If the number is not zero, srtlist[1] would be the number of the second sort variable or, if there is not a second sort variable, 0, and so on.

fmtlist contains the formats of the variables $1, \ldots, $ nvar. Each format is 12 bytes long and includes a binary zero end-of-string marker. For instance,

'%9.0f\0......%8.2f\0......%20.0g\0.....%d\0.........%dD_m_Y\0....'

indicates that variable 1 has a %9.0f format, variable 2 a %8.2f format, variable 3 a %20.0g format, and so on. Note that these are Stata formats, not C formats. In particular, %d is not an integer format, it is Stata's default date format. %dD_m_Y is a detailed Stata date format. Be aware,

1. Formats beginning with '%d', '%-d', '%t', or '%-t' are date formats.

2. Nondate formats ending in 'gc' or 'fc' are similar to C's g and f formats but with commas. Most translation routines would ignore the ending c (change it to \0).

3. Formats may contain commas rather than period, such as %9,2f, indicating European format.

If fmtlist is read into the C-array char fmtlist[], then &fmtlist[12*(i-1)] refers to the starting address of the format for the ith variable.

lbllist contains the names of the value formats associated with the variables 1...**nvar**. Each value-format name is 32 bytes long and includes a binary zero end-of-string marker. For instance,

```
0    33           66   99
|    |            |    |
\0...yesno\0...\0...yesno\0...
```

indicates that variables 1 and 3 have no value label associated with them, whereas variables 2 and 4 are both associated with the value label named **yesno**. If **lbllist** is read into the C-array **char lbllist[]**, then **&lbllist[33*(i-1)]** points to the start of the label name associated with the ith variable.

The Variable Labels are recorded as

Contents	Length	Format	Comments
Variable 1's label	81	char	\0 terminated
Variable 2's label	81	char	\0 terminated
.	.	.	.
.	.	.	.
Variable **nvar**'s label	81	char	\0 terminated

If there is no variable label, the first character of the label is \0.

The Expansion Fields are recorded as

Contents	Length	Format	Comments
data type	1	byte	coded, currently only 0 and 1 defined
len	4	int	encoded per **byteorder**
contents	len	varies	
data type	1	byte	coded
len	4	int	encoded per **byteorder**
contents	len	varies	
data type	1	byte	code 0 means end
len	4	int	0 means end

Expansion fields conclude with code 0 and len 0; before the termination marker, there may be no or many separate data blocks. Expansion fields are used to record information that is unique to Stata and has no equivalent in other data management packages. Expansion fields are always optional when writing data and, generally, programs reading Stata datasets will want to ignore the expansion fields. The format makes this easy. When writing, write 5 bytes of zeros for this field. When reading, read five bytes; the last four bytes now tell you the size of the next read, which you discard. You then continue like this until you read 5 bytes of zeros.

The only expansion fields currently defined are type 1 records for variable characteristics. The design, however, allows new types of expansion fields to be included in subsequent releases of Stata without changes in the data format since unknown expansion types can simply be skipped.

For those who care, the format of type 1 records is a binary-zero terminated variable name in bytes 0–32, a binary-zero terminated characteristic name in bytes 33–65, and a binary-zero terminated string defining the contents in bytes 66 through the end of the record.

The Data are recorded as

Contents	Length	Format
var 1, obs 1	per `typlist`	per `typlist`
var 2, obs 1	per `typlist`	per `typlist`
.	.	.
var `nvar`, obs 1	per `typlist`	per `typlist`
var 1, obs 2	per `typlist`	per `typlist`
.	.	.
.	.	.
var 1, obs `nobs`	per `typlist`	per `typlist`
.	.	.
var `nvar`, obs `nobs`	per `typlist`	per `typlist`

The data are written as all the variables on the first observation, followed by all the data on the second observation, and so on. Each variable is written in its own internal format, as given in `typlist`. All values are written per `byteorder`. Strings are null terminated if they are shorter than the allowed space, but they are not terminated if they occupy the full width.

End-of-file may occur at this point. If it does, there are no value labels to be read. End-of-file may similarly occur between value labels. On end-of-file, all data have been processed.

Each Value Label is written as

Contents	Length	Format	Comments
`len`	4	int	length of `value_label_table`
`labname`	33	char	\0 terminated
padding	3		
`value_label_table`	`len`	see below	

and this is repeated for each value label included in the file. The format of the `value_label_table` is

Contents	Length	Format	Comments
`n`	4	int	number of entries
`txtlen`	4	int	length of `txt[]`
`off[]`	4*n	int array	`txt[]` offset table
`val[]`	4*n	int array	sorted value table
`txt[]`	`txtlen`	char	text table

`n`, `txtlen`, `off[]`, and `val[]` are encoded per `byteorder`.

For example, the `value_label_table` for 1 ↔ yes and 2 ↔ no, shown in HILO format, would be

```
byte position:  00 01 02 03   04 05 06 07   08 09 10 11    12 13 14 15
     contents:  00 00 00 02   00 00 00 07   00 00 00 00    00 00 00 04
      meaning:        n = 2    txtlen = 7    off[0] = 0     off[1] = 4

byte position:  16 17 18 19   20 21 22 23   24 25 26 27 28 29 30
     contents:  00 00 00 01   00 00 00 02    y  e  s 00  n  o 00
      meaning:   val[0] = 1    val[1] = 2   txt --->
```

The interpretation is that there are `n` = 2 values being mapped. The values being mapped are `val[0]` = 1 and `val[1]` = 2. The corresponding text for `val[0]` would be at `off[0]` = 0 (and so be "yes") and for `val[1]` would be at `off[1]` = 4 (and so be "no").

Interpreting this table in C is not as daunting as it appears. Let (`char *`) `p` refer to the memory area into which `value_label_table` is read. Assume your C compiler uses 4-byte `int`s. The following manifests make interpreting the table easier:

```
#define SZInt                  4
#define Off_n                  0
#define Off_nxtoff             SZInt
#define Off_off                (SZInt+SZInt)
#define Off_val(n)             (SZInt+SZInt+n*SZInt)
#define Off_txt(n)             (Off_val(n) + n*SZInt)
#define Len_table(n,nxtoff)    (Off_txt(n) + nxtoff)

#define Ptr_n(p)               ( (int *) ( ((char *) p) + Off_n ) )
#define Ptr_nxtoff(p)          ( (int *) ( ((char *) p) + Off_nxtoff ) )
#define Ptr_off(p)             ( (int *) ( ((char *) p) + Off_off ) )
#define Ptr_val(p,n)           ( (int *) ( ((char *) p) + Off_val(n) ) )
#define Ptr_txt(p,n)           ( (char *) ( ((char *) p) + Off_txt(n) ) )
```

It is now the case that for(i=0; i < *Ptr_n(p); i++), the value *Ptr_val(p,i) is mapped to the character string Ptr_txt(p,i).

Remember in allocating memory for *p that the table can be big. The limits are $n = 65{,}536$ mapped values with each value being up to 81 characters long (including the null terminating byte). Such a table would be 5,823,712 bytes long. No user is likely to approach that limit and, in any case, after reading the 8 bytes preceding the table (n and txtlen), you can calculate the remaining length as 2*4*n+txtlen and malloc() as the exact amount.

Constructing a table is more difficult. The easiest approach is to set arbitrary limits equal to or smaller than Stata's as to the maximum number of entries and total text length you will allow and simply declare the three pieces off[], val[], and txt[] according to those limits:

```
int off[MaxValueForN] ;
int val[MaxValueForN] ;
char txt[MaxValueForTxtlen] ;
```

Stata's internal code follows a more complicated strategy of always keeping the table in compressed form and having a routine that will "add one position" in the table. This is slower but keeps memory requirements to be no more than the actual size of the table.

In any case, when adding new entries to the table, remember that val[] must be in ascending order: val[0] < val[1] < $\cdots$ < val[n]. It is not required that off[] or txt[] be kept in ascending order. We previously offered the example of the table that mapped 1 $\leftrightarrow$ yes and 2 $\leftrightarrow$ no:

```
byte position:   00 01 02 03   04 05 06 07   08 09 10 11    12 13 14 15
     contents:   00 00 00 02   00 00 00 07   00 00 00 00    00 00 00 04
      meaning:          n = 2    txtlen = 7    off[0] = 0     off[1] = 4

byte position:   16 17 18 19   20 21 22 23   24 25 26 27 28 29 30
     contents:   00 00 00 01   00 00 00 02   y  e  s 00  n  o 00
      meaning:    val[0] = 1    val[1] = 2    txt --->
```

This table could just as well be recorded as

```
byte position:   00 01 02 03   04 05 06 07   08 09 10 11    12 13 14 15
     contents:   00 00 00 02   00 00 00 07   00 00 00 03    00 00 00 00
      meaning:          n = 2    txtlen = 7    off[0] = 3     off[1] = 0

byte position:   16 17 18 19   20 21 22 23   24 25 26 27 28 29 30
     contents:   00 00 00 01   00 00 00 02   n  o 00  y  e  s 00
      meaning:    val[0] = 1    val[1] = 2    txt --->
```

but it could not be recorded as

```
byte position:  00 01 02 03   04 05 06 07   08 09 10 11   12 13 14 15
     contents:  00 00 00 02   00 00 00 07   00 00 00 04   00 00 00 00
      meaning:         n = 2   txtlen = 7    off[0] = 4    off[1] = 0
byte position:  16 17 18 19   20 21 22 23   24 25 26 27 28 29 30
     contents:  00 00 00 02   00 00 00 01   y  e  s 00  n  o 00
      meaning:   val[0] = 2    val[1] = 1    txt --->
```

It is not the out-of-order values of off[] that cause problems; it is out-of-order values of val[]. In terms of table construction, we find it easier to keep the table sorted as it grows. This way one can use a binary search routine to find the appropriate position in val[] quickly.

The following C routine will find the appropriate slot. It uses the manifests we previously defined and thus it assumes the table is in compressed form, but that is not important. Changing the definitions of the manifests to point to separate areas would be easy enough.

```
/*
        slot = vlfindval(char *baseptr, int val)
        Looks for value val in label at baseptr.
                If found:
                        returns slot number:  0, 1, 2, ...
                If not found:
                        returns k<0 such that val would go in slot -(k+1)
                                k== -1        would go in slot 0.
                                k== -2        would go in slot 1.
                                k== -3        would go in slot 2.
*/
int vlfindval(char *baseptr, int myval)
{
        int         n ;
        int         lb, ub, try ;
        int         *val ;
        char        *txt ;
        int         *off ;
        int         curval ;
        n   = *Ptr_n(baseptr) ;
        val = Ptr_val(baseptr, n) ;
        if (n==0) return(-1) ;   /* not found, insert into 0 */
                                 /* in what follows,              */
                                 /* we know result between [lb,ub] */
                                 /* or it is not in the table     */
        lb = 0 ;
        ub = n - 1 ;
        while (1) {
                try = (lb + ub) / 2 ;
                curval = val[try] ;
                if (myval == curval) return(try) ;
                if (myval<curval) {
                        ub = try - 1 ;
                        if (ub<lb) return(-(try+1)) ;
                        /* because want to insert before try, ergo,
                           want to return try, and transform is -(W+1). */
                }
                else /* myval>curval */ {
                        lb = try + 1 ;
                        if (ub<lb) return(-(lb+1)) ;
                        /* because want to insert after try, ergo,
                           want to return try+1 and transform is -(W+1) */
                }
        }
        /*NOTREACHED*/
}
```

Also See

Related: [G] **file formats .gph**

Title

foreach — Loop over items

Syntax

```
foreach lname { in | of listtype } list {
        stata commands referring to `lname´
}
```

Allowed are

foreach *lname* **in** *anylist*

foreach *lname* **of local** *lmacname*

foreach *lname* **of global** *gmacname*

foreach *lname* **of varlist** *varlist*

foreach *lname* **of newlist** *newvarlist*

foreach *lname* **of numlist** *numlist*

Description

foreach repeatedly sets local macro *lname* to each element of the list and executes the commands enclosed in braces. The loop is executed zero or more times; it is executed zero times if the list is null or empty. Also see [P] **forvalues**, which is the fastest way to loop over consecutive values, such as looping over numbers from 1 to k.

foreach *lname* in *anylist* allows a general list. Elements are separated from each other by one or more blanks.

foreach *lname* of local *lmacname* and foreach *lname* of global *gmacname* obtain the list from the indicated place. This method of using foreach produces the fastest executing code.

foreach *lname* of varlist *list*, foreach *lname* of newlist *list*, and foreach *lname* of numlist *list* are very much like foreach *lname* in *list*, except that the *list* is given the appropriate interpretation. For instance,

```
foreach x in mpg weight-turn {
        . . .
}
```

has two elements, "mpg" and "weight-turn", so the loop will be executed twice.

```
foreach x of varlist mpg weight-turn {
        . . .
}
```

96

has four elements, `mpg`, `weight`, `length`, and `turn`, because *list* was given the interpretation of a varlist.

`foreach` *lname* `of varlist` *list* gives *list* the interpretation of a *varlist*. The *list* is expanded according to standard variable abbreviation rules, and the existence of the variables is confirmed.

`foreach` *lname* `of newlist` *list* indicates that the list is to be interpreted as new variable names; see [U] **14.4.2 Lists of new variables**. A check is performed to see that the named variables could be created, but they are not automatically created.

`foreach` *lname* `of numlist` *list* indicates a number list and allows standard number list notation; see [U] **14.1.8 numlist**.

Remarks

Remarks are presented under the headings

> *Introduction*
> *foreach ... of local and foreach ... of global*
> *foreach ... of varlist*
> *foreach ... of newlist*
> *foreach ... of numlist*
> *Use of foreach with continue*
> *The unprocessed list elements*

Introduction

`foreach` has lots of forms, but it is just one command, and what it means is

```
foreach value of a list of things, set x equal to the each and {
        execute these instructions once per value
        and in the loop we can refer to `x´ to refer to the value
}
```

and this is coded

```
foreach x ... {
        ... `x´ ...
}
```

We use the name `x` for illustration; you may use whatever name you like. The list itself can come from a variety of places and can be given a variety of interpretations, but `for x in` is easiest to understand:

```
foreach x in a b mpg 2 3 2.2 {
        ... `x´ ...
}
```

The list is `a`, `b`, `mpg`, `2`, `3`, and `2.2`, and appears right in the command. In some programming instances, you might know the list ahead of time, but often what you know is that you want to do the loop for each value of the list contained in a macro, for instance `` `varlist´ ``. In that case, you could code

```
foreach x in `varlist´ {
        ... `x´ ...
}
```

but your code will execute more quickly if you code

```
foreach x of local varlist {
        ... `x´ ...
}
```

Both work, but the second is quicker to execute. In the first, Stata has to expand the macro and substitute it into the command line, whereupon foreach must then pull back the elements one at a time and store them. In the second, all that is already done and foreach can just grab the local macro varlist.

The two forms we have just shown,

```
foreach x in ... {
        ... `x' ...
}
```

and

```
foreach x of local ... {
        ... `x' ...
}
```

are the two ways foreach is most commonly used. The other forms are for special occasions.

In the unlikely event you have something that you want to be given the interpretation of a varlist, newvarlist, or numlist before it is interpreted as a list, you can code

```
foreach x of varlist mpg weight-turn g* {
        ... `x' ...
}
```

or

```
foreach x of newvarlist id values1-9 {
        ... `x' ...
}
```

or

```
foreach x of numlist 1/3 5 6/10 {
        ... `x' ...
}
```

Just as with foreach x in ..., you put the list right on the command line and, if you have the list in a macro, you can put `macroname´ on the command line.

If you have the list in a macro, you have no alternative but to code `macroname´; there is no special foreach x of local *macroname* variant for varlist, newvarlist, and numlist because, in those cases, foreach x of local *macroname* itself is probably sufficient. If you have the list in a macro, how did it get there? Well, it probably was something that the user typed and that your program has already parsed. In that case, the list has already been expanded, and treating the list as a general list is adequate; it need not be given the special interpretation again, at least as far as foreach is concerned.

▷ Example

foreach is generally used in programs, but it may be used interactively and, for illustration, we will use it that way. Three files are appended to the dataset in memory. The dataset currently in memory and each of the three files have only one string observation.

```
. list

                                 x
    1.              data in memory
. foreach file in this.dta that.dta theother.dta {
    2.              append using "`file´"
    3. }

. list

                                 x
    1.              data in memory
    2.        data from this.dta
    3.        data from that.dta
    4. data from theother.dta
```

Quotes may be used to allow elements with blanks.

```
. foreach name in "Christi Pechacek" "Ashley Johnson" "Marsha Martinez" {
    2.              display length("`name´") " characters long -- `name´"
    3. }
16 characters long -- Christi Pechacek
14 characters long -- Ashley Johnson
15 characters long -- Marsha Martinez
```

◁

foreach ... of local and foreach ... of global

foreach *lname* of local *lmacname* obtains the blank separated list (which may contain quotes) from local macro *lmacname*. For example,

```
foreach file of local flist {
        ...
}
```

produces the same results as typing

```
foreach file in `flist´ {
        ...
}
```

except that `foreach file of local flist` is faster, uses less memory, and allows the list to be modified in the body of the loop.

If the contents of `flist` are modified in the body of `foreach file in `flist´`, `foreach` will not notice and the original list will be used. The contents of `flist` may, however, be modified in `foreach file of local flist`, but only to add new elements onto the end.

foreach *lname* of global *gmacname* is the same as `foreach` *lname* in $*gmacname*, with the same three caveats as to speed, memory use, and modification in the loop body.

▷ Example

```
. local grains "rice wheat flax"

. foreach x of local grains {
    2.              display "`x´"
    3. }
rice
wheat
flax
```

```
. global money "Dollar Lira Pound"

. foreach y of global money {
  2.        display "`y´"
  3. }
Dollar
Lira
Pound
```

◁

foreach ... of varlist

foreach *lname* of `varlist` *varlist* { ... } allows specifying an existing variable list.

▷ Example

```
. foreach var of varlist pri-rep t* {
  2.        quietly summarize `var´
  3.        summarize `var´ if `var´ > r(mean)
  4. }
```

Variable	Obs	Mean	Std. Dev.	Min	Max
price	22	9814.364	3022.929	6229	15906

Variable	Obs	Mean	Std. Dev.	Min	Max
mpg	31	26.67742	4.628802	22	41

Variable	Obs	Mean	Std. Dev.	Min	Max
rep78	29	4.37931	.493804	4	5

Variable	Obs	Mean	Std. Dev.	Min	Max
trunk	40	17.1	2.351214	14	23

Variable	Obs	Mean	Std. Dev.	Min	Max
turn	41	43.07317	2.412367	40	51

◁

foreach *lname* of `varlist` *varlist* { ... } can be useful interactively, but is rarely used in programming contexts. You can code

```
syntax [varlist] ...
foreach var of varlist `varlist´ {
      ...
}
```

but that is not as efficient as coding

```
syntax [varlist] ...
foreach var of local varlist {
      ...
}
```

because `varlist´ has already been expanded by the **syntax** command according to the macro rules.

❑ Technical Note

```
syntax [varlist] ...
foreach var of local varlist {
        ...
}
```

is also preferable to coding

```
syntax [varlist] ...
tokenize `varlist'
while "`1'" ~= "" {
        ...
        macro shift
}
```

or

```
syntax [varlist] ...
tokenize `varlist'
local i = 1
while "``i''" ~= "" {
        ...
        local i = `i' + 1
}
```

not only because it is more readable, but because it is also faster.

❑

foreach … of newlist

newlist signifies to foreach that the list is composed of new variables. foreach verifies that the list contains valid new variable names, but it does not create the variables. For instance,

```
. foreach var of newlist z1-z4 {
  2.        gen `var' = uniform()
  3. }
```

would create variables z1, z2, z3, and z4.

foreach … of numlist

foreach *lname* of numlist *numlist* provides a method of looping through a list of numbers. Standard number list notation is allowed; see [U] **14.1.8 numlist**. For instance,

```
. foreach num of numlist 1/4 8 103 {
  2.        display `num'
  3. }
1
2
3
4
8
103
```

If you wish to loop over a large number of equally spaced values, do not code, for instance,

```
foreach x in 1/1000 {
        ...
}
```

Instead, code

```
forvalues x = 1/1000 {
        ...
}
```

see [P] **forvalues**. Understand that `foreach` must store the list of elements, whereas `forvalues` obtains the elements one at a time by calculation.

Use of foreach with continue

The *lname* in `foreach` is defined only in the loop body. If you code

```
foreach x ... {
        /* loop body, `x´ is defined */
}
/* `x´ is now undefined, meaning it contains "" */
```

`x´ is defined only within the loop body, and this is the case even if you use `continue`, `break` (see [P] **continue**) to exit the loop early:

```
foreach x ... {
        ...
        if ... {
                continue, break
        }
}
/* `x´ is still undefined, even if continue, break is executed */
```

If you subsequently need the value of `x´, code

```
foreach x ... {
        ...
        if ... {
                local lastx `"`x´"´
                continue, break
        }
}
/* `lastx´ defined */
```

The unprocessed list elements

The macro `ferest()´ may be used in the body of the `foreach` loop to obtain the unprocessed list elements.

▷ Example

```
. foreach x in alpha "one two" three four {
  2.            display
  3.            display `"        x is |`x´|"´
  4.            display `"ferest() is |`ferest()´|"´
  5. }
        x is |alpha|
ferest() is |"one two" three four|

        x is |one two|
ferest() is |three four|

        x is |three|
ferest() is |four|

        x is |four|
ferest() is ||
```
◁

`ferest()´ is only available within the body of the loop; outside of that `ferest()´ evaluates to "". Thus, you might code,

```
foreach x ... {
        ...
        if ... {
                local lastx `"`x´"´
                local rest `"`ferest()´"´
                continue, break
        }
}
/* `lastx´ and `rest´ are defined */
```

Also See

Complementary:	[P] **continue**
Related:	[P] **forvalues**, [P] **if**, [P] **while**, [R] **for**
Background:	[U] **21 Programming Stata**, [U] **21.3 Macros**

Title

forvalues — Loop over consecutive values

Syntax

> **<u>forva</u>lues** *lname* = *range* {
>> *stata commands referring to* `` `lname' ``
>
> }

where *range* is

$\#_1(\#_d)\#_2$	meaning $\#_1$ to $\#_2$ in steps of $\#_d$
$\#_1/\#_2$	meaning $\#_1$ to $\#_2$ in steps of 1
$\#_1 \ \#_t$ **to** $\#_2$	meaning $\#_1$ to $\#_2$ in steps of $\#_t - \#_1$
$\#_1 \ \#_t : \#_2$	meaning $\#_1$ to $\#_2$ in steps of $\#_t - \#_1$

The loop is executed as long as calculated values of `` `lname' `` are $\leq \#_2$.

Description

forvalues repeatedly sets local macro *lname* to each element of *range* and executes the commands enclosed in braces. The loop is executed zero or more times.

Remarks

forvalues is the fastest way to execute a block of code for different numeric values of *lname*.

▷ Example

With **forvalues** *lname* = $\#_1(\#_d)\#_2$, the loop is executed zero or more times, once for *lname* = $\#_1 + \#_d$, once for *lname* = $\#_1 + \#_d + \#_d$, and so on, as long as *lname* $\leq \#_2$ (assuming $\#_d$ is positive) or as long as *lname* $\geq \#_2$ (assuming $\#_d$ is negative). Specifying $\#_d$ as 0 is an error.

```
. forvalues i = 1(1)5 {
  2.          display `i´
  3. }
1
2
3
4
5
```

lists the numbers one to five, stepping by one, while

```
. forvalues i = 10(-2)1 {
  2.          display `i´
  3. }
10
8
6
4
2
```

lists the numbers starting from ten, stepping down by two until it reaches two. Notice that it stops at two instead of one or zero. The following

```
. forvalues i = 1(1)1 {
  2.          display `i´
  3. }
1
```

displays one, while

```
. forvalues i = 1(1)0 {
  2.          display `i´
  3. }
```

displays nothing.

◁

forvalues *lname* = $\#_1/\#_2$ is the same as using forvalues *lname* = $\#_1(1)\#_2$. Note that using / does not allow counting backwards.

▷ Example

```
. forvalues i = 1/3 {
  2.          display `i´
  3. }
1
2
3
```

lists the three values from one to three, but

```
. forvalues i = 3/1 {
  2.          display `i´
  3. }
```

lists nothing, since using this form of the forvalues command only allows incrementing by one.

◁

The forvalues *lname* = $\#_1 \#_t$ to $\#_2$ and forvalues *lname* = $\#_1 \#_t$: $\#_2$ forms of the forvalues command are equivalent to computing $\#_d = \#_t - \#_1$ and then using the forvalues *lname* = $\#_1(\#_d)\#_2$ form of the command.

▷ Example

```
. forvalues i = 5 10 : 25 {
  2.          display `i´
  3. }
5
10
15
20
25
```

```
. forvalues i = 25 20 to 5 {
  2.          display `i´
  3. }
25
20
15
10
5
```
◁

❑ Technical Note

The values of the loop bounds are determined once and for all the first time the loop is executed. Changing the loop bounds will have no effect. For instance,

```
. local n 3
. forvalues i = 1(1)`n´ {
  2.          local n = `n´ + 1
  3.          display `i´
  4. }
1
2
3
```

will not create an infinite loop. With `n´ originally equal to 3, the loop will be performed three times.

Similarly, modifying the loop counter will not affect **forvalues**' subsequent behavior. For instance,

```
. forvalues i = 1(1)3 {
  2.          display "Top of loop  i = `i´"
  3.          local i = `i´ * 4
  4.          display "After change i = `i´"
  5. }
Top of loop  i = 1
After change i = 4
Top of loop  i = 2
After change i = 8
Top of loop  i = 3
After change i = 12
```

will still execute three times, setting `i´ to 1, 2, and 3 at the beginning of each iteration.

❑

Also See

Complementary:	[P] **continue**
Related:	[P] **foreach**, [P] **if**, [P] **while**, [R] **for**
Background:	[U] **21 Programming Stata**, [U] **21.3 Macros**

Title

---
functions — Functions for programmers

Description

This entry provides a quick reference for functions that are of special interest to programmers. Matrix functions are not listed here; see [U] **17.8 Matrix functions**. See [U] **16.3 Functions** for a complete list of all non-matrix functions and for additional details about the functions listed here.

Remarks

Function	Description
Mathematical functions	See [U] **16.3.1 Mathematical functions**.
Statistical functions	See [U] **16.3.2 Statistical functions** for other functions and for additional details about this function.
uniform()	uniform pseudo-random number function; returns uniformly distributed pseudo-random numbers on the interval $[0, 1)$; it takes no arguments but the parentheses must be included; it can be seeded with the **set seed** command; see [R] **generate**
	Also see the inverse distribution functions such as normprob(), invF(), invchi2tail(), etc. Normally distributed random numbers, for instance, can be generated using invnorm(uniform()).
Date functions	See [U] **16.3.3 Date functions**.
String functions	See [U] **16.3.5 String functions** for additional details about these functions.
abbrev(s,n)	returns the name s, abbreviated to n characters. s may contain a name, a time-series operated name, or any string. If any of the characters of s are '.', and $n < 8$ or $n = .$, then the value of n defaults to a value of 8. Otherwise, if $n < 5$ or if $n = .$, then n defaults to a value of 5. abbrev() is typically used with variable names and variable names with time-series operators (the period case).
index(s_1,s_2)	returns the position in s_1 in which s_2 is first found or zero if s_1 does not contain s_2. index("this","is") is 3 and index("this","it") is 0.

(Continued on next page)

107

Function	Description
length(s)	returns the actual length of the string. length("ab") evaluates to 2.
lower(s)	returns the lowercased variant of s. lower("THIS") evaluates to "this".
ltrim(s)	returns s with any leading blanks removed. Thus, ltrim(" this") evaluates to "this".
match(s_1,s_2)	evaluates to 1 if s_1 matches the pattern s_2; otherwise, it returns 0. match("17.4","1??4") returns 1.
real(s)	converts s into a numeric argument. real("5.2")+1 evaluates to 6.2.
reverse(s)	returns reversed s. reverse("hello") evaluates to "olleh".
rtrim(s)	returns s with any trailing blanks removed. Thus, rtrim("this ") evaluates to "this".
string(n, %fmt)	converts n into a string with %fmt display format. string(14610, "%dM-D-CY") evaluates to "January-01-2000".
subinstr(s_1,s_2,s_3,n)	returns s_1 where the first n occurrences in s_1 of s_2 have been replaced with s_3. subinstr("this is this","is","X",1) evaluates to "thX is this".
subinword(s_1,s_2,s_3,n)	returns s_1 where the first n occurrences in s_1 of s_2 as a word have been replaced with s_3. A word is defined as a space-separated token; a token at the beginning or end of s also counts as being space-separated. subinword("this is this","is","X",1) evaluates to "this X this".
substr(s,n_1,n_2)	returns the substring of s starting at the n_1th column for a length of n_2. substr("abcdef",2,3) evaluates to "bcd". If $n_1 < 0$, the starting position is interpreted as distance from the end of the string. Thus, substr("abcdef",-2,1) evaluates to "e". If n_2 ==., the remaining portion of the string is returned. substr("abcdef",4,.) evaluates to "def".
trim(s)	returns s with any leading and trailing blanks removed. It is identical to ltrim(rtrim(s)). Thus, trim(" this ") evaluates to "this".
upper(s)	returns the uppercased variant of s. upper("this") evaluates to "THIS".

Function	Description
Special functions	See [U] **16.3.6 Special functions** for additional details about these functions.
autocode($x,n,xmin,xmax$)	partitions the interval from *xmin* to *xmax* into n equal-length intervals and returns the upper bound of the interval that contains x. This function is an automated version of recode() (see below). See [U] **28 Commands for dealing with categorical variables** for an example.
_caller()	returns version of the program or session that invoked the currently running program; see [P] **version**. For use by programmers.
cond(x,a,b)	returns a if x evaluates to *true* (not 0) and b if x evaluates to *false* (0). generate maxinc=cond(inc1>inc2,inc1,inc2) creates the variable maxinc as the maximum of inc1 and inc2 (assuming inc1 and inc2 are not *missing*).
e(*name*)	contains the value of saved result e(*name*). See [U] **21.8 Accessing results calculated by other programs**. Also see [U] **17.8.1 Matrix functions returning matrices**.
e(sample)	evaluates to 1 if the observation was part of the estimation sample; otherwise, 0. See [U] **23.4 Specifying the estimation subsample**.
float(x)	returns the value of x rounded to float. Although you may store your numeric variables as byte, int, long, float, or double, Stata converts all numbers to double before performing any calculations. As a consequence, difficulties can arise when numbers that have no finite binary representation are compared. See [U] **16.10 Precision and problems therein** for more information.
group(x)	creates a categorical variable that divides the dataset into x as nearly equal-sized subsamples as possible, numbering the first group 1, the second 2, and so on.
inlist($z,a,b,\ldots$)	evaluates to 1 if z is a member of the remaining arguments; otherwise, returns 0. The number of arguments is between 2 and 255. All must be reals or all must be strings.

(*Continued on next page*)

Function	Description
inrange(z,a,b)	evaluates to 1 if $a \leq z \leq b$; otherwise, returns 0. The following ordered rules apply: $z = .$ returns 0. $a = .$ and $b = .$ returns 1. $a = .$ returns 1 if $z \leq b$; otherwise it returns 0. $b = .$ returns 1 if $a \leq z$; otherwise it returns 0. Otherwise, 1 is returned if $a \leq z \leq b$ In the above, if the arguments are strings, '.' is interpreted as "".
int(x)	returns the integer obtained by truncating x. Thus, int(5.2) is 5 as is int(5.8); int(-5.2) is -5 as is int(-5.8). One way to obtain the closest integer to x is int(x+sign(x)/2), which simplifies to int(x+0.5) for $x \geq 0$. Use of the round() function, however, is preferred.
matrix(*exp*)	restricts name interpretation to scalars and matrices; see scalar() function below.
max(x_1,x_2,...,x_n)	returns the maximum of x_1, x_2, ..., x_n. Missing values are ignored. If all arguments are *missing, missing* is returned. For example, max(3+2,1) evaluates to 5.
min(x_1,x_2,...,x_n)	returns the minimum of x_1, x_2, ..., x_n. Missing values are ignored. If all arguments are *missing, missing* is returned.
missing(x)	returns 0 if $x \neq .$ (or $\neq$ "" for a string); otherwise, returns 1
recode(x,x_1,x_2,...,x_n)	returns *missing* if x is *missing*; x_1 if $x \leq x_1$; otherwise x_2 if $x \leq x_2$, ...; otherwise x_n if x is greater than x_1, x_2, ..., x_{n-1}. Also see [R] **recode** for another style of recode function.
r(*name*)	contains the value of saved result r(*name*). See [U] **21.8 Accessing results calculated by other programs**; also see [U] **17.8.1 Matrix functions returning matrices**.
reldif(x, y)	"relative" difference $\|x - y\|/(\|y\| + 1)$.
replay()	function for programmers; see [P] **estimates**.
return(*name*)	contains the value of to-be-saved result return(*name*). See [U] **21.10 Saving results**.

(*Continued on next page*)

Function	Description
round(x,y)	returns x rounded to units of y. For $y = 1$, this amounts to the closest integer to x; round(5.2,1) is 5 as is round(4.8,1); round(-5.2,1) is -5 as is round(-4.8,1). The rounding definition is generalized for $y \neq 1$. With $y = .01$, for instance, x is rounded to two decimal places; round(sqrt(2),.01) is 1.41. y may also be larger than 1; round(28,5) is 30, which is 28 rounded to the closest multiple of 5. For $y = 0$, the function is defined as returning x unmodified.
s(*name*)	contains the value of saved result s(*name*). See [U] **21.8 Accessing results calculated by other programs**.
scalar(*exp*)	restricts name interpretation to scalars and matrices.
sign(x)	returns *missing* if x is *missing*, -1 if $x < 0$, 0 if $x = 0$, and 1 if $x > 0$.
sum(x)	returns the running sum of x, treating missing values as zero. For example, following the command **generate y=sum(x)**, the ith observation on y contains the sum of the first through ith observations on x. Also see [R] **egen** for an alternative sum function that produces a constant equal to the overall sum.
Time-series functions	See [U] **16.3.4 Time-series functions**.

Also See

Related: [R] **egen**

Background: [U] **16.3 Functions**,
[U] **17.8 Matrix functions**

Title

gettoken — Low-level parsing

Syntax

gettoken *emname1* [*emname2*] : *emname3* [, p̲arse(*pchars*) q̲uotes

m̲atch(*lmacname*)]

where *pchars* are the parsing characters, *lmacname* is a local macro name, and *emname* is described in the following table:

emname is:	refers to a:
macroname	local macro
(local) *macroname*	local macro
(global) *macroname*	global macro

Description

The gettoken command is a low-level parsing command designed for programmers who wish to parse input for themselves. The **syntax** command (see [P] **syntax**) is an easier to use high-level parsing command.

gettoken obtains the next token from the macro *emname3* and stores it in the macro *emname1*. If macro *emname2* is specified, the remainder of the string from *emname3* is stored in the *emname2* macro. *emname1* and *emname3*, or *emname2* and *emname3*, may be the same name. The first token is determined based on the parsing characters *pchars* which default to a space if not specified.

Options

parse("*pchars*") specifies the parsing characters. If parse() is not specified, parse(" ") is assumed.

quotes indicates that the outside quotes are not to be stripped in what is stored in *emname1*. This option has no effect on what is stored in *emname2*, because it always retains outside quotes. quotes is a rarely specified option; in most cases, you want the quotes stripped. You would not want the quotes stripped if you wanted to make a perfect copy of the contents of the original macro for parsing at a later time.

match(*lmacname*) specifies that parentheses are to be matched in determining the token. The outer level of parentheses, if any, are removed before the token is stored in *emname1*. The local macro *lmacname* is set to "(" if parentheses were found; otherwise it is set to an empty string.

(Continued on next page)

112

Remarks

Often we apply `gettoken` to the macro `` `0´ `` (see [U] **21.4.6 Parsing nonstandard syntax**), as in

```
gettoken first : 0
```

which obtains the first token (with spaces as token delimiters) from `` `0´ `` and leaves `` `0´ `` unchanged. Or alternatively,

```
gettoken first 0 : 0
```

which obtains the first token from `` `0´ `` and saves the rest back in `` `0´ ``.

▷ Example

Even though `gettoken` is typically used as a programming command, we demonstrate its use interactively:

```
. local str "cat+dog    mouse++horse"
. gettoken left : str
. display `"`left´"´
cat+dog
. display `"`str´"´
cat+dog    mouse++horse
. gettoken left str : str, parse(" +")
. display `"`left´"´
cat
. display `"`str´"´
+dog    mouse++horse
. gettoken next str : str, parse(" +")
. display `"`next´"´
+
. display `"`str´"´
dog    mouse++horse
```

Both global and local variables may be used with `gettoken`. Strings with nested quotes are also allowed and the `quotes` option may be specified if desired. For more information on compound double quotes, see [U] **21.3.5 Double quotes**.

```
. global weird `"`""some" strings"´ are `"within "strings""´"´
. gettoken (local)left (global)right : (global)weird
. display `"`left´"´
"some" strings
. display `"$right"´
 are `"within "strings""´
. gettoken left (global)right : (global)weird , quotes
. display `"`left´"´
`""some" strings"´
. display `"$right"´
 are `"within "strings""´
```

The `match` option is illustrated below.

```
. local pstr "(a (b c)) ((d e f) g h)"
. gettoken left right : pstr
. display `"`left'"'
(a
. display `"`right'"'
 (b c)) ((d e f) g h)
. gettoken left right : pstr , match(parns)
. display `"`left'"'
a (b c)
. display `"`right'"'
 ((d e f) g h)
. display `"`parns'"'
(
```

◁

▷ Example

One use of `gettoken` is to process two-word commands. For example, `mycmd list` does one thing and `mycmd generate` does another. We wish to obtain the word following `mycmd`, examine it, and call the appropriate subroutine with a perfect copy of what followed.

```
program define mycmd
        version 7.0
        gettoken subcmd 0 : 0
        if "`subcmd'" == "list" {
                mycmd_l `0'
        }
        else if "`subcmd'" == "generate" {
                mycmd_g `0'
        }
        else    error 199
end

program define mycmd_l
        ...
end

program define mycmd_g
        ...
end
```

◁

▷ Example

Suppose we wish to create a general prefix command with syntax

```
newcmd ... :  stata_command
```

where the ... is some possibly complicated syntax. We want to split this entire command line on colon, making a perfect copy of what precedes the colon—which will be parsed by our program—and what follows the colon—which will be passed along to *stata_command*.

```
program define newcmd
        version 7.0
        gettoken part 0 : 0, parse(" :") quotes
        while `"`part'"' ~= ":" & `"`part'"' ~= "" {
                local left `"`left' `part'"'
                gettoken part 0 : 0, parse(" :") quotes
        }
```

> (`left´ *now contains what followed* newcmd *up to the colon*)
> (`0´ *now contains what followed the colon*)
>
> . . .

     end

Notice the use of the quotes option. Also notice that we used compound double quotes when accessing `part´ and `left´ because these macros might contain embedded quotation marks.

◁

❑ Technical Note

We strongly encourage you to specify space as one of your parsing characters. For instance, with the last example, you may have been tempted to use gettoken but parse only on colon instead of on colon and space as in

```
gettoken left 0 : 0, parse(":") quotes
gettoken colon 0 : 0, parse(":")
```

and thereby avoid the while loop. This is not guaranteed to work for two reasons. First, if the length of the string up to the colon is large, you run the risk of having it truncated. Second, if `left´ begins with a quotation mark, the result will not be what you expect.

Our recommendation is always to specify a space as one of your parsing characters and to grow your desired macro as was demonstrated in our last example.

❑

Also See

Complementary:	[P] **display**, [P] **while**
Related:	[P] **syntax**, [P] **tokenize**
Background:	[U] **21 Programming Stata**

Title

hexdump — Display hexadecimal report on file

Syntax

hexdump *filename* $\left[\text{, } \underline{\text{analyze}} \text{ } \underline{\text{tabulate}} \text{ } \underline{\text{noex}}\text{tended } \underline{\text{res}}\text{ults } \underline{\text{from}}(\#) \text{ } \underline{\text{to}}(\#) \right]$

Description

hexdump displays a hexadecimal dump of a file or, optionally, a report analyzing the dump.

Although hexdump is not a programming command, it is included in this manual because it is highly technical.

Options

analyze specifies that a report on the dump rather than the dump itself is to be presented.

tabulate specifies in the analyze report that a full tabulation of the ASCII characters is also to be presented.

noextended states that your screen cannot display printable extended ASCII characters, characters in the range 161–254 or, equivalently, 0xa1–0xfe. (hexdump does not display characters 128–160 and 255.)

results is for programmers. It specifies that in addition to other saved results, hexdump is to save $r(c0)$, $r(c1)$, ..., $r(c255)$, containing the frequency with which each character code was observed.

from(#) specifies the first byte of the file to be dumped or analyzed. The default is to start at the first byte of the file, from(0).

to(#) specifies the last byte of the file to be analyzed. The default is to continue to the end of the file.

Remarks

hexdump is useful when you are having difficulty reading a file using infile, infix, or insheet. Sometimes, the reason for the difficulty is often that the file does not contain what you think it contains, or that it does contain the format you have been told, and looking at the file in text mode is either not possible or not sufficiently revealing.

Pretend we had the file myfile.raw containing

```
Datsun 210      4589  35  5  1
VW Scirocco     6850  25  4  1
Merc. Bobcat    3829  22  4  0
Buick Regal     5189  20  3  0
VW Diesel       5397  41  5  1
Pont. Phoenix   4424  19  .  0
Merc. Zephyr    3291  20  3  0
Olds Starfire   4195  24  1  0
BMW 320i        9735  25  4  1
```

This file has no problems. hexdump produces output that looks like this

```
. hexdump myfile.raw
```

			hex representation					character representation
address	0 1	2 3	4 5	6 7	8 9	a b	c d	e f	0123456789abcdef

address	0 1	2 3	4 5	6 7	8 9	a b	c d	e f	0123456789abcdef
0	4461	7473	756e	2032	3130	2020	2020	2034	Datsun 210 4
10	3538	3920	2033	3520	2035	2020	310d	0a56	589 35 5 1..V
20	5720	5363	6972	6f63	636f	2020	2020	3638	W Scirocco 68
30	3530	2020	3235	2020	3420	2031	0d0a	4d65	50 25 4 1..Me
40	7263	2e20	426f	6263	6174	2020	2033	3832	rc. Bobcat 382
50	3920	2032	3220	2034	2020	300d	0a42	7569	9 22 4 0..Bui
60	636b	2052	6567	616c	2020	2020	3531	3839	ck Regal 5189
70	2020	3230	2020	3320	2030	0d0a	5657	2044	20 3 0..VW D
80	6965	7365	6c20	2020	2020	2035	3339	3720	iesel 5397
90	2034	3120	2035	2020	310d	0a50	6f6e	742e	41 5 1..Pont.
a0	2050	686f	656e	6978	2020	3434	3234	2020	Phoenix 4424
b0	3139	2020	2e20	2030	0d0a	4d65	7263	2e20	19 . 0..Merc.
c0	5a65	7068	7972	2020	2033	3239	3120	2032	Zephyr 3291 2
d0	3020	2033	2020	300d	0a4f	6c64	7320	5374	0 3 0..Olds St
e0	6172	6669	7265	2020	3431	3935	2020	3234	arfire 4195 24
f0	2020	3120	2030	0d0a	424d	5720	3332	3069	1 0..BMW 320i
100	2020	2020	2020	2039	3733	3520	2032	3520	9735 25
110	2034	2020	310d	0a					4 1..

but can also produce output that looks like this:

```
. hexdump myfile.raw, analyze
```

Line-end characters			Line length (tab=1)	
\r\n (DOS)		9	minimum	30
\r by itself (Mac)		0	maximum	30
\n by itself (Unix)		0		
Space/separator characters			Number of lines	9
[blank]		99	EOL at EOF?	yes
[tab]		0		
[comma] (,)		0	Length of first 5 lines	
Control characters			Line 1	30
binary 0		0	Line 2	30
CTL excl. \r, \n, \t		0	Line 3	30
DEL		0	Line 4	30
Extended (128-159,255)		0	Line 5	30
ASCII printable				
A-Z		20		
a-z		61	File format	ASCII
0-9		77		
Special (!@#$ etc.)		4		
Extended (160-254)		0		
Total		279		

```
Observed were:
    \n \r blank . 0 1 2 3 4 5 6 7 8 9 B D M O P R S V W Z a b c d e f g h i
    k l n o p r s t u x y
```

Of the two forms of output, the second is often the more useful because it summarizes the file and the length of the summary is not a function of the length of the file. Here is the summary for a file that is just over 4 megabytes long,

```
. hexdump bigfile.raw, analyze
Line-end characters                 Line length (tab=1)
   \r\n        (DOS)      147,456      minimum                    29
   \r by itself (Mac)          0      maximum                    30
   \n by itself (Unix)         2
Space/separator characters          Number of lines        147,458
   [blank]           1,622,039       EOL at EOF?                yes
   [tab]                     0
   [comma] (,)               0      Length of first 5 lines
Control characters                   Line 1                     30
   binary 0                  0       Line 2                     30
   CTL excl. \r, \n, \t      0       Line 3                     30
   DEL                       0       Line 4                     30
   Extended (128-159,255)    0       Line 5                     30
ASCII printable
   A-Z                 327,684
   a-z                 999,436      File format              ASCII
   0-9               1,261,587
   Special (!@#$ etc.)  65,536
   Extended (160-254)        0
                   _____
Total                4,571,196

Observed were:
   \n \r blank . 0 1 2 3 4 5 6 7 8 9 B D M O P R S V W Z a b c d e f g h i
   k l n o p r s t u x y
```

and here is the same file, but with a subtle problem:

```
. hexdump badfile.raw, analyze
Line-end characters                 Line length (tab=1)
   \r\n        (DOS)      147,456      minimum                    30
   \r by itself (Mac)          0      maximum                    90
   \n by itself (Unix)         0
Space/separator characters          Number of lines        147,456
   [blank]           1,622,016       EOL at EOF?                yes
   [tab]                     0
   [comma] (,)               0      Length of first 5 lines
Control characters                   Line 1                     30
   binary 0                  8       Line 2                     30
   CTL excl. \r, \n, \t      4       Line 3                     30
   DEL                       0       Line 4                     30
   Extended (128-159,255)   24       Line 5                     30
ASCII printable
   A-Z                 327,683
   a-z                 999,426      File format             BINARY
   0-9               1,261,568
   Special (!@#$ etc.)  65,539
   Extended (160-254)       16
                   _____
Total                4,571,196

Observed were:
   \0 ^C ^D ^G \n \r ^U blank & . 0 1 2 3 4 5 6 7 8 9 B D E M O P R S U V W
   Z a b c d e f g h i k l n o p r s t u v x y } ~ E^A E^C E^I E^M E^P
   ë é ö 255
```

In the above, note that the line length varies between 30 and 90 (we were told that each line would be 30 characters long). Also note that the file contains what `hexdump, analyze` labeled control characters. Finally, note that `hexdump, analyze` declared the file to be BINARY rather than ASCII.

We created the second file by removing two valid lines from `bigfile.raw` (60 characters) and substituting 60 characters of binary junk. We would defy you to find the problem without using `hexdump, analyze`. You would succeed, but only after a lot of work. Remember, this file has 147,456 lines and only 2 of them are bad. Printing 1,000 lines at random from the file, your chances of listing the bad part is only .013472. To have a 50% chance of finding the bad lines, you would have to list 52,000 lines, which is to say, review about 945 pages of output. On those 945 pages, each line would need to be drawn at random. More likely, you would list lines in groups, and that would greatly reduce your chances of encountering the bad lines.

The situation is not quite as dire as we make out because, were you to read `badfile.raw` using `infile`, it would complain and, in this case, it would tell you exactly where it was complaining. Still, at that point you might wonder whether the problem was with how you were using `infile` or with the data. Moreover, our 60 bytes of binary junk experiment corresponds to transmission error. If the problem were instead that the person who constructed the file constructed two of the lines differently, `infile` might not complain, but later you would notice some odd values in your data (because obviously you would review the summary statistics, right?). In this case, `hexdump, analyze` might be the only way you could prove to yourself and others that the raw data need to be reconstructed.

❏ Technical Note

In the full hexadecimal dump,

```
. hexdump myfile.raw
                                                            character
                           hex representation             representation
       address   0 1  2 3  4 5  6 7  8 9  a b  c d  e f   0123456789abcdef

             0   4461 7473 756e 2032 3130 2020 2020 2034  Datsun 210     4
            10   3538 3920 2033 3520 2035 2020 310d 0a56  589  35  5  1..V
            20   5720 5363 6972 6f63 636f 2020 2020 3638  W Scirocco    68
            30   3530 2020 3235 2020 3420 2031 0d0a 4d65  50   25  4  1..Me
```
(output omitted)

addresses (listed on the left) are listed in hexadecimal. 10 means decimal 16, 20 means decimal 32, and so on. Sixteen characters are listed across each line.

In some other dump, you might see something like

```
. hexdump myfile2.raw
                                                            character
                           hex representation             representation
       address   0 1  2 3  4 5  6 7  8 9  a b  c d  e f   0123456789abcdef

             0   4461 7473 756e 2032 3130 2020 2020 2034  Datsun 210     4
            10   3538 3920 2033 3520 2035 2020 3120 2020  589  35  5  1
            20   2020 2020 2020 2020 2020 2020 2020 2020
             *
           160   2020 2020 2020 0a56 5720 5363 6972 6f63         .VW Sciroc
           170   636f 2020 2020 3638 3530 2020 3235 2020  co    6850   25
```
(output omitted)

The ∗ in the address field indicates that the previous line is repeated, and repeated, and repeated, until we get to hexadecimal address 160 (decimal 352).

❏

Saved Results

hexdump, analyze and hexdump, results save in r():

Scalars

r(DOS)	number of \r\n
r(Mac)	number of \r by itself
r(Unix)	number of \n by itself
r(blank)	number of blanks
r(tab)	number of tab characters
r(comma)	number comma (,) characters
r(ctl)	number of binary 0s; A–Z, excluding \r, \n, \t; DELs; and 128–159, 255
r(uc)	number of A–Z
r(lc)	number of a–z
r(digit)	number of 0–9
r(special)	number of printable special characters (!@# etc.)
r(extended)	number of printable extended characters (160–254)
r(filesize)	number of characters
r(lmin)	minimum line length
r(lmax)	maximum line length
r(lnum)	number of lines
r(eoleof)	1 if EOL at EOF, otherwise 0
r(l1)	length of 1st line
r(l2)	length of 2nd line
r(l3)	length of 3rd line
r(l4)	length of 4th line
r(l5)	length of 5th line
r(c0)	number of binary 0s (results only)
r(c1)	number of binary 1s (^A) (results only)
r(c2)	number of binary 2s (^B) (results only)
...	...
r(255)	number of binary 255s (results only)

Macros

r(format)	ASCII, EXTENDED ASCII, or BINARY

Also See

Complementary: [R] **type**

Title

if — if programming command

Syntax

if *exp* {

          stata_commands

}

else   *stata_command*

Note that `else` must appear on a separate line from the closing brace (}) of the corresponding `if` statement.

Description

The `if` command (not to be confused with the `if` qualifier; see [U] **14.1.3 if exp**) evaluates *exp*. If the result is *true* (nonzero), the commands inside the braces are executed. If the result is *false* (zero), those statements are ignored and the statement (or statements if enclosed in braces) following the `else` is executed.

Remarks

The `if` command is intended for use inside programs and do-files; see [U] **21.3.4 Macros and expressions** for examples of its use.

▷ Example

Do not confuse the `if` command with the `if` qualifier. Typing `if age>21 {summarize age}` will summarize *all* the observations on `age` if the first observation on `age` is greater than 21. Otherwise, it will do nothing. Typing `summarize age if age>21`, on the other hand, summarizes all the observations on `age` that are greater than 21.

◁

▷ Example

`if` is typically used in do-files and programs. For instance, let's write a program to calculate the Tukey (1977, 90–91) "power" function of a variable x:

```
. program define power
        if `2´>0 {
                generate z=`1´^`2´
                label variable z "`1´^`2´"
        }
        else if `2´==0 {
                generate z=log(`1´)
                label variable z "log(`1´)"
        }
        else {
                 generate z=-(`1´^(`2´))
                 label variable z "-`1´^(`2´)"
        }
        end
```

121

This program takes two arguments. The first argument is the name of an existing variable, x. The second argument is a number, which we will call n. The program creates a new variable z. If $n > 0$, z is x^n; if $n = 0$, z is $\log x$; if $n < 0$, z is $-x^n$. No matter which path the program follows through the code, it labels the variable appropriately:

```
. power age 2

. describe z

                storage  display   value
variable name   type     format    label      variable label

z               float    %9.0g                age^2
```

◁

❑ Technical Note

If the expression refers to any variables, their values in the first observation are used unless explicit subscripts are specified.

❑

References

Tukey, J. W. 1977. *Exploratory Data Analysis.* Reading, MA: Addison–Wesley Publishing Company.

Also See

Related: [P] **while**

Background: [U] **21 Programming Stata**

Title

| **macro** — Macro definition and manipulation |

Syntax

<u>gl</u>obal *mname* [=*exp* | :*extended_fcn* | "[*string*]" | `"[*string*]"´]

<u>loc</u>al *lclname* [=*exp* | :*extended_fcn* | "[*string*]" | `"[*string*]"´]

tempvar *lclname* [*lclname* [...]]

tempname *lclname* [*lclname* [...]]

tempfile *lclname* [*lclname* [...]]

<u>ma</u>cro <u>dir</u>

<u>ma</u>cro <u>drop</u> { *mname* [*mname* [...]] | *mname*∗ | _all }

<u>ma</u>cro <u>l</u>ist [*mname* [*mname* [...]] | _all]

<u>ma</u>cro <u>sh</u>ift [*#*]

where *extended_fcn* is any of

{ <u>t</u>ype | <u>f</u>ormat | <u>val</u>ue <u>l</u>abel | <u>var</u>iable <u>l</u>abel } *varname*

<u>l</u>abel { *valuelabelname* | (*varname*) } { maxlength | *#* [*#*] }

data <u>l</u>abel

<u>sort</u>edby

set { adosize | graphics | level | linesize | logtype | matsize | more | pagesize | rmsg | textsize | trace | type | virtual }

sysdir [STATA | UPDATES | BASE | SITE | STBPLUS | PERSONAL | *dirname*]
pwd
dirsep

<u>en</u>vironment *name*

r({ scalars | macros | matrices | functions})

e({ scalars | macros | matrices | functions})

123

s(macros)

<u>di</u>splay ...   (see [P] **display**)

{ <u>rown</u>ames | <u>coln</u>ames | <u>rowe</u>q | <u>cole</u>q | <u>rowf</u>ullnames | <u>colf</u>ullnames } *matname*

tsnorm *string* [, <u>var</u>name]

word { count | # of } *string*

piece # # of { "[*string*]" | `"[*string*]"´ }

subinstr { <u>gl</u>obal *mname2* | <u>loc</u>al *lclname2* } { "*from*" | `"*from*"´ }

   { "*to*" | `"*to*"´ } [, all <u>c</u>ount({ <u>gl</u>obal *mname3* | <u>loc</u>al *lclname3* }) <u>w</u>ord]

tempvar | tempfile

Description

global assigns strings to specified global macro names (*mnames*). **local** assigns strings to local macro names (*lclnames*). Both regular quotes (" and ") and compound double quotes (`" and "´) are allowed; see [U] **21.3.5 Double quotes**. If the *string* has embedded quotes, then compound double quotes are needed.

tempvar assigns names to the specified local macro names that may be used as temporary variable names in the dataset. When the program or do-file concludes, any variables in the dataset with these assigned names are dropped.

tempname assigns names to the specified local macro names that may be used as temporary scalar or matrix names. When the program or do-file concludes, any scalars or matrices in the dataset with these assigned names are dropped.

tempfile assigns names to the specified local macro names that may be used as names for temporary files. When the program or do-file concludes, any datasets created with these assigned names are erased.

macro manipulates global and local macros.

Remarks

Remarks are presented under the headings

> *Formal definition of a macro*
> *Global and local macro names*
> *Macro assignment*
> *Macro extended functions*
> *Macro extended functions for extracting data attributes*
> *Macro extended functions for accessing Stata system parameters*
> *Macro extended functions for filenames and file paths*
> *Macro extended functions for accessing operating-system parameters*
> *Macro extended functions for names of saved results*
> *Macro extended functions for formatting results*

Macros are a tool used in programming Stata, and this entry assumes that you have read [U] **21 Programming Stata** and especially [U] **21.3 Macros**. This entry concerns advanced issues not previously covered. For your convenience, a table of the predefined system macros can be found in [P] **macro system**.

Formal definition of a macro

A *macro* has a *macro name* and *macro contents*. Everywhere a punctuated macro name appears in a command—punctuation is defined below—the macro contents are substituted for the macro name.

Macros come in two types, called global and local macros. Macro names are up to 32 characters long for global macros and 31 characters long for local macros. The contents of global macros are defined with the `global` command and local macros with the `local` command. Global macros are just that. Local macros exist solely within the program or do-file in which they are defined. If that program or do-file calls another program or do-file, the local macros previously defined temporarily cease to exist and their existence is reestablished when the calling program regains control. When a program or do-file ends, its local macros are permanently deleted.

To substitute the macro contents of a global macro name, the macro name is typed (punctuated) with a dollar sign ($) in front. To substitute the macro contents of a local macro name, the macro name is typed (punctuated) with surrounding left and right single quotes (` ´). In either case, braces ({ }) can be used to clarify meaning and to form nested constructions. When the contents of an undefined macro are substituted, the macro name (and punctuation) is removed and nothing is substituted in its place.

For example,

The input . . .	is equivalent to . . .
`global a "myvar"`	
`gen $a = oldvar`	`gen myvar = oldvar`
`gen a = oldvar`	`gen a = oldvar`
`local a "myvar"`	
`gen `a´ = oldvar`	`gen myvar = oldvar`
`gen a = oldvar`	`gen a = oldvar`
`global a "newvar"`	
`global i = 2`	
`gen $a$i = oldvar`	`gen newvar2 = oldvar`
`local a "newvar"`	
`local i = 2`	
`gen `a´`i´ = oldvar`	`gen newvar2 = oldvar`
`global b1 "newvar"`	
`global i=1`	
`gen ${b$i} = oldvar`	`gen newvar = oldvar`
`local b1 "newvar"`	
`local i=1`	
`gen `b`i´´ = oldvar`	`gen newvar = oldvar`

```
global b1 "newvar"
global a "b"
global i = 1
gen ${$a$i} = oldvar                          gen newvar = oldvar

local b1 "newvar"
local a "b"
local i = 1
gen ``a'`i'' = oldvar                         gen newvar = oldvar
```

Global and local macro names

What we next say is an exceedingly fine point: Global macro names that begin with an underscore are really local macros; this is why local macro names can have only 31 characters. The command `local` is formally defined as equivalent to `global _`. Thus, the following are equivalent:

```
local x                          global _x
local i=1                        global _i=1
local name "Bill"               global _name "Bill"
local fmt : format myvar        global _fmt : format myvar
local 3 `2'                      global _3 $_2
```

`tempvar` is formally defined as equivalent to `local name : tempvar` for each name specified after `tempvar`. Thus,

```
tempvar a b c
```

is equivalent to

```
local a : tempvar
local b : tempvar
local c : tempvar
```

which in turn is equivalent to

```
global _a : tempvar
global _b : tempvar
global _c : tempvar
```

`tempfile` is defined similarly.

Macro assignment

When you type

```
. local name "something"
```

or

```
. local name `"something"'
```

something becomes the contents of the macro. The compound double quotes (`` `" `` and `"'`) are needed when *something* contains quotation marks. When you type

```
. local name = something
```

something is evaluated as an expression, and the result becomes the contents of the macro. Note the presence and lack of the equal sign. That is, if you type

```
. local problem "2+2"
. local result = 2+2
```

then `problem` contains 2+2, whereas `result` contains 4.

Finally, when you type

    . local name : *something*

something is interpreted as an extended macro function. (Note the colon rather than nothing or the equal sign.) Of course, all of this applies to `global` as well as to `local`.

Macro extended functions

Macro extended functions are of the form

    . local *macname* : ...

For instance,

    . local x : type mpg
    . local y : matsize
    . local z : display %9.4f sqrt(2)

We document the macro extended functions below. Macro extended functions are typically used in programs, but you can experiment with them interactively. For instance, if you are unsure what '`local x : type mpg`' does, you could type

    . local x : type mpg
    . display "`x'"
    int

Macro extended functions for extracting data attributes

`type` *varname*
    returns the storage type of variable *varname*, which might be "`int`", "`long`", "`float`", "`double`", "`str1`", "`str2`", etc.

`format` *varname*
    returns the display format associated with *varname*, for instance, "`%9.0g`", "`%12s`", etc.

`value label` *varname*
    returns the name of the value label associated with *varname*, which might be "" (meaning no label) or, for example, "`make`", meaning the value label's name is `make`.

`variable label` *varname*
    returns the variable label associated with *varname*, which might be "" (meaning no label) or, for example, "`Repair Record 1978`".

`data label`
    returns the dataset label associated with the dataset currently in memory, which might be "" (meaning no label) or, for example, "`1978 Automobile Data`".

`sortedby`
    returns the names of the variables by which the data in memory are currently sorted, which might be "" (meaning not sorted) or, for example, "`foreign mpg`", meaning the data are in the order the variable `foreign` and, within that, in the order of `mpg` (the order that would be obtained from the Stata command `sort foreign mpg`).

label *valuelabelname* # $[#_2]$
> returns the label value of # in *valuelabelname*. For instance, "label forlab 1" might return "Foreign cars" if forlab were the name of a value label and 1 mapped to "Foreign cars". If 1 did not correspond to any mapping within the value label, or if the value label forlab were not defined, then "1" (the # itself) would be returned.
>
> $#_2$ optionally specifies the maximum length of the of the label to be returned. If 'label forlab 1' would return "Foreign cars", then 'label forlab 1 6' would return "Foreig".

label (*varname*) # $[#_2]$
> works exactly as the above, except that rather than specifying the *valuelabelname* directly, one indirectly specifies. The value label name associated with *varname* is used, if there is one. If not, it is treated just as if *valuelabelname* were undefined; the number itself is returned.

Macro extended functions for accessing Stata system parameters

set ...
> returns the current setting set by set and shown by query.

set adosize
> returns a number recording the current value of adosize; see [P] **sysdir**.

set graphics
> returns "on" or "off", recording whether graphics, when they are drawn, are to be rendered to the screen.

set level
> returns a number recording the default value of the confidence level for confidence intervals reported by Stata; see [R] **level**.

set linesize
> returns a number recording the current width to which lines on the screen are being formatted; see [R] **log**.

set logtype
> returns "smcl" or "text", depending on the default log type to be created by log using; see [R] **log**.

set matsize
> returns a number reflecting the current value of matsize; see [R] **matsize**.

set more
> returns "on" or "off", depending on whether —more— conditions have been turned off; see [R] **more**.

set pagesize
> returns the number of lines allowed to be output between —more— conditions; see [R] **more**.

set rmsg
> returns "on" or "off", depending on whether return messages are being displayed; see [P] **rmsg**.

set textsize
> returns a number reflecting the default *textsize* to be used on graphs.

set trace
> returns "on" or "off", depending on whether programs are currently being traced; see [P] **program**.

set type
> returns the default storage type being used by Stata when a storage type is not explicitly specified; this should be "float" or "double", although the user could set it to something that is not recommended, such as "int". See [R] **generate**.

set virtual
> returns "on" or "off", depending on whether virtual memory optimization is on or off; see [R] **memory**.

Macro extended functions for filenames and file paths

sysdir [UPDATES | BASE | SITE | STBPLUS | PERSONAL | OLDPLACE]
> returns the various Stata system directory path names; see [P] **sysdir**. The name is always returned with a trailing path separator, e.g., 'sysdir STATA' might return "D:\PROGRAMS\STATA\".

sysdir *dirname*
> returns *dirname*. This function is used to code 'local x `dir´', where `dir´ might contain the name of a directory specified by a user or a keyword, such as STATA, UPDATES, etc. The appropriate directory name will be returned. The name is always returned with a trailing path separator.

pwd
> returns the name of the current (working) directory.

dirsep
> returns "\", "/", or ":", according to the appropriate directory separator character on the system ("\" for Windows, "/" for Unix, and ":" for Macintosh).

Macro extended functions for accessing operating-system parameters

environment *name*
> returns the contents of the operating system's environment variable named *name*, or "" if *name* is undefined. (Windows and Unix operating systems have the concept of environment variables; Macintosh does not.)

Macro extended functions for names of saved results

e(scalars)
> returns the names of all the saved results in e() that are scalars, with the names listed one after the other and separated by one space. For instance, e(scalar) might return "N ll_0 ll df_m chi2 r2_p", meaning scalar saved results e(N), e(ll_0), ..., exist.

e(macros)
> returns the names of all the saved results in e() that are macros.

e(matrices)
> returns the names of all the saved results in e() that are matrices.

e(functions)
> returns the names of all the saved results in e() that are functions. e(functions) might return "sample", meaning that the function e(sample) exists.

r(scalars), r(macros), r(matrices), r(functions)
> does the same for the r() that the extended macro functions e() do for the saved results in e().

```
s(macros)
```
returns the names of all the saved results in s() that are macros. (Results saved in s() can only be macros.)

Macro extended functions for formatting results

```
display ...
```
returns the results from the display command. The display extended function is the display command, except that the output is rerouted, not appearing on the screen, but placed into the contents of a macro.

You can use all the features of display that make sense, which is to say, you may not set styles with as *style* because macros do not have colors, you may not use _continue to suppress going to a new line on the real display (it is not being displayed), you may not use _newline (for the same reason), and you may not use _request to obtain input from the console (because input and output have nothing to do with macro definition). With those exceptions, everything else works. See [P] **display**.

Example:
```
local x : display %9.4 sqrt(2)
```

Macro extended functions related to matrices

In understanding the functions below, remember that the *fullname* of a matrix row or column is defined as *eqname:name*. For instance, *fullname* might be outcome:weight, and then the *eqname* is outcome and the *name* is weight. Or, the *fullname* might be gnp:L.cpi, and then the *eqname* is gnp and the *name* is L.cpi. Or, the *fullname* might be mpg, in which case the *eqname* is " " and the *name* is mpg. For more information, see [P] **matrix define**.

rowfullnames *matname*
    returns the *fullnames* of the rows of *matname*, listed one after another and separated by one space. As many *fullnames* are listed as rows of *matname*.

colfullnames *matname*
    is like rowfullnames, but returns the *fullnames* of the columns.

rownames *matname*
    returns the *names* of the rows of *matname*, listed one after another and separated by one space. As many names are listed as rows of *matname*.

colnames *matname*
    is like rownames, but returns the *names* of the columns.

roweq *matname*
    returns the *eqnames* of the columns of *matname*, listed one after another and separated by one space. As many names are listed as columns of *matname*. If the eqname of a column is blank, _ (underscore) is substituted. Thus, roweq might return "Poor Poor Poor Average Average Average" for one matrix and "_ _ _ _ _ _" for another.

coleq *matname*
    is like roweq, but returns the *eqnames* of the columns.

Macro extended functions related to time-series operators

tsnorm *string*

returns the canonical form of *string* when *string* is interpreted as a time-series operator. For instance, if *string* is 1dl, "L2D" is returned and if string is 1.1dl, L3D is returned. If *string* is nothing, "" is returned.

tsnorm *string*, varname

returns the canonical form of *string* when *string* is interpreted as a time-series operated variable. For instance, if *string* is 1dl.gnp, "L2D.gnp" is returned, and if string is 1.1dl.gnp, "L3D.gnp" is returned. If string is just a variable name, the variable name is returned.

Macro extended functions for parsing

word count *string*

returns the number of tokens in *string*. A token is a word (characters separated by spaces) or set of words enclosed in quotes. Do *not* enclose *string* in double quotes, because then **word count** will return "1".

word # of *string*

returns the #th token from *string*. Do not enclose *string* in double quotes.

piece #$_1$ #$_2$ of "*string*"

returns a piece of *string*. This macro extended function provides a smart method of breaking a string into pieces of roughly the specified length. #$_1$ specifies which piece to obtain. #$_2$ specifies the maximum length of each piece. Each piece is built trying to fill to the maximum length without breaking in the middle of a word. However, when a word is longer than #$_2$, the word will be split.

Compound double quotes may be used around *string*, and must be used when *string* itself might contain double quotes.

subinstr local *mname* "*from*" "*to*"

returns the contents of '*mname*', with the first occurrence of "*from*" changed to "*to*".

subinstr local *mname* "*from*" "*to*", all

does the same thing, but changes all occurrences of "*from*" to "*to*".

subinstr local *mname* "*from*" "*to*", word

returns the contents of '*mname*', with the first occurrence of the word "*from*" changed to "*to*". A word is defined as a space-separated token or a token at the beginning or end of the string.

subinstr local *mname* "*from*" "*to*", word all

does the same thing, but changes all occurrences of the word "*from*" to "*to*".

subinstr global *mname* ...

is the same as the above, but obtains the original string from the global macro $mname rather than the local macro '*mname*'.

subinstr ... global *mname* ..., ... count({global | local} *mname2*)

in addition what is specified, places a count of the number of substitutions in the specified global or in local macro *mname2*.

▷ Example

```
. local str "a or b or c or d"
. global newstr : subinstr local str "c" "sand"
. display "$newstr"
```

```
a or b or sand or d
. local str2 : subinstr global newstr "or" "and", all count(local n)
. display "`str2´"
a and b and sand and d
. display "`n´"
3
. local str3: subinstr local str2 "and" "x", all word
. display "`str3´"
a x b x sand x d
```

Notice that the "and" in "sand" did not get replaced by "x" since the **word** option was specified.

◁

The tempvar, tempname, and tempfile commands

The **tempvar**, **tempname**, and **tempfile** commands generate names that may be used for temporary variables, temporary scalars and matrices, and temporary files. A temporary something exists while the program or do-file is running but, once it concludes, automatically ceases to exist.

Temporary variables

You are writing a program and, in the middle of it, you need to calculate a new variable equal to $var1^2 + var2^2$ for use in the calculation. You might be tempted to write

```
( code omitted )
gen sumsq = var1^2 + var2^2
( code continues )
( code uses sumsq  in subsequent calculations )
drop sumsq
```

This would be a poor idea. First, users of your program might already have a variable called **sumsq**, and if they did, your program will break at the **generate** statement with the error "sumsq already defined". Second, your program in the subsequent code might call some other program, and perhaps that program (poorly) also attempts to create a variable **sumsq**. Third, even if nothing goes wrong, if users press *Break* after your code executes the **generate** but before the **drop**, you would confuse them by leaving behind the **sumsq** variable.

The way around these problems is to use temporary variables. Your code should read:

```
( code omitted )
tempvar sumsq
gen `sumsq´ = var1^2 + var2^2
( code continues )
( code uses `sumsq´  in subsequent calculations )
( you do not bother to drop `sumsq´ )
```

The **tempvar sumsq** command created a local macro called **sumsq** and stored in it a name that is different from any name currently in the data. Subsequently, you then use `sumsq´ with single quotes around it rather than **sumsq** in your calculation, so that rather than naming your temporary variable **sumsq**, you are naming it whatever Stata wants you to name it. With that small change, your program works just as before.

Another advantage to temporary variables is that you do not have to drop them—Stata will do that for you when your program terminates, regardless of the reason for your program terminating. So, if users press *Break* after the `generate`, your program is stopped, the temporary variables are dropped, and things really are just as if the user had never run your program.

❏ Technical Note

So what do these temporary variable names assigned by Stata look like? It should not matter to you; however they look, they are guaranteed to be unique (`tempvar` will not hand out the same name to more than one concurrently executing program). Nevertheless, to satisfy your curiosity:

```
. tempvar var1 var2
. display "`var1´ `var2´"
__000009 __00000A
```

Although we reveal the style of the names created by `tempvar`, you should not depend on this style. All that is important is that

1. The names are unique; they differ from one call to the next.

2. You should assume that they are so long that you cannot prefix or suffix them with additional characters and make use of them.

3. Stata keeps track of any names created by `tempvar` and, when the program or do-file ends, searches the data for those names. Any variables found with those names are automatically dropped. This happens regardless of whether your program ends with an error.

❏

Temporary scalars and matrices

`tempname` is the equivalent of `tempvar` for obtaining names for scalars and matrices. This use is explained, with examples, in [P] **scalar**.

❏ Technical Note

The temporary names created by `tempname` look just like those created by `tempvar`. The same cautions and features apply to `tempname` as `tempvar`:

1. The names are unique; they differ from one call to the next.

2. You should assume that they are so long that you cannot prefix or suffix them with additional characters and make use of them.

3. Stata keeps track of any names created by `tempname` and, when the program or do-file ends, searches for scalars or matrices with those names. Any scalars or matrices so found are automatically dropped; see [P] **scalar**. This happens regardless of whether your program ends with an error.

❏

Temporary files

`tempfile` is the equivalent of `tempvar` for obtaining names for disk files. Before getting into that, let us discuss how you should not use `tempfile`. Sometimes, in the midst of your program, you will find it necessary to destroy the user's data to obtain your desired result. You do not want to change the data, but it cannot be helped, and therefore you would like to arrange things so that the user's original data are restored at the conclusion of your program.

In such a case, you might be tempted to save the user's data in a (temporary) file, do your damage, and then restore the data. You can do this, but it is complicated because you then have to worry about the user pressing *Break* after you have stored the data and done the damage but have not yet restored it. Working with `capture` (see [P] **capture**), you can program all of this, but you do not have to. Stata's `preserve` command (see [P] **preserve**) will handle saving the user's data and restoring it regardless of how your program ends.

Still, there may be times when you need temporary files. For example,

```
( code omitted )
preserve                              /* preserve user's data */
keep var1 var2 xvar
save master, replace
drop var2
save part1, replace
use master, clear
drop var1
rename var2 var1
append using part1
erase master.dta
erase part1.dta
( code continues )
```

This is poor code, even though it does use `preserve` so that, regardless of how this code concludes, the user's original data will be restored. It is poor because datasets called `master.dta` and `part1.dta` might already exist and, if they do, this program will replace the user's (assumably valuable) data. It is also poor because, if the user presses *Break* before both (temporary) datasets are erased, they will be left behind to consume (assumably valuable) disk space.

Here is how the code should read:

```
( code omitted )
preserve                              /* preserve user's data */
keep var1 var2 xvar
tempfile master part1                 /* declare temporary files */
save "`master'"
drop var2
save "`part1'"
use "`master'", clear
drop var1
rename var2 var1
append using "`part1'"
( code continues, temporary files are not erased )
```

In this draft, Stata was asked to provide the names of temporary files in local macros named `master` and `part1`. We then put single quotes around `master` and `part1` wherever we referred to them so that, rather than using the names `master` and `part1`, we used the names Stata handed us. At the end of our program, we no longer bother to erase the temporary files. Since Stata gave us the temporary filenames, it knows they are temporary, and will erase them for us if our program completes, has an error, or the user presses *Break*.

❑ Technical Note

So what do the temporary filenames look like? Again, it should not matter to you, but for the curious:

```
. tempfile file1 file2
. display "`file1' `file2'"
/tmp/St13310.0001 /tmp/St13310.0002
```

We were using the Unix version of Stata; had we been using the Windows version, the last line might read:

```
. display "`file1' `file2'"
C:\WIN\TEMP\__000003.tmp C:\WIN\TEMP\__000004.tmp
```

Under Windows, Stata uses the environment variable TEMP to determine where temporary files are to be located. This variable is typically set in your autoexec.bat file. Ours is set to C:\WIN\TEMP. If the variable is not defined, Stata locates temporary files in your current directory.

Under Unix, Stata uses the environment variable TMPDIR to determine where temporary files are to be located. If the variable is not defined, Stata locates temporary files in /tmp.

Although we reveal the style of the names created by tempfile, just as with tempvar, you should not depend on it. tempfile produces names the operating system finds pleasing, and all that is important is that

1. The names are unique; they differ from one call to the next.

2. You should assume that they are so long that you cannot prefix or suffix them with additional characters and make use of them.

3. Stata keeps track of any names created by tempfile and, when your program or do-file ends, looks for files with those names. Any files found are automatically erased. This happens regardless of whether your program ends with an error.

Actually, item 3 is true only for Stata versions 3.1 and above. If you set the version to a lower number (see [P] **version**), then item 3 should read: "You, as the programmer, are responsible for removing any temporary files—they are not automatically deleted". We turn off this feature in case some old, user-written programs depend on files being left around.

❑

Manipulation of macros

macro dir and macro list list the names and contents of all defined macros; both do the same thing:

```
. macro list
_file2:    /tmp/St27844.0002
_file1:    /tmp/St27844.0001
_var2:     __00000A
_var1:     __000009
_str3:     a x b x sand x d
S_FNDATE:  7 Jul 2000 13:51
S_FN:      auto.dta
_dl:       Employee Data
_lbl:      Employee name
_vl:       sexlbl
_fmt:      %9.0g
tofname:   str18
F1:        help
```

```
F2:        #review;
F3:        describe;
F7:        save
F8:        use
S_ADO:     UPDATES;BASE;SITE;.;PERSONAL;STBPLUS;~/ado/
S_FLAVOR:  Intercooled
S_OS:      Unix
S_MACH:    Sun Solaris
S_level:   95
```

`macro drop` eliminates macros from memory, although it is rarely used since most macros are local and automatically disappear when the program ends. Macros can also be eliminated by defining their contents to be nothing using `global` or `local`, but `macro drop` is more convenient.

Typing `macro drop` *base*∗ drops all global macros whose names begin with *base*.

Typing `macro drop` _all eliminates all macros except system macros—macros that begin with "S_".

Typing `macro drop S_*` does not drop all system macros that begin with S_. It leaves certain macros in place that should not be casually deleted.

▷ Example

```
. macro drop _var* _lbl tofname _fmt

. macro list
_file2:    /tmp/St27844.0002
_file1:    /tmp/St27844.0001
_str3:     a x b x sand x d
S_FNDATE:   7 Jul 2000 13:51
S_FN:      auto.dta
_dl:       Employee Data
_vl:       sexlbl
F1:        help
F2:        #review;
F3:        describe;
F7:        save
F8:        use
S_ADO:     UPDATES;BASE;SITE;.;PERSONAL;STBPLUS;~/ado/
S_FLAVOR:  Intercooled
S_OS:      Unix
S_MACH:    Sun Solaris
S_level:   95

. macro drop _all

. macro list
S_FNDATE:   7 Jul 2000 13:51
S_FN:      auto.dta
S_ADO:     UPDATES;BASE;SITE;.;PERSONAL;STBPLUS;~/ado/
S_FLAVOR:  Intercooled
S_OS:      Unix
S_MACH:    Sun Solaris
S_level:   95

. macro drop S_*

. macro list
S_ADO:     UPDATES;BASE;SITE;.;PERSONAL;STBPLUS;~/ado/
S_FLAVOR:  Intercooled
S_OS:      Unix
S_MACH:    Sun Solaris
S_level:   95
```

◁

❑ Technical Note

Stata usually requires that you explicitly drop something before redefining it. For instance, before redefining a value label with the `label define` command or redefining a program with the `program define` command, you must type `label drop` or `program drop`. This way you are protected from accidentally replacing something that might require considerable effort to reproduce.

Macros, however, may be redefined freely. It is *not* necessary to `drop` a macro before redefining it. Macros typically consist of short strings that could be easily reproduced if necessary. The inconvenience of the protection is not justified by the small benefit.

❑

Macros as arguments: macro shift

Sometimes programs have in a macro a list of things—numbers, variable names, etc.—that you wish to access one at a time. For instance, after parsing (see [U] **21.4 Program arguments**), you might have in the local macro `` `varlist' `` a list of variable names. The `tokenize` command (see [P] **tokenize**) will take any macro containing a list and assign the elements to local macros named `` `1' ``, `` `2' ``, and so on. That is, if `` `varlist' `` contained "mpg weight displ", then coding

```
tokenize `varlist'
```

will make `` `1' `` contain "mpg", `` `2' `` contain "weight", `` `3' `` contain "displ", and `` `4' `` contain "" (nothing). The empty fourth macro marks the end of the list.

`macro shift` is often used to work through these elements one at a time in constructs like

```
while "`1'" ~= "" {
        do something based on `1'
        macro shift
}
```

`macro shift` discards `` `1' ``, shifts `` `2' `` to `` `1' ``, `` `3' `` to `` `2' ``, and so on. For instance, in our example, after the first `macro shift`, `` `1' `` will contain "weight", `` `2' `` will contain "displ", and `` `3' `` will contain "" (nothing).

Some programmers prefer to avoid `macro shift` and instead code

```
local i = 1
while "``i''" ~= "" {
        do something based on ``i''
        local i = `i' + 1
}
```

Either form is equally acceptable; the second has the advantage that what is in `` `1' ``, `` `2' ``, ..., remains unchanged so that one can pass through the list multiple times without resetting it (coding "`tokenize` `` `varlist' ``" again).

Even simpler is avoiding `tokenize` and the numbered macros and instead looping over the variables in `` `varlist' `` directly:

```
foreach var of local varlist {
        do something based on `var'
}
```

This is easier to understand and executes faster; see [P] **foreach**.

`macro shift` *#* performs multiple macro shifts or, if *#* is 0, none at all. That is, `macro shift 2` is equivalent to two `macro shift` commands. `macro shift 0` does nothing.

Also See

Complementary:	[P] **char**, [P] **gettoken**, [P] **numlist**, [P] **return**, [P] **syntax**, [P] **tokenize**
Related:	[P] **matrix define**, [P] **preserve**, [P] **scalar**
Background:	[U] **15.8 Characteristics**,
	[U] **21 Programming Stata**,
	[U] **21.3 Macros**,
	[P] **macro system**

Title

macro system — Quick reference for system macros

Description

This entry provides a quick reference for system macros. See [U] **21.3.10 Built-in global system macros** for details on the system macros.

Remarks

See [U] **21.3 Macros** for an introduction to macros.
See [P] **macro** for advanced issues not covered in [U] **21.3 Macros**.

Macros that begin with the characters S_ are called *system macros* and some are predefined for you:

System macro	Definition
S_ADO	path over which Stata looks for its ado-files
S_DATE	11-character string expressing the current date
S_FLAVOR	"Small" or "Intercooled"
S_FN	filename last specified with a use or save
S_FNDATE	date and time the file in S_FN was last saved
S_level	significance level for confidence intervals
S_MACH	type of computer
S_MODE	(Unix only) indicates if in batch mode
S_OS	name of operating system
S_OSDTL	level of operating system, if significant
S_TIME	8-character string expressing current time

Also See

Related: [P] **macro**, [P] **return**

Background: [U] **21.3 Macros**

Title

> **mark** — Mark observations for inclusion

Syntax

> **marksample** *lmacname* $\left[, \underline{\text{nova}}\text{rlist} \ \underline{\text{s}}\text{trok} \ \underline{\text{zero}}\text{weight noby} \right]$
>
> **mark** *newmarkvar* $\left[weight \right]$ $\left[\text{if } exp \right]$ $\left[\text{in } range \right]$ $\left[, \underline{\text{zero}}\text{weight noby} \right]$
>
> **markout** *markvar* $\left[varlist \right]$ $\left[, \underline{\text{s}}\text{trok} \right]$

aweights, fweights, pweights, and iweights are allowed; see [U] **14.1.6 weight**.

varlist may contain time-series operators; see [U] **14.4.3 Time-series varlists**.

Description

marksample, **mark**, and **markout** are for use in Stata programs. They create a 0/1 variable recording which observations are to be used in subsequent code. The idea is to determine the relevant sample early in code:

```
program define ...
        (parse the arguments)
        (determine which observations are to be used)
        rest of code ... if  to be used
end
```

marksample, **mark**, and **markout** assist in this.

```
program define ...
        (parse the arguments)
        (use mark* to create temporary variable `touse´ containing 0 or 1)
        rest of code ... if `touse´
end
```

marksample is for use in programs where the arguments are parsed using the **syntax** command; see [P] **syntax**. **marksample** creates a temporary **byte** variable, stores the name of the temporary variable in *lmacname*, and fills in the temporary variable with 0s and 1s according to whether the observation should be used. This determination is made by accessing information stored by **syntax** concerning the *varlist*, **if** *exp*, etc., allowed by the program. It typical use is

```
program define ...
        syntax ...
        marksample touse
        rest of code ... if `touse´
end
```

mark starts with an already created temporary variable name. It fills in *newmarkvar* with 0s and 1s according to whether the observation should be used according to the *weight*, **if** *exp*, and **in** *range* specified. **markout** modifies the variable created by **mark** by resetting it to contain 0 in observations that have missing value recorded for any of the variables in *varlist*. These commands are typically used as

```
program define ...
        (parse the arguments)
        tempvar touse
        mark `touse' ...
        markout `touse' ...
        rest of code ... if `touse'
end
```

`marksample` is better than `mark` because there is less chance of your forgetting to include some part of the sample restriction. `markout` can be used after `mark` or `marksample` when there are variables other than the varlist, and when observations that contain missing values of those variables are also to be excluded. For instance, the following code is common:

```
program define ...
        syntax ... [, Denom(varname) ... ]
        marksample touse
        markout `touse' `denom'
        rest of code ... if `touse'
end
```

Regardless of whether you use `mark` or `marksample`, followed or not by `markout`, the following rules apply:

1. The marker variable is set to 0 in observations for which *weight* is 0 (but see option `zeroweight`).

2. The appropriate error message is issued and all stops if *weight* is invalid (such as being less than 0 in some observation, or being a noninteger in the case of frequency weights, etc.).

3. The marker variable is set to 0 in observations for which the `if` *exp* is not satisfied.

4. The marker variable is set to 0 in observations outside of the `in` *range*.

5. The marker variable is set to 0 in observations for which any of the numeric variables in *varlist* contain numeric missing value.

6. The marker variable is set to 0 in *all* observations if any of the variables in *varlist* are strings; see option `strok` below for an exception.

7. The marker variable is set to 1 in the remaining observations.

Options

`novarlist` is for use with `marksample`. It specifies that missing values among variables in *varlist* are not to cause the marker variable to be set to 0. Specify `novarlist` if you previously specified

```
syntax newvarlist ...
```

or

```
syntax newvarname ...
```

In addition, specify `novarlist` in instances where missing values are not to cause observations to be excluded (perhaps you are analyzing the pattern of missing values).

`strok` is used with `marksample` or `markout`. Specify this option if string variables in *varlist* are to be allowed. `strok` changes Rule 6 above to read

"The marker variable is set to 0 in observations for which any of the string variables in *varlist* contain ""."

`zeroweight` is for use with `marksample` or `mark`. It deletes Rules 1 above, meaning that observations will not be excluded because the weight is zero.

`noby` is used rarely and only in `byable(recall)` programs. It specifies that, in identifying the sample, the restriction to the `by` group is to be ignored. `mark` and `marksample` are to create the marker variable as they would had the user not specified the `by... :` prefix. If the user did not specify the `by` prefix, specifying `noby` has no effect. `noby` provides a way for `byable(recall)` programs to identify the overall sample. For instance, if the program needed to calculate the percentage of observations in the `by` group, the program would need to know both the sample to be used on this call and the overall sample. The program might be coded as

```
program define ..., byable(recall)
        ...
        marksample touse
        marksample alluse, noby
        ...
        quietly count if `touse´
        local curN = r(N)
        quietly count if `alluse´
        local totN = r(N)
        local frac = `curN´/`totN´
        ...
end
```

See [P] **byable**.

Remarks

By far the most common programming error—made by us at StataCorp and others—is to use different samples at different parts of a Stata program. We strongly recommend that programmers identify the sample at the outset. This is easy with `marksample` (or alternatively, `mark` and `markout`). Consider a Stata program that begins

```
program define myprog
        version 7.0
        syntax varlist [if] [in]
        ...
end
```

Pretend this program makes a statistical calculation based on the observations specified in *varlist* that do not contain missing values (such as a linear regression). The program must identify the observations that it will use. Moreover, since the user can specify if *exp* or in *range*, these restrictions must also be taken into account. `marksample` makes this easy:

```
        version 7.0
        syntax varlist [if] [in]
        marksample touse
        ...
end
```

To produce the same result, we could create the temporary variable `touse` and then use `mark` and `markout` as follows:

```
program define myprog
        version 7.0
        syntax varlist [if] [in]
        tempvar touse
        mark `touse´ `if´ `in´
        markout `touse´ `varlist´
        ...
end
```

The result will be the same.

The `mark` command creates temporary variable `` `touse´ `` (temporary because of the preceding `tempvar`; see [P] **macro**) based on the `if` *exp* and `in` *range*. If there is no `if` *exp* or `in` *range*, `` `touse´ `` will contain 1 for every observation in the data. If `if price>1000` was specified by the user, only observations for which `price` is greater than 1,000 will have `touse` set to 1; the remaining will have `touse` set to zero.

The `markout` command updates the `` `touse´ `` marker created by `mark`. For observations for which `` `touse´ `` is 1—observations that might potentially be used—the variables in *varlist* are checked for missing values. If such an observation has any of the variables equal to missing, the observation's `` `touse´ `` value is reset to 0.

Thus, observations to be used all have `` `touse´ `` set to 1. Including `if` `` `touse´ `` at the end of statistical or data-management commands will restrict the command to operate on the appropriate sample.

▷ Example

Let's write a program to do the same thing as `summarize`, except that our program will also engage in casewise deletion—if an observation has a missing value in any of the variables, it is to be excluded from all the calculations.

```
program define cwsumm
        version 7.0
        syntax [varlist(ts)] [if] [in] [aweight fweight] [, Detail noFormat]
        marksample touse
        summarize `varlist' [`weight'`exp'] if `touse', `detail' `format'
end
```

◁

Also See

Complementary: [P] **byable**, [P] **syntax**

Background: [U] **21 Programming Stata**

Title

> **matrix** — Introduction to matrix commands

Description

An introduction to matrices in Stata is found in [U] **17 Matrix expressions**. This entry provides an overview of the `matrix` commands and provides additional background information on matrices in Stata.

Remarks

An overview of the `matrix` commands is presented below. This is followed by information on matrices not covered elsewhere.

Overview of matrix commands

Documentation on matrices in Stata are grouped below into three categories—Basics, Programming, and Specialized. We recommend that you begin with [U] **17 Matrix expressions** and then read [P] **matrix define**. After that, feel free to skip around.

Basics

[U] **17 Matrix expressions**	Introduction to matrices in Stata
[P] **matrix define**	Matrix definition, operators, and functions
[P] **matrix utility**	Listing, renaming, and dropping matrices

Programming

[P] **matrix accum**	Forming cross-product matrices
[R] **ml**	Maximum likelihood estimation
[P] **estimates**	Posting and redisplaying estimation results
[P] **matrix rowname**	Naming rows and columns
[P] **matrix score**	Scoring data from coefficient vectors

Specialized

[P] **matrix constraint**	Constrained estimation
[P] **matrix mkmat**	Convert variables to matrix and vice versa
[P] **matrix svd**	Singular value decomposition
[P] **matrix symeigen**	Eigenvalues and vectors of symmetric matrices
[P] **matrix get**	Accessing system matrices

Creating and replacing matrices

In general, matrices do not have to be preallocated or dimensioned prior to creation, but the exception is when you want to create an $r \times c$ matrix and then fill in each element one-by-one; see the description of the J() function in [P] **matrix define**. Matrices are typically created by `matrix define` or `matrix accum`; see [P] **matrix accum**.

Stata takes a high-handed approach to redefining matrices. You know that, when dealing with data, you must distinguish between creating a new variable or replacing the contents of an existing variable—Stata has two commands for this: `generate` and `replace`. For matrices, there is no such distinction. If you define a new matrix, it is created. If you give the same command and the matrix already exists, the currently existing matrix is destroyed and then the new one is defined. This treatment is the same as that given to macros and scalars.

Name space

The term "name space" refers to how names are interpreted. For instance, the variables in your dataset occupy one name space—other things, such as value labels, macros, and scalars, can have the same name and there is no confusion.

Macros also have their own name space; macros can have the same names as other things and Stata can still tell by context when you are referring to a macro because of the punctuation. When you type `gen newvar=myname`, `myname` must refer to a variable. When you type `gen newvar=`myname`—note the single quotes around `myname`—`myname` must refer to a local macro. When you type `gen newvar=$myname`, `myname` must refer to a global macro.

Scalars and matrices share the same name space, which is to say, scalars and matrices may have the same names as variables in the dataset, etc., but they cannot have the same names as each other. Thus, when you define a matrix called, say, `myres`, if a scalar by that name already exists, it is destroyed and the matrix replaces it. Correspondingly, if you define a scalar called `myres`, if a matrix by that name exists, it is destroyed and the scalar replaces it.

Naming conventions in programs

If you are writing Stata programs or ado-files using matrices, you may have some matrices you wish to leave behind for other programs to build upon, but you will certainly have other matrices which are nothing more than leftovers from calculations. Such matrices are called *temporary*. You should use Stata's `tempname` facility (see [P] **macro**) to name such matrices. These matrices will be automatically discarded when your program ends. For example, a piece of your program might read

```
tempname YXX XX
matrix accum `YXX' = price weight mpg
matrix `XX' = `YXX'[2...,2...]
```

Note the single quotes around the names after they are obtained from `tempname`; see [U] **21.3 Macros**.

❏ Technical Note

Let us consider writing a regression program in Stata. (There is actually no need for such a program since Stata already has the `regress` command.) A well-written estimation command would allow the `level()` option for specifying the width of confidence intervals and it would replay results when the command is typed without arguments. Here is a well-written version:

```
program define myreg, eclass
        version 7.0
        if ~replay() {
                syntax varlist(min=2 numeric) [if] [in] [, Level(integer $S_level)]

                marksample touse        /* mark the sample */

                tokenize "`varlist'"   /* put varlist into numbered arguments */

                tempname YXX XX Xy b hat V

                /* compute cross products YXX = (Y'Y , Y'X \ X'Y , X'X) */
                quietly matrix accum `YXX' = `varlist' if `touse'
                local nobs = r(N)
                local df = `nobs' - (rowsof(`YXX') - 1)
                matrix `XX' = `YXX'[2...,2...]
                matrix `Xy' = `YXX'[1,2...]

                /* compute the beta vector */
                matrix `b' = `Xy' * syminv(`XX')

                /* compute the covariance matrix */
                matrix `hat' = `b' * `Xy''
                matrix `V' = syminv(`XX') * (`YXX'[1,1] - `hat'[1,1])/`df'

                /* post the beta vector and covariance matrix */
                estimates post `b' `V', dof(`df') obs(`nobs') depname(`1') /*
                                        */ esample(`touse')

                /* save estimation information */
                est local depvar "`1'"
                est local cmd "myreg"
        }
        else {  /* replay */
                syntax [, Level(integer $S_level)]
        }

        if "`e(cmd)'"~="myreg" { error 301 }

        if `level' < 10 | `level' > 99 {
                di as err "level() must be between 10 and 99 inclusive"
                exit 198
        }

        /* print the regression table */
        estimates display, level(`level')
end
```

The syntax of our new command is

$$\texttt{myreg } \textit{depvar indepvars } \left[\texttt{if } \textit{exp}\right] \left[\texttt{in } \textit{range}\right] \left[\texttt{, level}(\#) \right]$$

myreg, typed without arguments, redisplays the output of the last myreg command. After estimation with myreg, the user may use correlate to display the covariance matrix of the estimators, predict to obtain predicted values or standard errors of the prediction, and test to test linear hypotheses about the estimated coefficients. The command is indistinguishable from any other Stata estimation command.

Despite the excellence of our work, we do have some criticisms:

1. myreg does not display the ANOVA table, R^2, etc.; it should and could be made to, although we would have to insert our own display statements before the estimates display instruction.

2. The program makes copious use of matrices with different names, resulting in extra memory use while the estimation is being made; the code could be made more economical, if less readable, by reusing matrices.

3. `myreg` makes the least-squares calculation using the absolute cross-product matrix, an invitation to numerical problems if the data are not consistently scaled. Stata's own `regress` command is more careful and we could be, too: `matrix accum` does have an option for forming the cross-product matrix in deviation form, but its use would complicate this program. This does not overly concern us, although we should make a note of it when we document `myreg`. Nowadays, users expect to be protected in linear regression, but have no such expectations for more complicated estimation schemes because avoiding the problem can be difficult to nearly impossible.

There is one nice feature of our program that did not occur to us when we wrote it. We use `syminv()` to form the inverse of the cross-product matrix and `syminv()` can handle singular matrices. If there is a collinearity problem, `myreg` behaves just like `regress`: it drops the offending variables and notes that they are dropped when it displays the output (at the `estimates display` step).

❏

❏ Technical Note

Our linear regression program is quite a bit longer than one might have written in an exclusively matrix programming language. After all, the coefficients can be obtained from $(\mathbf{X}'\mathbf{X})^{-1}\mathbf{X}'\mathbf{y}$ and in a dedicated matrix language, one would type nearly that, and obtaining the standard errors would require only a couple more matrix calculations. In fact, we did type nearly that to make the calculation; the extra lines in our program mostly have to do with syntax issues and linking to the rest of Stata. In writing your own programs, you might be tempted not to bother linking to the rest of Stata. Fight this temptation.

Linking to the rest of Stata pays off: in this case, we do not merely display the numerical results, we display them in a readable form, complete with variable names. We made a command that is indistinguishable from Stata's other estimation commands. If the user wants to test `_b[denver]=_b[la]`, the user types literally that; there is no need to remember the matrix equation and to count variables (such as constrain the third minus the fifteenth variable to sum to zero).

❏

Also See

Related: [P] **estimates**, [P] **matrix define**,
[R] **ml**

Background: [U] **17 Matrix expressions**,
[U] **21 Programming Stata**

Title

> **matrix accum** — Form cross-product matrices

Syntax

> matrix <u>ac</u>cum **A** = *varlist* $\left[weight\right]$ $\left[\text{if } exp\right]$ $\left[\text{in } range\right]$ $\left[,\, \underline{\text{no}}\text{constant}\right.$
>
> <u>dev</u>iations <u>means</u>(m) $\left.\vphantom{]}\right]$

> matrix <u>gls</u>accum **A** = *varlist* $\left[weight\right]$ $\left[\text{if } exp\right]$ $\left[\text{in } range\right]$, <u>group</u>(*groupvar*)
>
> <u>gls</u>mat($\left\{\mathbf{W}\,|\,stringvarname\right\}$) <u>row</u>(*rowvar*) $\left[\underline{\text{no}}\text{constant}\right]$

> matrix <u>vec</u>accum **a** = *varlist* $\left[weight\right]$ $\left[\text{if } exp\right]$ $\left[\text{in } range\right]$ $\left[,\, \underline{\text{no}}\text{constant}\right]$

aweights, fweights, iweights, and pweights are allowed; see [U] **14.1.6 weight**.

varlist may contain time-series operators; see [U] **14.4.3 Time-series varlists**.

Description

matrix accum accumulates cross-product matrices from the data to form $\mathbf{A} = \mathbf{X}'\mathbf{X}$.

matrix glsaccum accumulates cross-product matrices from the data using a specified inner weight matrix to form $\mathbf{A} = \mathbf{X}'\mathbf{B}\mathbf{X}$ where $\mathbf{B}$ is a block diagonal matrix.

matrix vecaccum accumulates the first variable against remaining variables in *varlist* to form a row vector of accumulated inner products to form $\mathbf{a} = \mathbf{x}_1'\mathbf{X}$ where $\mathbf{X} = (\mathbf{x}_2, \mathbf{x}_3, \ldots)$.

Options

noconstant suppresses the addition of a "constant" to the $\mathbf{X}$ matrix. If noconstant is not specified, it is as if a column of 1s is added to $\mathbf{X}$ before the accumulation begins. For instance, in the case of accum without noconstant, $\mathbf{X}'\mathbf{X}$ is really $(\mathbf{X}, \mathbf{1})'(\mathbf{X}, \mathbf{1})$, resulting in

$$\begin{pmatrix} \mathbf{X}'\mathbf{X} & \mathbf{X}'\mathbf{1} \\ \mathbf{1}'\mathbf{X} & \mathbf{1}'\mathbf{1} \end{pmatrix}$$

Thus, the last row and column contain the sums of the columns of $\mathbf{X}$ and the element in the last row and column contains the number of observations. If p variables are specified in the *varlist*, the resulting matrix is $(p+1) \times (p+1)$. Specifying noconstant suppresses the addition of this row and column (or just column in the case of vecaccum).

deviations, allowed only with matrix accum, causes the accumulation to be performed in terms of deviations from the mean. If noconstant is not specified, the accumulation of $\mathbf{X}$ is done in terms of deviations, but the added row and column of sums are *not* in deviation format (in which case they would be zeros). With noconstant specified, the resulting matrix divided through by $N - 1$, where N is the number of observations, is a covariance matrix.

means(**m**), allowed only with accum, creates matrix **m**: $1 \times (p+1)$ or $1 \times p$ (depending on whether noconstant is also specified) containing the means of **X**.

group(*groupvar*), required with glsaccum and not allowed otherwise, specifies the name of a variable that identifies the groups of observations to be individually weighted by glsmat(). The data must be sorted by *groupvar*.

glsmat({**W** | *stringvarname*}), required with glsaccum and not allowed otherwise, specifies the name of the matrix or the name of a string variable in the dataset that contains the name of the matrix which is to be used to weight the observations in the group(). *stringvarname* must be str8 or less.

row(*rowvar*), required with glsaccum and not allowed otherwise, specifies the name of a numeric variable containing the row numbers that specify the row and column of the glsmat() matrix to use in the inner-product calculation.

Remarks

accum

matrix accum is a straightforward command that accumulates a single matrix that holds $\mathbf{X'X}$ and $\mathbf{X'y}$, which is typically used in $\mathbf{b} = (\mathbf{X'X})^{-1}\mathbf{X'y}$. Say we wish to run a regression of the variable price on mpg and weight. We can begin by accumulating the full cross-product matrix for all three variables:

```
. matrix accum A = price weight mpg
(obs=74)

. matrix list A

symmetric A[4,4]
              price        weight          mpg         _cons
 price    3.448e+09
weight    1.468e+09     7.188e+08
   mpg      9132716       4493720        36008
 _cons       456229        223440         1576            74
```

In our accumulation, accum automatically added a constant; we specified three variables and got back a 4×4 matrix. The constant term is always added last. In terms of our regression model, the matrix we just accumulated has $\mathbf{y} = $ price and $\mathbf{X} = $ (weight, mpg, _cons), and can be written

$$\mathbf{A} = (\mathbf{y}, \mathbf{X})'(\mathbf{y}, \mathbf{X}) = \begin{pmatrix} \mathbf{y'y} & \mathbf{y'X} \\ \mathbf{X'y} & \mathbf{X'X} \end{pmatrix}$$

Thus, we can extract $\mathbf{X'X}$ from the submatrix of $\mathbf{A}$ beginning at the second row and column and we can extract $\mathbf{X'y}$ from the first column of $\mathbf{A}$, omitting the first row:

```
. matrix XX = A[2...,2...]
. matrix list XX

symmetric XX[3,3]
              weight          mpg         _cons
weight    7.188e+08
   mpg      4493720        36008
 _cons       223440         1576            74
```

```
. matrix Xy = A[2...,1]
. matrix list Xy
Xy[3,1]
             price
weight   1.468e+09
   mpg     9132716
 _cons      456229
```

We can now calculate $\mathbf{b} = (\mathbf{X}'\mathbf{X})^{-1}\mathbf{X}'\mathbf{y}$:

```
. matrix b = syminv(XX)*Xy
. matrix list b
b[3,1]
             price
weight   1.7465592
   mpg  -49.512221
 _cons   1946.0687
```

The same result could have been obtained directly from $\mathbf{A}$:

```
. matrix b = syminv(A[2...,2...])*A[2...,1]
```

❑ Technical Note

matrix accum, with the deviations and noconstant options, can also be used to obtain covariance matrices. The covariance between variables x_i and x_j is defined as

$$C_{ij} = \frac{\sum_{k=1}^{n}(x_{ik} - \overline{x}_i)(x_{jk} - \overline{x}_j)}{n-1}$$

Without the deviations option, matrix accum calculates a matrix with elements

$$R_{ij} = \sum_{k=1}^{n} x_{ik}x_{jk}$$

and with the deviations option,

$$A_{ij} = \sum_{k=1}^{n}(x_{ik} - \overline{x}_i)(x_{jk} - \overline{x}_j)$$

Thus, the covariance matrix $\mathbf{C} = \mathbf{A}/(n-1)$.

```
. matrix accum Cov = price weight mpg, deviations noconstant
(obs=74)
. matrix Cov = Cov/(r(N)-1)
. matrix list Cov
symmetric Cov[3,3]
              price       weight          mpg
 price      8699526
weight    1234674.8    604029.84
   mpg   -7996.2829   -3629.4261    33.472047
```

In addition to calculating the cross-product matrix, matrix accum records the number of observations in r(N), a feature we use in calculating the normalizing factor. With the corr() matrix function defined in [P] **matrix define**, we can convert the covariance matrix into a correlation matrix:

```
. matrix P = corr(Cov)
. matrix list P
symmetric P[3,3]
              price       weight         mpg
  price           1
 weight    .53861146            1
    mpg  -.46859669   -.80717486           1
```

◁

glsaccum

`matrix glsaccum` is a generalization of `matrix accum` useful in producing GLS-style weighted accumulations. Whereas `matrix accum` produces matrices of the form $\mathbf{X}'\mathbf{X}$, `glsaccum` produces matrices of the form $\mathbf{X}'\mathbf{B}\mathbf{X}$, where

$$B = \begin{pmatrix} \mathbf{W}_1 & 0 & \cdots & 0 \\ 0 & \mathbf{W}_2 & \cdots & 0 \\ \vdots & \vdots & \ddots & \vdots \\ 0 & 0 & \cdots & \mathbf{W}_K \end{pmatrix}$$

The matrices $\mathbf{W}_k$, $k = 1, \ldots, K$, are called the weighting matrices for observation group k. In the above, each of the $\mathbf{W}_k$ matrices is square but there is no assumption that they are all the same dimension. Note that by writing

$$\mathbf{X} = \begin{pmatrix} \mathbf{X}_1 \\ \mathbf{X}_2 \\ \vdots \\ \mathbf{X}_K \end{pmatrix}$$

the accumulation made by `glsaccum` can be written as

$$\mathbf{X}'\mathbf{B}\mathbf{X} = \mathbf{X}_1'\mathbf{W}_1\mathbf{X}_1 + \mathbf{X}_2'\mathbf{W}_2\mathbf{X}_2 + \cdots + \mathbf{X}_K'\mathbf{W}_K\mathbf{X}_K$$

`glsaccum` requires you to specify three options: `group(`*groupvar*`)`, `glsmat(`*matname*`)` or `glsmat(`*matvar*`)`, and `row(`*rowvar*`)`. Observations sharing the same value of *groupvar* are said to be in the same observation group—this specifies the group k in which they are to be accumulated. How $\mathbf{W}_k$ is assembled is the subject of the other two options.

Think of there being a super weighting matrix for the group, which we will call $\mathbf{V}_k$. $\mathbf{V}_k$ is specified by `glsmat()`—the same super matrix can be used for all observations by specifying a *matname* as the argument to `glsmat` or, if a variable name is specified, different super matrices can be specified—the contents of the variable will be used to obtain the particular name of the super matrix. (More correctly, the contents of the variable for the first observation in the group will be used: super matrices can vary across groups, but must be the same within group.)

Weighting matrix $\mathbf{W}_k$ is made from the super matrix $\mathbf{V}_k$ by selecting the rows and columns specified in `row(`*rowvar*`)`. In the simple case, $\mathbf{W}_k = \mathbf{V}_k$. This happens when there are m observations in the group and the first observation in the group has *rowvar* $= 1$, the second *rowvar* $= 2$, and so on. To fix ideas, let $m = 3$ and write

$$\mathbf{V}_1 = \begin{pmatrix} v_{11} & v_{12} & v_{13} \\ v_{21} & v_{22} & v_{23} \\ v_{31} & v_{32} & v_{33} \end{pmatrix}$$

$\mathbf{V}$ need not be symmetric. Let's pretend the first four observations in our dataset contain

obs. no.	*groupvar*	*rowvar*
1	1	1
2	1	2
3	1	3
4	2	...

In these data, the first three observations are in the first group because they share an equal *groupvar*. It is not important that *groupvar* happens to equal 1; it is important that the values are equal. The *rowvars* are, in order, 1, 2, and 3, so $\mathbf{W}_1$ is formed by selecting the first row and column of $\mathbf{V}_1$, then the second row and column of $\mathbf{V}_1$, and finally the third row and column of $\mathbf{V}_1$; to wit,

$$\mathbf{W}_1 = \begin{pmatrix} v_{11} & v_{12} & v_{13} \\ v_{21} & v_{22} & v_{23} \\ v_{31} & v_{32} & v_{33} \end{pmatrix}$$

or $\mathbf{W}_1 = \mathbf{V}_1$. Now, consider the same data, but reordered:

obs. no.	*groupvar*	*rowvar*
1	1	2
2	1	1
3	1	3
4	2	...

$\mathbf{W}_1$ is now formed by selecting the second row and column, then the first row and column, and finally the third row and column of $\mathbf{V}_1$. These steps can be performed sequentially, reordering first the rows and then the columns; the result is

$$\mathbf{W}_1 = \begin{pmatrix} v_{22} & v_{21} & v_{23} \\ v_{12} & v_{11} & v_{13} \\ v_{32} & v_{31} & v_{33} \end{pmatrix}$$

This reorganization of the $\mathbf{W}_1$ matrix exactly undoes the reorganization of the $\mathbf{X}_1$ matrix, so $\mathbf{X}_1'\mathbf{W}_1\mathbf{X}_1$ remains unchanged. Given how $\mathbf{W}_k$ is assembled from $\mathbf{V}_k$, the order of the row numbers in the data does not matter.

`glsaccum` is willing to carry this concept even further. Consider the following data:

obs. no.	*groupvar*	*rowvar*
1	1	1
2	1	3
3	1	3
4	2	...

Note that now *rowvar* equals 1 followed by 3 twice, so the first row and column of $\mathbf{V}_1$ are selected, followed by the third row and column twice; the second column is never selected. The resulting weighting matrix is

$$\mathbf{W}_1 = \begin{pmatrix} v_{11} & v_{13} & v_{13} \\ v_{31} & v_{33} & v_{33} \\ v_{31} & v_{33} & v_{33} \end{pmatrix}$$

Such odd weighting would not occur in, say, time-series analysis where the matrix might be weighting lags and leads. It could very well occur in an analysis of individuals in families, where 1 might indicate head of household, 2 a spouse, and 3 a child. In fact, such a case could be handled with a 3×3 super weighting matrix V even if the family became quite large: the appropriate weighting matrix $\mathbf{W}_k$ would be assembled, on a group-by-group (family-by-family) basis, from the underlying super matrix.

vecaccum

The first variable in the *varlist* is treated differently from the others by vecaccum. Think of the first variable as specifying a vector $\mathbf{y}$ and the remaining variables as specifying matrix $\mathbf{X}$. vecaccum makes the accumulation $\mathbf{y}'\mathbf{X}$ to return a row vector with elements

$$a_i = \sum_{k=1}^{n} y_k x_{ki}$$

Like accum, vecaccum adds a constant _cons to $\mathbf{X}$ unless noconstant is specified.

vecaccum serves two purposes. First, terms like $\mathbf{y}'\mathbf{X}$ often occur in calculating derivatives of likelihood functions; vecaccum provides a fast way of calculating them. Second, it is useful in time-series accumulations of the form

$$\mathbf{C} = \sum_{t=1}^{T} \sum_{\delta=-k}^{k} \mathbf{x}'_{t-\delta} \mathbf{x}_t W_\delta r_{t-\delta} r_t$$

In this calculation, $\mathbf{X}$ is an observation matrix with elements x_{tj}, with t indexing time (observations) and j variables $t = 1, \ldots, T$ and $j = 1, \ldots, p$. $\mathbf{x}_t$ ($1 \times p$) refers to the tth row of this matrix. Thus, $\mathbf{C}$ is a $p \times p$ matrix.

The Newey–West covariance matrix uses the definition $W_\delta = 1 - |\delta|/(k + 1)$ for $\delta \le k$. To make the calculation, the user (programmer) cycles through each of the j variables, forming

$$z_{tj} = \sum_{\delta=-k}^{k} x_{(t-\delta)j} W_\delta r_{t-\delta} r_t$$

Writing $\mathbf{z}_j = (z_{1j}, z_{2j}, \ldots, z_{Tj})'$, $\mathbf{C}$ is then

$$\mathbf{C} = \sum_{j=1}^{p} \mathbf{z}'_j \mathbf{X}$$

In this derivation, the user must decide in advance the maximum lag length k such that observations that are far apart in time must have increasingly small covariances in order to establish the convergence results.

The Newey–West estimator is in the class of generalized methods of moments (GMM) estimators. The choice of a maximum lag length k is a reflection of the length in time beyond which the autocorrelation becomes negligible for the purposes of estimating the variance matrix. The code fragment given below is merely for illustration of the matrix commands as Stata includes estimation with the Newey–West covariance matrix in the newey command. See [R] **newey** or Greene (2000, 464–465) for details on this estimator.

Note that it is calculations like $\mathbf{z}'_j \mathbf{X}$ that are made by vecaccum. Also note that $\mathbf{z}_j$ can be treated as a temporary variable in the dataset.

```
assume `1´,`2´, etc. contain the x's including constant
assume `r´ contains the r variable
assume `k´ contains the k range
tempname C factor t c
tempvar z
```

```
local p : word count `*´
matrix `C´ = J(`p´,`p´,0)
gen double `z´ = 0
forvalues d = 0/`k´ {
        if `d´ > 0 { scalar `factor´ = 1 } /* Add each submatrix twice  */
        else scalar `factor´ = 0.5         /* except for the lag=0 case */

        local w = (1 - `d´/(`k´+1))
        capture mat drop `t´
        forvalues j = 1/`p´ {
                replace `z´ = ``j´´[_n-`d´]*`w´*`r´[_n-`d´]*`r´
                mat vecaccum `c´ = `z´ `*´, nocons
                mat `t´ = `t´ \ `c´
        }
        mat `C´ = `C´ + (`t´ + `t´´)*`factor´
}
local `p´ = "_cons"                     /* Rename last var to _cons */
mat rownames `C´ = `*´
mat colnames `C´ = `*´
```
assume inverse and scaling for standard error reports

Treatment of user-specified weights

accum, glsaccum, and vecaccum all allow weights. Here is how they are treated:

All three commands can be thought of as returning something of the form $X_1' B X_2$. In the case of accum, $X_1 = X_2$ and $B = I$; in the case of glsaccum, $X_1 = X_2$; and in the case of vecaccum, $B = I$, X_1 is a column vector and X_2 is a matrix.

In point of fact, the commands really calculate $X_1' W^{1/2} B W^{1/2} X_2$, where W is a diagonal matrix. If no weights are specified, $W = I$. Now assume weights are specified and let $v: 1 \times n$ be the specified weights. If fweights or pweights are specified, then $W = \text{diag}(v)$. If aweights are specified, then $W = \text{diag}\{v/(1'v)(1'1)\}$, which is to say, the weights are normalized to sum to the number of observations. If iweights are specified, they are treated like fweights except that the elements of v are not restricted to be positive integers.

Saved Results

matrix accum, glsaccum, and vecaccum save the number of observations in r(N). glsaccum (with aweights) and vecaccum also store the sum of the weight in r(sum_w), but accum does not.

References

Greene, W. H. 2000. *Econometric Analysis*. 4th ed. Upper Saddle River, NJ: Prentice–Hall.

Also See

Complementary:	[R] **ml**
Background:	[U] **17 Matrix expressions**,
	[P] **matrix**

Title

> **matrix constraint** — Constrained estimation

Syntax

<u>matr</u>ix makeCns [*numlist*]

<u>matr</u>ix dispCns

matcproc **T a C**

T, **a**, and **C** are names of new or existing matrices.

Description

matrix makeCns makes a constraint matrix; the matrix can be obtained by the **matrix get(Cns)** function (see [P] **matrix get**). **matrix dispCns** displays the system-stored constraint matrix in readable form. **matcproc** returns matrices helpful for performing constrained estimation, including the constraint matrix.

Remarks

Users of estimation commands that allow constrained estimation define constraints using the **constraint** command; they indicate which constraints they want to use by specifying the **constraints**(*numlist*) option to the estimation command. This entry concerns programming such sophisticated estimators. If you are programming using **ml**, you can ignore this entry. Constraints are handled automatically (and if you were to look inside the **ml** code, you would find that it uses **matrix makeCns**).

Before reading this entry, you should be familiar with constraints from a user's perspective; see [R] **constraint**. You should also be familiar with programming estimation commands that do not include constraints; see [P] **estimates**.

Overview

You have an estimation command and wish to allow a set of linear constraints to be specified for the parameters by the user and then to produce estimates subject to those constraints. Stata will do most of the work for you. First, it will collect the constraints—all you have to do is add an option to your estimation command to allow the user to specify which constraints to use. Second, it will process those constraints, converting them from algebraic form (such as **group1=group2**) to a constraint matrix. Third, it will convert the constraint matrix into two, almost magical matrices that will, in the case of maximum likelihood estimation, allow you to write your routine almost as if there were no constraints.

There will be a "reduced-form" parameter vector $\mathbf{b}_c$, which your likelihood-calculation routine will receive. That vector, multiplied by one of the almost magical matrices and then added to the other, can be converted into a regular parameter vector with the constraints applied, so, other than the few extra matrix calculations, you can calculate the likelihood function as if there were no constraints. You can do the same thing with respect to the first and second derivatives (if you are calculating them) except that, after getting them, you will need to perform another matrix multiplication or two to convert them into the reduced form.

Once the optimum is found, you will have reduced-form parameter vector $\mathbf{b}_c$ and variance–covariance matrix $\mathbf{V}_c$. Both can be easily converted into full-form-but-constrained $\mathbf{b}$ and $\mathbf{V}$.

Finally, you will post the results along with the constraint matrix Stata made up for you in the first place. You can, with a few lines of program code, arrange it so that, every time results are replayed, the constraints under which they were produced are redisplayed and in standard algebraic format.

Mathematics

Let $\mathbf{Rb}' = \mathbf{r}$ be the constraint for $\mathbf{R}$ a $c \times p$ constraint matrix imposing c constraints on p parameters, $\mathbf{b}$ a $1 \times p$ parameter vector, and $\mathbf{r}$ a $c \times 1$ vector of constraint values.

We wish to construct a $p \times k$ matrix $\mathbf{T}$ that takes $\mathbf{b}$ into a reduced-rank form where $k = p - c$. There are obviously lots of $\mathbf{T}$ matrices that will do this; we choose one with properties

$$\mathbf{b}_c = \mathbf{b}_0 \mathbf{T}$$
$$\mathbf{b} = \mathbf{b}_c \mathbf{T}' + \mathbf{a}$$

where $\mathbf{b}_c$ is a reduced-form projection of any solution $\mathbf{b}_0$, i.e., $\mathbf{b}_c$ is a vector of lesser dimension ($1 \times k$ rather than $1 \times p$) that can be treated as if it were unconstrained. The second equation says that $\mathbf{b}_c$ can be mapped back into a higher-dimensioned, properly constrained $\mathbf{b}$; $1 \times p$ vector $\mathbf{a}$ is a constant that depends only on $\mathbf{R}$ and $\mathbf{r}$.

With such a $\mathbf{T}$ matrix and $\mathbf{a}$ vector, one can engage in unconstrained optimization of $\mathbf{b}_c$. If the estimate $\mathbf{b}_c$ with variance–covariance matrix $\mathbf{V}_c$ is produced, it can be mapped back into $\mathbf{b} = \mathbf{b}_c \mathbf{T}' + \mathbf{a}$ and $\mathbf{V} = \mathbf{T}\mathbf{V}_c\mathbf{T}'$. The resulting $\mathbf{b}$ and $\mathbf{V}$ can then be posted.

❏ Technical Note

So how did we get so lucky? This happy solution arises if

$$\mathbf{T} = \text{first } k \text{ eigenvectors of } \mathbf{I} - \mathbf{R}'(\mathbf{RR}')^{-1}\mathbf{R} \qquad (p \times k)$$
$$\mathbf{L} = \text{last } c \text{ eigenvectors of } \mathbf{I} - \mathbf{R}'(\mathbf{RR}')^{-1}\mathbf{R} \qquad (p \times c)$$
$$\mathbf{a} = \mathbf{r}'(\mathbf{L}'\mathbf{R}')^{-1}\mathbf{L}'$$

because

$$\left(\mathbf{b}_c, \mathbf{r}'\right) = \mathbf{b}\left(\mathbf{T}, \mathbf{R}'\right)$$

If $\mathbf{R}$ consists of a set of consistent constraints, then it is guaranteed to have rank c. Thus, $\mathbf{RR}'$ is a $c \times c$ invertible matrix.

We will now show that $\mathbf{RT} = \mathbf{0}$ and $\mathbf{R}(\mathbf{LL}') = \mathbf{R}$.

Since $\mathbf{R}: c \times p$ is assumed to be of rank c, the first k eigenvalues of $\mathbf{P} = \mathbf{I} - \mathbf{R}'(\mathbf{RR}')^{-1}\mathbf{R}$ are positive and the last c are zero. Break $\mathbf{R}$ into a basis spanned by these components. If $\mathbf{R}$ had any components in the first k, they could not be annihilated by $\mathbf{P}$, contradicting

$$\mathbf{RP} = \mathbf{R} - \mathbf{RR}'(\mathbf{RR}')^{-1}\mathbf{R} = 0$$

Therefore, $\mathbf{T}$ and $\mathbf{R}$ are orthogonal to each other. Since $(\mathbf{T}, \mathbf{L})$ is an orthonormal basis, $(\mathbf{T}, \mathbf{L})'$ is its inverse, so $(\mathbf{T}, \mathbf{L})(\mathbf{T}, \mathbf{L})' = \mathbf{I}$. Thus,

$$\mathbf{TT}' + \mathbf{LL}' = \mathbf{I}$$
$$(\mathbf{TT}' + \mathbf{LL}')\mathbf{R}' = \mathbf{R}'$$
$$(\mathbf{LL}')\mathbf{R}' = \mathbf{R}'$$

So, we conclude that $\mathbf{r} = \mathbf{bR}(\mathbf{LL}')$. $\mathbf{RL}$ is an invertible $c \times c$ matrix, so

$$\left\{\mathbf{b}_c, \mathbf{r}'(\mathbf{L}'\mathbf{R})^{-1}\right\} = \mathbf{b}(\mathbf{T}, \mathbf{L})$$

Remember, $(\mathbf{T}, \mathbf{L})$ is a set of eigenvectors, meaning $(\mathbf{T}, \mathbf{L})^{-1} = (\mathbf{T}, \mathbf{L})'$, so $\mathbf{b} = \mathbf{b}_c\mathbf{T}' + \mathbf{r}'(\mathbf{L}'\mathbf{R}')^{-1}\mathbf{L}'$.
❏

If a solution is found by likelihood methods, the reduced form parameter vector will be passed to the maximizer and from there to the program that computes a likelihood value from it. In order to find the likelihood value, the inner routines can compute $\mathbf{b} = \mathbf{b}_c\mathbf{T}' + \mathbf{a}$. The routine may then go on to produce a set of $1 \times p$ first derivatives $\mathbf{d}$ and $p \times p$ second derivatives $\mathbf{H}$ even though the problem is of lesser dimension. These matrices can be reduced to the k-dimensional space via

$$\mathbf{d}_c = \mathbf{dT}$$
$$\mathbf{H}_c = \mathbf{T}'\mathbf{HT}$$

❏ Technical Note

Alternatively, if a solution were to be found by direct matrix methods, then the programmer must derive a new solution based on $\mathbf{b} = \mathbf{b}_c\mathbf{T}' + \mathbf{a}$. For example, the least-squares normal equations come from differentiating $(\mathbf{y} - \mathbf{Xb})^2$. Setting the derivative with respect to $\mathbf{b}$ to zero results in

$$\mathbf{T}'\mathbf{X}'\left\{\mathbf{y} - \mathbf{X}(\mathbf{Tb}'_c + \mathbf{a}')\right\} = 0$$

yielding

$$\mathbf{b}'_c = (\mathbf{T}'\mathbf{X}'\mathbf{XT})^{-1}(\mathbf{T}'\mathbf{X}'\mathbf{y} - \mathbf{T}'\mathbf{X}'\mathbf{Xa}')$$
$$\mathbf{b}' = \mathbf{T}\left\{(\mathbf{T}'\mathbf{X}'\mathbf{XT})^{-1}(\mathbf{T}'\mathbf{X}'\mathbf{y} - \mathbf{T}'\mathbf{X}'\mathbf{Xa}')\right\} + \mathbf{a}'$$

Using the matrices $\mathbf{T}$ and $\mathbf{a}$, the solution is not merely to constrain the $\mathbf{b}'$ obtained from an unconstrained solution $(\mathbf{X}'\mathbf{X})^{-1}\mathbf{X}'\mathbf{y}$, even though you might know that, in this case, with further substitutions this could be reduced to

$$\mathbf{b}' = (\mathbf{X}'\mathbf{X})^{-1}\mathbf{X}'\mathbf{y} + (\mathbf{X}'\mathbf{X})^{-1}\mathbf{R}'\{\mathbf{R}(\mathbf{X}'\mathbf{X})^{-1}\mathbf{R}'\}^{-1}\{\mathbf{r} - \mathbf{R}(\mathbf{X}'\mathbf{X})^{-1}\mathbf{X}'\mathbf{y}\}$$

❏

Linkage of the mathematics to Stata

Users define constraints using the `constraint` command; see [R] **constraint**. The constraints are numbered and Stata stores them in algebraic format—the same format in which the user typed them. Stata does this because, until the estimation problem is defined, it cannot know how to interpret the constraint. Think of the constraint `_b[group1]=_b[group2]`, meaning two coefficients are to be constrained to equality, along with the constraint `_b[group3]=2`. The constraint matrices $\mathbf{R}$ and $\mathbf{r}$ are defined so that $\mathbf{R}\mathbf{b}' = \mathbf{r}$ imposes the constraint. The matrices *might* be

$$\begin{pmatrix} 0 & 0 & 1 & -1 & 0 & 0 \\ 0 & 0 & 0 & 0 & 1 & 0 \end{pmatrix} \begin{pmatrix} b_1 \\ b_2 \\ b_3 \\ b_4 \\ b_5 \\ b_6 \end{pmatrix} = \begin{pmatrix} 0 \\ 2 \end{pmatrix}$$

if it just so happened that the third and fourth coefficients corresponded to `group1` and `group2` and the fifth corresponded to `group3`. Then again, it might look different if the coefficients were organized differently.

Therefore, Stata must wait until estimation begins to define the $\mathbf{R}$ and $\mathbf{r}$ matrices. Stata learns about the organization of a problem from the names bordering the coefficient vector and variance–covariance matrix. Therefore, Stata requires you to `post` a dummy estimation result that has the correct names. Based on that, it can now determine the organization of the constraint matrix and make it for you. Once a (dummy) estimation result has been posted, `makeCns` can make the constraint matrices and, once they are built, you can obtain copies of them using `matrix` *mname*`=get(Cns)`. Stata stores the constraint matrices $\mathbf{R}$ and $\mathbf{r}$ as a single, $c \times (p+1)$ matrix $\mathbf{C} = (\mathbf{R}, \mathbf{r})$. Putting them together makes it easier to pass them to subroutines.

The second step in the process is to convert the constrained problem to a reduced-form problem. We outlined the mathematics above; the `matcproc` command will produce the $\mathbf{T}$ and $\mathbf{a}$ matrices. If you are performing maximum likelihood, your likelihood, gradient, and Hessian calculation subroutines can still work in the full metric by using the same $\mathbf{T}$ and $\mathbf{a}$ matrices to translate the reduced-format parameter vector back to the original metric. If you do this, and if you are calculating gradients or Hessians, you must remember to compress them to reduced form using the $\mathbf{T}$ and $\mathbf{a}$ matrices.

When you have a reduced-form solution, you translate this back to a constrained solution using $\mathbf{T}$ and $\mathbf{a}$. You then `post` the constrained solutions, along with the original `Cns` matrix, and use `estimates display` to display the results.

Thus, the outline of a program to perform constrained estimation is

```
program define myest, eclass
        version 7.0
        if ~replay() {
                #delimit ;
                syntax whatever [, whatever Constraints(numlist)
                        Level(integer $S_level)];
                #delimit cr
                any other parsing of the user's estimation request
                tempname b V C T a bc Vc
                local p=number of parameters
                 define the model ( set the row and column names)  in `b'
```

```
                    if "`constra´"~="" {
                            matrix `V´=`b´´*`b´
                            estimates post `b´ `V´            /* a dummy solution */
                            matrix makeCns `constra´
                            matrix dispCns              /* display constraints */
                            local shown "yes"
                            matcproc `T´ `a´ `C´
                            obtain solution in `bc´ and `Vc´
                            matrix `b´ = `bc´*`T´ + `a´
                            matrix `V´ = `T´*`Vc´*`T´´   /* note prime */
                            estimates post `b´ `V´ `C´, options
                    }
                    else {
                            obtain standard solution in `b´ and `V´
                            estimates post `b´ `V´, options
                    }
                    store whatever else you want in e()
                    est local cmd "myest"
            }
            else {    /* replay */
                    if "`e(cmd)´"~="myest" { error 301 }
                    syntax [, Level(integer $S_level)]
            }
            if `level´<10 | `level´>99 {
                    di as err "level() must be between 10 and 99 inclusive"
                    exit 198
            }
            if "`shown´"~="yes" {
                    matrix dispCns  /* display any constraints on replay */
            }
            output any header above the coefficient table
            estimates display, level(`level´)
    end
```

There is one point that might escape your attention: Immediately after obtaining the constraint, we display the constraints even before we undertake the estimation. This way, a user who has made a mistake may press *Break* rather than waiting until the estimation is complete to discover the error.

Our code also redisplays the constraints every time the problem output is repeated (by typing *myest* without arguments). So that the constraints are not shown twice at the time of estimation, we set the local macro `shown` to contain `yes`. If the output is ever repeated, the local macro `shown` will never be defined (and so will not contain `yes`) and we will redisplay the constraints along with the results of our estimation.

Also See

Complementary:	[P] **estimates**, [P] **matrix get**,
	[R] **constraint**
Related:	[R] **cnsreg**, [R] **ml**
Background:	[U] **17 Matrix expressions**,
	[U] **21 Programming Stata**,
	[U] **23 Estimation and post-estimation commands**,
	[P] **matrix**

Title

matrix define — Matrix definition, operators, and functions

Syntax

<u>mat</u>rix [<u>define</u>] *matname = matrix_expression*

<u>mat</u>rix [<u>in</u>put] *matname =* (# [,# ...] [\ # [, # ...] [\ [...]]])

Description

matrix define performs matrix computations. The word **define** may be omitted.

matrix input provides a method of inputting matrices. The word **input** may be omitted (see discussion that follows).

For an introduction and overview of matrices in Stata, see [U] **17 Matrix expressions**.

Remarks

matrix define calculates matrix results from other matrices. For instance,

```
. matrix define D = A + B + C
```

creates D containing the sum of A, B, and C. The word **define** may be omitted,

```
. matrix D = A + B + C
```

and the command may be further abbreviated:

```
. mat D=A+B+C
```

The same matrix may appear on both the left and the right of the equals sign in all contexts and Stata will not become confused. Complicated matrix expressions are allowed.

With **matrix input** you define the matrix elements rowwise; commas are used to separate elements within a row and backslashes are used to separate the rows. Spacing does not matter.

```
. matrix input A = (1,2\3,4)
```

The above would also work if you omitted the **input** subcommand.

```
. matrix A = (1,2\3,4)
```

There is a subtle difference: The first method uses the **matrix input** command; the second uses the matrix expression parser. Omitting **input** allows expressions in the command. For instance,

```
. matrix X = (1+1, 2*3/4 \ 5/2, 3)
```

is understood but

```
. matrix input X = (1+1, 2*3/4 \ 5/2, 3)
```

would produce an error.

`matrix input`, however, has two advantages. First, it allows input of very large matrices. (The expression parser is limited because it must "compile" the expressions and, if the result is too long, will produce an error.) Second, `matrix input` allows you to omit the commas.

Further remarks are presented under the headings

> *Inputting matrices by hand*
> *Matrix operators*
> *Matrix functions*
> *Matrix functions returning scalars*
> *Subscripting and element-by-element definition*
> *Name conflicts in expressions (name spaces)*
> *Macro extended functions*

Inputting matrices by hand

Before turning to operations on matrices, let's examine how matrices are created. Typically, at least in programming situations, you obtain matrices by accessing one of Stata's internal matrices (`e(b)` and `e(V)`; see [P] **matrix get**) or by accumulating it from the data (see [P] **matrix accum**). Nevertheless, the easiest way to create a matrix is to enter it using `matrix input`—this may not be the normal way one creates matrices, but it is useful for performing small, experimental calculations.

▷ Example

To create the matrix

$$\mathbf{A} = \begin{pmatrix} 1 & 2 \\ 3 & 4 \end{pmatrix}$$

type

```
. matrix A = (1,2 \ 3,4)
```

The spacing does not matter. To define the matrix

$$\mathbf{B} = \begin{pmatrix} 1 & 2 & 3 \\ 4 & 5 & 6 \end{pmatrix}$$

type

```
. matrix B = (1,2,3 \ 4,5,6)
```

To define the matrix

$$\mathbf{C} = \begin{pmatrix} 1 & 2 \\ 3 & 4 \\ 5 & 6 \end{pmatrix}$$

type

```
. matrix C = (1,2 \ 3,4 \ 5,6)
```

If you need more than one line and are working interactively, you merely keep typing; Stata will wrap the line around the screen. If you are working in a do- or ado-file, see [U] **19.1.3 Long lines in do-files**.

So how do you create vectors? You enter the elements, separating them by commas or backslashes. To create the row vector

$$\mathbf{D} = (1 \quad 2 \quad 3)$$

type

```
. matrix D = (1,2,3)
```

To create the column vector

$$\mathbf{E} = \begin{pmatrix} 1 \\ 2 \\ 3 \end{pmatrix}$$

type

```
. matrix E = (1\2\3)
```

To create the 1×1 matrix $\mathbf{F} = (2)$, type

```
. matrix F = (2)
```

In these examples we have omitted the `input` subcommand. They would work either way.

◁

Matrix operators

In what follows, uppercase letters $\mathbf{A}$, $\mathbf{B}$, ..., stand for matrix names. The matrix operators are

+ meaning addition. `matrix C=A+B`, $\mathbf{A}$: $r \times c$ and $\mathbf{B}$: $r \times c$, creates $\mathbf{C}$: $r \times c$ containing the elementwise addition $\mathbf{A} + \mathbf{B}$. An error is issued if the matrices are not conformable. Row and column names are obtained from $\mathbf{B}$.

− meaning subtraction or negation. `matrix C=A-B`, $\mathbf{A}$: $r \times c$ and $\mathbf{B}$: $r \times c$, creates $\mathbf{C}$ containing the elementwise subtraction $\mathbf{A} - \mathbf{B}$. An error is issued if the matrices are not conformable. `matrix C=-A` creates $\mathbf{C}$ containing the elementwise negation of $\mathbf{A}$. Row and column names are obtained from $\mathbf{B}$.

∗ meaning multiplication. `matrix C=A*B`, $\mathbf{A}$: $a \times b$ and $\mathbf{B}$: $b \times c$, returns $\mathbf{C}$: $a \times c$ containing the matrix product $\mathbf{AB}$; an error is issued if $\mathbf{A}$ and $\mathbf{B}$ are not conformable. The row names of $\mathbf{C}$ are obtained from the row names of $\mathbf{A}$, and the column names of $\mathbf{C}$ from the column names of $\mathbf{B}$.

matrix `C=A*s` or matrix `C=s*A`, $\mathbf{A}$: $a \times b$ and s a Stata scalar (see [P] **scalar**) or a literal number, returns $\mathbf{C}$: $a \times b$ containing the elements of $\mathbf{A}$ each multiplied by s. The row and column names of $\mathbf{C}$ are obtained from $\mathbf{A}$. For example, `matrix VC=MYMAT*2.5` multiplies each element of `MYMAT` by 2.5 and stores the result in `VC`.

/ meaning matrix division by scalar. `matrix C=A/s`, $\mathbf{A}$: $a \times b$ and s a Stata scalar (see [P] **scalar**) or a literal number, returns $\mathbf{C}$: $a \times b$ containing the elements of $\mathbf{A}$ each divided by s. The row and column names of $\mathbf{C}$ are obtained from $\mathbf{A}$.

meaning Kronecker product. `matrix C=A#B`, $\mathbf{A}$: $a \times b$ and $\mathbf{B}$: $c \times d$, returns $\mathbf{C}$: $ac \times bd$ containing the Kronecker product $\mathbf{A} \otimes \mathbf{B}$, all elementwise products of $\mathbf{A}$ and $\mathbf{B}$. The upper-left submatrix of $\mathbf{C}$ is the product $A_{1,1}\mathbf{B}$; the submatrix to the right is $A_{1,2}\mathbf{B}$; and so on. Row and column names are obtained by using the subnames of $\mathbf{A}$ as resulting equation names and the subnames of $\mathbf{B}$ for the subnames of $\mathbf{C}$ in each submatrix.

Nothing meaning copy. `matrix B=A` copies $\mathbf{A}$ into $\mathbf{B}$. The row and column names of $\mathbf{B}$ are obtained from $\mathbf{A}$. The `matrix rename` command (see [P] **matrix utility**) will rename instead of copy a matrix.

´ meaning transpose. `matrix B=A´`, $\mathbf{A}$: $r \times c$, creates $\mathbf{B}$: $c \times r$ containing the transpose of $\mathbf{A}$. The row names of $\mathbf{B}$ are obtained from the column names of $\mathbf{A}$ and the column names of $\mathbf{B}$ from the row names of $\mathbf{A}$.

, meaning join columns by row. `matrix C=A,B`, $\mathbf{A}$: $a \times b$ and $\mathbf{B}$: $a \times c$, returns $\mathbf{C}$: $a \times (b + c)$ containing $\mathbf{A}$ in columns 1 through b and $\mathbf{B}$ in columns $b + 1$ through $b + c$ (the columns of $\mathbf{B}$ are appended to the columns of $\mathbf{A}$). An error is issued if the matrices are not conformable. The row names of $\mathbf{C}$ are obtained from $\mathbf{A}$. The column names are obtained from $\mathbf{A}$ and $\mathbf{B}$.

\ meaning join rows by column. `matrix C=A\B`, $\mathbf{A}$: $a \times b$ and $\mathbf{B}$: $c \times b$, returns $\mathbf{C}$: $(a + c) \times b$ containing $\mathbf{A}$ in rows 1 through a and $\mathbf{B}$ in rows $a + 1$ through $a + c$ (the rows of $\mathbf{B}$ are appended to the rows of $\mathbf{A}$). An error is issued if the matrices are not conformable. The column names of $\mathbf{C}$ are obtained from $\mathbf{A}$. The row names are obtained from $\mathbf{A}$ and $\mathbf{B}$.

`matrix define` allows complicated matrix expressions. Parentheses may be used to control order of evaluation. The default order of precedence for the matrix operators (from highest to lowest) is

Matrix operator precedence

Operator	symbol
parentheses	( )
transpose	´
negation	–
Kronecker product	#
division by scalar	/
multiplication	*
subtraction	–
addition	+
column join	,
row join	\

▷ Example

The following examples are artificial but informative:

```
. matrix A = (1,2\3,4)
. matrix B = (5,7\9,2)
. matrix C = A+B
. matrix list C
C[2,2]
     c1  c2
r1    6   9
r2   12   6
. matrix B = A-B
. matrix list B
B[2,2]
     c1  c2
r1   -4  -5
r2   -6   2
. matrix X = (1,1\2,5\8,0\4,5)
. matrix C = 3*X*A´*B
```

```
. matrix list C

C[4,2]
       c1    c2
r1  -162    -3
r2  -612   -24
r3  -528    24
r4  -744   -18

. matrix D = (X´*X - A´*A)/4

. matrix rownames D = dog cat        /* see [R] matrix rowname */

. matrix colnames D = bark meow      /* see [R] matrix rowname */

. matrix list D

symmetric D[2,2]
       bark    meow
dog  18.75
cat   4.25    7.75

. matrix rownames A = aa bb          /* see [R] matrix rowname */

. matrix colnames A = alpha beta     /* see [R] matrix rowname */

. matrix list A

A[2,2]
      alpha    beta
aa        1       2
bb        3       4

. matrix D=A#D

. matrix list D

D[4,4]
         alpha:  alpha:   beta:   beta:
          bark    meow    bark    meow
aa:dog   18.75    4.25    37.5     8.5
aa:cat    4.25    7.75     8.5    15.5
bb:dog   56.25   12.75      75      17
bb:cat   12.75   23.25      17      31

. matrix G=A,B\D

. matrix list G

G[6,4]
         alpha    beta      c1      c2
    aa       1       2      -4      -5
    bb       3       4      -6       2
aa:dog   18.75    4.25    37.5     8.5
aa:cat    4.25    7.75     8.5    15.5
bb:dog   56.25   12.75      75      17
bb:cat   12.75   23.25      17      31

. matrix Z = (B - A)´*(B + A´*-B)/4  /* complex expressions ok */

. matrix list Z

Z[2,2]
           c1      c2
alpha     -81    -1.5
 beta    -44.5    8.5
```

◁

❑ Technical Note

Programmers: Watch out for confusion when combining ´, meaning transpose with local macros, where ´ is one of the characters that enclose macro names: `` `mname´ ``. Stata will not become confused, but you might. Compare:

```
. matrix `new1´ = `old´
```

and

```
. matrix `new2´ = `old´´
```

Note that matrix `new2´ contains matrix `old´, transposed. Stata will become confused if you type

```
. matrix `C´ = `A´\`B´
```

because the backslash in front of the `B´ makes the macro processor take the left quote literally. No substitution is ever made for `B´. Even worse, the macro processor assumes the backslash was meant for it and so removes the character! Pretend `A´ contained a, `B´ contained b, and `C´ contained c. After substitution, the line would read

```
. matrix c = a`B´
```

which is not at all what was intended. To make your meaning clear, put a space after the backslash:

```
. matrix `C´ = `A´\ `B´
```

which would then be expanded to read

```
. matrix c = a\ b
```

❑

Matrix functions

In addition to matrix operators, Stata has matrix functions. The matrix functions allow expressions to be passed as arguments. The following matrix functions are provided:

matrix **A**=I(*dim*) defines **A** as the *dim* × *dim* identity matrix where *dim* is a scalar expression and will be rounded to the nearest integer. matrix **A**=I(3) defines **A** as the 3 × 3 identity matrix.

matrix **A**=J(*r*,*c*,*z*) defines **A** as an *r* × *c* matrix containing elements *z*. *r*, *c*, and *z* are scalar expressions with *r* and *c* rounded to the nearest integer. matrix **A**=J(2,3,0) returns a 2 × 3 matrix containing 0 for each element.

matrix **L**=cholesky(*mexp*) performs Cholesky decomposition. An error is issued if the matrix expression *mexp* does not evaluate to a square, symmetric matrix. matrix **L**=cholesky(**A**) produces the lower-triangular (square root) matrix **L** such that $\mathbf{LL}' = \mathbf{A}$. The row and column names of **L** are obtained from **A**.

matrix **B**=syminv(*mexp*), for *mexp* evaluating to a square, symmetric, and positive definite matrix, returns the inverse. If *mexp* does not evaluate to a positive definite matrix, rows will be inverted until the diagonal terms are zero or negative; the rows and columns corresponding to these terms will be set to 0, producing a g2 inverse. The row names of **B** are obtained from the column names of *mexp* and the column names of **B** are obtained from the row names of *mexp*.

matrix **B**=inv(*mexp*), for *mexp* evaluating to a square but not necessarily symmetric or positive definite matrix, returns the inverse. A singular matrix will result in an error. The row names of **B** are obtained from the column names of *mexp* and the column names of **B** are obtained from the row names of *mexp*. syminv() should be used in preference to inv(), which is less accurate, whenever possible. (Also see [P] **matrix svd** for singular value decomposition.)

matrix **B**=sweep(*mexp*,*n*) applies the sweep operator to the *n*th row and column of the square matrix resulting from the matrix expression *mexp*. *n* is a scalar expression and will be rounded to the nearest integer. The names of **B** are obtained from *mexp* except that the *n*th row and column names are interchanged. For **A**: $n \times n$, $\mathbf{B} = \text{sweep}(\mathbf{A}, k)$ produces **B**: $n \times n$, defined as

$$B_{kk} = \frac{1}{A_{kk}}$$

$$B_{ik} = -\frac{A_{ik}}{A_{kk}}, \qquad i \neq k \qquad (kth\ column)$$

$$B_{kj} = \frac{A_{ij}}{A_{kk}}, \qquad j \neq k \qquad (jth\ row)$$

$$B_{ij} = A_{ij} - \frac{A_{ik}A_{kj}}{A_{kk}}, \qquad i \neq k, j \neq k$$

matrix **B**=corr(*mexp*), for *mexp* evaluating to a covariance matrix, stores the corresponding correlation matrix in **B**. The row and column names are obtained from *mexp*.

matrix **B**=diag(*mexp*), for *mexp* evaluating to a row or column vector ($1 \times c$ or $c \times 1$), creates **B**: $c \times c$ with diagonal elements from *mexp* and off-diagonal elements 0. The row and column names are obtained from the column names of *mexp* if *mexp* is a row vector or the row names if *mexp* is a column vector.

matrix **B**=vecdiag(*mexp*), for *mexp* evaluating to a square $c \times c$ matrix, creates **B**: $1 \times c$ containing the diagonal elements from *mexp*. vecdiag() is the opposite of diag(). The row name is set to r1. The column names are obtained from the column names of *mexp*.

nullmat(**B**) may only be used with the row-join (,) and column-join (\) operators and informs Stata that **B** might not exist. If **B** does not exist, the row-join or column-join operator simply returns the other matrix operator argument. An example of the use of nullmat() is given in [U] **17.8.1 Matrix functions returning matrices**.

matrix **B**=get(*systemname*) returns in **B** a copy of the Stata internal matrix *systemname*; see [P] **matrix get**. You can obtain the coefficient vector and variance–covariance matrix after an estimation command either with matrix get or by reference to e(b) and e(V).

▷ Example

The examples are, once again, artificial but informative.

```
. matrix myid = I(3)
. matrix list myid
symmetric myid[3,3]
     c1  c2  c3
r1    1
r2    0   1
r3    0   0   1
. matrix new = J(2,3,0)
. matrix list new
new[2,3]
     c1  c2  c3
r1    0   0   0
r2    0   0   0
. matrix A = (1,2\2,5)
. matrix Ainv = syminv(A)
. matrix list Ainv
symmetric Ainv[2,2]
     r1  r2
c1    5
c2   -2   1
```

```
. matrix L = cholesky(4*I(2) + A´*A)

. matrix list L

L[2,2]
          c1          c2
c1         3           0
c2         4   4.1231056

. matrix B = (1,5,9\2,1,7\3,5,1)

. matrix Binv = inv(B)

. matrix list Binv

Binv[3,3]
            r1           r2           r3
c1  -.27419355    .32258065    .20967742
c2   .15322581   -.20967742    .08870968
c3   .05645161    .08064516   -.07258065

. matrix C = sweep(B,1)

. matrix list C

C[3,3]
       r1    c2    c3
c1      1     5     9
r2     -2    -9   -11
r3     -3   -10   -26

. matrix C = sweep(C,1)

. matrix list C

C[3,3]
      c1  c2  c3
r1     1   5   9
r2     2   1   7
r3     3   5   1

. matrix Cov = (36.6598,-3596.48\-3596.48,604030)

. matrix R = corr(Cov)

. matrix list R

symmetric R[2,2]
            c1          c2
r1           1
r2  -.7642815            1

. matrix d = (1,2,3)

. matrix D = diag(d)

. matrix list D

symmetric D[3,3]
      c1  c2  c3
c1     1
c2     0   2
c3     0   0   3

. matrix e = vecdiag(D)

. matrix list e

e[1,3]
      c1  c2  c3
r1     1   2   3

. * matrix function arguments can be other matrix functions and expressions
. matrix F = diag(inv(B) * vecdiag(diag(d) + 4*sweep(B+J(3,3,10),2)´*I(3))´)
```

```
. matrix list F

symmetric F[3,3]
             c1            c2            c3
c1  -3.2170088
c2           0    -7.686217
c3           0            0     2.3548387
```

◁

Matrix functions returning scalars

In addition to the above functions used with `matrix define`, functions that can be described as matrix functions returning matrices, there are matrix functions that return mathematical scalars. The list of functions that follow should be viewed as a continuation of [U] **16.3 Functions**. If the functions listed below are used in a scalar context (for example used with `display` or `generate`) then **A**, **B**, ..., below stand for matrix names (possibly as a string literal or string variable name—details later). If the functions below are used in a matrix context (in `matrix define` for instance) then **A**, **B**, ..., may also stand for matrix expressions.

`rowsof(A)` and `colsof(A)` return the number of rows or columns of **A**.

`rownumb(A,`*string*`)` and `colnumb(A,`*string*`)` return the row or column number associated with the name specified by *string*. For instance, `rownumb(MYMAT,"price")` returns the row number (say, 3) in `MYMAT` that has name `price` (subname `price` and equation name blank). `colnumb(MYMAT,"out2:price")` returns the column number associated with name `out2:price` (subname `price` and equation name `out2`). If row or column name is not found, missing is returned.

`rownumb()` and `colnumb()` can also return the first row or column number associated with an equation name. For example, `colnumb(MYMAT,"out2:")` returns the first column number in `MYMAT` that has equation name `out2`. Missing is returned if the equation name `out2` is not found.

`trace(A)` returns the sum of the diagonal elements of square matrix **A**. If **A** is not square, missing is returned.

`det(A)` returns the determinant of square matrix **A**. The determinant is the volume of the $p-1$ dimensional manifold described by the matrix in p-dimensional space. If **A** is not square, missing is returned.

`diag0cnt(A)` returns the number of zeros on the diagonal of the square matrix **A**. If **A** is not square, missing is returned.

`mreldif(A,B)` returns the relative difference of matrix **A** and **B**. If **A** and **B** do not have the same dimensions, missing is returned. The matrix relative difference is defined as

$$\max_{i,j}\left(\frac{|\mathbf{A}[i,j]-\mathbf{B}[i,j]|}{|\mathbf{B}[i,j]|+1}\right)$$

`el(A,`i,j`)` and **A**$[i,j]$ return the i,j element of **A**. In most cases, either construct may be used; `el(MYMAT,2,3)` and `MYMAT[2,3]` are equivalent although `MYMAT[2,3]` is more readable. In the case of the second construct, however, **A** must be a matrix name—it cannot be a string literal or string variable. The first construct allows **A** to be a matrix name, string literal, or string variable. For instance, assume `mymat` (as opposed to `MYMAT`) is a string variable in the dataset containing matrix names. `mymat[2,3]` refers to the $(2,3)$ element of the matrix named `mymat`, a matrix which probably does not exist and so produces an error. `el(mymat,2,3)` refers to the data variable mymat; the contents of that variable will be taken to obtain the matrix name and el() will then return the $(2,3)$ element of that matrix. If that matrix does not exist, Stata will not issue an error; because you referred to it indirectly, the el() function will return missing.

In either construct, i and j may be any expression (an *exp*) evaluating to a real. MYMAT[2,3+1] returns the $(2,4)$ element. In programs that loop, you might refer to MYMAT[`i´,`j´+1].

In a matrix context (like matrix define), the first argument of el() may be a matrix expression. For instance, matrix $\mathbf{A} = \mathbf{B}$*el($\mathbf{B}$-$\mathbf{C}$,1,1) is allowed but display el($\mathbf{B}$-$\mathbf{C}$,1,1) would be an error since display is in a scalar context.

The matrix functions returning scalars defined above can be used in any context that allows an expression—what is abbreviated *exp* in the syntax diagrams throughout this manual. For instance, trace() returns the (scalar) trace of a matrix. Say you have a matrix called MYX. You could type

    . generate tr = trace(MYX)

although this would be a silly thing to do. It would be silly because it would force Stata to evaluate the trace of the matrix many times, once for each observation in the data, and it would then store that same result over and over again in the new data variable tr. But you could do it because, if you examine the syntax diagram for generate (see [R] **generate**), generate allows an *exp*.

If you just wanted to see the trace of MYX, you could type

    . display trace(MYX)

because the syntax diagram for display also allows an *exp*; see [P] **display**. More usefully, you could do either of the following:

    . local tr = trace(MYX)
    . scalar tr = trace(MYX)

This is more useful because it will evaluate the trace only once and then store the result. In the first case, the result will be stored in a local macro (see [P] **macro**); in the second, it will be stored in a Stata scalar (see [P] **scalar**).

▷ Example

Storing the number as a scalar is better for two reasons: it is more accurate (scalars are stored in double precision) and it is faster (macros are stored as printable characters and this conversion is a time-consuming operation). Not too much should be made of the accuracy issue; macros are stored with at least 13 digits, but it can make a difference in some cases.

In any case, let us demonstrate that both methods work with the simple trace function:

    . matrix A = (1,6\8,4)
    . local tr = trace(A)
    . display `tr´
    5
    . scalar sctr = trace(A)
    . scalar list sctr
        sctr =   5

◁

❑ Technical Note

The use of a matrix function returning scalar with **generate** does not have to be silly because, instead of specifying a matrix name, you may specify a string variable in the dataset. If you do, in each observation the contents of the string variable will be taken as a matrix name and the function will be applied to that matrix for that observation. If there is no such matrix, missing will be returned. Thus, if your dataset contained

```
. list

        matname
1.          X1
2.          X2
3.           Z
```

you could type

```
. generate tr = trace(matname)
(1 missing value generated)

. list

        matname      tr
1.          X1        5
2.          X2        .
3.           Z       16
```

Evidently, we have no matrix called **X2** stored. All the matrix functions returning scalars allow you to specify either a matrix name directly or a string variable that indirectly specifies the matrix name. When you indirectly specify the matrix and the matrix does not exist—as happened above—the function evaluates to missing. When you directly specify the matrix and it does not exist, you get an error:

```
. display trace(X2)
X2 not found
r(111);
```

This is true not only for **trace()**, but for every matrix function that returns a scalar described above.

❑

Subscripting and element-by-element definition

matrix **B=A**$[r_1,r_2]$, for range expressions r_1 and r_2 (defined below), extracts a submatrix from **A** and stores it in **B**. Row and column names of **B** are obtained from the extracted rows and columns of **A**. In what follows, assume **A** is $a \times b$.

A range expression can be a literal number. matrix **B=A**[1,2] would return a 1×1 matrix containing $A_{1,2}$.

A range expression can be a number followed by two periods followed by another number, meaning the rows or columns from the first number to the second. matrix **B=A**[2..4,1..5] would return a 3×5 matrix containing the second through fourth rows and the first through fifth columns of **A**.

A range expression can be a number followed by three periods, meaning all the remaining rows or columns from that number. matrix **B=A**[3,4...] would return a $1 \times b-3$ matrix (row vector) containing the fourth through last elements of the third row of **A**.

A range expression can be a quoted string, in which case it refers to the row or column with the specified name. `matrix B=A["price","mpg"]` returns a 1×1 matrix containing the element whose row name is `price` and column name `mpg`, which would be the same as `matrix B=A[2,3]` if the second row were named `price` and the third column `mpg`. `matrix B=A["price",1...]` would return the $1 \times b$ vector corresponding to the row named `price`. In either case, if there is no matrix row or column with the specified name, an error is issued and the return code is set to 111. If the row and/or column names include both an equation name and a subname, the fully qualified name must be specified, as in `matrix B=A["eq1:price",1...]`.

A range expression can be a quoted string containing only an equation name, in which case it refers to all rows or columns with the specified equation name. `matrix B=A["eq1:","eq1:"]` would return the submatrix of rows and columns that have equation names `eq1`.

A range expression containing a quoted string referring to an element (not to an entire equation) can be combined with the `..` and `...` syntaxes above: `matrix B=A["price"...,"price"...]` would define **B** as the submatrix of **A** beginning with the rows and columns corresponding to `price`. `matrix B=A["price".."mpg","price".."mpg"]` would define **B** as the submatrix of **A** starting at rows and columns corresponding to `price` and continuing through the rows and columns corresponding to `mpg`.

A range expression can be mixed. `matrix B=A[1.."price",2]` defines **B** as the column vector extracted from the second column of **A** containing the first element through the element corresponding to `price`.

Scalar expressions may be used in place of literal numbers. The resulting number will be rounded to the nearest integer. Subscripting with scalar expressions may be used in any expression context (such as `generate`, `replace`, etc.). Subscripting with row and column names may only be used in a matrix expression context. This is really not a constraint; see the `rownumb()` and `colnumb()` functions discussed previously in the section titled *Matrix functions returning scalars*.

`matrix A[r,c]=`*exp* changes the *r,c* element of **A** to contain the result of the evaluated scalar expression, as defined in [U] **16 Functions and expressions**, and as further defined in *Matrix functions returning scalars*. *r* and *c* may be scalar expressions and will be rounded to the nearest integer. The matrix **A** must already exist; the matrix function `J()` can be used to achieve this.

`matrix A[r,c]=`*mexp* places the matrix resulting from the *mexp* matrix expression into the already existing matrix **A** with the upper left corner of the *mexp* matrix located at the *r,c* element of **A**. If there is not enough room to place the *mexp* matrix at that location, a conformability error will be issued and the return code will be set to 503. *r* and *c* may be scalar expressions and will be rounded to the nearest integer.

▷ Example

Continuing with our artificial but informative examples,

```
. matrix A = (1,2,3,4\5,6,7,8\9,10,11,12\13,14,15,16)
. matrix rownames A = mercury venus earth mars
. matrix colnames A = poor average good exc
. matrix list A
A[4,4]
            poor  average    good     exc
mercury        1        2       3       4
  venus        5        6       7       8
  earth        9       10      11      12
   mars       13       14      15      16
. matrix b = A[1,2..3]
```

```
. matrix list b
b[1,2]
          average      good
mercury         2         3
. matrix b = A[2...,1..3]
. matrix list b
b[3,3]
          poor   average      good
venus        5         6         7
earth        9        10        11
 mars       13        14        15
. matrix b = A["venus".."earth","average"...]
. matrix list b
b[2,3]
          average      good       exc
venus           6         7         8
earth          10        11        12
. matrix b = A["mars",2...]
. matrix list b
b[1,3]
          average      good       exc
mars          14        15        16
. matrix b = A[sqrt(9)+1..substr("xmars",2,4),2.8..2*2] /* strange but valid */
. mat list b
b[1,2]
          good       exc
mars        15        16
. matrix rownames A = eq1:alpha eq1:beta eq2:alpha eq2:beta
. matrix colnames A = eq1:one eq1:two eq2:one eq2:two
. matrix list A
A[4,4]
            eq1:   eq1:   eq2:   eq2:
            one    two    one    two
eq1:alpha     1      2      3      4
 eq1:beta     5      6      7      8
eq2:alpha     9     10     11     12
 eq2:beta    13     14     15     16
. matrix b = A["eq1:","eq2:"]
. matrix list b
b[2,2]
            eq2:   eq2:
            one    two
eq1:alpha     3      4
 eq1:beta     7      8
. matrix A[3,2] = sqrt(9)
. matrix list A
A[4,4]
            eq1:   eq1:   eq2:   eq2:
            one    two    one    two
eq1:alpha     1      2      3      4
 eq1:beta     5      6      7      8
eq2:alpha     9      3     11     12
 eq2:beta    13     14     15     16
. matrix X = (-3,0\-1,-6)
```

```
. matrix A[1,3] = X
. matrix list A
A[4,4]
            eq1:   eq1:   eq2:   eq2:
            one    two    one    two
eq1:alpha     1      2     -3      0
 eq1:beta     5      6     -1     -6
eq2:alpha     9      3     11     12
 eq2:beta    13     14     15     16
```

◁

❑ Technical Note

matrix $\mathbf{A}[i,j]=exp$ can be used to implement matrix formulas that perhaps Stata does not have built in. Let's pretend Stata could not multiply matrices. We could still multiply matrices, and after some work, we could do so conveniently. Given two matrices, $\mathbf{A}$: $a \times b$ and $\mathbf{B}$: $b \times c$, the (i,j) element of $\mathbf{C} = \mathbf{AB}$, $\mathbf{C}$: $a \times c$, is defined as

$$C_{ij} = \sum_{k=1}^{b} A_{ik} B_{kj}$$

Here is a Stata program to make that calculation:

```
program define matmult            /* arguments A B C, creates C=A*B    */
        version 7.0
        args A B C                /* unload arguments into better names */
        if colsof(`A')~=rowsof(`B') {   /* check conformability          */
                error 503
        }
        local a = rowsof(`A')     /* obtain dimensioning information   */
        local b = colsof(`A')     /*    see Matrix functions returning */
        local c = colsof(`B')     /*    scalars above                  */
        matrix `C' = J(`a',`c',0) /* create result containing 0s       */
        forvalues i = 1/`a' {
                forvalues `j' = 1/`c' {
                        forvalues `k' = 1/`b' {
                                matrix `C'[`i',`j'] = `C'[`i',`j'] + /*
                                */ `A'[`i',`k']*`B'[`k',`j']
                        }
                }
        }
end
```

Now, if in some other program, we needed to multiply matrix XXI by Xy to form result **beta**, we could type matmult XXI Xy beta and never use Stata's built-in method for multiplying matrices (matrix beta=XXI*Xy). If we typed the program matmult into a file named matmult.ado, we would not even have to bother to load matmult before using it—it would be loaded automatically; see [U] **20 Ado-files**.

❑

Name conflicts in expressions (name spaces)

See [P] **matrix** for a description of name spaces. A matrix might have the same name as a variable in the dataset and, if it does, Stata might appear confused when evaluating an expression (an *exp*). When the names conflict, Stata uses the rule that it always takes the data-variable interpretation. You can override this.

First, when working interactively, you can avoid the problem by simply naming your matrices differently from your variables.

Second, when writing programs, you can avoid name conflicts by obtaining names for matrices from `tempname`; see [P] **macro**.

Third, whether working interactively or writing programs, when using names that might conflict, you can use the `matrix()` pseudo-function to force Stata to take the matrix name interpretation.

`matrix(`*name*`)` says that *name* is to be interpreted as a matrix name. For instance, consider the statement `local new=trace(xx)`. This might work and it might not. If `xx` is a matrix and there is no variable named `xx` in your dataset, it will work. If there is also a numeric variable named `xx` in your dataset, it will not. Typing the statement will produce a type-mismatch error—Stata assumes when you type `xx` you are referring to the data variable `xx` because there is a data variable `xx`. Typing `local new=trace(matrix(xx))` will produce the desired result in that case. When writing programs using matrix names not obtained from `tempname`, you are strongly advised to state explicitly that all matrix names are matrix names by using the `matrix()` function.

The only exception to this recommendation has to do with the construct $A[i,j]$. The two subscripts key Stata that A must be a matrix name and not an attempt to subscript a variable and so `matrix()` is not needed. This exception applies only to $A[i,j]$; it does not apply to `el(`A,i,j`)` which would be more safely written `el(matrix(A)`$,i,j$`)`.

❑ Technical Note

The `matrix()` and `scalar()` pseudo-functions (see [P] **scalar**) are really the same function, but you do not need to understand this fine point to program Stata successfully. Understanding might, however, lead to producing more readable code. The formal definition is this:

`scalar(`*exp*`)` (and therefore `matrix(`*exp*`)`) evaluates *exp*, but restricts Stata to interpreting all names in *exp* as scalar or matrix names. Recall that scalars and matrices share the same name space.

Ergo, since `scalar()` and `matrix()` are the same function, you can type `trace(matrix(xx))` or `trace(scalar(xx))`: both do the same thing even though the second looks wrong. Since `scalar()` and `matrix()` allow an *exp*, you could also type `scalar(trace(xx))` and achieve the same result. `scalar()` evaluates the *exp* inside the parentheses: it merely restricts how names are interpreted, so now `trace(xx)` clearly means the trace of the matrix named `xx`.

How can you make your code more readable? Pretend you wanted to calculate the trace plus the determinant of matrix `xx` and store it in the Stata scalar named `tpd` (no, there is no reason you would ever want to make such a silly calculation). You are writing a program and so want to protect yourself from `xx` also existing in the dataset. One solution would be

```
scalar tpd = trace(matrix(xx)) + det(matrix(xx))
```

Knowing the full interpretation rule, however, you realize you can shorten this to

```
scalar tpd = matrix(trace(xx) + det(xx))
```

and then, to make it more readable, you substitute `scalar()` for `matrix()`:

```
scalar tpd = scalar(trace(xx) + det(xx))
```

❑

Macro extended functions

The following macro extended functions (see [P] **macro**) are also defined:

rownames **A** and colnames **A** return the list of all the row or column subnames (with time-series operators if applicable) of **A**, separated by single blanks. Note that the equation names, even if present, are not included.

roweq **A** and coleq **A** return the list of all row equation names or column equation names of **A**, separated by single blanks, and with each name appearing however many times it appears in the matrix.

rowfullnames **A** and colfullnames **A** return the list of all the row or column names including equation names of **A**, separated by single blanks.

▷ Example

These functions are provided as macro functions and standard expression functions because Stata's expression evaluator is limited to working with strings of no more than 80 characters in length, something not true of Stata's macro parser. A matrix with many rows or columns can produce an exceedingly long list of names.

In sophisticated programming situations, you sometimes want to process the matrices by row and column names rather than by row and column number. For instance, assume you are programming and have two matrices, xx and yy. You know they contain the same column names but they might be in a different order. You want to reorganize yy to be in the same order as xx. The following code fragment will create `newyy´ (a matrix name obtained from tempname) containing yy in the same order as xx:

```
tempname newyy newcol
local names : colfullnames(xx)
foreach name of local names {
        local j = colnumb(yy,"`name´")
        if `j´==. {
                display as error "column for `name´ not found"
                exit 111
        }
        matrix `newcol´ = yy[1...,`j´]
        matrix `newyy´ = nullmat(`newyy´),`newcol´
}
```

◁

References

Cox, N. J. 1999. dm69: Further new matrix commands. *Stata Technical Bulletin* 50: 5–9. Reprinted in *Stata Technical Bulletin Reprints*, vol. 9, pp. 29–34.

——. 2000. dm79: Yet more new matrix commands. *Stata Technical Bulletin* 56: 4–8.

Weesie, J. 1997. dm49: Some new matrix commands. *Stata Technical Bulletin* 39: 17–20. Reprinted in *Stata Technical Bulletin Reprints*, vol. 7, pp. 43–48.

Also See

Complementary:	[P] **macro**, [P] **matrix get**, [P] **matrix utility**, [P] **scalar**
Background:	[U] **16.3 Functions**, [U] **17 Matrix expressions**, [P] **matrix**

Title

matrix get — Access system matrices

Syntax

<u>matrix</u> [<u>define</u>] *matname* = get(*internal_Stata_matrix_name*)

where *internal_Stata_matrix_name* is

_b	coefficients after any estimation command
VCE	covariance matrix of estimators after any estimation command
Rr	constraint matrix after `test`
Cns	constraint matrix after any estimation command
Ld	factor loadings after `factor`
Ev	eigenvalues after `factor`
Psi	uniquenesses after `factor`
Co	correlation matrix after `factor`
SD	standard deviations after `factor`
Mean	means after `factor`

Description

The `get()` matrix function obtains a copy of an internal Stata system matrix. Some system matrices can also be obtained more easily by directly referring to the returned result after a command. In particular, the coefficient vector can be referred to as `e(b)` and the variance–covariance matrix of estimators as `e(V)` after an estimation command.

Remarks

`get()` obtains copies of matrices containing coefficients and the covariance matrix of the estimators after estimation commands (such as `regress`, `probit`, etc.) and obtains copies of matrices left behind by other Stata commands. The other side of `get()` is `estimates post`, which allows ado-file estimation commands to post results to Stata's internal areas; see [P] **estimates**.

▷ Example

After any model estimation command the coefficients are available in _b and the variance–covariance matrix of the estimators in VCE.

```
. regress price weight mpg
(output omitted)
```

In this case we can directly use `e(b)` and `e(V)` to obtain the matrices.

```
. matrix list e(b)
e(b)[1,3]
        weight         mpg       _cons
y1   1.7465592  -49.512221   1946.0687
```

```
. matrix list e(V)
symmetric e(V)[3,3]
              weight         mpg       _cons
weight    .41133468
   mpg    44.601659    7422.863
 _cons   -2191.9032  -292759.82    12938766
```

We can also use the `matrix get` command to obtain these matrices.

```
. matrix b = get(_b)
. matrix V = get(VCE)
. matrix list b
b[1,3]
         weight         mpg       _cons
y1    1.7465592  -49.512221   1946.0687
. matrix list V
symmetric V[3,3]
              weight         mpg       _cons
weight    .41133468
   mpg    44.601659    7422.863
 _cons   -2191.9032  -292759.82    12938766
```

Note that the columns of b and both dimensions of V are properly labeled.

◁

▷ Example

After `test`, the restriction matrix is available in `Rr`. Having just estimated a regression of `price` on `weight` and `mpg`, we will run a test and then get the restriction matrix:

```
. test weight=1, notest
 ( 1)   weight = 1.0
. test mpg=40, accum
 ( 1)   weight = 1.0
 ( 2)   mpg = 40.0
       F(  2,    71) =    6.29
            Prob > F =    0.0030
. matrix rxtr=get(Rr)
. matrix list rxtr
rxtr[2,4]
     c1  c2  c3  c4
r1    1   0   0   1
r2    0   1   0  40
```

◁

Also See

Background: [U] **16.5 Accessing coefficients and standard errors**,
              [U] **17 Matrix expressions**,
              [P] **matrix**

Title

matrix mkmat — Convert variables to matrix and vice versa

Syntax

mkmat *varlist* [if *exp*] [in *range*] [, <u>matrix</u>(*matname*)]

svmat [*type*] **A** [, <u>n</u>ames({col | eqcol | matcol | *string*})]

matname **A** *namelist* [, <u>r</u>ows(*range*) <u>c</u>olumns(*range*) <u>e</u>xplicit]

where **A** is the name of an existing matrix, *type* is a storage type for the new variables, and *namelist* is one of (1) a *varlist*, i.e., names of existing variables possibly abbreviated; (2) _cons and the names of existing variables possibly abbreviated; or (3) arbitrary names when the explicit option is specified.

Description

mkmat stores the variables listed in *varlist* in column vectors of the same name; that is, $N \times 1$ matrices where $N = \_N$, the number of observations in the dataset. Optionally, they can be stored as a $N \times k$ matrix, where k is the number of variables in *varlist*.

svmat takes a matrix and stores its columns as new variables. It is the reverse of the mkmat command, which creates a matrix from existing variables.

matname renames the rows and columns of a matrix. matname differs from the matrix rownames and matrix colnames commands in that matname expands varlist abbreviations and also allows a restricted range for the rows or columns. See [P] **matrix rowname**.

Options

matrix() requests that the vectors be combined in a matrix, instead of creating the column vectors.

names({col | eqcol | matcol | *string*}) specifies how the new variables are to be named.
names(col) uses the column names of the matrix to name the variables.
names(eqcol) uses the equation names prefixed to the column names.
names(matcol) uses the matrix name prefixed to the column names.
names(*string*) names the variables *string*1, *string*2, ..., *string*n, where *string* is a user-specified *string* and *n* is the number of columns of the matrix.
If names() is not specified, the variables are named **A**1, **A**2, ..., **A**n, where **A** is the name of the matrix. If necessary, names will be truncated to 8 characters; if these names are not unique, an error message will be returned.

rows(*range*) and columns(*range*) specify the rows and columns of the matrix to rename. The number of rows or columns specified must be equal to the number of names in *namelist*. If both rows() and columns() are given, then the specified rows are named *namelist* and the specified columns are also named *namelist*. The range must be given in one of the following forms:

        `rows(.)`   renames all the rows;
        `rows(2..8)`   renames rows 2 through 8;
        `rows(3)`   renames only row 3;
        `rows(4...)`   renames row 4 to the last row.

If neither `rows()` nor `columns()` is given, then `rows(.) columns(.)` is the default. That is, the matrix must be square, and both the rows and the columns are named *namelist*.

`explicit` suppresses the expansion of varlist abbreviations and omits the verification that the names are those of existing variables. That is, the names in *namelist* are used explicitly and can be any valid row or column names.

Remarks

mkmat

Although cross-products of variables can be loaded into a matrix using the `matrix accum` command, in some instances, programmers may find it more convenient to work with the variables in their datasets as vectors instead of as cross products. `mkmat` allows the user a simple way to load specific variables into matrices in Stata's memory.

▷ Example

`mkmat` uses the variable name to name the single column in the vector. This feature guarantees that the variable name will be carried along in any additional matrix calculations. This feature is also useful when vectors are combined in a general matrix.

```
. describe
Contains data from test.dta
  obs:            10
  vars:            3                          19 Jul 2000 11:24
  size:          160 (99.9% of memory free)
```

variable name	storage type	display format	value label	variable label
x	float	%9.0g		
y	float	%9.0g		
z	float	%9.0g		

```
Sorted by:
. list
             x            y            z
  1.         1           10            2
  2.         2            9            4
  3.         3            8            3
  4.         4            7            5
  5.         5            6            7
  6.         6            5            6
  7.         7            4            8
  8.         8            3           10
  9.         9            2            1
 10.        10            1            9
. mkmat x y z, matrix(xyzmat)
```

```
. matrix list xyzmat

xyzmat[10,3]
       x   y   z
  r1   1  10   2
  r2   2   9   4
  r3   3   8   3
  r4   4   7   5
  r5   5   6   7
  r6   6   5   6
  r7   7   4   8
  r8   8   3  10
  r9   9   2   1
 r10  10   1   9
```

If any of the variables have missing values, you will receive an error message and no matrices will be created.

```
. matrix drop _all

. replace y = . in 5
(1 real change made, 1 to missing)

. mkmat x y z
matrix y would have missing values
r(504);

. matrix dir

.
```

This problem can be taken care of by restricting the matrix to nonmissing values.

◁

❑ Technical Note

`mkmat` provides a useful addition to Stata's matrix commands, but it will work only with small datasets.

Stata limits matrices to being no more than matsize × matsize which, by default, means 40 × 40, and, even with Intercooled Stata, this can be increased to a maximum of 800 × 800. Such limits appear to contradict Stata's claims of being able to process large datasets. By limiting Stata's matrix capabilities to matsize × matsize, has not Stata's matrix language itself been limited to datasets no larger than matsize? It would certainly appear so; in the simple matrix calculation for regression coefficients $(\mathbf{X}'\mathbf{X})^{-1}\mathbf{X}'\mathbf{y}$, $\mathbf{X}$ is an $n \times k$ matrix (n being the number of observations and k the number of variables) and, given the matsize constraint, n must certainly be less than 800.

Our answer is as follows: Yes, $\mathbf{X}$ is limited in the way stated but note that $\mathbf{X}'\mathbf{X}$ is a mere $k \times k$ matrix and, similarly, $\mathbf{X}'\mathbf{y}$ only $k \times 1$. Both these matrices are well within Stata's matrix-handling capabilities and Stata's `matrix accum` command (see [P] **matrix accum**) can directly create both of them.

Moreover, even if Stata could hold the $n \times k$ matrix $\mathbf{X}$, it would still be more efficient to use `matrix accum` to form $\mathbf{X}'\mathbf{X}$. $\mathbf{X}'\mathbf{X}$, interpreted literally, says to load a copy of the dataset, transpose it, load a second copy of the dataset, and then form the matrix product. Thus, two copies of the dataset occupy memory in addition to the original copy Stata already had available (and from which `matrix accum` could directly form the result with no additional memory use). For small n, the inefficiency is not important but, for large n, the inefficiency could make the calculation infeasible. For instance, with $n = 12,000$ and $k = 6$, the additional memory use is 1,125K bytes.

More generally, matrices in statistical applications tend to have dimension $k \times k$, $n \times k$, and $n \times n$, with k small and n large. Terms dealing with the data are of the generic form $\mathbf{X}'_{k_1 \times n} \mathbf{W}_{n \times n} \mathbf{Z}_{n \times k_2}$. ($\mathbf{X}'\mathbf{X}$ fits the generic form with $\mathbf{X} = \mathbf{X}$, $\mathbf{W} = \mathbf{I}$, and $\mathbf{Z} = \mathbf{X}$.) Matrix programming languages are not capable of dealing with the deceivingly simple calculation $\mathbf{X}'\mathbf{W}\mathbf{Z}$ because of the staggering size of the $\mathbf{W}$ matrix. For $n = 12,000$, storing $\mathbf{W}$ requires a little more than a gigabyte of memory. In statistical formulas, however, $\mathbf{W}$ is given by formula and, in fact, never needs to be stored in its entirety. Exploitation of this fact is all that is needed to resurrect the use of a matrix programming language in statistical applications. Matrix programming languages may be inefficient because of copious memory use, but in statistical applications, the inefficiency is minor for matrices of size $k \times k$ or smaller. Our design of the various `matrix accum` commands allow calculating terms of the form $\mathbf{X}'\mathbf{W}\mathbf{Z}$, and this one feature is all that is necessary to allow efficient and robust use of matrix languages.

Programs for creating data matrices such as that offered by `mkmat` are useful for pedagogical purposes and for a specific application where Stata's matsize constraint is not binding, it seems so natural. On the other hand, it is important that general tools not be implemented by forming data matrices because such tools will be drastically limited in terms of the dataset size. Coding the problem in terms of the various `matrix accum` commands (see [P] **matrix accum**) is admittedly more tedious but, by abolishing data matrices from your programs, you will produce tools suitable for use on large datasets.

❏

svmat

▷ Example

Let us get the vector of coefficients from a regression and use `svmat` to save the vector as a new variable, save the dataset, load the dataset back into memory, use `mkmat` to create a vector from the variable, and finally, use `matname` to rename the columns of the row vector.

```
. quietly regress mpg weight gear_ratio foreign
. matrix b = e(b)
. matrix list b
b[1,4]
        weight  gear_ratio     foreign       _cons
y1  -.00613903   1.4571134  -2.2216815   36.101353
. matrix c = b´
. svmat double c, name(bvector)
. list bvector1 in 1/5
        bvector1
  1.  -.00613903
  2.   1.4571134
  3.  -2.2216815
  4.   36.101353
  5.           .
. save example
file example.dta saved
. use example
. mkmat bvector1 if bvector1~=.
```

```
. matrix list bvector1
bvector1[4,1]
       bvector1
r1  -.00613903
r2   1.4571134
r3  -2.2216815
r4   36.101353
. matrix d = bvector1´
. matname d wei gear for _cons, c(.)
. matrix list d
d[1,4]
              weight  gear_ratio      foreign       _cons
bvector1  -.00613903   1.4571134   -2.2216815   36.101353
```

◁

Methods and Formulas

mkmat, svmat, and matname are implemented as ado-files.

Acknowledgment

mkmat was written by Ken Heinecke of CIMCO, Madison, Wisconsin.

References

Gould, W. W. 1994. ip6.1: Data and matrices. *Stata Technical Bulletin* 20: 10. Reprinted in *Stata Technical Bulletin Reprints*, vol. 4, pp. 70–71.

Heinecke, K. 1994. ip6: Storing variables in vectors and matrices. *Stata Technical Bulletin* 20: 8–9. Reprinted in *Stata Technical Bulletin Reprints*, vol. 4, pp. 68–70.

Sribney, W. M. 1995. ip6.2: Storing matrices as variables. *Stata Technical Bulletin* 24: 9–10. Reprinted in *Stata Technical Bulletin Reprints*, vol. 4, pp. 71–73.

Also See

Related:	[P] **matrix accum**
Background:	[U] **17 Matrix expressions**,
	[P] **matrix**

Title

> **matrix rowname** — Name rows and columns

Syntax

matrix <u>rown</u>ames **A** = *name(s)*

matrix <u>coln</u>ames **A** = *name(s)*

matrix <u>rowe</u>q **A** = *name(s)*

matrix <u>cole</u>q **A** = *name(s)*

Description

matrix rownames and colnames reset the row and column names of an already existing matrix. Row and column names may have three parts: *equation_name:ts_operator.subname*. Here, *name* can be: *subname*, *ts_operator.subname*, *equation_name:*, *equation_name:subname*, or *equation_name:ts_operator.subname*.

matrix roweq and coleq also reset the row and column names of an already existing matrix but, if a simple name is specified (a name without a colon), it is interpreted as an equation name.

In either case, the part of the name not specified is left unchanged.

Remarks

See [U] **17.2 Row and column names** for a description of the row and column names bordering a matrix.

▷ Example

In general, the names bordering matrices are set correctly by Stata due to the tracking of the matrix algebra and you will not need to reset them. Nevertheless, imagine you have formed $\mathbf{X}'\mathbf{X}$ in the matrix named XX and that it corresponds to the underlying variables price, weight, and mpg:

```
. matrix list XX
symmetric XX[3,3]
           c1          c2          c3
r1   3.448e+09
r2   1.468e+09   7.188e+08
r3     9132716     4493720       36008
```

You did not form this matrix with matrix accum because, had you done so, the rows and columns would already be correctly named. However you formed it, you now want to reset the names:

```
. matrix rownames XX = price weight mpg
. matrix colnames XX = price weight mpg
. matrix list XX

symmetric XX[3,3]
              price      weight         mpg
 price   3.448e+09
weight   1.468e+09   7.188e+08
   mpg     9132716     4493720       36008
```
◁

▷ Example

We now demonstrate setting the equation names, time-series operator, and subnames.

```
. matrix list AA

symmetric AA[4,4]
             c1          c2          c3          c4
r1     .2967663
r2    .03682017   .57644416
r3   -.87052852   .32713601   20.274957
r4    -1.572579  -.63830843  -12.150097   26.099582
. matrix rownames AA = length L3D2.length mpg L.mpg
. matrix colnames AA = length L3D2.length mpg L.mpg
. matrix roweq AA = eq1 eq1 eq2 eq2
. matrix coleq AA = eq1 eq1 eq2 eq2
. matrix list AA

symmetric AA[4,4]
                       eq1:        eq1:        eq2:        eq2:
                                   L3D2.                   L.
                     length      length         mpg         mpg
    eq1:length     .2967663
eq1:L3D2.length    .03682017   .57644416
       eq2:mpg    -.87052852   .32713601   20.274957
     eq2:L.mpg     -1.572579  -.63830843  -12.150097   26.099582
```
◁

❑ Technical Note

`matrix rownames` and `colnames` sometimes behave in surprising ways. Among the surprises are

1. If your list of names includes no colons — does not mention the equation names — whatever equation names are in place are left in place; they are not changed.

2. If your list of names has every name ending in a colon — so that it mentions only the equation names and not the subnames — whatever subnames are in place are left in place; they are not changed.

3. If your list of names has fewer names than are required to label all the rows or columns, the last name in the list is replicated. (If you specify too many names, you will get the conformability error message and no names will be changed.)

These surprises have their uses but, if you make a mistake, the result really may surprise you. For instance, rule 3, by itself, is just odd. Combined with rule 2, however, rule 3 allows you to set all the equation names in a matrix easily. If you type 'matrix rownames XX = myeq:', all the equation names in the row are reset while the subnames are left unchanged:

```
. matrix rownames XX = myeq:

. matrix list XX

symmetric XX[3,3]
                    price        weight           mpg
  myeq:price   3.448e+09
 myeq:weight   1.468e+09    7.188e+08
   myeq:mpg      9132716      4493720        36008
```

Setting equation names is often done before forming a partitioned matrix so that, when the components are assembled, each has the correct equation name.

Thus, to review, to get the result above, we could have typed

```
. matrix rownames XX = myeq:price myeq:weight myeq:mpg
```

or

```
. matrix rownames XX = price weight mpg

. matrix rownames XX = myeq:
```

or even

```
. matrix rownames XX = myeq:

. matrix rownames XX = price weight mpg
```

All would have resulted in the same outcome. The real surprise comes, however, when you make a mistake:

```
. matrix rownames XX = myeq:

. matrix rownames XX = price weight

. matrix list XX

symmetric XX[3,3]
                    price        weight           mpg
  myeq:price   3.448e+09
 myeq:weight   1.468e+09    7.188e+08
 myeq:weight      9132716      4493720        36008
```

Our mistake above is that we listed only two names for the subnames of the rows of XX and **matrix rownames** then labeled both of the last rows with the subname **weight**.

❑

❑ Technical Note

The equation name _: by itself is special; it means the null equation name. For instance, as of the last technical note, we were left with

```
. matrix list XX

symmetric XX[3,3]
                    price        weight           mpg
  myeq:price   3.448e+09
 myeq:weight   1.468e+09    7.188e+08
 myeq:weight      9132716      4493720        36008
```

Let's fix it:

```
. matrix rownames XX = price weight mpg

. matrix rownames XX = _:

. matrix list XX
symmetric XX[3,3]
             price      weight         mpg
 price   3.448e+09
weight   1.468e+09   7.188e+08
   mpg     9132716     4493720       36008
```

❑

❑ Technical Note

matrix roweq and **coleq** are really the same commands as **matrix rownames** and **colnames**. They differ in only one respect: If a specified name does not contain a colon, **roweq** and **coleq** interpret that name as if it did end in a colon.

matrix rownames, colnames, roweq, and **coleq** are often used in conjunction with the **rowfullnames, colfullnames, rownames, colnames, roweq,** and **coleq** macro extended functions introduced in [P] **matrix define**. It is important to remember that the **rownames** and **colnames** extended macro functions return only the subname and, if present, the time-series operator:

```
. matrix list AA
symmetric AA[4,4]
                          eq1:          eq1:          eq2:          eq2:
                                        L3D2.                       L.
                        length        length           mpg           mpg
      eq1:length    .2967663
 eq1:L3D2.length    .03682017     .57644416
        eq2:mpg    -.87052852     .32713601     20.274957
      eq2:L.mpg     -1.572579    -.63830843    -12.150097     26.099582
. local rsubs : rownames AA

. display "The row subnames of AA are -- `rsubs´ --"
The row subnames of AA are -- length L3D2.length mpg L.mpg --
```

Similarly, the **roweq** extended macro function returns only the equation names without the trailing colon:

```
. local reqs : roweq AA

. display "The row equations of AA are -- `reqs´ --"
The row equations of AA are -- eq1 eq1 eq2 eq2 --
```

Thus, now consider the problem that you have two matrices named **A** and **B** which have the same number of rows. **A** is correctly labeled and includes equation names. You want to copy the names of **A** to **B**. You might be tempted to type

```
. local names : rownames A

. matrix rownames B = `names´
```

This is not adequate. You will have copied the subnames but not the equation names. To copy both parts of the names, you can type

```
. local subs : rownames A

. local eqs : roweq A

. matrix rownames B = `subs´

. matrix roweq B = `eqs´
```

This method can be used even when there might not be equation names. The equation name _ is special: not only does setting an equation to that name remove the equation name but, when there is no equation name, the `roweq` and `coleq` macro extended functions return that name.

A better way to copy the names is to use the `rowfullnames` and `colfullnames` extended macro functions (see [P] **matrix define** and [P] **macro**). You can more compactly type

```
. local rname : rowfullnames A
. matrix rownames B = `rname´
```

❑

Also See

Complementary: [P] **macro**, [P] **matrix define**

Background: [U] **17 Matrix expressions**,
                    [P] **matrix**

Title

> **matrix score** — Score data from coefficient vectors

Syntax

<u>ma</u>trix <u>sco</u>re [*type*] *newvar* = **b** [if *exp*] [in *range*] [, { eq(# #) | eq(*eqname*) }

<u>missval</u>(#) replace]

where **b** is a $1 \times p$ matrix.

Description

matrix score creates $newvar_j = \mathbf{x}_j \mathbf{b}'$ (**b** a row vector), where $\mathbf{x}_j$ is the row vector of values of the variables specified by the column names of **b**. The name _cons is treated as a variable equal to 1.

Options

eq(# #) or eq(*eqname*) specify the equation—by either number or name—for selecting coefficients from **b** to use in scoring. See [U] **17.2 Row and column names** and [P] **matrix rowname** for more on equation labels with matrices.

missval(#) specifies the value to be assumed if any values are missing from the variables referenced by the coefficient vector. By default, this value is taken to be missing (.) and any missing value among the variables produces a missing score.

replace specifies that *newvar* already exists. In this case, observations not included by if *exp* and in range are left unchanged; that is, they are not changed to missing. Be warned that replace does not promote the storage type of the existing variable; if the variable was stored as an int, the calculated scores would be truncated to integers when stored.

Remarks

Scoring refers to forming linear combinations of variables in the data with respect to a coefficient vector. For instance, consider the vector **coefs**:

```
. matrix list coefs
coefs[1,3]
         weight        mpg      _cons
y1    1.7465592  -49.512221  1946.0687
```

Scoring the data with this vector would create a new variable equal to the linear combination:

$$1.7465592\,\text{weight} - 49.512221\,\text{mpg} + 1946.0687$$

The vector is interpreted as coefficients; the corresponding names of the variables are obtained from the column names (row names if **coefs** were a column vector). To form this linear combination, we type

```
. matrix score lc = coefs
```

```
. summarize lc
    Variable |      Obs        Mean    Std. Dev.        Min        Max
------------+-----------------------------------------------------------
          lc |       74    6165.257    1597.606     3406.46   9805.269
```

If the coefficient vector has equation names, `matrix score` with the `eq()` option selects the appropriate coefficients for scoring. `eq(#1)` is assumed if no `eq()` option is specified.

```
. matrix list coefs
coefs[1,5]
          price:      price:      price:      displ:      displ:
         weight         mpg       _cons      weight       _cons
y1     1.7358275  -51.298249   2016.5101  .10574552  -121.99702
. matrix score lcnoeq = coefs
. matrix score lca = coefs , eq(price)
. matrix score lc1 = coefs , eq(#1)
. matrix score lcb = coefs , eq(displ)
. matrix score lc2 = coefs , eq(#2)
. summarize lcnoeq lca lc1 lcb lc2
    Variable |      Obs        Mean    Std. Dev.        Min        Max
------------+-----------------------------------------------------------
      lcnoeq |       74    6165.257    1598.264    3396.859   9802.336
         lca |       74    6165.257    1598.264    3396.859   9802.336
         lc1 |       74    6165.257    1598.264    3396.859   9802.336
         lcb |       74    197.2973    82.18474     64.1151   389.8113
         lc2 |       74    197.2973    82.18474     64.1151   389.8113
```

❏ Technical Note

If the same equation name is scattered in different sections of the coefficient vector, the results may not be what you expect.

```
. matrix list bad
bad[1,5]
          price:      price:      displ:      price:      displ:
         weight         mpg      weight       _cons       _cons
y1     1.7358275  -51.298249  .10574552   2016.5101  -121.99702
. matrix score badnoeq = bad
. matrix score bada = bad , eq(price)
. matrix score bad1 = bad , eq(#1)
. matrix score badb = bad , eq(displ)
. matrix score bad2 = bad , eq(#2)
. matrix score bad3 = bad , eq(#3)
. matrix score bad4 = bad , eq(#4)
. summarize bad*
    Variable |      Obs        Mean    Std. Dev.        Min        Max
------------+-----------------------------------------------------------
     badnoeq |       74    4148.747    1598.264    1380.349   7785.826
        bada |       74    4148.747    1598.264    1380.349   7785.826
        bad1 |       74    4148.747    1598.264    1380.349   7785.826
        badb |       74    319.2943    82.18474    186.1121   511.8083
        bad2 |       74    319.2943    82.18474    186.1121   511.8083
        bad3 |       74     2016.51           0     2016.51    2016.51
        bad4 |       74    -121.997           0    -121.997   -121.997
```

Coefficient vectors created by Stata estimation commands will have equation names together.

❏

Also See

Background: [U] **17 Matrix expressions,**
[P] **matrix**

Title

matrix svd — Singular value decomposition

Syntax

<u>matrix</u> <u>svd</u> **U** **w** **V** = **A**

where **U**, **w**, and **V** are matrix names (the matrices may exist or not) and **A** is the name of an existing $m \times n, m \geq n$ matrix.

Description

The **svd** matrix command produces the singular value decomposition (SVD) of **A**.

Remarks

The singular value decomposition of $m \times n$ matrix **A**, $m \geq n$, is defined as

$$\mathbf{A} = \mathbf{U} \operatorname{diag}(\mathbf{w}) \mathbf{V}'$$

U: $m \times n$, **w**: $1 \times n$ (diag(**w**): $n \times n$), and **V**: $n \times n$, where **U** is column orthogonal ($\mathbf{U}'\mathbf{U} = \mathbf{I}$ if $m = n$), all the elements of **w** are positive or zero, and $\mathbf{V}'\mathbf{V} = \mathbf{I}$.

Singular value decomposition can be used to obtain a g2-inverse of **A** ($\mathbf{A}^*$: $n \times m$, such that $\mathbf{A}\mathbf{A}^*\mathbf{A} = \mathbf{A}$ and $\mathbf{A}^*\mathbf{A}\mathbf{A}^* = \mathbf{A}^*$—the first two Moore–Penrose conditions) via $\mathbf{A}^* = \mathbf{V}\{\operatorname{diag}(1/w_j)\}\mathbf{U}'$, where $1/w_j$ refers to individually taking the reciprocal of the elements of **w** and substituting 0 if $w_j = 0$ or is small. If **A** is square and of full rank, $\mathbf{A}^* = \mathbf{A}^{-1}$.

▷ Example

Singular value decomposition is used to obtain accurate inverses of nearly singular matrices and to obtain g2-inverses of matrices which are singular, to construct orthonormal bases, and to develop approximation matrices. Our example will prove that **matrix svd** works:

```
. matrix A = (1,2,9\2,7,5\2,4,18)
. matrix svd U w V = A
. matrix list U
U[3,3]
           c1          c2          c3
r1   -.42313293    .89442719    -.1447706
r2    -.3237169   -6.016e-17    .94615399
r3   -.84626585   -.4472136    -.2895412
. matrix list w
w[1,3]
           c1          c2          c3
r1   21.832726   2.612e-16   5.5975071
```

```
. matrix list V

V[3,3]
             c1          c2          c3
c1  -.12655765  -.96974658     .2087456
c2  -.29759672   .23786237    .92458514
c3  -.94626601   .05489132   -.31869671

. matrix newA = U*diag(w)*V´

. matrix list newA

newA[3,3]
    c1  c2  c3
r1   1   2   9
r2   2   7   5
r3   2   4  18
```

As claimed, **newA** is equal to our original **A**.

The g2-inverse of **A** is computed below. The second element of **w** is small, so we decide to set the corresponding element of $\text{diag}(1/w_j)$ to zero. We then show that the resulting **Ainv** matrix has the properties of a g2-inverse for **A**.

```
. matrix Winv = J(3,3,0)

. matrix Winv[1,1] = 1/w[1,1]

. matrix Winv[3,3] = 1/w[1,3]

. matrix Ainv = V*Winv*U´

. matrix list Ainv

Ainv[3,3]
             r1          r2          r3
c1   -.0029461   .03716103   -.0058922
c2   -.0181453   .16069635  -.03629059
c3   .02658185   -.0398393    .05316371

. matrix AAiA = A*Ainv*A

. matrix list AAiA

AAiA[3,3]
    c1  c2  c3
r1   1   2   9
r2   2   7   5
r3   2   4  18

. matrix AiAAi = Ainv*A*Ainv

. matrix list AiAAi

AiAAi[3,3]
             r1          r2          r3
c1   -.0029461   .03716103   -.0058922
c2   -.0181453   .16069635  -.03629059
c3   .02658185   -.0398393    .05316371
```

◁

Also See

Complementary: [P] **matrix define**

Background: [U] **17 Matrix expressions**,
                    [P] **matrix**

Title

> **matrix symeigen** — Eigenvalues and vectors of symmetric matrices

Syntax

matrix symeigen X v = A

Description

Given an $n \times n$ symmetric matrix $\mathbf{A}$, matrix symeigen returns the eigenvectors in the columns of $\mathbf{X}$: $n \times n$ and the corresponding eigenvalues in $\mathbf{v}$: $1 \times n$. The eigenvalues are sorted; $\mathbf{v}[1,1]$ contains the largest eigenvalue (and $\mathbf{X}[1\ldots,1]$ its corresponding eigenvector) and $\mathbf{v}[1,n]$ contains the smallest eigenvalue (and $\mathbf{X}[1\ldots,n]$ its corresponding eigenvector).

Remarks

Typing matrix symeigen X v = A for $\mathbf{A}$ $n \times n$ returns

$$\mathbf{v} = \left(\lambda_1, \lambda_2, \ldots, \lambda_n\right)$$
$$\mathbf{X} = \left(\mathbf{x}_1, \mathbf{x}_2, \ldots, \mathbf{x}_n\right)$$

where $\lambda_1 \geq \lambda_2 \geq \ldots \geq \lambda_n$. Each $\mathbf{x}_i$ and λ_i is a solution to

$$\mathbf{A}\mathbf{x}_i = \lambda_i \mathbf{x}_i$$

or, more compactly,

$$\mathbf{A}\mathbf{X} = \mathbf{X}\operatorname{diag}(\mathbf{v})$$

▷ Example

Eigenvalues and eigenvectors have many uses. We will demonstrate that symeigen returns matrices meeting the definition:

```
. matrix list A
symmetric A[3,3]
             weight        mpg       length
weight     44094178
   mpg   -264948.11   2443.4595
length   1195077.3   -7483.5135   36192.662
. matrix symeigen X lambda = A
. matrix list lambda
lambda[1,3]
          e1          e2          e3
r1   44128163   3830.4869   820.73955
. matrix list X
X[3,3]
              e1          e2          e3
weight   .99961482   -.02756261   .00324179
   mpg  -.00600667    -.1008305   .99488549
length   .02709477    .99452175   .10095722
```

193

```
. matrix AX = A*X

. matrix XLambda = X*diag(lambda)

. matrix list AX

AX[3,3]
                 e1            e2            e3
weight     44111166    -105.57823     2.6606641
   mpg    -265063.5    -386.22991     816.54187
length    1195642.6     3809.5025     82.859585

. matrix list XLambda

XLambda[3,3]
                 e1            e2            e3
weight     44111166    -105.57823     2.6606641
   mpg    -265063.5    -386.22991     816.54187
length    1195642.6     3809.5025     82.859585
```

◁

Methods and Formulas

Stata's internal eigenvalue and eigenvector extraction routines are translations of the public domain EISPACK routines, Smith et al. (1976), which are in turn based on Wilkinson and Reinsch (1971). EISPACK was developed under contract for the Office of Scientific and Technical Information, U.S. Department of Energy, by Argonne National Laboratory and supported by funds provided by the Nuclear Regulatory Commission. Stata's use of these routines is by permission of the National Energy Software Center of the Argonne National Laboratory. A brief but excellent introduction to the techniques employed by these routines can be found in Press et al. (1992, 456–495).

References

Press, W. H., S. A. Teukolsky, W. T. Vetterling, and B. P. Flannery. 1992. *Numerical Recipes in C: The Art of Scientific Computing*. 2d ed. Cambridge University Press.

Smith, B. T., et al. 1976. *Matrix Eigen System Routines—EISPACK Guide*. 2d ed. vol. 6 of Lecture Notes in Computer Science. New York: Springer-Verlag.

Wilkinson, J. H. and C. Reinsch. 1971. *Linear Algebra*, vol. 2 of *Handbook for Automatic Computation*. New York: Springer-Verlag.

Also See

Background: [U] **17 Matrix expressions**,
                    [P] **matrix**

Title

> **matrix utility** — List, rename, and drop matrices

Syntax

<u>mat</u>rix <u>d</u>ir

<u>mat</u>rix <u>l</u>ist *mname* $\left[\right.$, <u>nobl</u>ank <u>noh</u>alf <u>noh</u>eader <u>non</u>ames <u>f</u>ormat(%*fmt*) <u>t</u>itle(*string*) $\left.\right]$

<u>mat</u>rix <u>ren</u>ame *oldname newname*

<u>mat</u>rix drop $\left\{\right.$ _all $\mid$ *mname(s)* $\left.\right\}$

Description

matrix dir lists the names of currently existing matrices. **matrix list** lists the contents of a matrix. **matrix rename** changes the name of a matrix. **matrix drop** eliminates a matrix.

Options

noblank suppresses printing a blank line before printing the matrix. This is useful in programs.

nohalf specifies that, even if the matrix is symmetric, the full matrix is to be printed. The default is to print only the lower triangle in such cases.

noheader suppresses the display of the matrix name and dimension before the matrix itself. This is useful in programs.

nonames suppresses the display of the bordering names around the matrix.

format(%*fmt*) specifies the format to be used to display the individual elements of the matrix. The default is **format(%10.0g)**.

title(*string*) adds the specified title *string* to the header displayed before the matrix itself. If **noheader** is specified, **title()** does nothing because displaying the header is suppressed.

Remarks

▷ Example

Little needs to be said by way of introduction. In the example below, however, note that **matrix list** normally displays only the lower half of symmetric matrices. **nohalf** prevents this.

```
. matrix dir
            a[2,2]
            b[3,3]
. matrix rename a z
. matrix dir
            z[2,2]
            b[3,3]
```

```
. matrix list b

symmetric b[3,3]
      c1   c2   c3
r1    2
r2    5    8
r3    4    6    3
. matrix list b, nohalf

symmetric b[3,3]
      c1   c2   c3
r1    2    5    4
r2    5    8    6
r3    4    6    3
. matrix drop b

. matrix dir
            z[2,2]
. matrix drop _all

. matrix dir
```

◁

❏ Technical Note

When writing programs and using matrix names obtained through `tempname` (see [P] **macro**), it is not necessary to explicitly drop matrices; the matrices are removed automatically at the conclusion of the program.

```
. program define example
  1.            tempname a
  2.            matrix `a´ = (1,2\3,4)                /* this is temporary  */
  3.            matrix b = (5,6\7,8)                  /* and this permanent */
  4.            display "The temporary matrix a contains"
  5.            matrix list `a´, noheader
  6. end
. example
The temporary matrix a contains
      c1   c2
r1    1    2
r2    3    4
. matrix dir
            b[2,2]
```

Nevertheless, dropping matrices with temporary names in programs when they are no longer needed is recommended unless the program is about to exit (when they will be dropped anyway). Matrices consume memory; dropping them frees memory.

❏

Also See

Background: [U] **17 Matrix expressions**,
                     [P] **matrix**

Title

> **more** — Pause until key is pressed

Syntax

> more

Description

> more causes Stata to display —more— and pause until any key is pressed if more is set on and does nothing if more is set off; see [R] **more** for information on set more on and set more off.

Remarks

> Ado-file programmers need take no special action to have —more— conditions arise when the screen is full. Stata handles that automatically.

> If, however, you wish to force a —more— condition early, you can include the more command in your program. The syntax of more is

> more

> more takes no arguments.

Also See

> **Complementary:**   [R] **query**
>
> **Background:**   [U] **10 —more— conditions**

Title

> **numlist** — Parse numeric lists

Syntax

> numlist "*numlist*" $\left[\right.$, <u>asc</u>ending <u>desc</u>ending <u>int</u>eger <u>miss</u>ingokay min(#) max(#)
>
> <u>r</u>ange(*operator#* $\left[\text{operator#}\right]$) sort $\left.\right]$

where *operator* is   { < | <= | > | >= };

there is no space between *operator* and #;

and where *numlist* consists of one or more *numlist_elements* shown below.

numlist_element	Example	Expands to	Definition
#	3.82	3.82	a number
.	.	.	a missing value
$\#_1/\#_2$	4/6 2.3/5.7	4 5 6 2.3 3.3 4.3 5.3	starting at $\#_1$ increment by 1 to $\#_2$
$\#_1(\#_2)\#_3$	2(3)10 4.8(2.1)9.9	2 5 8 4.8 6.9 9	starting at $\#_1$ increment by $\#_2$ to $\#_3$
$\#_1[\#_2]\#_3$	2[3]10 4.8[2.1]9.9	2 5 8 4.8 6.9 9	starting at $\#_1$ increment by $\#_2$ to $\#_3$
$\#_1\ \#_2:\#_3$	5 7:13 1.1 2.4:5.8	5 7 9 11 13 1.1 2.4 3.7 5	starting at $\#_1$ increment by $(\#_2 - \#_1)$ to $\#_3$
$\#_1\ \#_2$ to $\#_3$	5 7 to 13 1.1 2.4 to 5.8	same	same

Description

The `numlist` command expands the numeric list supplied as a string argument and performs error checking based on the options specified. Any numeric sequence operators in the *numlist* string are evaluated and the expanded list of numbers is returned in `r(numlist)`. See [U] **14.1.8 numlist** for a discussion of numeric lists.

Options

ascending indicates that the user must give the numeric list in ascending order without repeated values. This is different from the sort option.

descending indicates that the numeric list must be given in descending order without repeated values.

integer specifies that the user may only give integer values in the numeric list.

missingokay indicates that missing values are allowed in the numeric list. By default, missing values are not allowed.

min(#) specifies the minimum number of elements allowed in the numeric list. The default is min(1). If you want to allow empty numeric lists, specify min(0).

max(#) specifies the maximum number of elements allowed in the numeric list. The default is max(1600), which is the largest allowed maximum.

range(*operator #* [*operator #*]) specifies the acceptable range for the values in the numeric list. The *operator*s are: < (less than), <= (less than or equal to), > (greater than), and >= (greater than or equal to). No space is allowed between the *operator* and the *#*.

sort specifies that the returned numeric list is to be sorted. This is different from the ascending option. ascending places the responsibility for providing a sorted list on the user who will not be allowed to enter a nonsorted list. sort, on the other hand, puts no restriction on the user and will take care of sorting the list. Repeated values are also allowed with sort.

Remarks

Programmers rarely use the numlist command because syntax will also expand numeric lists and it will handle the rest of the parsing problem, too, at least if the command being parsed follows standard syntax. numlist is used for expanding numeric lists when what is being parsed does not follow standard syntax.

▷ Example

We demonstrate the numlist command interactively.

```
. numlist "5.3 1.0234 3 6:18 -2.0033 5.3/7.3"
. display "`r(numlist)'"
5.3 1.0234 3 6 9 12 15 18 -2.0033 5.3 6.3 7.3

. numlist "5.3 1.0234 3 6:18 -2.0033 5.3/7.3", integer
invalid numlist has noninteger elements
r(126);

. numlist "1 5 8/12 15", integer descending
invalid numlist has elements out of order
r(124);

. numlist "1 5 8/12 15", integer ascending
. display "`r(numlist)'"
1 5 8 9 10 11 12 15
```

```
. numlist "100 1 5 8/12 15", integer ascending
invalid numlist has elements out of order
r(124);
. numlist "100 1 5 8/12 15", integer sort
. display "`r(numlist)'"
1 5 8 9 10 11 12 15 100
. numlist "3 5 . 28 -3(2)5"
invalid numlist has missing values
r(127);
. numlist "3 5 . 28 -3(2)5", missingokay min(3) max(25)
. display "`r(numlist)'"
3 5 . 28 -3 -1 1 3 5
. numlist "28 36", min(3) max(6)
invalid numlist has too few elements
r(122);
. numlist "28 36 -3 5 2.8 7 32 -8", min(3) max(6)
invalid numlist has too many elements
r(123);
. numlist "3/6 -4 -1 to 5", range(>=1)
invalid numlist has elements outside of allowed range
r(125);
. numlist "3/6", range(>=0 <30)
. display "`r(numlist)'"
3 4 5 6
```

◁

Saved Results

numlist saves in r():

Macros
    r(numlist)   the expanded numeric list

Also See

Related: [P] **syntax**

Background: [U] **14.1.8 numlist**

Title

pause — Program debugging command

Syntax

pause { on | off | [*message*] }

Description

If pause is on, 'pause [*message*]' command displays *message* and temporarily suspends execution of the program, returning control to the keyboard. Execution of keyboard commands continues until you type **end** or **q**, at which time execution of the program resumes. Typing BREAK in pause mode (as opposed to pressing the *Break* key) also resumes program execution, but the break signal is sent to the calling program.

If pause is off, pause does nothing.

Pause is off by default. Type **pause on** to turn pause on. Type **pause off** to turn it back off.

Remarks

pause assists in debugging Stata programs. The line pause or 'pause *message*' is placed in the program where problems are suspected (more than one pause may be placed in a program). For instance, you have a program that is not working properly. A piece of this program reads

```
gen `tmp´=exp(`1´)/`2´
summarize `tmp´
local mean=r(mean)
```

You think the error may be in the creation of `tmp´. You change the program to read:

```
gen `tmp´=exp(`1´)/`2´
pause Just created tmp          /* this line is new */
summarize `tmp´
local mean=r(mean)
```

Let's pretend your program is named **myprog**; interactively, you now type

```
. myprog
( output from your program appears )
```

That is, **pause** does nothing because pause is off, so **pause**s in your program are ignored. If you turn pause on,

```
. pause on
. myprog
( any output myprog creates up to the pause appears )
pause:  Just created tmp
-> . describe
  (output omitted )
-> . list
  (output omitted )
-> . end
execution resumes...
( remaining output from myprog appears)
```

The "->" is called the pause-mode prompt. You can give any Stata command. You can examine variables and, if you wish, even change them. If while in pause mode, you wish to terminate execution of your program, you type BREAK (in capitals):

```
. myprog
( any output myprog creates up to the pause appears )
pause:  Just created tmp
-> . list
  (output omitted )
-> . BREAK
sending Break to calling program...
--Break--
r(1);

. _
```

The results are the same as if you pressed *Break* while your program were executing. If you press the *Break* key in pause mode (as opposed to typing BREAK), however, it means only that the execution of the command you have just given interactively is to be interrupted.

Notes:

1. You may put many **pause**s in your programs.

2. By default, pause is off, so the **pause**s will not do anything. Even so, you should remove the pauses after your program is debugged because each execution of a do-nothing **pause** will slow your program slightly.

3. **pause** is implemented as an ado-file; this means the definitions of local macros in your program are unavailable to you. To see the value of local macros, display them in the **pause** message; for instance,

```
        pause Just created tmp, i=`i´
```

Then, when the line is executed, you will see something like

```
    pause:  Just created tmp, i=1
    -> . _
```

4. Remember, temporary variables (e.g., **tempvar tmp** ... **gen** `tmp´=...) are assigned real names such as __00424 by Stata; see [P] **macro**. Thus, in pause mode you want to examine __00424 and not **tmp**. Generally, you can determine the real name of your temporary variables from **describe**'s output, but in the example above, it would be better had **pause** been invoked with

```
        pause Just created tmp, called `tmp´, i=`i´
```

Then, when the line is executed, you will see something like

```
    pause:  Just created tmp, called __00424, i=1
    -> . _
```

5. When giving commands that include double quotes, you may occasionally see the error message "type mismatch", but then the command will work properly:

```
    pause:  Just created tmp, called __00424, i=1
    -> . list if __00424=="male"
    type mismatch
    ( output from request appears as if nothing is wrong)
    -> . _
```

Methods and Formulas

pause is implemented as an ado-file.

References

Becketti, S. 1993. ip4: Program debugging command. *Stata Technical Bulletin* 13: 13–14. Reprinted in *Stata Technical Bulletin Reprints*, vol. 3, pp. 57–58.

Also See

Complementary:	[P] **program**
Related:	[P] **more**
Background:	[U] **21 Programming Stata**

Title

> **postfile** — Save results in Stata dataset

Syntax

> **postfile** *postname varlist* **using** *filename* [, **d**ouble **e**very(*#*) **replace**]
>
> **post** *postname* (*exp*) (*exp*) ... (*exp*)
>
> **postclose** *postname*

Description

These commands are utilities to assist Stata programmers in performing Monte Carlo-type experiments. **postfile** declares the variable names and the filename of a (new) Stata dataset where results will be stored. **post** adds a new observation to the declared dataset. **postclose** declares an end to the posting of observations. All three commands manipulate the new dataset without disturbing the data in memory. After **postclose**, the new dataset contains the posted results and may be loaded with **use**; see [R] **save**.

filename, if specified without a suffix, is taken to mean *filename*.**dta**.

Options

double specifies that the results collected are to be stored as Stata **double**s, meaning 8-byte reals. If **double** is not specified, results are stored as Stata **float**s, meaning 4-byte reals.

every(*#*) specifies results are to be written to disk every *#*th call to **post**. **post** temporarily holds results in memory and periodically opens the Stata dataset being built to append the stored results. **every()** should typically not be specified as you are unlikely to choose a value for *#* that is as efficient as the number **post** chooses on its own, which is a function of the number of results being written and their storage type.

replace indicates that the file specified may already exist and, if it does, **postfile** may erase the file and create a new one.

Remarks

The typical use of the post commands is

```
tempname memhold
tempfile results
...
postfile `memhold´ ... using "`results´"
...
while ... {
        ...
        post `memhold´ ...
        ...
}
postclose `memhold´
...
use "`results´", clear
...
```

Two names are specified with `postfile`, *postname* and *filename*. *postname* is a name assigned to internal memory buffers and *filename* is the name of the file to be created. Subsequent `post`s and the `postclose` are followed by *postname* so Stata will know to what file they refer.

In our sample, we obtain both names from Stata's temporary name facility (see [P] **macro**) although, in some programming situations, you may wish to substitute a hard-coded *filename*. We recommend that *postname* always be obtained from `tempname`. This ensures that your program can be nested within any other program and ensures that the memory used by `post` is freed if anything goes wrong. Using a temporary filename, too, ensures that the file will be erased if the user presses *Break*. In some cases, however, you may wish to leave the file of incomplete results behind. That is okay, but remember that the file is not fully up to date if `postclose` has not been executed. `post` buffers results in memory and only periodically updates the file.

▷ Example

We wish to write a program to collect means and variances from 10,000 randomly constructed 100-observation samples of lognormal data and store the results in `results.dta`. Suppose we are evaluating the coverage of the 95%, *t*-based confidence interval when applied to lognormal data. As background, we can obtain a single 100-observation lognormal sample by typing

```
drop _all
set obs 100
gen z = exp(invnorm(uniform()))
```

We can obtain the mean and standard deviation by then typing

```
summarize z
```

Moreover, `summarize` stores the sample mean in `r(mean)` and variance in `r(Var)`. It is those two values we wish to collect. Our program is

```
program define lnsim
        version 7.0
        tempname sim
        postfile `sim' mean var using results, replace
        quietly {
                forvalues i = 1/10000 {
                        drop _all
                        set obs 100
                        gen z = exp(invnorm(uniform()))
                        summarize z
                        post `sim' (r(mean)) (r(Var))
                }
        }
        postclose `sim'
end
```

The command `postfile` begins the accumulation of results. `sim` is the name assigned to the internal memory buffers where results will be held; `mean` and `var` are the names to be given to the two variables which will contain the information we collect; and variables will be stored in the file named `results.dta`. Since two variable names were specified on the `postfile`, two expressions must be specified following the `post`. In this case, the expressions are simply `r(mean)` and `r(Var)`. Had we wanted, however, to save the mean divided by the standard deviation and the standard deviation, we could have typed

```
post `sim' (r(mean)/sqrt(r(Var))) (sqrt(r(Var)))
```

Finally, `postclose` `sim` concluded the simulation. The dataset `results.dta` is now complete.

```
. lnsim
. use results, clear
. describe
Contains data from results.dta
  obs:         10,000
  vars:             2                        23 Sep 2000 12:59
  size:       120,000 (88.4% of memory free)
```

variable name	storage type	display format	value label	variable label
mean	float	%9.0g		
var	float	%9.0g		

```
Sorted by:
. summarize
```

Variable	Obs	Mean	Std. Dev.	Min	Max
mean	10000	1.649879	.216586	1.069133	2.896868
var	10000	4.689451	4.458131	.7389911	106.0029

◁

References

Gould, W. 1994. ssi6: Routines to speed Monte Carlo experiments. *Stata Technical Bulletin* 20: 18–22. Reprinted in *Stata Technical Bulletin Reprints*, vol. 4, pp. 202–207.

Also See

Related: [R] **bstrap**, [R] **simul**

Title

> **_predict** — Obtain predictions, residuals, etc., after estimation programming command

Syntax

After `regress`

>   _predict [*type*] *newvarname* [if *exp*] [in *range*] [, xb stdp stdf
>
>   stdr hat cooksd residuals rstandard rstudent
>
>   nooffset nolabel]

After single-equation (SE) *estimators*

>   _predict [*type*] *newvarname* [if *exp*] [in *range*] [, xb stdp
>
>   nooffset nolabel]

After multiple-equation (ME) *estimators*

>   _predict [*type*] *newvarname* [if *exp*] [in *range*] [, xb stdp stddp
>
>   nooffset nolabel equation(*eqno*[, *eqno*])]

If no prediction options are specified, the following are calculated:

after `logit`	probability of a positive outcome
after `probit`	probability of a positive outcome
after `mlogit`	probability of a positive outcome
after `cox`	relative hazard
after `cox, tvc()`	log relative hazard (linear prediction)
after other commands	linear prediction

Description

_predict is for use by programmers as a subroutine for implementing the predict command for use after estimation; see [R] **predict**.

Options

xb calculates the linear prediction from the estimated model. That is, all models can be thought of as estimating a set of parameters $b_1, b_2, \ldots, b_k$, and the linear prediction is $\widehat{y}_j = b_1 x_{1j} + b_2 x_{2j} + \cdots + b_k x_{kj}$, often written in matrix notation as $\widehat{\mathbf{y}}_j = \mathbf{x}_j \mathbf{b}$. In the case of linear regression, the values $\widehat{y}_j$ are called the predicted values or, for out-of-sample predictions, the forecast. In the case of logit and probit, for example, $\widehat{y}_j$ is called the logit or probit index.

It is important to understand that the x_{1j}, x_{2j}, ..., x_{kj} used in the calculation are obtained from the data currently in memory and do not have to correspond to the data on the independent variables used in estimating the model (obtaining the b_1, b_2, ..., b_k).

stdp calculates the standard error of the prediction after any estimation command. Here, the prediction is understood to mean the same thing as the "index", namely $\mathbf{x}_j\mathbf{b}$. The statistic produced by stdp can be thought of as the standard error of the predicted expected value, or mean index, for the observation's covariate pattern. This is also commonly referred to as the standard error of the fitted value.

stdf calculates the standard error of the forecast. This is the standard error of the point prediction for a single observation. It is commonly referred to as the standard error of the future or forecast value. By construction, the standard errors produced by stdf are always larger than those by stdp; see *Methods and Formulas* in [R] **predict**.

stdr calculates the standard error of the residuals.

stddp is allowed only after you have previously estimated a multiple-equation model. The standard error of the difference in linear predictions $(\mathbf{x}_{1j}\mathbf{b} - \mathbf{x}_{2j}\mathbf{b})$ between equations 1 and 2 is calculated.

hat or leverage calculates the diagonal elements of the projection hat matrix.

cooksd calculates the Cook's D influence statistic (Cook 1977).

residuals calculates the residuals.

rstandard calculates the standardized residuals.

rstudent calculates the studentized (jackknifed) residuals.

nooffset may be combined with most statistics and specifies that the calculation should be made ignoring any offset or exposure variable specified when the model was estimated.

This option is available, even if not documented, for **predict** after a specific command. If neither the offset(*varname*) option nor the exposure(*varname*) option was specified when the model was estimated, specifying nooffset does nothing.

nolabel prevents _predict from labeling the newly created variable.

equation(*eqno*[,*eqno*]) is relevant only when you have previously estimated a multiple-equation model. It specifies to which equation you are referring.

equation() is typically filled in with one *eqno*—it would be filled in that way with options xb and stdp, for instance. equation(#1) would mean the calculation is to be made for the first equation, equation(#2) would mean the second, and so on. Alternatively, you could refer to the equations by their names. equation(income) would refer to the equation named income and equation(hours) to the equation named hours.

If you do not specify equation(), the results are as if you specified equation(#1).

Other statistics refer to between-equation concepts; stddp is an example. In those cases, you might specify equation(#1,#2) or equation(income,hours). When two equations must be specified, equation() is not optional.

Methods and Formulas

See *Methods and Formulas* in [R] **predict** and [R] **regress**.

References

Cook, R. D. 1977. Detection of influential observations in linear regression. *Technometrics* 19: 15–18.

Also See

Related: [R] **predict**

Background: [U] **23 Estimation and post-estimation commands**

Title

preserve — Preserve and restore data

Syntax

preserve [, <u>ch</u>anged]

restore [, not <u>pre</u>serve]

Description

preserve preserves the data, guaranteeing a restore on program termination.

restore forces a restore of the data now.

Options

changed instructs preserve to preserve only the data-has-changed-since-last-save flag. Use of this option is strongly discouraged, as explained below.

not instructs restore to cancel the previous preserve.

preserve instructs restore to restore the data now but not to cancel the restoration of the data again at program conclusion. If preserve is not specified, the scheduled restoration at program conclusion is canceled.

Remarks

preserve and restore deal with the programming problem where the user's data must be changed in order to achieve the desired result but, when the program concludes, the programmer wishes to undo the damage done to the data. When preserve is issued, the user's data are preserved. The data in memory remain unchanged. When the program or do-file concludes, the user's data are automatically restored.

Alternatively, after a preserve, the programmer can instruct Stata to restore the data now with the restore command. This is useful when the programmer needs the original data back and knows no more damage will be done to it. restore, preserve can be used when the programmer needs the data back but plans further damage. restore, not can be used when the programmer wishes to cancel the previous preserve and have the data currently in memory returned to the user.

▷ Example

In most cases, preserve is used by itself and is used early in the program. You are writing a program to report some statistic, but the statistic cannot be calculated without changing the user's data. Here, changing does not mean merely adding a variable or two; that could be done with temporary variables as described in [P] **macro**. Changing means that the data really must be changed: observations might be discarded, the contents of existing variables changed, and the like. Although the programmer could just ignore the destruction of the user's data, the programmer might actually want to use the program herself and knows she will become exceedingly irritated when she uses it without remembering to first save her data. In other words, the programmer wishes to write a programmingly correct, or PC, command. It is not difficult:

210

```
program define myprog
        ( code for interpreting — parsing — the user's request )
        preserve
        ( code that destroys the data )
        ( code that makes the calculation )
        ( code that reports the result )
end
```

To preserve the data, `preserve` must make a copy of it on disk. Therefore, our programmer smartly performs all the parsing and setup, where errors are likely, before the `preserve`. Once she gets to the point in the code where the damage must be done, however, she preserves the data. After that, she forgets the problem. Stata will handle restoring the user's data even if the user presses *Break* in the middle of the program.

◁

▷ Example

Now let's consider a program that must destroy the user's data but needs it back again and, once it is recovered, will do no more damage. The outline is

```
program define myprog
        ( code for interpreting — parsing — the user's request )
        preserve
        ( code that destroys the data )
        ( code that makes the first part of the calculation )
        restore
        ( code that makes the second part of the calculation )
        ( code that reports the result )
end
```

While there are other ways the programmer could have arranged to save the data and get it back (`save` and `use` with temporary files as described in [P] **macro** comes to mind), this method is better because, should the user press *Break* after the data are damaged but before the data are restored, Stata will handle restoring the data.

◁

▷ Example

This time the program must destroy the user's data, bring the data back and destroy the data again, and finally report its calculation. The outline is

```
program define myprog
        ( code for interpreting — parsing — the user's request )
        preserve
        ( code that destroys the data )
        ( code that makes the first part of the calculation )
        restore, preserve
        ( code that makes the second part of the calculation )
        ( code that reports the result )
end
```

Alternatively, the programmer could have coded a `restore` on one line and a `preserve` on the next. It would have the same result but would be inefficient, since Stata would then rewrite the data to disk. `restore, preserve` tells Stata to reload the data but to leave the copy on disk for ultimate restoration.

◁

▷ Example

You are writing a program that intends to change the user's data in memory—the damage you are about to do is not damage at all. Nevertheless, were the user to press *Break* while you are in the midst of your machinations, what would be left in memory would be useless. The programmingly correct outline is

```
program define myprog
        ( code for interpreting—parsing—the user's request )
        preserve
        ( code that reforms the data )
        restore, not
end
```

Before undertaking the reformation, the programmer smartly preserves the data. Then, when everything is complete, the programmer cancels the restoration by saying `restore, not`.

◁

❑ Technical Note

`preserve, changed` is best avoided, although it is very fast. `preserve, changed` does not preserve the data: it merely records whether the data have changed since the data were last saved (as mentioned by `describe` and as checked by `exit` and `use` when the user does not also say `clear`), and restores the flag at the conclusion of the program. It is the programmer's responsibility to ensure that the data really have not changed.

As long as your programs use temporary variables as created by `tempvar` (see [P] **macro**), the changed-since-last-saved flag would not be changed anyway—Stata is able to track such temporary changes to the data that it will, itself, be able to undo. In fact, we cannot think of a single use for `preserve, changed`, and included it only to preserve the happiness of our more imaginative users.

❑

Also See

Background: [P] **macro**

Title

> **program** — Define and manipulate programs

Syntax

<u>program</u> <u>def</u>ine *program_name* $\big[$, $\big[$ nclass | rclass | eclass | sclass $\big]$

<u>by</u>able({ <u>rec</u>all $\big[$,<u>noh</u>eader $\big]$ | <u>one</u>call })

<u>sort</u>preserve $\big]$

<u>program</u> <u>dir</u>

<u>program</u> drop { *program_name* $\big[$ *program_name* $\big[$ ... $\big]$ $\big]$ | _all }

<u>program</u> <u>list</u> $\big[$ *program_name* $\big[$ *program_name* $\big[$ ... $\big]$ $\big]$ | _all $\big]$

<u>set</u> <u>trace</u> { on | off }

Description

program defines and manipulates programs.

set trace on traces the execution of programs for debugging. set trace off turns off tracing after it has been set on.

See [U] **21 Programming Stata** for a complete description of programs. The remarks below address only the use of the program dir, program drop, and program list commands along with set trace. The table of *Useful commands for programmers* repeats the quick reference information given in [U] **21.12 A compendium of useful commands for programmers**.

Options

nclass states that the program being defined does not return results in r(), e(), or s() and is the default.

rclass states that the program being defined returns results in r(). This is done using the return command; see [P] **return**. If the program is not explicitly declared to be rclass, then it may not change or replace results in r().

eclass states that the program being defined returns results in e() or modifies already existing results in e(). This is done using the estimates command, but still see [P] **return** because that is where it is documented. If the program is not explicitly declared to be eclass, then it may not replace or change results in e().

sclass states that the program being defined returns results in s(). This is done using the sreturn command; see [P] **return**. If the program is not explicitly declared to be sclass, then it may not change or replace results in s(), but it still may clear s() using 'sreturn clear'; see [P] **return**.

byable() states that the program is to allow Stata's by *varlist*: prefix. There are two styles for writing byable programs: byable(recall) and byable(onecall). The writing of byable programs is discussed in [P] **byable**; see [P] **byable** for a discussion of this important option.

`sortpreserve` states that the program will change the sort order of the data and that Stata is to restore the original sort order of the data upon the program's conclusion. See [P] **sortpreserve** for a discussion of this important option.

Remarks

(*Table of useful commands for programmers on next page*)

Useful commands for programmers

Basics

[P] **program**	Define and manipulate programs
[P] **sortpreserve**	Sorting within programs
[P] **byable**	Making programs byable
[P] **macro**	Macro definition and manipulation

Parsing and program arguments

[P] **syntax**	Parse Stata syntax
[P] **confirm**	Argument verification
[P] **gettoken**	Low-level parsing

Program control

[P] **version**	Version control
[P] **if**	if programming command
[P] **foreach**, [P] **forvalues**, [P] **while**	Looping
[P] **continue**	Loop breaking
[P] **error**	Display generic error message and exit
[P] **exit**	Exit from a program or do-file
[P] **capture**	Capture return code

Console output

[P] **display**	Display strings and values of scalar expressions
[P] **tabdisp**	Display tables

Commonly used programming commands

[P] **return**	Return saved results
[P] **#delimit**	Change delimiter
[P] **quietly**	Quietly and noisily perform Stata command
[P] **mark**	Mark observations for inclusion
[P] **matrix**	Introduction to matrix commands
[P] **preserve**	Preserve and restore data
[P] **scalar**	Scalar variables

Debugging

[P] **pause**	Program debugging command
[P] **program**	set trace debugging command

Advanced programming commands

[P] **break**	Suppress *Break* key
[P] **char**	Characteristics
[P] **estimates**	Temporarily preserve results from estimation command
[R] **ml**	Maximum likelihood estimation
[P] **more**	Pause until key is pressed
[P] **postfile**	Save results in Stata dataset
[P] **tokenize**	Divide strings into tokens
[P] **unab**	Unabbreviate variable list
[P] **window**	Programming menus, dialogs, and windows

The `program dir` command lists the names of all the programs stored in memory. `program list` lists contents of the program or programs.

▷ Example

When you start Stata, there are no programs stored in memory. If you type `program dir`, Stata displays an empty list:

```
. program dir
.
```

Later during the session:

```
. program dir
ado       720  _pred_se
ado       336  logit_p.GetRhs
ado      3728  logit_p
ado       272  predict
ado      1456  logistic
        _____
          6512
```

The `ado` after the program name indicates that the program was automatically loaded and thus is eligible to be automatically dropped should memory become scarce; see [U] **20 Ado-files**. The number is the size, in bytes, of the program. The total amount of memory occupied by programs is currently 6,464 bytes. Notice the `logit_p.GetRhs` entry. The `GetRhs` program is defined in the `logit_p.ado` file and was loaded when `logit_p` was loaded.

Let's now create two of our own programs using `program define`:

```
. program define rng
  1. args n a b
  2. if "`b´"=="" {
  3.    display "You must type three arguments: n a b"
  4.    exit
  5. }
  6. drop _all
  7. set obs `n´
  8. generate x = (_n-1)/(_N-1)*(`b´-`a´)+`a´
  9. end
. program define smooth
  1. args v1 v2
  2. confirm variable `v1´
  3. confirm new variable `v2´
  4. generate `v2´ = cond(_n==1|_n==_N,`v1´,(`v1´[_n-1]+`v1´+`v1´[_n+1])/3)
  5. end
```

After typing `program define`, lines are collected until you type a line with the word **end**. For our purposes, it does not matter what these programs do. If we were now to type `program dir`, we would see

```
. program dir
          256  smooth
          288  rng
ado       720  _pred_se
ado       336  logit_p.GetRhs
ado      3728  logit_p
ado       272  predict
ado      1456  logistic
        _____
          7056
```

We can list a program using the `program list` command:

```
. program list smooth
smooth:
  1. args v1 v2
  2. confirm variable `v1´
  3. confirm new variable `v2´
  4. generate `v2´ = cond(_n==1|_n==_N,`v1´,(`v1´[_n-1]+`v1´+`v1´[_n+1])/3)
```

If we do not specify the program we want listed, `program list` lists all the programs stored in memory.

The `program drop` command eliminates programs from memory. Typing `program drop` *program_name* eliminates *program_name* from memory. Typing `program drop _all` eliminates *all* programs from memory.

```
. program drop smooth
. program dir
          288  rng
ado       720  _pred_se
ado       336  logit_p.GetRhs
ado      3728  logit_p
ado       272  predict
ado      1456  logistic
        _____
         6800
. program drop _all
. program dir
  .
```

◁

Debugging programs

▷ Example

Stata does not normally display the lines of your program as it executes them. With `set trace on`, however, it does:

```
. program list simple
simple:
  1. args msg
  2. if `"`msg´"´=="hello" {
  3.         display "you said hello"
  4. }
  5. else display "you did not say hello"
  6. display "good-bye"
. set trace on
. simple
- args msg
- if `"`msg´"´=="hello" {
  display "you said hello"
  }
- else display "you did not say hello"
you did not say hello
- display "good-bye"
good-bye

. set trace off
```

Lines that are executed are preceded by a dash. We see that Stata executed the first two lines of our program, skipped the next two lines, and executed the last two lines.

The output from our program is interspersed with the lines that caused the output. This can be greatly useful when our program has an error. For instance, we have written a more useful program called `myprog`; here is what happens when we run it:

```
. myprog mpg, prefix("new")
invalid syntax
r(198);
```

We did not expect this and, look as we will at our program code, we cannot spot the error. Our program contains many lines of code, however, so we have no idea even where to look. By setting `trace` on, we can quickly find the error:

```
. set trace on

. myprog mpg, prefix("new")
- version 7.0
- syntax varname , [ PRefix(string)]
- local newname "`prefix'`varname'
invalid syntax
r(198);
```

The error was close to the top—we omitted the closing quote in the definition of the local `newname` macro.

◁

Also See

Complementary: [P] **byable**, [P] **discard**, [P] **sortpreserve**, [R] **query**

Background: [U] **21 Programming Stata**

Title

> **quietly** — Quietly and noisily perform Stata command

Syntax

<u>qu</u>ietly *command*

<u>n</u>oisily *command*

<u>set</u> <u>ou</u>tput { <u>proc</u> | <u>inform</u> | <u>e</u>rror }

Description

`quietly` suppresses all terminal output for the duration of *command*.

`noisily` turns back on terminal output, if appropriate, for the duration of *command*. It is useful only in programs.

`set output` specifies the output to be displayed.

Remarks

quietly used interactively

▷ Example

`quietly` is useful in situations where you are using Stata interactively and want to temporarily suppress the terminal output. For instance, to estimate a regression of `mpg` on the variables `weight`, `weightsq`, and `foreign` and to suppress the terminal output, type

```
. quietly regress mpg weight weightsq foreign
.
```

Admittedly, it is unlikely you would ever want to do this in real life.

◁

quietly used in programs

❑ Technical Note

`quietly` is often used in programs. For instance, let's say you have the following program to run a regression of y on x, calculate the residuals, and then list the outliers, defined as points with residuals below the fifth percentile or above the 95th percentile:

```
program define myprog
        regress `1´ `2´
        predict resid, resid
        sort resid
        summarize resid, detail
        list `1´ `2´ resid if resid< r(p5) | resid> r(p95)
        drop resid
end
```

While the program will work, it will also fill the screen with the regression output, any notes predict feels obligated to mention, and the detailed output from summarize. A better version of this program might read

```
program define myprog
        quietly regress `1´ `2´
        quietly predict resid, resid
        quietly sort resid
        quietly summarize resid, detail
        list `1´ `2´ resid if resid< r(p5) | resid> r(p95)
        drop resid
end
```

You can also combine quietly with { }:

```
program define myprog
        quietly {
                regress `1´ `2´
                predict resid, resid
                sort resid
                summarize resid, detail
        }
        list `1´ `2´ resid if resid< r(p5) | resid> r(p95)
        drop resid
end
```

❑

❑ Technical Note

noisily is the antonym of quietly and it too can be used in programs and do-files. In fact, that is its only real use. We could recode our example program to read as follows:

```
program define myprog
        quietly {
                regress `1´ `2´
                predict resid, resid
                sort resid
                summarize resid, detail
                noisily list `1´ `2´ resid if resid< r(p5) | resid> r(p95)
                drop resid
        }
end
```

In this case, we have not improved readability.

❑

❑ Technical Note

noisily is not really the antonym of quietly. If the user types quietly myprog yvar xvar, the output will be suppressed because that is what the user wanted. In this case, a noisily inside myprog will not display the output—noisily means noisily only if the program was allowed to be noisy when it was invoked.

❑

❑ Technical Note

If you think you understand all of this, take the following test. Is there any difference between quietly do *filename* and run *filename*? How about noisily run *filename* and do *filename*? What would happen if you typed quietly noisily summarize *myvar*? If you typed noisily quietly summarize *myvar*?

When you are ready, we will tell you the answers.

quietly do *filename* is equivalent to run *filename*. Typing run is easier, however.

noisily run *filename* is not at all the same as do *filename*. run produces no output, and no matter how noisily you run run, it is still quiet.

Typing quietly noisily summarize *myvar* is the same as typing summarize myvar. Think of it as quietly {noisily summarize *myvar*}. It is the inside noisily that takes precedence.

Typing noisily quietly summarize *myvar* is the same as typing quietly summarize *myvar*—it does nothing but burn computer time. Again, it is the inside term, quietly this time, that takes precedence.

❑

❑ Technical Note

set output proc means that all output, including procedure (command) output, is displayed. inform suppresses procedure output but displays informative messages and error messages. error suppresses all output except error messages. In practice, set output is seldom used.

❑

Also See

Background: [U] **21 Programming Stata**

Title

> **return** — Return saved results

Syntax

<u>retu</u>rn clear

<u>retu</u>rn scalar *name* = *exp*

<u>retu</u>rn local *name* = *exp*

<u>retu</u>rn local *name* ["] *string* ["]

<u>retu</u>rn matrix *name* *matname*

<u>retu</u>rn add

<u>sretu</u>rn clear

<u>sretu</u>rn local *name* = *exp*

<u>sretu</u>rn local *name* ["] *string* ["]

<u>esti</u>mates clear

<u>esti</u>mates post **b** **V** [**C**] [, <u>dep</u>name(*string*) <u>o</u>bs(*#*) <u>d</u>of(*#*) <u>e</u>sample(*varname*)]

<u>esti</u>mates scalar *name* = *exp*

<u>esti</u>mates local *name* = *exp*

<u>esti</u>mates local *name* ["] *string* ["]

<u>esti</u>mates matrix *name* *matname*

<u>esti</u>mates repost [**b** = **b**] [**V** = **V**] [, <u>e</u>sample(*varname*) <u>ren</u>ame]

where **b**, **V**, and **C** are *matnames*.

Description

Results of calculations are saved by many Stata commands so that they can be easily accessed and substituted into subsequent commands. This entry summarizes for programmers how to save results. If your interest is in using previously saved results, see [R] **saved results**.

return saves results in r().

sreturn saves results in s().

estimates saves results in e().

Options

depname(*string*) is for use with **estimates post**. It supplies the name of the dependent variable to appear in the estimation output. The name specified need not be the name of an existing variable.

obs(*#*) is for use with estimates post. It specifies the number of observations on which the estimation was performed. This number is stored in e(N), and obs() is provided simply for convenience. Results are no different than estimates post followed by estimates scalar N = *#*.

dof(*#*) is for use with estimates post. It specifies the number of denominator degrees of freedom to be used with t and F statistics and so is used in calculating significance levels and confidence intervals. The number specified is saved in e(df_r), and dof() is provided simply for convenience. Results are no different than estimates post followed by estimates scalar df_r = *#*.

esample(*varname*) is for use with estimates post and estimates repost. It specifies the name of a 0/1 variable that is to become the e(sample) function. *varname* must contain 0 and 1 values only, with 1 indicating the observation is in the estimation subsample. matrix post and matrix repost will be able to execute a little more quickly if *varname* is stored as a byte variable.

varname is dropped from the dataset or, more correctly, it is stolen and stashed in a secret place.

rename is for use with the b = b syntax of estimates repost. All numeric estimation results remain unchanged but the labels of **b** are substituted for the variable and equation names of the already posted results.

Remarks

This entry summarizes information that is presented in greater detail in other parts of the Stata documentation. Most particularly, we recommend you read [U] **21 Programming Stata**. The commands listed above are used by programmers to save results, results which are accessed by others using r(), e(), and s(); see [R] **saved results**.

The commands listed above may be used only in programs—see [U] **21 Programming Stata** and [P] **program**—and then only when the program is declared explicitly as being rclass, eclass, or sclass:

```
program define ..., rclass
        ...
        return ...
        ...
end
program define ..., eclass
        ...
        estimates ...
        ...
end
program define ..., sclass
        ...
        sreturn ...
        ...
end
```

Saving results in r()

1. The program must be declared explicitly to be r class: program define ... , rclass.

2. Distinguish between r() (returned results) and return() (results being assembled that will be returned). The program you write actually stores results in return(). Then, when your program completes, whatever is in return() is copied to r(). Thus, the program you write can consume r() results from other programs and there is no conflict.

3. `return clear` clears the `return()` class. This command is seldomly used because `return()` starts out empty when your program begins. If your program ends with a nonzero return code, `r()` is cleared but the partially assembled results in `return()` are not copied to `r()`. Thus, `return clear` is for those instances when you have started assembling results and all is going well, but given the problem at hand, you need to start all over again.

4. `return scalar` *name* = *exp* evaluates *exp* and stores the result in the scalar `return(`*name*`)`. *exp* must evaluate to a numeric result or missing. If your code has previously stored something in `return(`*name*`)`, whether that be a scalar, matrix, or whatever else, the previous value is discarded and this result replaces it.

5. `return local` *name* = *exp* evaluates *exp* and stores the result in the macro `return(`*name*`)`. *exp* may evaluate to a numeric or string result. If your code has previously stored something in `return(`*name*`)`, whether that be a scalar, matrix, or whatever else, the previous value is discarded and this result replaces it.

   Be careful with this syntax: do not code

   ```
   return local name = `mymacro´
   ```

   because that will copy just the first 80 characters of `` `mymacro´ ``. Instead code

   ```
   return local name "`mymacro´"
   ```

6. `return local` *name* *string* copies *string* to macro `return(`*name*`)`. If your code has previously stored something in `return(`*name*`)`, whether that be a scalar, matrix, or whatever else, the previous value is discarded and this result replaces it.

   If you do not enclose *string* in double quotes, multiple blanks in *string* are compressed into single blanks.

7. `return matrix` *name* *matname* destructively copies `matname` into matrix `return(`*name*`)`, which is to say, *matname* is erased. What actually occurs is that *matname* is renamed `return(`*name*`)`. If your code has previously stored something in `return(`*name*`)`, whether that be a scalar, matrix, or whatever else, the previous value is discarded and this result replaces it.

8. `return add` copies everything new in `r()` into `return()`. For instance, say your program performed a `summarize`. `return add` lets you add everything just returned by `summarize` to the to-be-returned results of your program. The emphasis is on add. If your program had already set `return(N)`, `summarize`'s `r(N)` would not replace the previously set result. The remaining `r()` results set by `summarize` would be copied.

Saving results in s()

1. The program must be declared explicitly to be s class: `program define ... , sclass`.

2. The s class is not cleared automatically. It is a static, single-level class. Results are posted to `s()` the instant they are saved.

3. `sreturn clear` clears `s()`. It is recommended that this command be used near the top of s-class routines. `sreturn clear` may be used in non s-class programs, too.

4. The s class provides macros only. The s class is intended for returning results of subroutines that parse input. At the parsing step, it is important that the r class not be changed or cleared because some of what still awaits being parsed might refer to `r()` and the user expects those results to substitute according to what was in `r()` at the time he or she typed the command.

5. `sreturn local` *name* = *exp* evaluates *exp* and stores the result in the macro `s`(*name*). *exp* may evaluate to a numeric or string result. If your code has previously stored something else in `s`(*name*), the previous value is discarded and this result replaces it.

   Be careful with this syntax: do not code

   > `sreturn local` *name* = `` `mymacro´ ``

   because that will copy just the first 80 characters of `` `mymacro´ ``. Instead code

   > `sreturn local` *name* `` "`mymacro´" ``

6. `sreturn local` *name string* copies *string* to macro `s`(*name*). If your code has previously stored something else in `s`(*name*), the previous value is discarded and this result replaces it.

   If you do not enclose *string* in double quotes, multiple blanks in *string* are compressed into single blanks.

Saving results in e()

1. The program must be declared explicitly to be e class: `program define ... , eclass`.

2. The e class is cleared whenever an `estimates post` is executed. The e class is a static, single-level class, meaning results are posted to the class the instant they are stored.

3. `estimates clear` clears `e()`. This is a rarely used command.

4. `estimates post` is how you must begin saving results in `e()`. Because `estimates post` clears `e()`, anything saved in `e()` prior to the `estimates post` is lost.

   `estimates post` saves matrix (vector, really) `e(b)`, matrix `e(V)`, and function `e(sample)`. The recommended syntax is

   > `estimates post` `` `b´ `` `` `V´ ``, `esample(` `` `touse´ ``) ...

   where `` `b´ `` is a row vector containing the parameter estimates, `` `V´ `` is a symmetric matrix containing the variance estimates, and `` `touse´ `` is a 0/1 variable recording 1 in observations that appear in the estimation subsample.

   The result of this command will be that `` `b´ ``, `` `V´ ``, and `` `touse´ `` will all disappear. In fact, `estimates post` examines what you specify and, if it is satisfied with them, renames them `e(b)`, `e(V)`, and `e(sample)`.

   In terms of `estimates post`'s other options,

   a. We recommend that you specify `depname(`*string*`)` if there is a single dependent variable name that you want to appear on the output. Whether you specify `depname()` or not, remember later to define macro `e(depvar)` to contain the name(s) of the dependent variable(s).

   b. Specify `obs(`#`)` or remember later to define scalar `e(N)` to contain the number of observations.

   c. Few models require specifying `dof(`#`)` or, if that is not done, remembering to later define scalar `e(df_r)`. This all has to do with substituting t and F statistics based on # (denominator) degrees of freedom for asymptotic z and χ^2 statistics in the estimation output.

5. `estimates scalar` *name* = *exp* evaluates *exp* and stores the result in the scalar `e`(*name*). *exp* must evaluate to a numeric result or missing. If your code has previously stored something in `e`(*name*), whether that be a scalar, matrix, or whatever else, the previous value is discarded and this result replaces it.

6. `estimates local` *name* = *exp* evaluates *exp* and stores the result in the macro `e`(*name*). *exp* may evaluate to a numeric or string result. If your code has previously stored something in `e`(*name*), whether that be a scalar, matrix, or whatever else, the previous value is discarded and this result replaces it.

   Be careful with this syntax: do not code

   > `estimates local` *name* = `` `mymacro' ``

   because that will copy just the first 80 characters of `` `mymacro' ``. Instead code

   > `estimates local` *name* `` "`mymacro'" ``

7. `estimates local` *name string* copies *string* to macro `e`(*name*). If your code has previously stored something in `e`(*name*), whether that be a scalar, matrix, or whatever else, the previous value is discarded and this result replaces it.

   If you do not enclose *string* in double quotes, multiple blanks in *string* are compressed into single blanks.

8. `estimates matrix` *name matname* destructively copies `matname` into matrix `e`(*name*), which is to say, *matname* is erased. What actually occurs is that *matname* is renamed `e`(*name*). If your code has previously stored something in `e`(*name*), whether that be a scalar, matrix, or whatever else, the previous value is discarded and this result replaces it, with two exceptions:

   `estimates matrix` cannot be used to save in `e(b)` or `e(V)`. The only way to post matrices to these special names is `estimates post` and `estimates repost`. The reason for that is so that various tests can be run on them before they are made official. Other Stata commands will use `e(b)` and `e(V)` and expect to see a valid estimation result. If `e(b)` is $1 \times k$, they expect `e(V)` to be $k \times k$. They expect that the names of rows and columns will be the same, so that the ith column of `e(b)` corresponds to the ith row and column of `e(V)`. They expect `e(V)` to be symmetric. They expect `e(V)` to have positive or zero elements along its diagonal, and so on. `estimates post` and `estimates repost` check these assumptions.

9. `estimates repost` allows changing `e(b)`, `e(V)`, and `e(sample)` without clearing the estimation results and starting all over again. As with `estimates post`, specified matrices and variables disappear after reposting because they are renamed `e(b)`, `e(V)`, or `e(sample)` as appropriate.

10. Programmers posting estimation results should remember to save
    a. Macro `e(cmd)` containing the name of the estimation command. Make this the last thing you save in `e()`.
    b. Macro `e(depvar)` containing the name(s) of the dependent variable(s).
    c. Scalar `e(N)` containing the number of observations.
    d. Scalar `e(df_m)` containing the model degrees of freedom.
    e. Scalar `e(df_r)` containing the "denominator" degrees of freedom if estimates are nonasymptotic; otherwise, do not define this result.
    f. Scalar `e(ll)` containing the log-likelihood value, if relevant.
    g. Scalar `e(ll_0)` containing the log-likelihood value for the constant-only model, if relevant.
    h. Scalar `e(chi2)` containing the χ^2 test of the model against the constant-only model, if relevant.
    i. Macro `e(chi2type)` containing "LR", "Wald", or other depending on how `e(chi2)` was obtained.
    j. Scalar `e(r2_p)` containing the value of the pseudo-R^2 if it is calculated.
    k. Macro `e(vcetype)` containing the text to appear above standard errors in estimation output; typically "Robust" or it is undefined.

    l. Macro e(clustvar) containing the name of the cluster variable, if any.

    m. Scalar e(N_clust) containing the number of clusters.

    n. Macro e(predict) containing the name of the command that predict is to use; if this is blank, predict uses the default _predict.

11. estimates has other subcommands beyond the ones shown in this section. They have to do with aspects other than posting results when programming estimation commands. See [P] **estimates** for more information about posting estimation results.

Recommended names for saved results

Users will appreciate it if you use predictable names for your saved results. The rules we use are

1. Mathematical and statistical concepts such as number of observations, degrees of freedom, etc., are given mathematical-style, short names. Subscripting is indicated with '_'. Names are to proceed from the general to the specific. If N means number of observations, then N_1 might be the number of observations in the first group.

    Suffixes are to be avoided where possible. For instance, a χ^2 statistic would be recorded in a variable starting with chi2. If, in the context of the command, a statement about "the χ^2 statistic" would be understood as referring to this statistic, then the name would be chi2. If it required further modification, such as χ^2 for the comparison test, then the name might be chi2_c.

    Common prefixes are

N	number of observations
df	degrees of freedom
k	count of variables
n	generic count
lb and ub	lower- and upper-bound of confidence interval
chi2	χ^2 statistic
t	t statistic
F	F statistic
p	significance
p and pr	probability
ll	log likelihood
D	deviance
r2	R^2

2. Programming concepts such as lists of variable names, etc., are given English style names. Names should proceed from the specific to the general. The name of the dependent variable is depvar, not vardep.

    Some examples are

depvar	dependent variable name(s)
eqnames	equation names
model	name of model estimated
xvar	x variable
title	title used

3. Popular usage takes precedence over the rules. For example:

    a. mss is model's sum of squares even though, per Rule 1, it ought to be ss_m.

    b. mean is used as the prefix to record means.

    c. Var is used as the prefix to mean variance.

    d. The returned results from most Stata commands follow Rule 3.

Also See

Related:	[P] **estimates**,
	[R] **saved results**
Background:	[U] **21 Programming Stata**,
	[U] **21.10 Saving results**

Title

> **_rmcoll** — Remove collinear variables

Syntax

> _rmcoll *varlist* [in *range*] [if *exp*] [*weight*] [, <u>noconst</u>ant]
>
> _rmdcoll *depvar varlist* [in *range*] [if *exp*] [*weight*] [, <u>noconst</u>ant <u>nocollin</u>]

fweights, aweights, pweights, and iweights are allowed; see [U] **14.1.6 weight**.

Description

_rmcoll returns in r(varlist) the names of the variables from the varlist that form a noncollinear set.

If any variables are collinear, in addition to each not being included in r(varlist), a message is displayed for each:

    Note: _____ dropped due to collinearity.

ml users: It is not necessary to call _rmcoll because ml removes the collinear variables for you, assuming that you do not specify ml model's collinear option. Even so, ml programmers sometimes use _rmcoll because they need the noncollinear set of variables and, in such cases, they specify ml model's collinear option so that ml does not waste time looking for collinearity again.

_rmdcoll identifies collinearity, including collinearity with the dependent variable. _rmdcoll returns in r(varlist) a variable list from which collinear variables have been removed and displays a message

    _____ collinear with _____

with an error code 459 when the dependent variable is collinear with the independent variables.

Options

noconstant specifies that, in looking for collinearity, an intercept should not be included. That is, a variable that contains the same nonzero value in every observation should not be considered collinear.

nocollin specifies that collinear variables have already been removed from the varlist. Otherwise, _rmcoll is called first to remove any such collinearity.

Remarks

_rmcoll and _rmdcoll are typically used when writing estimation commands.

_rmcoll is used if the programmer wants to drop the collinear variables from the independent variables.

_rmdcoll is used if the programmer wants to detect the collinearity of the dependent variable with the independent variables.

A code fragment for the caller of _rmcoll might read as

```
...
syntax varlist [fweight iweight] ... [, noCONStant ... ]
marksample touse
if "`weight'" = ""
        tempvar w
        quietly gen double `w' = `exp' if `touse'
        local wgt [`weight'=`w']
else    local wgt /* is nothing */
tokenize `varlist'
local depvar `1'
mac shift
_rmcoll `*' `wgt' if `touse', `constant'
local xvars `r(varlist)'
...
```

In this code fragment, *varlist* contains a single dependent and zero or more independent variables. The dependent variable is split off and stored in *depvar*, and then the remaining variables are passed through _rmcoll and the resulting noncollinear set stored in *xvars*.

Saved Results

_rmcoll and _rmdcoll save in r():

r(varlist)   names of noncollinear variables

Also See

Complementary: [R] **ml**

Background: [U] **21 Programming Stata**

Title

rmsg — Return messages

Syntax

set rmsg { on | off }

Description

set rmsg determines whether the return message is to be displayed at the completion of each command. The initial setting is off.

Remarks

See [U] **11 Error messages and return codes** for a description of return messages and use of this command.

Also See

Complementary: [P] **error**,
                       [R] **query**

Background: [U] **11 Error messages and return codes**

Title

_robust — Robust variance estimates

Syntax

_robust *varlist* [*weight*] [if *exp*] [in *range*] [, variance(*matname*) minus(#)

    strata(*varname*) psu(*varname*) cluster(*varname*) fpc(*varname*)

    subpop(*varname*) vsrs(*matname*) srssubpop zeroweight]

pweights, aweights, fweights, and iweights are allowed; see [U] **14.1.6 weight**.

Description

   _robust is a programmer's command. It computes a robust variance estimator based on a *varlist* of scores and a covariance matrix. It produces estimators for ordinary data (each observation independent), clustered data (data not independent within groups, but independent across groups), and complex survey data with stratified cluster sampling.

   The robust variance estimator goes by many names: Huber/White/sandwich are typically used in the context of robustness against heteroskedasticity. Survey statisticians often refer to this variance calculation as a first-order Taylor-series linearization method. Despite the different names, the estimator is the same.

   The score *varlist* consists of a single variable for single-equation models or multiple variables for multiple-equation models—one variable for each equation. The "covariance" matrix before adjustment is either posted using estimates post (see [P] **estimates**) or specified with the variance(*matname*) option. In the former case, _robust replaces the covariance in the post with the robust covariance matrix. In the latter case, the matrix *matname* is overwritten with the robust covariance matrix. Note: The robust covariance formula is $V = DMD$, where D is what we are calling the "covariance" matrix before adjustment; this is not always a true covariance. See *Remarks* below.

   Before tackling this section, readers should be familiar with [U] **23.11 Obtaining robust variance estimates** and the *Methods and Formulas* section of [R] **regress**. It is presumed that readers have already programmed an estimator in Stata and now wish to have it compute robust variance estimates. If you have not yet programmed your estimator, see [U] **21 Programming Stata**, [R] **ml**, and [P] **estimates**. Users who wish to program an estimator for survey data should be intimately familiar with [R] **svymean** and [R] **svy estimators**. See [R] **estimation commands** for a complete list of commands that compute robust variance estimators.

Options

   variance(*matname*) specifies a matrix containing the unadjusted "covariance" matrix; i.e., the D in $V = DMD$. The matrix must have its rows and columns labeled with the appropriate corresponding variable names; i.e., the names of the x's in $x\beta$. If there are multiple equations, the matrix must have equation names; see [P] **matrix rowname**. The D matrix is overwritten with the robust covariance matrix V. If this option is not specified, it is assumed that D has been posted using estimates post; _robust will then automatically post the robust covariance matrix V and replace D.

232

minus(#) specifies $k = \#$ for the multiplier $n/(n - k)$ of the robust variance estimator. Stata's maximum likelihood commands use $k = 1$, as do all the svy commands. regress, robust uses, by default, this multiplier with k equal to the number of explanatory variables in the model including the constant. The default is $k = 1$. See Methods and Formulas for details.

strata(varname) specifies the name of a variable (numeric or string) that contains stratum identifiers.

psu(varname) specifies the name of a variable (numeric or string) that contains identifiers for the primary sampling unit (PSU). psu() and cluster() are synonyms; they both specify the same thing.

cluster(varname) is a synonym for psu().

fpc(varname) requests a finite population correction for the variance estimates. If the variable specified has values less than or equal to 1, it is interpreted as a stratum sampling rate $f_h = n_h/N_h$, where n_h = number of PSUs sampled from stratum h and N_h = total number of PSUs in the population belonging to stratum h. If the variable specified has values greater than or equal to n_h, it is interpreted as containing N_h.

subpop(varname) specifies that estimates be computed for the single subpopulation defined by the observations for which $varname \neq 0$ (and not missing). This option would typically be used only with survey data.

vsrs(matname) creates a matrix containing $\widehat{V}_{\mathrm{srswor}}$, an estimate of the variance that would have been observed had the data been collected using simple random sampling without replacement. This is used for the computation of deff and deft for survey data; see [R] svymean for details.

srssubpop can only be specified if vsrs() and subpop() are specified. srssubpop requests that the estimate of simple-random-sampling variance vsrs() be computed assuming sampling within a subpopulation. If srssubpop is not specified, it is computed assuming sampling from the entire population.

zeroweight specifies whether observations with weights equal to zero should be omitted from the computation. This option does not apply to frequency weights; observations with zero frequency weights are always omitted. If zeroweight is specified, observations with zero weights are included in the computation. If zeroweight is not specified (the default), observations with zero weights are omitted. Including the observations with zero weights affects the computation in that it may change the counts of PSUs (clusters) per stratum. Stata's svy commands include observations with zero weights; all other commands exclude them. This option would typically be used only with survey data.

Remarks

We will proceed to explain the formulas behind the robust variance estimator and how to use _robust through an informal development with some simple examples. For an alternative discussion, see [U] 23.11 Obtaining robust variance estimates. See the references cited at the end of this entry for more formal expositions.

Let us first consider ordinary least-squares regression. The estimator for the coefficients is

$$\widehat{\beta} = (\mathbf{X}'\mathbf{X})^{-1}\mathbf{X}'\mathbf{y}$$

where $\mathbf{y}$ is an $n \times 1$ vector representing the dependent variable and $\mathbf{X}$ is an $n \times k$ matrix of covariates.

Since we consider everything conditional on $\mathbf{X}$, $(\mathbf{X}'\mathbf{X})^{-1}$ can be regarded as a constant matrix. Hence, the variance of $\widehat{\beta}$ is

$$V(\widehat{\beta}) = (\mathbf{X}'\mathbf{X})^{-1} V(\mathbf{X}'\mathbf{y}) (\mathbf{X}'\mathbf{X})^{-1}$$

What is the variance of $\mathbf{X}'\mathbf{y}$, a $k \times 1$ vector? Let's look at its first element; it is

$$\mathbf{X}_1'\mathbf{y} = x_{11}y_1 + x_{21}y_2 + \cdots + x_{n1}y_n$$

where $\mathbf{X}_1$ is the first column of $\mathbf{X}$. Since $\mathbf{X}$ is treated as a constant, we can write the variance as

$$V(\mathbf{X}_1'\mathbf{y}) = x_{11}^2 V(y_1) + x_{21}^2 V(y_2) + \cdots + x_{n1}^2 V(y_n)$$

The only assumption that we have made here is that the y_j are independent.

The obvious estimate for $V(y_j)$ is $\widehat{e}_j^2$, the square of the residual $\widehat{e}_j = y_j - \mathbf{x}_j\widehat{\boldsymbol{\beta}}$, where $\mathbf{x}_j$ is the jth row of $\mathbf{X}$. We must estimate the off-diagonal terms of the covariance matrix for $\mathbf{X}'\mathbf{y}$ as well. Working this out, we have

$$\widehat{V}(\mathbf{X}'\mathbf{y}) = \sum_{j=1}^n \widehat{e}_j^2\, \mathbf{x}_j'\mathbf{x}_j$$

Note that we defined $\mathbf{x}_j$ as a row vector, so that $\mathbf{x}_j'\mathbf{x}_j$ is a $k \times k$ matrix.

We have just derived the robust variance estimator for linear regression coefficient estimates for independent observations:

$$\widehat{V}(\widehat{\boldsymbol{\beta}}) = (\mathbf{X}'\mathbf{X})^{-1} \left(\sum_{j=1}^n \widehat{e}_j^2\, \mathbf{x}_j'\mathbf{x}_j \right) (\mathbf{X}'\mathbf{X})^{-1}$$

You can see why it is called the "sandwich" estimator.

❑ Technical Note

The only detail that we have overlooked is the multiplier. We will see later that survey statisticians like to view the center of the sandwich as a variance estimator for totals. As such, they use a multiplier of $n/(n-1)$, just as $1/(n-1)$ is used for the variance estimator of a mean. However, for survey data, n is no longer the total number of observations, but the number of clusters in a stratum. See *Methods and Formulas* at the end of this entry.

The case of linear regression is, however, special. If we assume homoskedasticity and normality, we can derive the expectation of $\widehat{e}_j^2$ for finite n. This is discussed in [R] **regress**. Under the assumptions of homoskedasticity and normality, $n/(n-k)$ is a better multiplier than $n/(n-1)$.

If you specify the **minus(#)** option, _robust will use $n/(n-\#)$ as the multiplier. **regress, robust** also gives two other options for the multiplier: **hc2** and **hc3**. Since these multipliers are special to linear regression, _robust does not compute them.

❑

▷ Example

Before we show how _robust is used, let's compute the robust variance estimator "by hand" for linear regression for the case in which observations are independent (i.e., no clusters).

We need to compute $\mathbf{D} = (\mathbf{X}'\mathbf{X})^{-1}$ and the residuals $\widehat{e}_j$. **regress** with the **mse1** option will allow us to compute both easily; see [R] **regress**.

```
. use auto
(1978 Automobile Data)
. quietly regress mpg weight gear_ratio foreign, mse1
. matrix D = e(V)
. predict double e, residual
```

We can write the center of the sandwich as

$$\mathbf{M} = \sum_{j=1}^{n} \widehat{e}_j^2 \mathbf{x}_j' \mathbf{x}_j = \mathbf{X}' \mathbf{W} \mathbf{X}$$

where $\mathbf{W}$ is a diagonal matrix with $\widehat{e}_j^2$ on the diagonal. `matrix accum` with `iweight`s can be used to calculate this (see [P] **matrix accum**):

```
. matrix accum M = weight gear_ratio foreign [iweight=e^2]
(obs=813.7814109)
```

We now assemble the sandwich. In order to match `regress, robust`, we use a multiplier of $n/(n-k)$.

```
. matrix V = 74/70 * D*M*D

. matrix list V

symmetric V[4,4]
                   weight   gear_ratio      foreign         _cons
    weight     3.788e-07
gear_ratio    .00039798    1.9711317
   foreign    .00008463   -.55488334    1.4266939
     _cons   -.00236851   -6.9153285    1.2149035    27.536291
```

The result is exactly the same as that from `regress, robust`:

```
. quietly regress mpg weight gear_ratio foreign, robust

. matrix Vreg = e(V)

. matrix list Vreg

symmetric Vreg[4,4]
                   weight   gear_ratio      foreign         _cons
    weight     3.788e-07
gear_ratio    .00039798    1.9711317
   foreign    .00008463   -.55488334    1.4266939
     _cons   -.00236851   -6.9153285    1.2149035    27.536291
```

If we use `_robust`, the initial steps are the same. We still need $\mathbf{D}$, the "bread" of the sandwich, and the residuals. The residuals $\mathbf{e}$ are the *varlist* for `_robust`. $\mathbf{D}$ is passed via the `variance()` option (abbreviation `v()`). $\mathbf{D}$ is overwritten and contains the robust variance estimate.

```
. quietly regress mpg weight gear_ratio foreign, mse1

. matrix D = e(V)

. predict double e, residual

. _robust e, v(D) minus(4)

. matrix list D

symmetric D[4,4]
                   weight   gear_ratio      foreign         _cons
    weight     3.788e-07
gear_ratio    .00039798    1.9711317
   foreign    .00008463   -.55488334    1.4266939
     _cons   -.00236851   -6.9153285    1.2149035    27.536291
```

Rather than specifying the `variance()` option, $\mathbf{D}$ and the point estimates can be first posted using `estimates post`. `_robust` alters the post, substituting the robust variance estimates.

```
. quietly regress mpg weight gear_ratio foreign, mse1
. gen byte samp = e(sample)
. matrix D = e(V)
. matrix b = e(b)
. local n = e(N)
. local k = colsof(D)
. local dof = `n´ - `k´
. predict double e, residual
. estimates post b D, dof(`dof´) esample(samp)
. _robust e, minus(`k´)
. estimates display
```

	Coef.	Robust Std. Err.	t	P>|t|	[95% Conf. Interval]	
weight	-.006139	.0006155	-9.97	0.000	-.0073666	-.0049115
gear_ratio	1.457113	1.40397	1.04	0.303	-1.343016	4.257243
foreign	-2.221682	1.194443	-1.86	0.067	-4.603923	.1605597
_cons	36.10135	5.247503	6.88	0.000	25.63554	46.56717

Again, what we did matches **regress, robust**:

```
. regress mpg weight gear_ratio foreign, robust
```

Regression with robust standard errors

```
Number of obs =      74
F(  3,     70) =   48.30
Prob > F       =  0.0000
R-squared      =  0.6670
Root MSE       =  3.4096
```

mpg	Coef.	Robust Std. Err.	t	P>|t|	[95% Conf. Interval]	
weight	-.006139	.0006155	-9.97	0.000	-.0073666	-.0049115
gear_ratio	1.457113	1.40397	1.04	0.303	-1.343016	4.257243
foreign	-2.221682	1.194443	-1.86	0.067	-4.603923	.1605597
_cons	36.10135	5.247503	6.88	0.000	25.63554	46.56717

◁

❑ Technical Note

Note the simple ways in which _robust was called. When we used the **variance()** option, we called it by typing

```
. _robust e, v(D) minus(4)
```

As we described, _robust computed

$$\widehat{V}(\widehat{\beta}) = \mathbf{D} \left(\frac{n}{n-k} \sum_{j=1}^{n} \widehat{e}_j^2 \mathbf{x}_j' \mathbf{x}_j \right) \mathbf{D}$$

We passed $\mathbf{D}$ to _robust using the option v(D) and specified $\widehat{e}_j$ as the variable e. So how did _robust know what variables to use for $\mathbf{x}_j$? It got them from the row and column names of the matrix D. Recall how we generated D initially:

```
. quietly regress mpg weight gear_ratio foreign, mse1
. matrix D = e(V)
. matrix list D
symmetric D[4,4]
                weight  gear_ratio      foreign      _cons
    weight    5.436e-08
gear_ratio    .00006295   .20434146
   foreign    .00001032  -.08016692    .1311889
     _cons   -.00035697    -.782292   .17154326   3.3988878
```

Stata's estimation commands and the `ml` commands produce matrices with appropriately labeled rows and columns. So if that is how you generate your **D**, this will be taken care of automatically. But if you generate **D** in another manner, be sure you label it appropriately; see [P] **matrix rowname**.

When `_robust` is used after `estimates post`, it gets the variable names from the row and column names of the posted matrices. So again, the matrices must be labeled appropriately.

Let us make another rather obvious comment. `_robust` uses the variables from the row and column names of the **D** matrix at the time `_robust` is called. It is the programmer's responsibility to ensure that the data in these variables have not changed and that `_robust` selects the appropriate observations for the computation, using an `if` restriction if necessary (for instance, `if e(sample)`).

❑

Clustered data

To get robust variance estimates for clustered data or for complex survey data, you simply use the `cluster()`, `strata()`, etc., options when you call `_robust`.

The first steps are the same as before. For clustered data, the degrees of freedom of the t statistic are the number of clusters minus one (we will discuss this later).

```
. quietly regress mpg weight gear_ratio foreign, mse1
. gen byte samp = e(sample)
. matrix D = e(V)
. matrix b = e(b)
. predict double e, residual
. local k = colsof(D)
. tabulate rep78
```

Repair Record 1978	Freq.	Percent	Cum.
1	2	2.90	2.90
2	8	11.59	14.49
3	30	43.48	57.97
4	18	26.09	84.06
5	11	15.94	100.00
Total	69	100.00	

```
. local nclust = r(r)
. di `nclust'
5
. local dof = `nclust' - 1
. estimates post b D, dof(`dof') esample(samp)
. _robust e, minus(`k') cluster(rep78)
```

```
. estimates display
```
                    (standard errors adjusted for clustering on rep78)

	Coef.	Robust Std. Err.	t	P>|t|	[95% Conf.	Interval]
weight	-.006139	.0008399	-7.31	0.002	-.008471	-.0038071
gear_ratio	1.457113	1.801311	0.81	0.464	-3.544129	6.458355
foreign	-2.221682	.8144207	-2.73	0.053	-4.482876	.0395129
_cons	36.10135	3.39887	10.62	0.000	26.66458	45.53813

And what we get is, of course, the same as `regress, robust cluster()`. Wait a minute, it is not the same!

```
. regress mpg weight gear_ratio foreign, robust cluster(rep78)
```

Regression with robust standard errors

Number of obs =	69
F(3, 4) =	78.61
Prob > F =	0.0005
R-squared =	0.6631
Root MSE =	3.4827

Number of clusters (rep78) = 5

mpg	Coef.	Robust Std. Err.	t	P>|t|	[95% Conf.	Interval]
weight	-.005893	.0008214	-7.17	0.002	-.0081735	-.0036126
gear_ratio	1.904503	2.18322	0.87	0.432	-4.157088	7.966093
foreign	-2.149017	1.20489	-1.78	0.149	-5.49433	1.196295
_cons	34.09959	4.215275	8.09	0.001	22.39611	45.80307

Not even the point estimates are the same. We made the classic programmer's mistake of not using the same sample for our initial `regress, mse1` call as we did with _robust. Our cluster variable rep78 is missing for 5 observations. _robust omitted these observations, but `regress, mse1` did not.

_robust is best used only in programs for just this reason. So let's write a program and use marksample and markout (see [P] **mark**) to determine the sample in advance of running regress and _robust.

(Continued on next page)

```
                                                          ─── top of myreg.ado ───────
program define myreg, eclass
        version 7.0
        syntax varlist [if] [in] [, CLuster(varname) ]
        marksample touse
        markout `touse' `cluster', strok

        tempvar e count
        tempname D b

        quietly {
                regress `varlist' if `touse', mse1
                matrix `D' = e(V)
                matrix `b' = e(b)
                local n = e(N)
                local k = colsof(`D')
                predict double `e' if `touse', residual

                if "`cluster'"~="" {
                        sort `touse' `cluster'
                        by `touse' `cluster': gen byte `count' = 1 if _n==1 & `touse'
                        summarize `count', meanonly
                        local nclust =  r(sum)
                        local dof = `nclust' - 1
                        local clopt "cluster(`cluster')"
                }
                else    local dof = `n' - `k'

                estimates post `b' `D', dof(`dof') esample(`touse')

                _robust `e' if e(sample), minus(`k') `clopt'
        }
        estimates display
end
                                                          ─── end of myreg.ado ───────
```

When we run this program, we do get the same results as **regress, robust cluster()**.

```
. myreg mpg weight gear_ratio foreign, cluster(rep78)
                          (standard errors adjusted for clustering on rep78)
```

| | | Robust | | | | |
	Coef.	Std. Err.	t	P>|t|	[95% Conf.	Interval]
weight	-.005893	.0008214	-7.17	0.002	-.0081735	-.0036126
gear_ratio	1.904503	2.18322	0.87	0.432	-4.157088	7.966093
foreign	-2.149017	1.20489	-1.78	0.149	-5.49433	1.196295
_cons	34.09959	4.215275	8.09	0.001	22.39611	45.80307

Survey data

We will now modify our **myreg** command so that it handles complex survey data. Our new version will allow **pweights** and **iweights**, stratification, and clustering.

(Continued on next page)

```
──────────────────────────────────────────── top of myreg.ado ──────────
program define myreg, eclass
        version 7.0
        syntax varlist [if] [in] [pweight iweight] [, /*
                */ STRata(varname) CLuster(varname) ]
        marksample touse, zeroweight
        markout `touse' `cluster' `strata', strok
        if "`weight'"~="" {
                tempvar w
                quietly gen double `w' `exp' if `touse'
                local iwexp "[iw=`w']"
                if "`weight'" == "pweight" {
                        capture assert `w' >= 0 if `touse'
                        if _rc { error 402 }
                }
        }
        if "`cluster'"~="" {
                local clopt "cluster(`cluster')"
        }
        if "`strata'"~="" {
                local stopt "strata(`strata')"
        }
                tempvar e
        tempname D b
        quietly {
                regress `varlist' `iwexp' if `touse', mse1
                matrix `D' = e(V)
                matrix `b' = e(b)
                predict double `e' if `touse', residual
                _robust `e' `iwexp' if `touse', v(`D') `clopt' `stopt' zeroweight
                local dof = r(N_clust) - r(N_strata)
                local depn : word 1 of `varlist'
                estimates post `b' `D', depn(`depn') dof(`dof') esample(`touse')
        }
        di
        estimates display
end
──────────────────────────────────────────── end of myreg.ado ──────────
```

Note the following details about our version of myreg for survey data:

1. We called _robust before we posted the matrices with estimates post, whereas in our previous version of myreg we called estimates post and then _robust. Here we called _robust first so that we could use its r(N_strata), containing the number of strata, and r(N_clust), containing the number of clusters; see *Saved Results* at the end of this entry. We did this so that we could pass the correct degrees of freedom (= number of clusters − number of strata) to estimates post.

   Note that this works even if the strata() and cluster() options are not specified: r(N_strata) = 1 if strata() is not specified (there truly is one stratum); and r(N_clust) = number of observations if cluster() is not specified (each observation is a cluster).

2. The call to _robust was made with iweights regardless of whether myreg was called with pweights or iweights. Computationally, _robust treats pweights and iweights exactly the same. The only difference is that it puts out an error message if it encounters a negative pweight whereas negative iweights are allowed. As good programmers, we put out the error message early before any time-consuming computations are done.

3. We used the `zeroweight` option with the `marksample` command so that zero weights would not be excluded from the sample. We gave the `zeroweight` option with _robust so that it, too, would not exclude zero weights.

   Observations with zero weights affect final results only by their effect (if any) on the counts of the clusters. Setting some weights temporarily to zero will, for example, produce subpopulation estimates. If subpopulation estimates are desired, however, it would be better to implement _robust's `subpop()` option and restrict the call to `regress, mse1` to this subpopulation.

4. Stata's `svy` commands always use `psu` rather than `cluster`. This is only a matter of style. They are synonyms as far as _robust is concerned.

   Our program gives the same results as `svyreg`. Indeed, `svyreg` is implemented as an ado-file that calls `regress, mse1` and then _robust.

```
. myreg mpg weight gear_ratio foreign [pw=displ], strata(strata) cluster(psu)
```

mpg	Coef.	Std. Err.	t	P>|t|	[95% Conf. Interval]	
weight	-.0057248	.0004042	-14.16	0.000	-.0066055	-.0048441
gear_ratio	.7775839	1.084891	0.72	0.487	-1.586191	3.141359
foreign	-1.86776	1.242491	-1.50	0.159	-4.574914	.8393952
_cons	36.64061	3.912454	9.37	0.000	28.1161	45.16511

```
. svyreg mpg weight gear_ratio foreign [pw=displ], strata(strata) psu(psu)
```

Survey linear regression

```
pweight:  displacement
Strata:   strata
PSU:      psu
```

Number of obs	=	74
Number of strata	=	3
Number of PSUs	=	15
Population size	=	14600
F(3, 10)	=	77.04
Prob > F	=	0.0000
R-squared	=	0.6900

mpg	Coef.	Std. Err.	t	P>|t|	[95% Conf. Interval]	
weight	-.0057248	.0004042	-14.16	0.000	-.0066055	-.0048441
gear_ratio	.7775839	1.084891	0.72	0.487	-1.586191	3.141359
foreign	-1.86776	1.242491	-1.50	0.159	-4.574914	.8393952
_cons	36.64061	3.912454	9.37	0.000	28.1161	45.16511

Controlling the header display

Compare the output for our survey version of `myreg` with the earlier version that only handled clustering. The header for the earlier version was

(standard errors adjusted for clustering on rep78)

		Robust				
	Coef.	Std. Err.	t	P>|t|	[95% Conf. Interval]	

The header for the survey version lacked the word "Robust" above "Std. Err." and it also lacked the banner "(standard errors adjusted for clustering on ...)".

Both of these headers were produced by `estimates display`, and programmers can control what it produces. The word above "Std. Err." is controlled by setting `e(vcetype)`. The banner "(standard errors adjusted for clustering on ...)" is controlled by setting `e(clustvar)` to the cluster variable name. These can be set using the `estimates local` command; see [P] **estimates**.

When _robust is called after `estimates post` (as it did in the earlier version that produced the above header), it automatically sets these macros. If you do not want the banner displayed, your code should read

```
estimates post ...
_robust ...
estimates local clustvar ""
```

You can also change the phrase displayed above "Std. Err." by resetting `e(vcetype)`. If you want nothing there, reset `e(vcetype)` to empty—`estimates local vcetype ""`.

For our survey version of `myreg`, we called _robust before calling `estimates post`. In this case, _robust does not set these macros. Trying to do so would be futile since `estimates post` clears all previous estimation results including all `e()` macros, but you can set them yourself after calling `estimates post`. We make this addition to our survey version of `myreg`:

```
_robust ...
estimates post ...
estimates local vcetype "Design-based"
```

The output is

```
. myreg mpg weight gear_ratio foreign [pw=displ], strata(strata) cluster(psu)
```

mpg	Coef.	Design-based Std. Err.	t	P>|t|	[95% Conf. Interval]	
weight	−.0057248	.0004042	−14.16	0.000	−.0066055	−.0048441
gear_ratio	.7775839	1.084891	0.72	0.487	−1.586191	3.141359
foreign	−1.86776	1.242491	−1.50	0.159	−4.574914	.8393952
_cons	36.64061	3.912454	9.37	0.000	28.1161	45.16511

Maximum likelihood estimators

Maximum likelihood estimators are basically no different from linear regression when it comes to the use of _robust. We will first do a little statistics and then give a simple example.

We can write our maximum-likelihood estimation equation as

$$\mathbf{G}(\boldsymbol{\beta}) = \sum_{j=1}^{n} \mathbf{S}(\boldsymbol{\beta}; y_j, \mathbf{x}_j) = \mathbf{0}$$

where $\mathbf{S}(\boldsymbol{\beta}; y_j, \mathbf{x}_j) = \partial l_j / \partial \boldsymbol{\beta}$ is the score vector and l_j the log-likelihood for the jth observation. Here $\boldsymbol{\beta}$ represents all the parameters in the model, including any auxiliary parameters. We will discuss how to use _robust when there are auxiliary parameters or multiple equations in the next section. But for now, all the theory works out fine for any set of parameters.

Using a first-order Taylor-series expansion (i.e., the delta method), we can write the variance of $\mathbf{G}(\boldsymbol{\beta})$ as

$$\widehat{V}\{\mathbf{G}(\boldsymbol{\beta})\}\big|_{\beta=\widehat{\beta}} = \frac{\partial \mathbf{G}(\boldsymbol{\beta})}{\partial \boldsymbol{\beta}}\bigg|_{\beta=\widehat{\beta}} \widehat{V}(\widehat{\boldsymbol{\beta}}) \frac{\partial \mathbf{G}(\boldsymbol{\beta})}{\partial \boldsymbol{\beta}}'\bigg|_{\beta=\widehat{\beta}}$$

Solving for $\widehat{V}(\widehat{\beta})$ gives

$$\widehat{V}(\widehat{\beta}) = \left[\left\{\frac{\partial \mathbf{G}(\beta)}{\partial \beta}\right\}^{-1} \widehat{V}\{\mathbf{G}(\beta)\}\left\{\frac{\partial \mathbf{G}(\beta)}{\partial \beta}\right\}'^{-1}\right]\Bigg|_{\beta=\widehat{\beta}}$$

but

$$\mathbf{H} = \frac{\partial \mathbf{G}(\beta)}{\partial \beta}$$

is the Hessian (matrix of second-derivatives) of the log-likelihood. Thus, we can write

$$\widehat{V}(\widehat{\beta}) = \mathbf{D}\,\widehat{V}\{\mathbf{G}(\beta)\}\big|_{\beta=\widehat{\beta}}\,\mathbf{D}$$

where $\mathbf{D} = -\mathbf{H}^{-1}$ is the traditional covariance estimate.

Now $\mathbf{G}(\beta)$ is simply a sum, and we can estimate its variance just as we would the sum of any other variable—it is n^2 times the standard estimator of the variance of a mean:

$$\frac{n}{n-1}\sum_{j=1}^{n}(z_j - \bar{z})^2$$

But, here, the scores $\mathbf{u}_j = \mathbf{S}(\widehat{\beta}; y_j, \mathbf{x}_j)$ are (row) vectors. Also note that their sum, and thus their mean, is zero. So we have

$$\widehat{V}\{\mathbf{G}(\beta)\}\big|_{\beta=\widehat{\beta}} = \frac{n}{n-1}\sum_{j=1}^{n}\mathbf{u}_j'\mathbf{u}_j$$

Putting it all together, our robust variance estimator is

$$\widehat{V}(\widehat{\beta}) = \mathbf{D}\left(\frac{n}{n-1}\sum_{j=1}^{n}\mathbf{u}_j'\mathbf{u}_j\right)\mathbf{D}$$

so we see that the robust variance estimator is just the delta method combined with a simple estimator for totals!

The above estimator for the variance of the total (the center of the sandwich) is only appropriate when observations are independent. For clustered data and complex survey data, this estimator is replaced by one appropriate for the independent units of the data. Clusters (or PSUs) are independent, so we can sum the scores within a cluster to create a "super-observation" and then use the standard formula for a total on these independent super-observations. Our robust variance estimator thus becomes

$$\widehat{V}(\widehat{\beta}) = \mathbf{D}\left\{\frac{n_c}{n_c-1}\sum_{i=1}^{n_c}\left(\sum_{j\in C_i}\mathbf{u}_j\right)'\left(\sum_{j\in C_i}\mathbf{u}_j\right)\right\}\mathbf{D}$$

where C_i contains the indices of the observations belonging to the ith cluster for $i = 1, 2, \ldots, n_c$ with n_c the total number of clusters.

See [R] **svymean** for the variance estimator for a total that is appropriate for complex survey data. Our development here has been quite heuristic. We have, for instance, purposefully omitted sampling weights from our discussion; see [R] **svy estimators** for a better treatment.

See Gould and Sribney (1999) for a discussion of maximum likelihood and of Stata's `ml` command.

❏ Technical Note

It is easy to see where the appropriate degrees of freedom for the robust variance estimator come from. The center of the sandwich is n^2 times the standard estimator of the variance for the mean of n observations. A mean divided by its standard error has exactly a Student's t distribution with $n - 1$ degrees of freedom for normal i.i.d. variables, but also has approximately this distribution under many other conditions. Thus, a point estimate divided by the square root of its robust variance estimate is approximately distributed as a Student's t with $n - 1$ degrees of freedom.

More importantly, this also applies to clusters, where each cluster is considered a "super-observation". Here the degrees of freedom are $n_c - 1$, where n_c is the number of clusters (super-observations). Note that if there are only a small number of clusters, confidence intervals using t statistics can become quite large. It is just like estimating a mean with only a small number of observations.

When there are strata, the degrees of freedom are $n_c - L$, where L is the number of strata; see [R] **svymean** for details.

Note that not all of Stata's maximum likelihood estimators that produce robust variance estimators for clustered data use t statistics. Obviously, it only matters when the number of clusters is small. Users who want to be rigorous in their handling of clustered data should use the **svy** commands, where t statistics and adjusted Wald tests (see [R] **svytest**) are always used. Programmers who want to inflict similar rigor should do likewise.

❏

We have not yet given any details about the functional form of our scores $\mathbf{u}_j = \partial l_j / \partial \boldsymbol{\beta}$. In many cases, the log-likelihood l_j is a function of $\mathbf{x}_j \boldsymbol{\beta}$ (the "index"). Logistic regression, probit, and poisson regression are examples. There are no auxiliary parameters and there is only one equation.

In these cases, we can write $\mathbf{u}_j = s_j \mathbf{x}_j$, where

$$s_j = \frac{\partial l_j}{\partial (\mathbf{x}_j \boldsymbol{\beta})}$$

We refer to s_j as the score index. Our formula for the robust estimator when observations are independent becomes

$$\widehat{V}(\widehat{\boldsymbol{\beta}}) = \mathbf{D} \left(\frac{n}{n - 1} \sum_{j=1}^{n} s_j^2 \, \mathbf{x}_j' \mathbf{x}_j \right) \mathbf{D}$$

This is precisely the formula that we used for linear regression with $\widehat{e}_j$ replaced by s_j and $k = 1$ in the multiplier.

Before we discuss auxiliary parameters, let's show how to implement _robust for single-equation models.

▷ Example

The robust variance implementation for single-equation maximum-likelihood estimators with no auxiliary parameters is almost exactly the same as it is for linear regression. The only differences are that $\mathbf{D}$ is now the traditional covariance matrix (the negative of the inverse of the matrix of second derivatives) and that the variable passed to _robust is the score index s_j rather than the residuals $\widehat{e}_j$.

Let's alter our last **myreg** program for survey data to make a program that does logistic regression for survey data. We only have to change a few lines of the program.

―― top of mylogit.ado ――――――――

```
program define mylogit, eclass
        version 7.0
        syntax varlist [if] [in] [pweight] [, /*
                */ STRata(varname) CLuster(varname) ]
        marksample touse, zeroweight
        markout `touse' `strata' `cluster', strok

        if "`weight'"~="" {
                tempvar w
                quietly gen double `w' `exp' if `touse'
                local awexp "[aw=`w']"
                capture assert `w' >= 0 if `touse'
                if _rc { error 402 }
        }
        if "`cluster'"~="" {
                local clopt "cluster(`cluster')"
        }
        if "`strata'"~="" {
                local stopt "strata(`strata')"
        }
        tempvar s
        tempname D b
        quietly {
                logit `varlist' `awexp' if `touse'
                matrix `D' = e(V)
                matrix `b' = e(b)

                predict double `s' if e(sample)
                local depn : word 1 of `varlist'
                replace `s' = (`depn'~=0) - `s' if e(sample)

                _robust `s' `awexp' if e(sample), v(`D') `clopt' `stopt' zeroweight

                local dof = r(N_clust) - r(N_strata)

                replace `touse' = e(sample)
                estimates post `b' `D', depn(`depn') dof(`dof') esample(`touse')
                estimates local vcetype "Design-based"
        }
        di /* display blank line */
        estimates display
end
```

―― end of mylogit.ado ――――――――

Note the following about our program:

1. This time we used aweights in both the call to logit and the call to _robust. Unfortunately, logit does not allow iweights; otherwise we would have used them. If you examine the robust estimator formula $V = DMD$, you will see that $D \propto w^{-1}$ and $M \propto w^2$, where w represents the weights (any weights other than frequency weights). logit scales the weights when it computes D and _robust scales the weights when it computes M; thus, these two scalings cancel each other out and we are left with what we would have computed had we used unscaled weights. See *Methods and Formulas* at the end of this entry.

2. Since logit only allows nonnegative weights, so must mylogit. Negative weights are, admittedly, a rather odd item; they only arise when using some very specialized techniques.

3. We obtained the scores by first calling predict to compute the predicted probabilities and then doing the necessary computation ourselves. logit has a score() option which computes the scores. This would have been a better way to get the scores, but using predict is a more typical procedure.

4. `logit` is a unique command in that it will drop observations in some cases for reasons (e.g., when success or failure is predicted perfectly) other than missing values, so our `touse` variable may not represent the true estimation sample. That is why we used the `if e(sample)` condition with the `predict`, `replace`, and `_robust` commands. Then, to provide `estimates post` with an appropriate `esample()` option, we set the `touse` variable equal to the `e(sample)` from the `logit` command and then use this `touse` variable in the `esample()` option.

Our `mylogit` program gives the same results as `svylogit`:

```
. mylogit foreign mpg weight gear_ratio [pw=displ], strata(strata) cluster(psu)
```

foreign	Coef.	Design-based Std. Err.	t	P>|t|	[95% Conf. Interval]	
mpg	-.3489011	.1263689	-2.76	0.017	-.6242353	-.0735669
weight	-.0040789	.001226	-3.33	0.006	-.00675	-.0014077
gear_ratio	6.324169	1.263861	5.00	0.000	3.570453	9.077886
_cons	-2.189748	7.220947	-0.30	0.767	-17.92284	13.54334

```
. svylogit foreign mpg weight gear_ratio [pw=displ], strata(strata) psu(psu)
```

Survey logistic regression

pweight:	displacement	Number of obs	=	74
Strata:	strata	Number of strata =		3
PSU:	psu	Number of PSUs	=	15
		Population size	=	14600
		F(3, 10)	=	11.14
		Prob > F	=	0.0016

foreign	Coef.	Std. Err.	t	P>|t|	[95% Conf. Interval]	
mpg	-.3489011	.1263689	-2.76	0.017	-.6242353	-.0735669
weight	-.0040789	.001226	-3.33	0.006	-.00675	-.0014077
gear_ratio	6.324169	1.263861	5.00	0.000	3.570453	9.077886
_cons	-2.189748	7.220947	-0.30	0.767	-17.92284	13.54334

◁

❑ Technical Note

The theory developed here applies to full-information maximum-likelihood estimators. Conditional likelihoods such as conditional (fixed-effects) logistic regression (`clogit`) and Cox regression (`stcox`) use variants on this theme. The `robust` option on `stcox` uses a similar, but different, formula; see [R] **st stcox** and Lin and Wei (1989) for details.

On the other hand, the theory developed here applies to more estimators than just maximum likelihood estimators. The theory can also be applied to general estimating equations

$$\mathbf{G}(\beta) = \sum_{j=1}^{n} \mathbf{g}(\beta; y_j, \mathbf{x}_j) = \mathbf{0}$$

See, for example, Binder (1983) for a formal development of the theory.

Programmers are cautioned that they are responsible for the theory behind their implementation.

❑

Multiple-equation estimators

The theory for auxiliary parameters and multiple-equation models is no different from what we described in the previous section. For independent observations, just as before, our robust variance estimator is

$$\widehat{V}(\boldsymbol{\beta}) = \mathbf{D}\left(\frac{n}{n-1}\sum_{j=1}^{n}\mathbf{u}_j'\mathbf{u}_j\right)\mathbf{D}$$

where $\mathbf{u}_j = \partial l_j/\partial\boldsymbol{\beta}$ is the score (row) vector and $\mathbf{D}$ is the traditional covariance estimate (the negative of the inverse of the matrix of second derivatives).

With auxiliary parameters and/or multiple equations, we simply view $\boldsymbol{\beta}$ as the vector of all the parameters in the model. Without loss of generality, we can write the log-likelihood as

$$l_j = l_j(\mathbf{x}_j^{(1)}\boldsymbol{\beta}^{(1)}, \mathbf{x}_j^{(2)}\boldsymbol{\beta}^{(2)}, \ldots, \mathbf{x}_j^{(p)}\boldsymbol{\beta}^{(p)})$$

An auxiliary parameter is regarded as $\mathbf{x}_j^{(i)}\boldsymbol{\beta}^{(i)}$ with $\mathbf{x}_j \equiv 1$ and $\boldsymbol{\beta}^{(i)}$ a scalar. Our score vector becomes

$$\mathbf{u}_j = [\, s_j^{(1)}\mathbf{x}_j^{(1)} \quad s_j^{(2)}\mathbf{x}_j^{(2)} \quad \cdots \quad s_j^{(p)}\mathbf{x}_j^{(p)} \,]$$

where $s_j^{(i)} = \partial l_j/\partial(\mathbf{x}_j\boldsymbol{\beta}^{(i)})$ is the score index for the ith equation.

This notation has been introduced so that it is clear how to call _robust. You use

. _robust $s_j^{(1)}$ $s_j^{(2)}$ $\ldots$ $s_j^{(p)}$, *options*

where $s_j^{(1)}$, etc., are variables that contain the score indexes. The $\mathbf{D}$ matrix that you pass to _robust or post with `estimates post` must be labeled with exactly p equation names.

_robust takes the first score index $s_j^{(1)}$ and matches it to the first equation on the $\mathbf{D}$ matrix to determine $\mathbf{x}_j^{(1)}$, takes the second score index and matches it to the second equation, etc. Some examples will make this perfectly clear.

▷ Example

Here is what a matrix with equation names looks like:

```
. matrix list D
symmetric D[6,6]
                     1:           1:           1:           2:           2:
                  price      foreign        _cons        price      foreign
   1:price    1.240e-08
 1:foreign   -1.401e-06     .593554
   1:_cons   -.00007592   -.13992997    .61347545
   2:price    4.265e-09   -5.366e-07   -.00002693    1.207e-08
 2:foreign   -1.590e-06    .37202357   -.02774147   -3.184e-06    .56833685
   2:_cons    -.0000265   -.0343682     .20468675   -.00007108   -.1027108
                     2:
                  _cons
   2:_cons    .54017838
```

The call to _robust would then be

```
. _robust s1 s2, v(D)
```

where s1 and s2 are the score indexes for equation 1 and equation 2 respectively.

Covariance matrices from models with auxiliary parameters look just like multiple-equation matrices:

```
. matrix list D
symmetric D[5,5]
                     eq1:        eq1:        eq1:        eq1:      sigma:
                  weight  gear_ratio     foreign       _cons       _cons
   eq1:weight   5.978e-07
eq1:gear_ratio   .00069222   2.2471526
  eq1:foreign   .00011344  -.88159935   1.4426905
    eq1:_cons  -.00392566  -8.6029018   1.8864693   37.377729
   sigma:_cons  -7.217e-15  -1.663e-10   2.147e-10  -6.464e-09   .07430437
```

The second equation consists of the auxiliary parameter only. The call to _robust would be the same as before:

```
. _robust s1 s2, v(D)
```

◁

▷ Example

We will now give an example using ml and _robust to produce an estimation command that has robust and cluster() options. You can actually accomplish all of this easily using ml without using the _robust command since ml has robust and cluster() options. We will pretend that these two options are unavailable to illustrate the use of _robust.

To keep the example simple, we will do linear regression as a maximum likelihood estimator. In this case, the log-likelihood is

$$l_j = -\frac{1}{2}\left\{\left(\frac{y_j - \mathbf{x}_j\boldsymbol{\beta}}{\sigma}\right)^2 + \ln\left(2\pi\sigma^2\right)\right\}$$

There is an auxiliary parameter σ, and we have two score indexes:

$$\frac{\partial l_j}{\partial(\mathbf{x}_j\boldsymbol{\beta})} = \frac{y_j - \mathbf{x}_j\boldsymbol{\beta}}{\sigma^2}$$

$$\frac{\partial l_j}{\partial\sigma} = \frac{1}{\sigma}\left\{\left(\frac{y_j - \mathbf{x}_j\boldsymbol{\beta}}{\sigma}\right)^2 - 1\right\}$$

Here are programs to compute this estimator. We have two ado-files: mymle.ado and likereg.ado. The first ado-file contains two programs mymle and Scores. mymle is the main program and Scores is a subprogram that computes the score indexes after we compute the maximum likelihood solution. Since Scores is only called by mymle, we can nest it in the mymle.ado file; see [U] **20 Ado-files**.

──────────────────────────── top of mymle.ado ────────────

```
program define mymle, eclass
        version 7.0
        local options "Level(integer $S_level)"
        if replay() {
                if "`e(cmd)´"~="mymle" {
                        error 301
                }
                syntax [, `options´]
                ml display, level(`level´)
                exit
        }
        syntax varlist [if] [in] [, /*
                */ `options´ Robust CLuster(varname) ]
/* Determine estimation sample. */
        marksample touse
        if "`cluster´"~="" {
                markout `touse´ `cluster´, strok
                local clopt "cluster(`cluster´)"
        }
/* Get starting values. */
        tokenize `varlist´
        local depn "`1´"
        macro shift
        quietly summarize `depn´ if `touse´
        local cons = r(mean)
        local sigma = sqrt(r(Var))
/* Do ml. */
        ml model lf likereg (`depn´=`*´) /sigma if `touse´, /*
                */ init(/eq1=`cons´ /sigma=`sigma´)  max /*
                */ title("MLE linear regression") nooutput `options´
        if "`robust´"~="" | "`cluster´"~="" {
                tempvar s1 s2
                Scores `depn´ `s1´ `s2´
                _robust `s1´ `s2´ if `touse´, `clopt´
        }
        est local cmd "mymle"
        ml display, level(`level´)
end

program define Scores
        version 7.0
        args depn s1 s2
        quietly {
                predict double `s1´
                gen double `s2´ = (((`depn´ - `s1´)/[sigma][_cons])^2 - 1) /*
                */                /[sigma][_cons]
                replace `s1´ = (`depn´ - `s1´)/([sigma][_cons]^2)
        }
end
```

──────────────────────────── end of mymle.ado ────────────

Our `likereg` program computes the likelihood. Since it is called by Stata's `ml` commands, we cannot nest it in the other file.

```
                                                ─────── top of likereg.ado ───────
program define likereg
        version 7.0
        args lf xb s
        qui replace `lf´ = -0.5*((($ML_y1 - `xb´)/`s´)^2 + log(2*_pi*`s´^2))
end
                                                ─────── end of likereg.ado ───────
```

Note the following:

1. Our command `mymle` will produce robust variance estimates if either the `robust` or the `cluster()` option is specified. Otherwise, it will display the traditional estimates.

2. We used the `lf` method with `ml`; see [R] **ml**. We could have used the `deriv1` or `deriv2` methods. Since you will probably include code to compute the first derivatives analytically for the `robust` option, there is no point in using `deriv0`. (However, one could compute the first derivatives numerically and pass these to `_robust`.)

3. Our `Scores` program uses `predict` to compute the index $x_j\beta$. Since we had already posted the results using `ml`, `predict` is available to us. Note that, by default, `predict` computes the index for the first equation.

4. Again, since we had already posted the results using `ml`, we can use [sigma][_cons] to get the value of σ; see [U] **16.5 Accessing coefficients and standard errors** for the syntax of accessing coefficients from multiple-equation models.

5. `ml` calls `estimates post`, so when we call `_robust` it alters the posted covariance matrix, replacing it with the robust covariance matrix. `_robust` also sets `e(vcetype)`, and if the `cluster()` option is specified, it sets `e(clustvar)` as well.

6. We let `ml` produce Z statistics, even when we specified the `cluster()` option. If the number of clusters is small, it would be better to use t statistics. To do this, you could specify the `dof()` option on the `ml` command, but you would have to compute the number of clusters in advance. Alternatively, you could get the number of clusters from `_robust`'s `r(N_clust)` and then re-post the matrices using `estimates post`.

   If we run our command with the `cluster()` option, we get

```
. mymle mpg weight gear_ratio foreign, cluster(rep78)
initial:       log likelihood =  -219.4845
rescale:       log likelihood =  -219.4845
rescale eq:    log likelihood =  -219.4845
Iteration 0:   log likelihood =  -219.4845  (not concave)
Iteration 1:   log likelihood = -207.02829  (not concave)
Iteration 2:   log likelihood =  -202.6134
Iteration 3:   log likelihood = -189.81321
Iteration 4:   log likelihood = -181.94707
Iteration 5:   log likelihood = -181.94473
Iteration 6:   log likelihood = -181.94473
```

```
MLE linear regression                           Number of obs    =          69
                                                Wald chi2(3)     =      135.82
Log likelihood = -181.94473                     Prob > chi2      =      0.0000
                             (standard errors adjusted for clustering on rep78)
```

mpg	Coef.	Robust Std. Err.	z	P>|z|	[95% Conf. Interval]	
eq1						
weight	-.005893	.000803	-7.34	0.000	-.0074669	-.0043191
gear_ratio	1.904503	2.134518	0.89	0.372	-2.279075	6.08808
foreign	-2.149017	1.178012	-1.82	0.068	-4.457879	.1598441
_cons	34.09959	4.121243	8.27	0.000	26.02211	42.17708
sigma						
_cons	3.380223	.8840543	3.82	0.000	1.647508	5.112937

These results are similar to the earlier results that we got with our first myreg program and regress, cluster.

Note that our likelihood is not globally concave. Linear regression is not globally concave in β and σ. ml's lf convergence routine encountered a little trouble in the beginning, but had no problem coming to the right solution.

◁

Saved Results

_robust saves in r():

Scalars
   r(N)   number of observations
   r(N_strata)   number of strata
   r(N_clust)   number of clusters (PSUs)
   r(sum_w)   sum of weights (if weights are specified)
   r(N_subpop)   number of observations for subpopulation (subpop() only)
   r(sum_wsub)   sum of weights for subpopulation (subpop() and weights only)

Note that r(N_strata) and r(N_clust) are always set. If the strata() option is not specified, r(N_strata) = 1 (there truly is one stratum). If neither the cluster() nor the psu() option is specified, r(N_clust) equals the number of observations (each observation is a PSU).

When _robust alters the post of estimates post, it also saves in e():

Macros
   e(vcetype)   "Robust"
   e(clustvar)   name of cluster (PSU) variable

e(vcetype) controls the phrase estimates display displays above "Std. Err."; e(vcetype) can be set to another phrase (or to empty for no phrase) if you wish. e(clustvar) displays the banner "(standard errors adjusted for clustering on *varname*)", or it can be set to empty (estimates local clustvar "") if you do not wish this banner to be displayed.

Methods and Formulas

We give the formulas here for complex survey data, this being the most general case.

Our parameter estimates $\widehat{\beta}$ are the solution to the estimating equation

$$\mathbf{G}(\beta) = \sum_{h=1}^{L} \sum_{i=1}^{n_h} \sum_{j=1}^{m_{hi}} w_{hij} \mathbf{S}(\beta; y_{hij}, \mathbf{x}_{hij}) = \mathbf{0}$$

where (h, i, j) index the observations: $h = 1, \ldots, L$ are the strata, $i = 1, \ldots, n_h$ are the sampled PSUs (clusters) in stratum h, and $j = 1, \ldots, m_{hi}$ are the sampled observations in PSU (h, i). The outcome variable is represented by y_{hij}, the explanatory variables are $\mathbf{x}_{hij}$ (a row vector), and w_{hij} are the weights.

If no weights are specified, $w_{hij} = 1$. If the weights are aweights, they are first normalized to sum to the total number of observations in the sample: $n = \sum_{h=1}^{L} \sum_{i=1}^{n_h} m_{hi}$. If the weights are fweights, the formulas below do not apply; fweights are treated in such a way to give the same results as unweighted observations duplicated the appropriate number of times.

For maximum likelihood estimators, $\mathbf{S}(\beta; y_{hij}, \mathbf{x}_{hij}) = \partial l_j / \partial \beta$ is the score vector where l_j is the log-likelihood. Note that for survey data, this is not a true likelihood but a "pseudo" likelihood; see [R] svy estimators.

Let

$$\mathbf{D} = -\left. \frac{\partial \mathbf{G}(\beta)}{\partial \beta} \right|_{\beta=\widehat{\beta}}^{-1}$$

For maximum likelihood estimators, $\mathbf{D}$ is the traditional covariance estimate—the negative of the inverse of the Hessian. Note that in the following the sign of $\mathbf{D}$ does not matter.

The robust covariance estimate calculated by _robust is

$$\widehat{V}(\widehat{\beta}) = \mathbf{DMD}$$

where $\mathbf{M}$ is computed as follows. Let $\mathbf{u}_{hij} = \mathbf{S}(\beta; y_{hij}, \mathbf{x}_{hij})$ be a row vector of scores for the (h, i, j) observation. Let

$$\mathbf{u}_{hi\bullet} = \sum_{j=1}^{m_{hi}} w_{hij} \mathbf{u}_{hij} \qquad \text{and} \qquad \overline{\mathbf{u}}_{h\bullet\bullet} = \frac{1}{n_h} \sum_{i=1}^{n_h} \mathbf{u}_{hi\bullet}$$

$\mathbf{M}$ is given by

$$\mathbf{M} = \frac{n-1}{n-k} \sum_{h=1}^{L} (1 - f_h) \frac{n_h}{n_h - 1} \sum_{i=1}^{n_h} (\mathbf{u}_{hi\bullet} - \overline{\mathbf{u}}_{h\bullet\bullet})'(\mathbf{u}_{hi\bullet} - \overline{\mathbf{u}}_{h\bullet\bullet})$$

where k is the value given in the minus() option. By default, $k = 1$ and the term $(n-1)/(n-k)$ vanishes. Stata's regress, robust and regress, robust cluster() use k equal to the number of explanatory variables in the model including the constant (Fuller et al. 1986). All svy commands use $k = 1$.

The specification $k = 0$ is handled differently. If minus(0) is specified, $(n-1)/(n-k)$ and $n_h/(n_h - 1)$ are both replaced by 1. Note that the "huberized" commands in Stata 4.0 (hreg, hlogit, etc.) used $k = 0$.

The factor $(1 - f_h)$ is the finite population correction. If the `fpc()` option is not specified, $f_h = 0$ is used. If `fpc()` is specified and the variable is greater than or equal to n_h, it is assumed to contain the values of N_h, and f_h is given by $f_h = n_h / N_h$, where N_h is the total number of PSUs in the population belonging to the hth stratum. If the `fpc()` variable is less than or equal to 1, it is assumed to contain the values of f_h. See [R] **svymean** for details and cautionary remarks.

For the `vsrs()` option and the computation of $\widehat{V}_{\mathrm{srswor}}$, the `subpop()` option, and the `srssubpop` option, see [R] **svymean**.

References

Binder, D. A. 1983. On the variances of asymptotically normal estimators from complex surveys. *International Statistical Review* 51: 279–292.

Fuller, W. A. 1975. Regression analysis for sample survey. *Sankhyā, Series C* 37: 117–132.

Fuller, W. A., W. Kennedy, D. Schnell, G. Sullivan, H. J. Park. 1986. *PC Carp*. Ames, IA: Statistical Laboratory, Iowa State University.

Gail, M. H., W. Y. Tan, and S. Piantadosi. 1988. Tests for no treatment effect in randomized clinical trials. *Biometrika* 75: 57–64.

Gould, W. W. and W. M. Sribney. 1999. *Maximum likelihood estimation with Stata*. College Station, TX: Stata Press.

Huber, P. J. 1967. The behavior of maximum likelihood estimates under non-standard conditions. In *Proceedings of the Fifth Berkeley Symposium on Mathematical Statistics and Probability*. Berkeley, CA: University of California Press, vol. 1, 221–233.

Kent, J. T. 1982. Robust properties of likelihood ratio tests. *Biometrika* 69: 19–27.

Kish, L. and M. R. Frankel. 1974. Inference from complex samples. *Journal of the Royal Statistical Society* B 36: 1–37.

Lin, D. Y. and L. J. Wei. 1989. The robust inference for the Cox proportional hazards model. *Journal of the American Statistical Association* 84: 1074–1078.

MacKinnon, J. G. and H. White. 1985. Some heteroskedasticity consistent covariance matrix estimators with improved finite sample properties. *Journal of Econometrics* 29: 305–325.

Rogers, W. H. 1993. sg17: Regression standard errors in clustered samples. *Stata Technical Bulletin* 13: 19–23. Reprinted in *Stata Technical Bulletin Reprints*, vol. 3, pp. 88–94.

Royall, R. M. 1986. Model robust confidence intervals using maximum likelihood estimators. *International Statistical Review* 54: 221–226.

White, H. 1980. A heteroskedasticity-consistent covariance matrix estimator and a direct test for heteroskedasticity. *Econometrica* 48: 817–830.

——. 1982. Maximum likelihood estimation of misspecified models. *Econometrica* 50: 1–25.

Also See

Complementary:	[P] **estimates**, [R] **ml**
Related:	[R] **estimation commands**, [R] **regress**, [R] **svy estimators**, [R] **svymean**
Background:	[U] **21 Programming Stata**, [U] **23.11 Obtaining robust variance estimates**, [U] **29 Overview of model estimation in Stata**

Title

scalar — Scalar variables

Syntax

scalar [define] *scalar_name* = *exp*

scalar { dir | list } [_all | *scalar_name(s)*]

scalar drop { _all | *scalar_name(s)* }

Description

scalar define defines the contents of the scalar variable *scalar_name*.

scalar dir and list are the same command—both list the contents of currently defined scalars.

scalar drop eliminates defined scalars from memory.

Remarks

Stata scalars are named entities that store numbers which may include missing values. For instance,

```
. scalar a = 2
. display a+2
4
. scalar b = a+3
. display b
5
. scalar root2 = sqrt(2)
. display %18.0g root2
 1.414213562373095
. scalar im = sqrt(-1)
. display im
.
```

scalar list can be used to display the contents of macros (as can display for reasons that will be explained below) and scalar drop can be used to eliminate scalars from memory:

```
. scalar list
       im =          .
    root2 =  1.4142136
        b =          5
        a =          2
. scalar list a b
        a =          2
        b =          5
. scalar drop a b
. scalar list
       im =          .
    root2 =  1.4142136
. scalar drop _all
. scalar list
```

254

While scalars can be used interactively, their real use is in programs. Stata has macros and Stata has scalars, and deciding when to use which can be confusing.

▷ Example

Let's examine a problem where either macros or scalars could be employed in the solution. There will be occasions in your programs where you need something that we will describe as a mathematical scalar—a single number. For instance, let us assume that you are writing a program and need the mean of some variable for use in a subsequent calculation. You can obtain the mean after `summarize` from `r(mean)` (see *Saved Results* in [R] **summarize**), but you must obtain it immediately because the numbers stored in `r()` are reset almost every time you give a statistical command.

Let us complicate the problem: to make some calculation, you need to calculate the difference in the means of two variables which we will call `var1` and `var2`. One solution to your problem is to use macros:

```
summarize var1, meanonly
local mean1 = r(mean)
summarize var2, meanonly
local mean2 =  r(mean)
local diff = `mean1´ - `mean2´
```

Subsequently, you use `` `diff´ `` in your calculation. Let's understand how this works: You `summarize var1, meanonly`; inclusion of the `meanonly` option suppresses the output from the `summarize` command and the calculation of the variance. You then save the contents of `r(mean)`—the just-calculated mean—in the local macro `mean1`. You then `summarize var2`, again suppressing the output, and store that just-saved result in the local macro `mean2`. Finally, you create another local macro called `diff` that contains the difference. In making this calculation, you must put the `mean1` and `mean2` local macro names in single quotes because you want the contents of the macros. If the mean of `var1` is 3 and `var2` is 2, you want the numbers 3 and 2 substituted into the formula for `diff` to produce 1. If you omitted the single quotes, Stata would think you are referring to the difference not of the contents of macros named `mean1` and `mean2`, but of two variables named `mean1` and `mean2`. Those variables probably do not exist, so Stata would then produce an error message. In any case, you put the names in the single quotes.

Now let's consider the solution using Stata scalars:

```
summarize var1, meanonly
scalar m1 = r(mean)
summarize var2, meanonly
scalar m2 = r(mean)
scalar df = m1 - m2
```

The program fragments are quite similar, although note that this time we did not put the names of the scalars used in calculating the difference—which we called `df` this time—in single quotes. Stata scalars are allowed only in mathematical expressions—they are a kind of variable—and Stata knows you want the contents of those variables.

So, which solution is better? There is certainly nothing to recommend one over the other in terms of program length—both programs have the same number of lines and, in fact, there is a one-to-one correspondence between what each of the lines does. Nevertheless, the scalar-based solution is better, and here is why:

Macros are printable representations of things. When we said `local mean1 = r(mean)`, Stata took the contents of `r(mean)`, converted it into a printable form from its internal (and highly accurate) binary representation, and stored that string of characters in the macro `mean1`. When we created `mean2`, Stata did the same thing again. Then, when we said `local diff = `mean1´ - `mean2´`, Stata first substituted the contents of the macros `mean1` and `mean2`—which are really strings—into the command. If the means of the two variables are 3 and 2, then the printable string representations stored in `mean1` and `mean2` are "3" and "2". After substitution, Stata was looking at the command `local diff = 3 - 2`. It then processed that, converting the 3 and 2 back into internal binary representation to take the difference, producing the number 1, which it then converted into the printable representation "1", which it finally stored in the macro `diff`.

All of this conversion from binary to printable representation and back again is a lot of work for Stata. Moreover, while there are no accuracy issues with numbers like 3 and 2, had the first number been $3.67108239891 \times 10^{-8}$, there would have been. When converting to printable form, Stata produces representations containing up to 17 digits and, if necessary, uses scientific notation. The first number would have become `3.6710823989e-08` and the last digit would have been lost. In computer scientific notation, 17 printable positions provides you with a minimum of 13 significant digits. This is quite a lot, but not as many as Stata carries internally.

Now let us trace the execution of the solution using scalars. `scalar m1 = r(mean)` quickly copied the binary representation stored in `r(mean)` into the scalar `m1`. Similarly, executing `scalar m2 = r(mean)` did the same thing, although it saved it in `m2`. Finally, `scalar df = m1 - m2` took the two binary representations, subtracted them, and copied the result to the scalar `df`. This produces a more accurate result.

◁

❏ Technical Note

Since scalars are more accurate, why use macros at all? First, scalars cannot store strings—scalars are numbers. Second, macros do have their use even when the contents are numeric. Scalars can only be used in the context of a mathematical expression, which is abbreviated *exp* in the syntax diagrams throughout this manual. Macros can be used anywhere. For instance, pretend that in a time-series context, you need to obtain the mean of the first through the next-to-last observations of a variable called `x`. You can do this in Stata by typing

```
summarize x in 1/-2
```

but pretend that Stata could not count observations backwards in an `in` *range*. You could do the following:

```
local end = _N - 1
summarize x in 1/`end'
```

You could not do this with scalars because there is no way to substitute the value stored in a scalar into the context of an `in` *range*. It is only when Stata is expecting an expression that you can use scalars.

❏

Naming scalars

Scalars can have the same names as variables in the data and Stata will not become confused. You, however, may. Consider the following Stata command:

```
. generate newvar = alpha*beta
```

What does it mean? It certainly means to create a new data variable named `newvar`, but what will be in `newvar`? There are four possibilities:

1. Take the data variable `alpha` and the data variable `beta` and multiply the corresponding observations together.

2. Take the scalar `alpha` and the data variable `beta`, multiply each observation of `beta` by `alpha`.

3. Take the data variable `alpha` and the scalar `beta`, multiply each observation of `alpha` by `beta`.

4. Take the scalar `alpha` and the scalar `beta`, multiply them together, and store the result repeatedly into `newvar`.

How Stata decides among these four possibilities is the topic of this section.

Stata's first rule is that if there is only one `alpha`, be it a data variable or a scalar, and one `beta`, be it a data variable or a scalar, Stata selects the single feasible solution and does it. If, however, there is more than one `alpha` or more than one `beta`, Stata always selects the data-variable interpretation in preference to the scalar.

For instance, assume you have a data variable called `alpha` and a scalar called `beta`:

```
. list

           alpha
  1.           1
  2.           3
  3.           5
. scalar list
        beta =           3
. gen newvar = alpha*beta
. list

           alpha     newvar
  1.           1          3
  2.           3          9
  3.           5         15
```

The result was to take the data variable `alpha` and multiply it by the scalar `beta`. Now let's start again, but this time, assume you have a data variable called `alpha` and both a data variable and a scalar called `beta`:

```
. scalar list
        beta =           3
. list

           alpha       beta
  1.           1          2
  2.           3          3
  3.           5          4
. gen newvar = alpha*beta
. list

           alpha       beta     newvar
  1.           1          2          2
  2.           3          3          9
  3.           5          4         20
```

The result is to multiply the data variables, ignoring the scalar `beta`. In situations like this, you can force Stata to use the scalar by specifying `scalar(beta)` rather than merely `beta`:

```
. gen newvar2 = alpha*scalar(beta)
```

```
. list
            alpha       beta      newvar    newvar2
     1.         1          2           2          3
     2.         3          3           9          9
     3.         5          4          20         15
```

The `scalar()` pseudo-function, placed around a name, says that the name is to be interpreted as the name of a scalar even if a data variable by the same name exists. You can use `scalar()` around all your scalar names if you wish; it is not required that there be a name conflict. Obviously, it will be easiest if you give your data and scalars different names.

❏ Technical Note

The advice to name scalars and data variables differently may work interactively, but in programming situations, you cannot know whether the name you have chosen for a scalar conflicts with the data variables because the data are typically provided by the user and could have any names whatsoever.

One solution—and not a very good one—is to place the `scalar()` pseudo-function around the names of all your scalars when you use them. A much better solution is to obtain the names for your scalars from Stata's `tempname` facility; see [P] **macro**. There are other advantages as well. Let us go back to calculating the sum of the means of variables `var1` and `var2`. Our original draft looked like this:

```
summarize var1, meanonly
scalar m1 = r(mean)
summarize var2, meanonly
scalar m2 = r(mean)
scalar df = m1 - m2
```

A well-written draft would look like this:

```
tempname m1 m2 df
summarize var1, meanonly
scalar `m1´ = r(mean)
summarize var2, meanonly
scalar `m2´ = r(mean)
scalar `df´ = `m1´ - `m2´
```

We first declared the names of our temporary scalars. Actually, what `tempname` does is create three new local macros named `m1`, `m2`, and `df`, and place in those macros names that Stata makes up, names that are guaranteed to be different from the data. (`m1`, for your information, probably contains something like `__000001`.) When we use the temporary names, we put single quotes around them—`m1` is not the name we want; we want the name that is stored in the local macro named `m1`.

That is, if we type

```
scalar m1 = r(mean)
```

we create a scalar named `m1`. After `tempname m1 m2 df`, if we type

```
scalar `m1´ = r(mean)
```

we create a scalar named with whatever name happens to be stored in `m1`. It is Stata's responsibility to make sure that name is valid and unique and Stata did that when we issued the `tempname` command. As programmers, we never need to know what is really stored in the macro `m1`: all we need to do is put single quotes around the name whenever we use it.

There is a second advantage to naming scalars with names obtained from `tempname`. Stata knows they are temporary—when our program concludes, all temporary scalars will be automatically dropped from memory. And, if our program calls another program, that program will not accidentally use one of our scalars even if the programmer happened to use the same name. Consider

```
program define myprog
        ( lines omitted )
        tempname m1
        scalar `m1´ = something
        mysub
        ( lines omitted )
end
program define mysub
        ( lines omitted )
        tempname m1
        scalar `m1´ = something else
        ( lines omitted )
end
```

Both `myprog` and `mysub` refer to a scalar `m1´; `myprog` defines `m1´ and then calls `mysub`, and `mysub` then defines `m1´ differently. When `myprog` regains control, however, `m1´ is just as it was before calling `mysub`!

It is unchanged because the scalar is not named m1: it is named something as returned by `tempname`—a guaranteed unique name—and that name is stored in the local macro m1. When `mysub` is executed, Stata safely hides all local macros, so the local macro m1 in `mysub` has no relation to the local macro m1 in `myprog`. `mysub` now puts a temporary name in its local macro m1—a different name because `tempname` always returns unique names—and `mysub` goes forth to use that different name. When `mysub` completes, Stata discards the temporary scalars and macros, restores the definitions of the old temporary macros, and `myprog` is off and running again.

Even if `mysub` had been poorly written in the sense of not obtaining its temporary names from `tempname`, `myprog` would have no difficulty. The use of `tempname` by `myprog` is sufficient to guarantee that no other program can harm it. For instance, pretend `mysub` looked like

```
program define mysub
        ( lines omitted )
        scalar m1 = something else
        ( lines omitted )
end
```

Note that `mysub` is now directly using a scalar named m1. That will not interfere with `myprog`, however, because `myprog` has no scalar named m1. Its scalar is named `m1´, a name obtained from `tempname`.

❑

❑ Technical Note

One result of the above is that scalars are not automatically shared between programs. The scalar `m1´ in `myprog` is different from either of the scalars m1 or `m1´ in `mysub`. What if `mysub` needs `myprog`'s `m1´?

One solution is not to use `tempname`: write `myprog` to use the scalar m1 and `mysub` to use the scalar m1. Both will be accessing the same scalar. This, however, is not recommended.

A better solution is to pass `m1´ as an argument. For instance,

```
program define myprog
        ( lines omitted )
        tempname m1
        scalar `m1´ = something
        mysub `m1´
        ( lines omitted )
end
```

```
program define mysub
        args m1
        ( lines omitted )
        commands using `m1´
        ( lines omitted )
end
```

We passed the name of the scalar given to us by tempname—`m1´—as the first argument to mysub. mysub picked up its first argument and stored that in its own local macro by the same name—m1. Actually, mysub could have stored the name in any macro name of its choosing; the line reading args m1 could read args m2 as long as we changed the rest of mysub to use the name `m2´ wherever it uses the name `m1´.

❏

Also See

Complementary:	[P] **matrix**
Related:	[P] **macro**
Background:	[U] **21.3 Macros**,
	[U] **21.7.2 Temporary scalars and matrices**

Title

> **sleep** — Pause for a specified time

Syntax

```
sleep #
```

where # is number of milliseconds.

Description

sleep tells Stata to pause for # milliseconds before continuing with the next command.

Remarks

Use sleep when you want Stata to wait for some amount of time before executing the next command.

```
. sleep 10000
```

pauses Stata for 10 seconds.

Also See

Background: [P] **window**

Title

smcl — Stata Markup and Control Language

Description

SMCL, which stands for Stata Markup and Control Language and is pronounced "smicle", is Stata's output language. SMCL directives, such as "{it:...}" in the following,

```
One can output {it:italics} using SMCL
```

affect how output appears:

One can output *italics* using SMCL

All Stata output is processed by SMCL: help files, statistical results, and even the output of `display` in the programs you write.

Remarks

Remarks are presented under the headings

Introduction
SMCL modes
Command summary—general syntax
Formatting commands for use in line and paragraph modes
Link commands for use in line and paragraph modes
Formatting commands for use in line mode
Formatting commands for use in paragraph mode
Commands for use in As-Is mode
Commands for use in Stata 6 help mode
The {char} directive
Advice on using display
Advice on formatting help files

Introduction

The two main uses of SMCL are in the programs you compose and in the help files you write to document them, although SMCL may be used in any context. Everything Stata displays on the screen is processed by SMCL.

Your first encounter with SMCL was probably the Stata session logs created by the `log using` command. By default, Stata creates logs in SMCL format and even gives them the file suffix `.smcl`. The file suffix does not matter, that the output is in SMCL format does. Files containing SMCL can be redisplayed in their original rendition, and SMCL output can be translated to other formats using the `translate` command; see [R] **translate**.

SMCL is mostly just ASCII text. For instance,

```
. display "this is SMCL"
this is SMCL
```

but throughout that can be SMCL directives. SMCL directives are enclosed in braces. Try the following:

```
. display "{title:this is SMCL, too}"
this is SMCL, too
```

The "{title:...}" directive told SMCL to output what followed the colon in title format. Exactly how title format appears on your screen—or on paper should you print it—will vary, but SMCL will ensure that it always appears as a recognizable title.

Now try this:

```
. display "now we will try {help summarize:clicking}"
now we will try clicking
```

Type the above into Stata. The word *clicking* will appear as clickable text—probably in some shade of blue. Click on the word. This will bring up Stata's Viewer and show you help for the summarize command. The SMCL {help:...} directive is an example of a *link*. The directive {help summarize:clicking} displayed the word *clicking* and arranged things so that when the user clicked on the highlighted word, help for summarize appeared.

Here is another example of a link:

```
. display "You can also run Stata commands by {stata summarize mpg:clicking}"
You can also run Stata commands by clicking
```

Click on the word and this time the result will be exactly as if you had typed the command "summarize mpg" into Stata. If you have the automobile data loaded, you will see the summary statistics for the variable mpg.

That is how SMCL is used. You can use it to make your output look better and to add clickable links.

SMCL modes

At all times, SMCL is in one of four modes:

1. SMCL line mode
2. SMCL paragraph mode
3. As-Is mode
4. Stata 6 help mode

Modes 1 and 2 are nearly alike—in these two modes, SMCL directives are understood, and the modes differ only in that blanks and carriage returns are taken seriously in line mode and less seriously in paragraph mode. In paragraph mode—so called because it is useful for formatting text into paragraphs—SMCL will join one line to the next and split lines to form output with lines that are of nearly equal length. In line mode, SMCL shows the line very much as you entered it. For instance, in line mode, the input text

```
Variable name          mean           standard error
```

(which might appear in a help file) would be spaced in the output exactly as we entered it. In paragraph mode, the above would be output as "Variable name mean standard error", which is to say, all run together. On the other hand, the text

```
The two main uses of SMCL are in the programs you compose and in the help files
you write to document them,  although SMCL may be used in any context.
Everything Stata displays on the screen is processed by SMCL.
```

would be set into a nicely formatted paragraph in paragraph mode.

In mode 3, As-Is mode, SMCL directives are not interpreted. `{title:...}`, for instance, has no special meaning—it is just the characters open brace, t, i, and so on. If `{title:...}` appeared in SMCL input text,

```
{title:My Title}
```

it would be displayed exactly as it appears: `{title:My Title}`. In As-Is mode, text is taken just as it is and SMCL just displays it. As-Is mode is of little use to people other than those wishing to document how SMCL works, because with As-Is mode, they can show examples of what SMCL input looks like.

Mode 4, Stata 6 help mode, you want to avoid; it is included for backwards compatibility. Prior to Stata 7, Stata's help files had an odd and special encoding that would allow some words to be highlighted, and it also allowed the creation of clickable links to other help files. However, it does not have nearly the features of SMCL and, moreover, it can only be used in `.hlp` files. In Stata 6 help mode, SMCL recreates this old environment so that old help files continue to display correctly even if they have not been updated.

Those are the four modes, and the most important of them are the first two, the SMCL modes, and the single most important mode is SMCL line mode—mode 1. Line mode is the mother of all modes in that SMCL continually returns to it, and it is only from line mode that you can get to the other modes. For instance, to enter paragraph mode you use the `{p}` directive, and you use it from line mode, although you typically do not think of that. Paragraphs end when a blank line is encountered, and what *end* means is that SMCL returns to line mode. Consider the following lines appearing in some help file:

```
{p}
The two main uses of SMCL are in the programs you compose and
the
help files you write to document them,
although SMCL may be used in any context.
Everything Stata displays on the screen is processed by SMCL.
{p}
Your first encounter with SMCL was probably the Stata session
...
```

Between the paragraphs above, SMCL returned to line mode. SMCL stayed in paragraph mode as long as the paragraph continued without a blank line but, once the paragraph ended, SMCL returned to line mode. There are ways of ending paragraphs other than blank lines, but blank lines are the most common. Regardless of how paragraphs end, SMCL returns to line mode.

In another part of our help file, we might have

```
{p}
SMCL, which stands for Stata Markup and Control Language
and is pronounced "smicle", is Stata's output language.
SMCL directives, for example, the {c -(}it:...{c )-} in the following,
        One can output {it:italics} using SMCL
{p} affects how output appears:  ...
```

Between the paragraphs, we entered line mode, so the "One can output..." part will appear as we have spaced it, namely indented. It will appear that way because we are in line mode.

The other two modes are invoked using the `{asis}` and `{s6hlp}` directives and do not end with blank lines. They continue until you enter the `{smcl}` directive and, in this case `{smcl}` must be followed by a carriage return. You may put a carriage return at the end of `{asis}` or the `{s6hlp}` directives—it will make no difference—but to return to SMCL line mode, you must put a carriage return directly after the `{smcl}` directive.

To summarize, when dealing with SMCL, begin by assuming you are in line mode; you almost certainly will be. If you wish to enter a paragraph, you will use the {p} directive but, once the paragraph ends, you will be back in line mode and ready to start another paragraph if you desire. If you want to enter As-Is mode, perhaps because you are including a piece of ASCII text output, use the {asis} directive, and at the end of the piece, use the {smcl}(carriage return) directive to return to line mode. If you want to include a piece of an old Stata 6 help file, use the {s6hlp} directive to enter Stata 6 help mode and, at its conclusion, use {smcl}(carriage return) to return to line mode.

Command summary—general syntax

Pretend that {xyz} is a SMCL directive, although it is not. {xyz} might have any of the following syntaxes:

Syntax 1: {xyz}

Syntax 2: {xyz:*text*}

Syntax 3: {xyz *args*}

Syntax 4: {xyz *args*:*text*}

Syntax 1 means, "do whatever it is that {xyz} does". Syntax 2 means, "do whatever it is that {xyz} does, do it on the text *text*, and then stop doing it." Syntax 3 means, "do whatever it is that {xyz} does, as modified by *args*." Finally, Syntax 4 means, "do whatever it is that {xyz} does, as modified by *args*, do it on the text *text*, and then stop doing it."

Not every SMCL directive has all four syntaxes, and which syntaxes are allowed is made clear in the descriptions below.

Also note that in syntaxes 3 and 4, *text* may contain other SMCL directives, so the following is valid:

```
{center:The use of {ul:SMCL} in help files}
```

The *text* of one SMCL directive may itself contain other SMCL directives. There is, however, one important limitation of which you need be aware: Not only must the braces match, but they must match on the same physical (input) line. To wit,

```
{center:The use of {ul:SMCL} in help files}
```

is correct, but

```
{center:The use of {ul:SMCL} in
help files}
```

is an error. When SMCL encounters an error, it simply displays the text in the output it does not understand, so the result of making the error above would be to display

```
{center:The use of SMCL in
help files}
```

The {ul:...} SMCL understood, but the {center:...} it did not because the braces did not match on the input line, so that part is just displayed. If you see SMCL directives in your output, you have made an error.

Formatting commands for use in line and paragraph modes

{sf}, {it}, and {bf} follow syntaxes 1 and 2.
These directives specify how the font is to appear. {sf} indicates standard face (font), {it} italic face, and {bf} boldface.

Used in syntax 1, these directives switch to the font face specified, and that rendition will continue to be used until another one of the commands is given.

Used in syntax 2, they display *text* in the specified way and then switch the font face back to whatever it previously was.

Examples:
```
the value of {it}varlist {sf}may be specified ...
the value of {it:varlist} may be specified ...
```

{input}, {error}, {result}, and {text} follow syntaxes 1 and 2.
These directives specify how the text should be rendered: in the style that indicates user input, an error, a calculated result, or the text around calculated results.

These styles are often rendered in terms of color. In the results window, on a black background, Stata by default shows input in white, error messages in red, calculated results in yellow, and text in green. As a result, many users think of these four directives as the "color" directives:

$$\{input\} = white$$

$$\{error\} = red$$

$$\{result\} = yellow$$

$$\{text\} = green$$

It is fine to think of them in this way, but do not get carried away with the metaphor. The relationship between the real colors and {input}, {error}, {result}, and {text} may not be the default (the user could reset it) and, in fact, these renditions may not be shown in color at all. The user might have set {result}, for instance, to show in boldface, or in highlight, or in something else. However the styles are rendered, SMCL tries to distinguish among {input}, {error}, {result}, and {text}.

Examples:
```
{text}the variable mpg has mean {result:21.3} in the sample.
{text}mpg     {c |} {result}21.3
{text}mpg     {c |} {result:21.3}
{error:variable not found}
```

{inp}, {err}, {res}, and {txt}, follow syntaxes 1 and 2.
These four commands are synonyms for {input}, {error}, {result}, and {text}.

Examples:
```
{txt}the variable mpg has mean {res:21.3} in the sample.
{txt}mpg     {c |} {res}21.3
{txt}mpg     {c |} {res:21.3}
{err:variable not found}
```

{cmd} follows syntaxes 1 and 2.

{cmd} is another style not unlike the "color" styles, and it is the recommended way to show Stata commands in help files. Do not confuse {cmd} with {inp}. {inp} is the way commands actually typed are shown, and {cmd} is the recommended way you show commands you might type. We recommend that help files be presented in terms of {txt} and that commands be shown using {cmd}; use any of {sf}, {it}, or {bf} in a help file, but we recommend that you do not use any of the "colors" {inp}, {err}, or {res} except in places where you are showing actual Stata output.

Example:
When using the {cmd:summarize} command, specify ...

{cmdab:*text1*:*text2*} follows a variation on syntax 2 (note the double colons).

{cmdab} is the recommended way to show minimal abbreviations for Stata commands and options in help files; *text1* represents the minimum abbreviation and *text2* represents the rest of the text. When the entire command or option name is the minimal abbreviation, *text2* may be omitted along with the extra colon. In that case, {cmdab:*text*} is equivalent to {cmd:*text*}; it makes no difference which you use.

Examples:
{cmdab:su:mmarize} [{it:varlist}] [{it:weight}] [{cmdab:if} {it:exp}]
the option {cmdab:ef:orm}{cmd:({it:varname})} ...

{hilite} and {hi} follow syntaxes 1 and 2.

{hilite} and {hi} are synonyms. {hilite} is the recommended way to highlight (draw attention to) something in help files. You might highlight, for example, a reference to a manual, the STB, or a book.

Examples:
see {hilite:[R] anova} for more details.
see {hi:[R] anova} for more details.

{ul} follows syntaxes 2 and 3.

{ul on} starts underlining mode. {ul off} ends it. {ul:*text*} underlines *text*.

Examples:
You can {ul on}underline{ul off} this way or
you can {ul:underline} this way

{*} follows syntax 2 and 4.

{*} is the comment indicator. What follows it (inside the braces) is ignored.

Examples:
{* this text will be ignored}
{*:as will this}

{hline} follows syntaxes 1 and 3.

{hline} (syntax 1) draws a horizontal line the rest of the way across the page.
{hline #} (syntax 3) draws a horizontal line of # characters.
{hline} (either syntax) is generally used in line mode.

Examples:
{hline}
{hline 20}

{.-} follows syntax 1.

{.-} is a synonym for {hline} (syntax 1).

Examples:
{.-}

{dup #:*text*} follows syntax 4.

{dup} repeats *text* # times.

Examples:
{dup 20:A}
{dup 20:ABC}

{char *code*} and {c *code*} are synonyms and follow syntax 3.

These directives display the specified characters which otherwise might be difficult to type on your keyboard. See the section *The* {char} *directive* below.

Examples:
C{c o´}rdoba es una joya arquitect{c o´}nica.
{c S|}57.20
The ASCII character 206 in the current font is {c 206}
The ASCII character 5a (hex) is {c 0x5a}
{c -(} is open brace and {c)-} is close brace

{reset} follows syntax 1.

{reset} is equivalent to coding {result}{sf}.

Examples:
{reset}

Link commands for use in line and paragraph modes

All the link commands share the feature that when syntax 4 is allowed,

Syntax 4: {xyz *args*:*text*}

then syntax 3 is also allowed,

Syntax 3: {xyz *args*}

and, if syntax 3 is specified, it is treated as if you specified syntax 4, inserting a colon and then repeating the argument. For instance, {help} is defined below as allowing syntaxes 3 and 4. Thus, the directive

```
{help summarize}
```

is equivalent to the directive

```
{help summarize:summarize}
```

Coding {help summarize} or {help summarize:summarize} both display the word summarize and, if the user clicks on that, the action of help summarize is taken. Thus, you might code

```
See help for {help summarize} for more information.
```

This would display "See help for **summarize** for more information" and make the word summarize clickable. If you wanted to make the words describing the action different from the action, use syntax 4,

> You can also {help summarize:examine the summary statistics} if you wish.

which results in "You can also **examine the summary statistics** if you wish."

The link commands, which may be used in either line mode or paragraph mode, are

{help *args*[:*text*]} follows syntaxes 3 and 4.

> {help} displays *text* as clickable and, if the user clicks on the text, displays in the Viewer help on *args*; see [R] **help**. *args* can be omitted since the help command is valid without arguments; {help:*text*} presents the same results as {help help:*text*}.

> *Examples:*
> {help summarize}
> {help summarize:the mean}

{help_d:*text*} follows syntax 2.

> {help_d} displays *text* as clickable and, if the user clicks the text, displays a help dialog box from which the user may obtain interactive help on any Stata command of his or her choosing.

> *Example:*
> ... using the {help_d:help system} ...

{search *args*[:*text*]} follows syntaxes 3 and 4.

> {search} displays *text* as clickable and, if the user clicks on the text, displays in the Viewer the results of search on *args*; see [R] **search**.

> *Examples:*
> {search anova:click here} for the latest information on ANOVA
> Various programs are available for {search anova}

{search_d:*text*} follows syntax 2.

> {search_d} displays *text* as clickable and, if the user clicks on the text, displays a search dialog box from which the user may obtain interactive help based on keywords of his or her choosing.

> *Example:*
> ... using the {search_d:search system} ...

{browse *args*[:*text*]} follows syntaxes 3 and 4.

> {browse} displays *text* as clickable and, if the user clicks on the text, launches the user's browser pointing at *args*. Since *args* is typically a URL and so contains a colon, it is usually necessary that *args* be specified in quotes.

> *Example:*
> ... you can {browse "http://www.stata.com":visit the Stata web site} ...

{view *args*[:*text*]} follows syntaxes 3 and 4.

> {view} displays *text* as clickable and, if the user clicks on the text, presents in the Viewer the filename *args*. If *args* is a URL, be sure to specify it in quotes. {view} would seldom be used in a SMCL file (such as a help file), because one would seldom know of a fixed location for the file unless it was a URL. {view} is sometimes used from programs because the program knows the location of the file it created.

> *Examples:*
> see {view "http://www.stata.com/man/readme.smcl"}

> display `"{view "`newfile'":click here} to view the file created"'

{view_d:*text*} follows syntax 2.

>   {view_d} displays *text* as clickable and, if the user clicks on the text, displays a view dialog box from which the user may type the name of a file or a URL to be displayed in the viewer.

>   *Example:*
>   {view_d:Click here} to view your current log

{news:*text*} follows syntax 2.

>   {news} displays *text* as clickable and, if the user clicks on the text, displays in the Viewer the latest news from www.stata.com.

>   *Example:*
>   For the latest NetCourse offerings, see the {news:news}.

{net *args*[:*text*]} follows syntaxes 3 and 4.

>   {net} displays *text* as clickable and, if the user clicks on the text, displays in the Viewer the results of net *args*; see [R] **net**. For security reasons, net get and net install cannot be executed in this way. Instead, use {net:describe ...} to show the page and, from there, the user can click the appropriate spots if he or she wishes to install the materials. Whenever *args* contains a colon, as it does when *args* is a URL, be sure to enclose *args* in quotes.

>   *args* can be omitted because the net command is valid without arguments. {net:*text*} performs the equivalent of {net cd .:*text*}; it presents the contents of the current net location.

>   *Examples:*
>   programs are available from {net "from http://www.stata.com":Stata}
>   Nicholas Cox has written a series of matrix commands which you can obtain
>   by {net "describe http://www.stata.com/stb/stb56/dm79":clicking here}

{net_d:*text*} follows syntax 2.

>   {net_d} displays *text* as clickable and, if the user clicks on the text, displays a search dialog box from which the user may search the net for additions to Stata.

>   *Example:*
>   To search the net for the latest additions to Stata available,
>   {net_d:click here}.

{netfrom_d:*text*} follows syntax 2.

>   {netfrom_d} displays *text* as clickable and, if the user clicks on the text, displays a dialog box into which the user may enter a URL and then see the contents of the site. This directive is seldom used.

>   *Example:*
>   If you already know the URL, {netfrom_d:click here}.

{ado *args*[:*text*]} follows syntaxes 3 and 4.

>   {ado} displays *text* as clickable and, if the user clicks on the text, displays in the Viewer the results of ado *args*; see [R] **net**. For security reasons, ado uninstall cannot be executed in this way. Instead, use {ado:describe ...} to show the package and, from there, the user can click to uninstall if he or she wishes to delete the material.

>   *args* can be omitted because the ado command is valid without arguments. {ado:*text*} presents a complete directory of installed packages.

>   *Example:*
>   You can see the user-written packages you have installed (and uninstall
>   any that you wish) by {ado dir:clicking here}

{ado_d:*text*} follows syntax 2.

   {ado_d} displays *text* as clickable and, if the user clicks on the text, displays a dialog box from which the user may search for user-written routines he or she previously installed (and uninstall them if desired).

   Example:
   You can search the user-written ado-files you have installed
   by {ado_d:clicking here}.

{update *args*[:*text*]} follows syntaxes 3 and 4.

   {update} displays *text* as clickable and, if the user clicks on the text, displays in the Viewer the results of update *args*; see [R] **update**. If *args* contains a URL, be careful to place the *args* in quotes.

   args can be omitted because the update command is valid without arguments. {update:*text*} is really the best way to use the {update} directive because it allows the user to choose whether and from where to update their Stata.

   Examples:
   Check whether your Stata is {update:up-to-date}.
   Check whether your Stata is {update "from http://www.stata.com":up-to-date}.

{update_d:*text*} follows syntax 2.

   {update_d} displays *text* as clickable and, if the user clicks on the text, displays an update dialog box into which the user may type a source (typically http://www.stata.com, but perhaps a local CD drive) from which he or she can then install official updates to Stata.

   Example:
   If you are installing from CD or some other source,
   {update_d:click here}.

{back:*text*} follows syntax 2.

   {back} displays *text* as clickable and, if the user clicks on the text, takes an action equivalent to pressing the Viewer's Back button.

   Example:
   {back:go back to the previous page}

{clearmore:*text*} follows syntax 2.

   {clearmore} displays *text* as clickable and, if the user clicks on the text, takes an action equivalent to pressing Stata's clear-more-condition button. {clearmore} is of little use, but remember that all Stata output goes through SMCL. When —more— appears at the bottom of the screen, you can click on it to clear it. You can do that because, to display the —more— at the bottom of the screen, Stata displays

   Example:
   {clearmore:{hline 2}more{hline 2}}

(Continued on next page)

{stata *args*[:*text*]} follows syntaxes 3 and 4.

{stata} displays *text* as clickable and, if the user clicks on the text, executes the Stata command *args* in the Results window. Stata will first ask before executing the command, but most users will turn off the asking for locally installed files (and leave it on for files over the web). If *args* (the Stata command) contains a colon, remember to enclose the command in quotes.

Example:

```
... {stata summarize mpg:to obtain the mean of mpg}...
```

Remember, like all SMCL directives, {stata} can be used in programs as well as files, Thus, you could code

```
display "... {stata summarize mpg:to obtain the mean of mpg}..."
```

or, if you were in the midst of outputting a table,

```
di "{stata summarize mpg:mpg}     {c |}" ...
```

However, it is more likely that, rather than hardcoding the variable name, the variable name would be in a macro, say `vn´,

```
di "{stata summarize `vn´:`vn´}     {c |}" ...
```

and you probably would not know how many blanks to put after the variable name, since it could be of any length. Thus, you might code

```
di "{ralign 12:{stata summ `vn´:`vn´}} {c |}" ...
```

thus allocating 12 spaces for the variable name, which would be followed by a blank and the vertical bar. Then you would want to handle the problem that `vn´ might be longer than 12 characters,

```
local vna = abbrev(`vn´,12)
di "{ralign 12:{stata summ `vn´:`vna´}} {c |}" ...
```

and there you have a line that will output a part of a table, with the clickable variable name on the left, and with the action of clicking on the variable name being to summ `vn´ except, of course, you could make the action whatever else you wanted.

Note concerning paragraph mode: In paragraph mode, you can arrange to have either one space or two spaces at the end of sentences, which is to say, following the characters '.', '?', '!', and ':'. In the output, SMCL puts two spaces after each of those characters if you put two or more spaces after them in your input, or if you put a carriage return; SMCL puts one space if you put one space. Thus,

```
{p}
Dr. Smith was near panic.  He could not reproduce the result.
Now he wished he had read about logging output in Stata.
```

will display as

```
Dr. Smith was near panic.  He could not reproduce the result.  Now he wished he
had read about logging output in Stata.
```

(Continued on next page)

Formatting commands for use in line mode

{title:*text*}(carriage return) follows syntax 2.

{title:*text*} displays *text* as a title. {title:...} should be followed by a carriage return and, usually, by one more blank lines so that the title is offset from what follows. (In help files, we precede titles by two blank lines and follow them by one.)

Example:
{title:Command summary -- general syntax}

{p}
Pretend {cmd:{c -({xyz}c)-}} were a SMCL directive, although ...

{center:*text*} and {centre:*text*} follow syntax 2.

{center:*text*} and {centre:*text*} are synonyms; they center the text on the line. {center:*text*} should usually be followed by a carriage return because any text that follows it will appear on the same line.

Examples:
{center:This text will be centered}
{center:This text will be centered} and this will follow it

{right:*text*} follows syntax 2.

{right} displays *text* with its last character aligned on the right margin. {right:*text*} should be followed by a carriage return.

Examples:
{right:this is right aligned}
{right:this is shifted left one character }

{lalign #:*text*} and {ralign #:*text*} follow syntax 4.

{lalign} left aligns *text* in a field # characters wide, and {ralign} right aligns *text*.

Example:
{lalign 12:mpg}{ralign 15:21.2973}

{...} follows syntax 1.

{...} specifies that the next carriage return is to be treated as if it were a blank.

Example:
Sometimes you need to type a long line and, while {...}
that is fine with SMCL, some word processors balk. {...}
In line mode, the above will appear as one long line to SMCL.

{col #} follows syntax 3.

{col #} skips forward to column #. If you are already at or beyond that column on the output, {col #} does nothing.

Example:
mpg{col 20}21.3{col 30}5.79

{space #} follows syntax 3.

space is equivalent to typing # blank characters.

Example:
20.5{space 20}17.5

{tab} follows syntax 1.

{tab} has the same effect as typing a tab character. Tab stops are set every 8 spaces.

Examples:
{tab}This begins one tab stop in
{tab}{tab}This begins two tab stops in

Note: SMCL also understands tab characters and treats them the same as the {tab} command, so you may include tabs in your files.

Formatting commands for use in paragraph mode

{p} follows syntax 3. The full syntax is {p # # #}.

{p # # #} enters paragraph mode. The first # specifies how much to indent the first line, the second # how much to indent the second and subsequent lines, and the third # how much to bring in the right margin on all lines. Numbers, if not specified, default to zero, so typing {p} without numbers is equivalent to typing {p 0 0 0}, {p #} is equivalent to {p # 0 0}, and so on. {p} (with or without numbers) may be followed by a carriage return or not; it makes no difference.

Paragraph mode ends when a blank line is encountered, the {p_end} directive is encountered, or {smcl}(carriage return) is encountered.

Examples:
{p}
{p 4}
{p 0 4}
{p 8 8 8}

{p_end} follows syntax 1.

{p_end} is a way of ending a paragraph without having a blank line between paragraphs. {p_end} may be followed by a carriage return or not; it will make no difference in the output.

Example:
{p_end}

{bind:*text*} follows syntax 2.

{bind:...} keeps *text* together on a line even if that makes one line of the paragraph uncommonly short. {bind:...} can also be used to insert one or more real spaces into the paragraph if you specify *text* as one or more spaces.

Example:
Commonly, bind is used {bind:to keep words together} on a line.

{break} follows syntax 1.

{break} is used to force a line break without ending the paragraph.

Example:
{p 4 8 4}
{it:Example:}{break} Commonly, ...

Commands for use in As-Is mode

{asis} follows syntax 1.

{asis} begins As-Is mode, which continues until {smcl}(carriage return) is encountered. {asis} may be followed by a carriage return or not; it makes no difference, but {smcl} must be immediately followed by a carriage return. {smcl} returns you to SMCL line mode. No other SMCL commands are interpreted in As-Is mode.

Commands for use in Stata 6 help mode

{s6hlp} follows syntax 1.

{s6hlp} begins Stata 6 help mode, which continues until {smcl}(carriage return) is encountered. {s6hlp} may be followed by a carriage return or not; it makes no difference, but {smcl} must be immediately followed by a carriage return. {smcl} returns you to SMCL line mode. No other SMCL commands are interpreted in Stata 6 help mode. In this mode, text surrounded by ^carets^ is highlighted, and there are some other features, but those are not documented here. The purpose of Stata 6 help mode is to properly display old help files.

The {char} directive

The {char} directive—synonym {c}—allows the output of any ASCII character. For instance, {c 106} is equivalent to typing the letter j, because ASCII code 106 is defined as the letter j.

One way you can get to all the ASCII characters is by typing {c #}, where # is between 1 and 255. Or, if you prefer, you can type {c 0x#}, where # is a hexadecimal number between 1 and ff. Thus, {c 0x6a} is also j because the hexadecimal number 6a is equal to the decimal number 106.

In addition, so that you do not have to remember the ASCII numbers, {c} provides special codes for characters that are, for one reason or another, difficult to type. These include

{c S|}	$ (dollar sign)
{c 'g}	` (open single quote)
{c -(}	{ (left curly brace)
{c)-}	} (right curly brace)

{c S\|} and {c 'g} are included not because they are difficult to type or cause SMCL any problems, but because in Stata display statements, they can be difficult to make display because they are Stata's macro substitution characters and tend to be interpreted by Stata. For instance,

```
. display "shown in $US"
shown in
```

drops the $US part because Stata interpreted $US as a macro and the global macro was undefined. A way around this problem is to code

```
. display "shown in {c S|}US"
shown in $US
```

{c -(} and {c)-} are included because { and } have special meanings to SMCL. { and } are used to enclose SMCL directives. Although { and } have special meaning to SMCL, SMCL usually displays the two characters correctly when they do not have a special meaning. This is because SMCL follows the rule that, when it does not understand when it thinks ought to be a directive, it shows what it did not understand in unmodified form. Thus, this works:

```
. display "among the alternatives {1, 2, 4, 7}"
among the alternatives {1, 2, 4, 7}
```

but this does not:

```
. display "in the set {result}"
in the set
```

because SMCL interpreted {result} as a SMCL directive to set the output style (color) to that for results. The way to code the above is

```
. display "in the set {c -(}result{c )-}"
in the set {result}
```

In addition, SMCL provides the following line-drawing characters:

{c -}	a wide — (dash) character
{c |}	a tall | character
{c +}	a wide — on top of a tall |
{c TT}	a top T
{c BT}	a bottom T
{c LT}	a left T
{c RT}	a right T
{c TLC}	a top-left corner
{c TRC}	a top-right corner
{c BRC}	a bottom-right corner
{c BLC}	a bottom-left corner

When you use {hline}, it constructs the line using the {c -} character. The above are not really ASCII, they are instructions to SMCL to draw lines. The "characters" are, however, one-character wide and one-character tall, so you can use them as characters in your output. The result is that Stata output that appears on your screen can look like this:

```
. summarize mpg weight

    Variable |      Obs       Mean    Std. Dev.      Min        Max
         mpg |       74    21.2973    5.785503        12         41
      weight |       74   3019.459    777.1936      1760       4840
```

but, if the result is translated into straight ASCII, it will look like this:

```
. summarize mpg weight

    Variable |      Obs       Mean    Std. Dev.      Min        Max
-------------+-----------------------------------------------------
         mpg |       74    21.2973    5.785503        12         41
      weight |       74   3019.459    777.1936      1760       4840
```

because SMCL will be forced to restrict itself to the ASCII characters.

Finally, SMCL provides the following West European characters:

{c a´}	á	{c e´}	é	{c i´}	í	{c o´}	ó	{c u´}	ú
{c A´}	Á	{c E´}	É	{c I´}	Í	{c O´}	Ó	{c U´}	Ú
{c a´g}	à	{c e´g}	è	{c i´g}	ì	{c o´g}	ò	{c u´g}	ù
{c A´g}	À	{c E´g}	È	{c I´g}	Ì	{c O´g}	Ò	{c U´g}	Ù
{c a^}	â	{c e^}	ê	{c i^}	î	{c o^}	ô	{c u^}	û
{c A^}	Â	{c E^}	Ê	{c I^}	Î	{c O^}	Ô	{c U^}	Û
{c a~}	ã					{c o~}	õ		
{c A~}	Ã					{c O~}	Õ		
{c a:}	ä	{c e:}	ë	{c i:}	ï	{c o:}	ö	{c u:}	ü
{c A:}	Ä	{c E:}	Ë	{c I:}	Ï	{c O:}	Ö	{c U:}	Ü
{c ae}	æ	{c c,}	ç	{c n~}	ñ	{c o/}	ø	{c y´}	ý
{c AE}	Æ	{c C,}	ç	{c N~}	Ñ	{c O/}	Ø	{c Y´}	Ý
{c y:}	ÿ	{c ss}	ß	{c r?}	¿	{c r!}	¡		
{c L-}	£	{c Y=}	(yen)	{c E=}	€				

SMCL uses ISO-8859-1 (Latin1) to render the above characters. For instance, {c e´} is equivalent to {c 0xe9}, if you care to look it up. {c 0xe9} will display as é if you are using an ISO-8859-1 (Latin1) compatible font. Most are.

In the case of the Macintosh, however, Stata uses the Macintosh encoding in which, for instance, {c e´} is equivalent to {c 8e}. This should work for Macintosh users unless they are using an ISO-8859-1 (Latin1) encoded font. To find out, run the following experiment:

```
. display "{c e´}"
é
```

Do you see é as we do? If not, and you are on a Macintosh, type

```
. set charset latin1
```

and try the experiment again. If that solves the problem, you will want to include that line in your profile.do. You can set the encoding back to Macintosh style by typing set charset mac. set charset typed without an argument will display the current setting. (set charset works on all platforms but is really only useful on the Macintosh.)

Advice on using display

Do not think twice; you can just use SMCL directives in your display statements and they will work. What we are really talking about, however, is programming, and there are two things to know.

First, remember how display lets you display results as text, as result, as input, and as error, with the abbreviations as txt, as res, as inp, and as err. For instance, a program might contain the lines

```
program define ...
        ...
        qui summarize `varname´
        display as txt "the mean of `varname´ is " as res r(mean)
        ...
    end
```

Results would be the same if the display statement were coded

```
        display "{txt}the mean of `varname´ is {res}" r(mean)
```

That is, the `display` directive `as txt` just sends `{txt}` to SMCL, the display directive `as res` just sends `{res}` to SMCL, and so on.

However, `as err` does not just send `{err}`. In addition, `as err` tells Stata that what is about to be displayed is an error message so that, if output is being suppressed, Stata knows to display this message anyway. To wit,

```
display as err "varname undefined"
```

is the right way to issue the error message "varname undefined".

```
display "{err}varname undefined"
```

would not work as well because, if the program was having its output suppressed, the error message would not be displayed because Stata would not know to stop suppressing output. You could code

```
display as err "{err}varname undefined"
```

but that is redundant. `display`'s `as error` directive both tells Stata that this is an error message and sends the `{err}` directive to SMCL. The last part makes output appear in the form of error messages, probably in red. The first part is what guarantees that the error message appears even if output is being suppressed.

If you think about this, you will now realize that you could code

```
display as err "{txt}varname undefined"
```

to produce an error message that would appear as ordinary text (meaning it would probably be in green) and yet still display in all cases. Please do not do this. By convention, all error messages should be displayed in SMCL's `{err}` (default red) rendition.

The second thing to know is how Stata sets the state of SMCL the instant before `display` displays its output. When you use `display` interactively—when you use it at the keyboard or in a do-file—Stata sets SMCL in line mode, font face `{sf}`, and style `{res}`. For instance, if you type

```
. display 2+2
4
```

the 4 will appear in `{sf}{res}`, meaning in standard font face and in result style, which probably means in yellow. On the other hand, consider the following:

```
. program define demonstrate_display
  1. display 2+2
  2. end
. demonstrate_display
4
```

In this case, the 4 will appear in `{sf}{inp}`, meaning the result is probably shown in white!

When `display` is executed from inside a program, no settings are made to SMCL. SMCL is just left in the mode it happens to be in and, in this case, it happened to be in line mode `{sf}{inp}` because that was the mode it was in after the user typed the command `demonstrate_display`.

This is an important feature of `display` because it means that, in your programs, one `display` can pick up where the last left off. Perhaps you have four or five `displays` in a row that produce the text to appear in a paragraph. The first `display` might begin paragraph mode and the rest of the `displays` finish it off, with the last `display` displaying a blank line to end paragraph mode. In this case, it is of great importance that SMCL stay in the mode you left it in between `displays`.

That leaves only the question of what mode SMCL is in when your program begins. You should assume SMCL is in line mode, but make no assumptions about the style (color) `{txt}`, `{res}`, `{err}`, or `{inp}`. Within a program, all `display` commands should be coded as

```
        display as ... ...
```

or

```
        display "one of {txt}, {res}, {err}, or {inp} ..." ...
```

with the exception that you may violate this rule if you really intend one `display` to pick up where another left off. For example,

```
        display as text "{p}"
        display "This display violates the rule but that is all right"
        display "because it is setting a paragraph and we want all"
        display "these displays to be treated as a whole.  Note that"
        display "we did follow the rule with the first display in the"
        display "sequence."
        display
        display "Now we are back in line mode, because of the blank line"
```

You could even code

```
    program define example2
        display as text "{p}"
        display "Below we will call a subroutine to contribute a sentence"
        display "to this paragraph being constructed by example2:"
        example2_subroutine
        display "The text that example2_subroutine contributed became"
        display "part of this single paragraph.  Now we will end the paragraph."
        display
    end
    program define example2_subroutine
        display "This sentence is being displayed by"
        display "example2_subroutine."
    end
```

The result of running this would be:

```
. example2
Below we will call a subroutine to contribute a sentence to this paragraph
being constructed by example2: This sentence is being displayed by
example2_subroutine.  The text that example2_subroutine contributed became
part of this single paragraph.  Now we will end the paragraph.
```

Advice on formatting help files

Help files are just files named *whatever*.hlp that Stata displays when the user types "`help` *whatever*". The first line of a help file should read

```
{smcl}
```

Because of help files that exist in old format, before displaying a help file, Stata issues a {s6hlp} directive to SMCL before displaying the text, thus putting SMCL in Stata 6 help mode. The {smcl} at the top of your help file returns SMCL to line mode. Old help files do not have that and, since SMCL faithfully reproduces the old Stata 6 help file formatting commands, they display correctly, too.

After that, it is a matter of style. Our style is to put a header at the top of the page along with a manual reference, skip one line, and follow that by a title.

```
{smcl}
{.-}
help for {cmd:whatever} {right:manual:  {hi:[R] whatever}}
{.-}
{title:Title of help entry}
```

For your personal help files, you might want to use

```
{smcl}
{.-}
help for {cmd:whatever}
{.-}

{title:Title of help entry}
```

or

```
{smcl}
{.-}
help for {cmd:whatever} {right:my name or email address}
{.-}

{title:Title of help entry}
```

After the title, we put the syntax diagrams. This is going to surprise you: we format the syntax diagrams as paragraphs, but with the first line not indented as much as the second and subsequent lines. For instance, we might code

```
{p 8 27}
{cmdab:wh:atever}
[{it:varlist}]
[{it:weight}]
[{cmd:if} {it:exp}]
[{cmd:in} {it:range}]
[{cmd:,}
    {cmdab:d:etail}
    {cmdab:mean:only}
    {cmdab:f:ormat}
    {cmdab:gen:erate}{cmd:(}{it:newvar}{cmd:)}
    {cmdab:s:kip}
]
```

which will produce the reasonable looking syntax diagram

> <u>wh</u>atever [*varlist*] [*weight*] [**if** *exp*] [**in** *range*] [, <u>det</u>ail <u>mean</u>only
> <u>f</u>ormat <u>gen</u>erate(*newvar*) <u>s</u>kip]

That done, it is just a matter of following that with the titles and contents for

> Description
> Options
> Remarks and/or Examples
> Also see

For the titles, we precede them by two blank lines, use {title} to display the title, and follow that by one more blank line.

Text we always set in paragraphs, generally using {p} (meaning no indenting of the first line or the subsequent lines). For the options, we use {p 0 4}, thus using a hanging indent and, if the option needs more than one paragraph to be described, subsequent paragraphs are set using {p 4 4}. For example,

```
{p 0 4}
{cmd:generate(}{it:newvar}{cmd:)} creates {it:newvar} containing the values
at each of the knots.  If {cmd:skip} is also specified, ...
```

will produce

> **generate**(*newvar*) creates *newvar* containing the values at each of the knots. If
>   **skip** is also specified, ...

For examples, we would also use paragraphs,

```
{p 8 16}
. {cmd:whatever mpg weight displ}
{p_end}
{p 8 16}
. {cmd:whatever mpg weight displ, generate(knots) skip}
{p_end}
```

Note our use of {p_end} to end paragraphs without putting a blank line between paragraphs. The result of the above is

```
. whatever mpg weight displ
. whatever mpg weight displ, generate(knots) skip
```

Note that we set the second and subsequent line indentation to a number greater than the first-line indentation so that, should a line wrap, it would be obvious. Although we tend to use paragraphs for examples, we would not hesitate to use line mode if we found that more convenient.

If we wanted to show actual Stata output, we could. We could fire up Stata, use log using to create a Stata log, use our command on an example dataset, and then copy that log right into the middle of help file. If we wanted to do that, we would probably do something like the following:

```
{.-}
{* log begins here -------------------------------------------- }
```
copy the .smcl log file to here
```
{* log ends here -------------------------------------------- }
{sf}{txt}
{.-}
```

There are two things to note in the above: (1) we used {.-} to set off the log, and (2) after the log, we included {sf}{txt} to get SMCL reset. Concerning the second, help files are done in {sf}{txt} and, when Stata started our help file, it did that for us. After the inclusion of the log, we may no longer be in that mode so, to be safe, we reset it.

Finally, for the *Also see* section, we would use paragraph mode:

```
{title:Also see}
{p 0 21}
{bind: }Manual:  {hi:[R] whatever}, {hi:[R] summarize}
{p_end}
{p 0 21}
On-line:  help for
    {help centile},
    {help cf},
    {help ci},
    {help codebook},
    {help compare},
    {help egen},
    {help inspect},
    {help lv},
    {help means},
    {help tabsum}
{p_end}
```

which results in

Also see
```
 Manual:  [R] whatever, [R] summarize
 On-line:  help for centile, cf, ci, codebook, compare, egen, inspect, lv, means,
               tabsum
```

We included {p_end} at the end of the final "paragraph" rather than a blank line so that a blank line would not appear at the end of our help file.

Pay attention to the number of spaces we typed after "Manual:" and "On-line:". We put two spaces following the colon, and thus SMCL did the same in the output. SMCL puts one space after a colon when we put one space and two spaces when we put two or more spaces, or a carriage return. If we preferred to have one space after the colon, we could do that, but then we would need to change {p 0 21} to be {p 0 20}, since we would then want subsequent lines indented one less space.

Also See

Complementary: [P] **display**,
                       [GS] **3 The Viewer**

Related: [R] **log**

Title

sortpreserve — Sorting within programs

Description

This entry discusses the use of sort (see [R] sort) within programs.

Remarks

Properly written programs do one of three things:

1. Report results
2. Add new variables to the dataset
3. Modify the data in memory

A properly written program does only one of those three things, but you do not want to get carried away with the idea. A properly written program might, for instance, (1) report results and yet still have an option to (2) add a new variable to the dataset, but a properly written program would not do all three. The user should be able to obtain reports over and over again by simply retyping the command, and if a command both reports results and modifies the data, that will not be possible.

Properly written programs of the first two types should also not change the sort order of the data. If the data are sorted on mpg and foreign before the command is given, and all the command does is report results, then the data should still be sorted on mpg and foreign at the conclusion of the command. Yet, the command might find it necessary to sort the data to obtain the results it calculates.

This entry deals with how to satisfy both needs. It is easy.

sortpreserve

You may include sort commands inside your programs and leave the user's data in the original order when your program concludes by specifying the option sortpreserve on the program define line:

```
program define whatever, sortpreserve
        ...
end
```

That, in a nutshell, is all there is to it. sortpreserve tells Stata when it starts your program to first record the information about how the data are currently sorted, and then later uses that information to restore the order to what it previously was. Stata will do this no matter how your program ends, whether as you expected, or with an error, or because the user pressed the *Break* key.

The cost of sortpreserve

There is a cost to sortpreserve, so you do not want to specify the option when it is not needed, but the cost is not much. sortpreserve will consume a little computer time in restoring the sort order at the conclusion of your program. Rather than talking about this time in seconds or milliseconds, which can vary according to the computer you use, let's define our unit of time as the time to execute:

```
. generate long x = _n
```

283

Pretend that you added that command to your program, just as we have typed it, without using temporary variables. You could then make careful timings of your program to find out just how much extra time your program would take to execute. It would not be much. Let's call that amount of time one *genlong* unit. Then,

- `sortpreserve`, if it has to restore the order because your program has changed it, takes 2 *genlong* units.

- `sortpreserve`, if it does not need to change the order because your program has not changed it yet, takes one-half a *genlong* unit.

The above results are based on empirical timings using 100,000 and 1,000,000 observations.

How sortpreserve works

`sortpreserve` works by adding a temporary variable to the dataset before your program starts and, if you are curious about the name of that variable, it is recorded in the macro `sortindex`. There are times when you will want to know that name. It is important that the variable `sortindex` still exist at the conclusion of your program. If your program concludes with something like

        keep `id' `varlist'

it is of vital importance that you change that line to read

        keep `id' `varlist' `sortindex'

If you fail to do that, Stata will report the error message "could not restore sort order because variables were dropped". Actually, even that little change may be insufficient because the dataset in its original form might have been sorted on something other than `id` and `varlist`. What you really need to do is add, early in your program and before you change the sort order,

        local sortvars : sort

and then change the `keep` statement to read

        keep `id' `varlist' `sortvars' `sortindex'

Understand, however, that all of this discussion is only about the use of the command `keep`, and that very few programs would even include a `keep` statement because we are skirting the edge of what is a properly written program.

`sortpreserve` is intended for use in programs that report results or add new variables to the dataset, not programs that modify the data in memory. The inclusion of `keep` at the end of your program really makes it a class-3 program, and in that case, the idea of preserving the sort order really makes no sense anyway.

Use of sortpreserve with preserve

`sortpreserve` may be used with `preserve` (see [P] **preserve** for a description of `preserve`). We can imagine a complicated program that re-sorts the data and then, under certain conditions, discovers it has to do real damage to the data in order to calculate its results, and so then **preserves** the data to boot:

```
program define ..., sortpreserve
        ...
        sort ...
        ...
        if ... {
                preserve
                ...
        }
        ...
end
```

The above will work. When the program ends, Stata will first restore any `preserve`d data and then reestablish the sort of the original dataset.

Use of sortpreserve with subroutines that use sortpreserve

Programs that use `sortpreserve` may call other programs that use `sortpreserve`, and this can be a good way to speed up code. Consider a calculation where you need the data first sorted by `` `i´ ``
`` `j´ ``, then by `` `j´ `` `` `i´ ``, and finally by `` `i´ `` `` `j´ `` again. You might code

```
program define ..., sortpreserve
        ...
        sort `i´ `j´
        ...
        sort `j´ `i´
        ...
        sort `i´ `j´
        ...
end
```

but faster to execute will be

```
program define ..., sortpreserve
        ...
        sort `i´ `j´
        mysubcalculation `i´ `j´ ...
        ...
end
program define mysubcalculation, sortpreserve
        args i j ...
        sort `j´ `i´
        ...
end
```

Also See

Complementary: [P] **byable**, [P] **program**

Title

> **st st_is** — Survival analysis subroutines for programmers

Syntax

st_is 2 { full | analysis }

st_show [noshow]

st_ct "[*byvars*]" _-> *newtvar newpopvar newfailvar* [*newcensvar* [*newentvar*]]

These commands are for use with survival-time data; see [R] **st**. You must have **stset** your data before using these commands.

Description

These commands are provided for programmers—persons wishing to write new st commands.

st_is verifies that the data in memory are survival-time (st) data. If not, it issues the error message "data not st", r(119).

st is currently "release 2", meaning that this is the second design of the system. Programs written for the previous release continue to work. (The previous release of st corresponds to Stata 5.)

Modern programs code **st_is 2 full** or **st_is 2 analysis**. The **st_is 2** part verifies that the dataset in memory is in release 2 format; if it is in the prior format, it is converted to release 2 format. (Older programs simply code **st_is**. This verifies that no new features are **stset** about the data that would cause the old program to break.)

The **full** and **analysis** parts indicate whether the dataset may be past, future, or past and future. Code **st_is 2 full** if the command is suitable for running on the analysis sample and the past and future data (many data-management commands fall into this category). Code **st_is 2 analysis** if the command is suitable for use only with the analysis sample (most statistical commands fall into this category). See [R] **st stset** for the definitions of past and future.

st_show displays the summary of the survival-time variables or does nothing, depending on what the user specified when **stset**ing the data.

st_ct is a low-level utility that provides risk-group summaries from survival-time data.

Options

noshow requests that **st_show** display nothing.

Remarks

Remarks are presented under the headings

> *Definitions of characteristics and st variables*
> *Outline of an st command*
> *Using the st_ct utility*
> *Comparison of st_ct with sttoct*
> *Data verification*
> *Data conversion*

Definitions of characteristics and st variables

From a programmer's perspective, st is a set of conventions that specify where certain pieces of information are stored and how to interpret that information together with a few subroutines that make it easier to follow the conventions.

At the lowest level, st is nothing more than a set of Stata characteristics that programmers may access:

char _dta[_dta]	st (marks that the data is st)
char _dta[st_ver]	2 (version number)
char _dta[st_id]	*varname* or nothing; id() variable
char _dta[st_bt0]	*varname* or nothing; t0() variable
char _dta[st_bt]	*varname*; *t* variable from stset t, ...
char _dta[st_bd]	*varname* or nothing; failure() variable
char _dta[st_ev]	list of numbers or nothing; *numlist* from failure(*varname*[==*numlist*])
char _dta[st_enter]	contents of enter() or nothing; *numlist* expanded
char _dta[st_exit]	contents of exit() or nothing; *numlist* expanded
char _dta[st_orig]	contents of origin() or nothing; *numlist* expanded
char _dta[st_bs]	# or 1; scale() value
char _dta[st_o]	_origin or #
char _dta[st_s]	_scale or #
char _dta[st_ifexp]	*exp* or nothing; from stset ... if exp ...
char _dta[st_if]	*exp* or nothing; contents of if()
char _dta[st_ever]	*exp* or nothing; contents of ever()
char _dta[st_never]	*exp* or nothing; contents of never()
char _dta[st_after]	*exp* or nothing; contents of after()
char _dta[st_befor]	*exp* or nothing; contents of before()
char _dta[st_wt]	weight type or nothing; user-specified weight
char _dta[st_wv]	*varname* or nothing; user-specified weighting variable
char _dta[st_w]	[*weighttype*=*weightvar*] or nothing
char _dta[st_show]	noshow or nothing
char _dta[st_t]	_t (for compatibility with release 1)
char _dta[st_t0]	_t0 (for compatibility with release 1)
char _dta[st_d]	_d (for compatibility with release 1)
char _dta[st_n0]	# or nothing; number of st notes
char _dta[st_n1]	text of first note or nothing
char _dta[st_n2]	text of second note or nothing
char _dta[st_set]	text or nothing. If filled in, streset will refuse to execute and present this text as the reason

In addition, all st datasets have the following four variables:

_t0	time of entry (in t units) into risk pool
_t	time of exit (in t units) from risk pool
_d	contains 1 if failure, 0 if censoring
_st	contains 1 if observation is to be used and 0 otherwise

Thus, in a program, you might code

```
display "the failure/censoring base time variable is _t"
display "and its mean in the uncensored subsample is"
summarize _t if _d
```

No matter how simple or complicated the data, these four variables exist and are filled in. For instance, in simple data, _t0 might contain 0 for every observation and _d might always contain 1.

Some st datasets also contain the variables

> _origin   contains evaluated value of origin()
> _scale   contains evaluated value of scale()

The characteristic `_dta[st_o]` contains the name `_origin` or it contains a number, often 0. It contains a number when the origin does not vary across observations. `_dta[st_s]` works the same way with the `scale()` value. Thus, the origin and scale are, in all cases, '`_dta[st_o]`' and '`_dta[st_s]`'. In fact, these characteristics are seldom used because variables `_t` and `_t0` are already adjusted.

Some st datasets have an `id()` variable that clusters together records on the same subject. The name of the variable varies and the name can be obtained from the characteristic `_dta[st_id]`. If there is no `id()` variable, the characteristic contains nothing.

Outline of an st command

If you are writing a new st command, place `st_is` near the top of your code. This ensures that your command does not execute on inappropriate data. In addition, place `st_show` following the parsing of your command's syntax; this will display the key st variables. The minimal outline for an st command is

```
program define st name
        version 7
        st_is 2 ...
        ... syntax command ...
        ... determined there are no syntax errors ...
        st_show
        ... guts of program ...
end
```

Note that `st_is 2` appears even before parsing of input. That is to avoid irritating users when they type a command, get a syntax error, work hard to eliminate the error, and then learn that "data not st".

A fuller outline for an st command, particularly one that performs analysis on the data, is

```
program define st name
        version 7
        st_is 2 ...
        syntax ... [, ... noSHow ... ]
        st_show `show´
        marksample touse
        quietly replace `touse´ = 0 if _st==0
        ... guts of program ...
end
```

Do not forget that all calculations and actions are to be restricted, at the least, to observations for which $\_st \neq 0$. Observations with $\_st = 0$ are to be ignored.

Using the st_ct utility

st_ct converts the data in memory to observations containing summaries of risk groups. Consider the code

```
st_is 2 analysis
preserve
st_ct "" -> t pop die
```

This would change the data in memory to contain something akin to count-time data. The transformed data would have observations containing

t	time
pop	population at risk at time t
die	number who fail at time t

There would be one record per time t and the data would be sorted by t. The original data are discarded, which is why you should code preserve; see [P] **preserve**.

The above three lines could be used as the basis for calculating the Kaplan–Meier product-limit survivor function estimate; the rest of the code being

```
keep if die
gen double hazard = die/pop
gen double km     = 1-hazard  if _n==1
replace    km     = (1-hazard)*km[_n-1] if _n>1
```

st_ct can be used to obtain risk groups separately for subgroups of the population. The code

```
st_is 2 analysis
preserve
st_ct "race sex" -> t pop die
```

would change the data in memory to contain

race	
sex	
t	time
pop	population at risk at time t
die	number who fail at time t

There will be one observation for each race–sex–t combination and the data will be sorted by race sex t.

With this data, you could calculate the Kaplan–Meier product-limit survivor function estimate for each race–sex group by coding

```
keep if die
gen double hazard = die/pop
by race sex: gen double km     = 1-hazard  if _n==1
by race sex: replace     km     = (1-hazard)*km[_n-1] if _n>1
```

st_ct is a convenient subroutine. The above code fragment works regardless of the complexity of the underlying survival-time data. It does not matter whether there is one record per subject, no censoring, and a single failure per subject, or multiple records per subject, gaps, and recurring failures for the same subject. st_ct forms risk groups that summarize the events recorded by the data.

st_ct can provide the number censored and the number who enter the risk group. The code

```
st_ct "" -> t pop die cens ent
```

creates records containing

t	time
pop	population at risk at time t
die	number who fail at time t
cens	number who are censored at t (after the failures)
ent	number who enter at t (after the censorings)

As before,

```
        st_ct "race sex" -> t pop die cens ent
```

would create a similar dataset with records for each **race-sex** group.

Comparison of st_ct with sttoct

sttoct—see [R] **st sttoct**—is related to st_ct and, in fact, sttoct is implemented in terms of st_ct. The differences between them are

1. sttoct creates ct data, meaning that the dataset is marked as being ct. st_ct merely creates a useful dataset; it does not **ctset** the data.

2. st_ct creates a total population at risk variable—which is useful in programming—but sttoct creates no such variable.

3. sttoct eliminates thrashings—censorings and reentries of the same subject as covariates change—if there are no gaps, strata shifting, etc. st_ct does not. Thus, at a particular time, sttoct might show that there are 2 lost to censoring and none entered, whereas st_ct might show 12 censorings and 10 entries. Note that this makes no difference to the calculations of the number at risk and the number who fail, which are the major ingredients in survival calculations.

4. st_ct is faster.

Data verification

As long as you code st_is at the top of your program, you need not verify the consistency of the data. That is, you need not verify that subjects do not fail before they enter, etc.

The dataset is verified when the user **stsets** it. It is hereby agreed between users and programmers that, if the user makes a substantive change to the data, the user will rerun **stset** (which can be done by typing **stset** or **streset** without arguments) to reverify that all is well.

Data conversion

If you write a program that converts the data from one form of st data to another, or from st data to something else, be sure to issue the appropriate **stset** command. For instance, a command we have written, **stbase**, converts the data from st to a simple cross-section in one instance. In our program, we coded **stset, clear** so that all other st commands would know that this is no longer st data and that making st calculations on it would be inappropriate.

In fact, even if we had forgotten, it would not have mattered. Other st programs would have found many of the key st variables missing and so ended with a "such-and-such not found" error.

Also See

Complementary:	[R] **st stset**, [R] **st sttoct**
Background:	[R] **st**

Title

syntax — Parse Stata syntax

Syntax

args *macroname1* [*macroname2* [*macroname3* ...]]

syntax *description_of_syntax*

Description

There are two ways that a Stata program can interpret what the user types:

1. positionally, meaning first argument, second argument, and so on;

2. according to a grammar such as standard Stata syntax.

args does the first. The first argument is assigned to *macroname1*, the second to *macroname2*, and so on. In the program, you subsequently refer to the contents of the macros by enclosing their names in single quotes: `` `macroname1´ ``, `` `macroname2´ ``, ... :

```
program define myprog
        args varname dof beta
        (the rest of the program would be coded in terms of `varname´, `dof´, and `beta´)
        ...
end
```

syntax does the second. You specify the new command's syntax on the **syntax** command; for instance, you might code

```
program define myprog
        syntax varlist [if] [in] [, DOF(integer 50) Beta(real 1.0)]
        (the rest of the program would be coded in terms of `varlist´, `if´, `in´, `dof´, and `beta´)
        ...
end
```

syntax examines what the user typed and attempts to match it to the syntax diagram. If it does not match, an error message is issued and the program is stopped (a nonzero return code is returned). If it does match, the individual components are stored in particular local macros where you can subsequently access them. In the example above, the result would be to define the local macros `` `varlist´ ``, `` `if´ ``, `` `in´ ``, `` `dof´ ``, and `` `beta´ ``.

For an introduction to Stata programming, see [U] **21 Programming Stata** and especially [U] **21.4 Program arguments**.

Syntax, continued

The *description_of_syntax* allowed by `syntax` includes

---

description_of_varlist:
    type   *nothing*
  or
    optionally type   [
    then type one of `varlist` `varname` `newvarlist` `newvarname`
    optionally type   (*varlist_specifiers*)
    type   ]   (if you typed [at the start)

                   varlist_specifiers are `default=none` `min=#` `max=#` <u>`numeric`</u> <u>`string`</u> `ts`
                                 <u>`generate`</u>   (`newvarlist` and `newvarname` only)

                  Examples: `syntax varlist ...`
                                   `syntax [varlist] ...`
                                   `syntax varlist(min=2) ...`
                                   `syntax varlist(max=4) ...`
                                   `syntax varlist(min=2 max=4 numeric) ...`
                                   `syntax varlist(default=none) ...`

                                   `syntax newvarlist(max=1) ...`

                                   `syntax varname ...`
                                   `syntax [varname] ...`

If you type nothing, then the command does not allow a varlist.

Typing [and] means that the varlist is optional.

`default=` specifies how the varlist is to be filled in when the varlist is optional and the user does not specify it. The default is to fill it in with all the variables. If `default=none` is specified, it is left empty.

`min=` and `max=` specify the minimum and maximum number of variables that may be specified. Typing `varname` is equivalent to typing `varlist(max=1)`.

`numeric` and `string` restrict the specified varlist to consist of entirely numeric or entirely string variables.

`ts` allows the varlist to contain time-series operators.

`generate` specifies, in the case of `newvarlist` or `newvarname`, that the new variables are to be created and filled in with missing values.

After the `syntax` command, the resulting varlist is returned in `` `varlist' ``. If there are new variables (you coded `newvarname` or `newvarlist`), the macro `` `typlist' `` is also defined containing the storage type of each of the new variables, listed one after the other.

---

description_of_if:
    type   *nothing*
  or
    optionally type   [
    type   `if`
    optionally type   /
    type   ]   (if you typed [at the start)

                  Examples: `syntax ... if ...`
                                   `syntax ... [if] ...`
                                   `syntax ... [if/] ...`
                                   `syntax ... if/ ...`

If you type nothing, then the command does not allow an `if` *exp*.

Typing [and] means that the `if` *exp* varlist is optional.

After the `syntax` command, the resulting `if` *exp* is returned in `` `if' ``. The macro contains `if` followed by the expression unless you specified /, in which case the macro contains just the expression.

description_of_in:
type	*nothing*

or

optionally type	[
type	in
optionally type	/
type	]	(if you typed [at the start)

Examples:	`syntax ... in ...`
	`syntax ... [in] ...`
	`syntax ... [in/] ...`
	`syntax ... in/ ...`

If you type nothing, then the command does not allow an in *range*.

Typing [and] means that the in *range* is optional.

After the `syntax` command, the resulting in *range* is returned in `` `in´ ``. The macro contains in followed by the range unless you specified /, in which case the macro contains just the range.

description_of_using:
type	*nothing*

or

optionally type	[
type	using
optionally type	/
type	]	(if you typed [at the start)

Examples:	`syntax ... using ...`
	`syntax ... [using] ...`
	`syntax ... [using/] ...`
	`syntax ... using/ ...`

If you type nothing, then the command does not allow using *filename*.

Typing [and] means that the using *filename* is optional.

After the `syntax` command, the resulting filename is returned in `` `using´ ``. The macro contains using followed by the filename in quotes unless you specified /, in which case the macro contains just the filename and without quotes.

description_of_=exp:
type	*nothing*

or

optionally type	[
type	=
optionally type	/
type	exp
type	]	(if you typed [at the start)

Examples:	`syntax ... =exp ...`
	`syntax ... [=exp] ...`
	`syntax ... [=/exp] ...`
	`syntax ... =/exp ...`

If you type nothing, then the command does not allow an =*exp*.

Typing [and] means that the =*exp* is optional.

After the `syntax` command, the resulting expression is returned in `` `exp´ ``. The macro contains =, a space, and the expression unless you specified /, in which case the macro contains just the expression.

description_of_weights:

type	*nothing*
or	
type	[
type any of	f̲weight a̲weight p̲weight i̲weight
optionally type	/
type	]
	Examples: syntax ... [fweight] ...
	syntax ... [fweight pweight] ...
	syntax ... [pweight fweight] ...
	syntax ... [fweight pweight iweight/] ...

If you type nothing, then the command does not allow weights. A command may not allow both a weight and =*exp*.

You must type [and]; they are not optional. Weights are always optional.

The first weight specified is the default weight type.

After the **syntax** command, the resulting weight and expression are returned in `weight´ and `exp´. `weight´ contains the weight type or nothing if no weights were specified. `exp´ contains =, a space, and the expression unless you specified /, in which case the macro contains just the expression.

description_of_options:

type	*nothing*	
or		
type	[,	
type	*option_descriptors*	(these options will be optional)
optionally type	*	
type	]	
or		
type	,	
type	*option_descriptors*	(these options will be required)
optionally type	[	
optionally type	*option_descriptors*	(these options will be optional)
optionally type	*	
optionally type	]	
	Examples: syntax ... [, MYopt Thisopt]	
	syntax ..., MYopt Thisopt	
	syntax ..., MYopt [Thisopt]	
	syntax ... [, MYopt Thisopt *]	

If you type nothing, then the command does not allow options.

The brackets distinguish optional from required options. All options can be optional, all options can be required, or some can be optional and others be required.

After the **syntax** command, options are returned to you in local macros based on the first 31 letters of each option's name. If you also specify *, any remaining options are collected and placed, one after the other, in `options´. If you do not specify *, then if the user specifies any options that you do not list, an error is returned.

option_descriptors are documented below.

(Continued on next page)

option_descriptor optionally_on:
 type   *OPname*   (capitalization indicates minimal abbreviation)

       Examples: `syntax ..., ... replace ...`
                `syntax ..., ... REPLACE ...`
                `syntax ..., ... detail ...`
                `syntax ..., ... Detail ...`
                `syntax ..., ... CONStant ...`

The result of the option is returned in a macro name formed by the first 31 letters of the option's name. Thus, option `replace` is returned in local macro `` `replace' `` and option `detail` in local macro `` `detail' ``.

The macro contains nothing if not specified or else it contains the macro's name, fully spelled out.

Warning: be careful if the first two letters of the option's name are `no`, such as the option called `notice`. You must capitalize at least the `N` in such cases.

---

option_descriptor optionally_off:
 type   `no`
 type   *OPname*   (capitalization indicates minimal abbreviation)

       Examples: `syntax ..., ... noreplace ...`
                `syntax ..., ... noREPLACE ...`
                `syntax ..., ... nodetail ...`
                `syntax ..., ... noDetail ...`
                `syntax ..., ... noCONStant ...`

The result of the option is returned in a macro name formed by the first 31 letters of the option's name excluding the `no`. Thus, option `noreplace` is returned in local macro `` `replace' ``, option `nodetail` in local macro `` `detail' ``.

The macro contains nothing if not specified or else it contains the macro's name, fully spelled out, with a `no` prefixed. That is, in the `noREPLACE` example above, macro `` `replace' `` contains nothing or it contains `noreplace`.

---

option_descriptor optional_integer_value:
 type   *OPname*   (capitalization indicates minimal abbreviation)
 type   `(integer`
 type   `#` (unless the option is required)   (the default integer value)
 type   `)`

       Examples: `syntax ..., ... Count(integer 3) ...`
                `syntax ..., ... SEQuence(integer 1) ...`
                `syntax ..., ... dof(integer -1) ...`

The result of the option is returned in a macro name formed by the first 31 letters of the option's name.

The macro contains the integer specified by the user or else it contains the default value.

---

option_descriptor optional_real_value:
 type   *OPname*   (capitalization indicates minimal abbreviation)
 type   `(real`
 type   `#` (unless the option is required)   (the default value)
 type   `)`

       Examples: `syntax ..., ... Mean(real 2.5) ...`
                `syntax ..., ... SD(real -1) ...`

The result of the option is returned in a macro name formed by the first 31 letters of the option's name.

The macro contains the integer specified by the user or else it contains the default value.

option_descriptor optional_numlist:

type	OPname	(capitalization indicates minimal abbreviation)
type	(numlist	
type	<u>asc</u>ending or <u>desc</u>ending or *nothing*	
optionally type	<u>int</u>eger	
optionally type	missingokay	
optionally type	min=#	
optionally type	max=#	
optionally type	># or >=# or *nothing*	
optionally type	<# or <=# or *nothing*	
optionally type	sort	
type	)	

Examples:
```
syntax ..., ... VALues(numlist) ...
syntax ..., ... VALues(numlist max=10 sort) ...
syntax ..., ... TIME(numlist >0) ...
syntax ..., ... FREQuency(numlist >0 integer) ...
syntax ..., ... OCCur(numlist missingokay >=0 <1e+9) ...
```

The result of the option is returned in a macro name formed by the first 31 letters of the option's name.

The macro contains the values specified by the user, but listed out, one after the other. For instance, the user might specify time(1(1)4,10) so that the local macro `time´ would contain "1 2 3 4 10".

min and max specify the minimum and maximum number of elements that may be in the list.

<, <=, >, and >= specify the range of elements allowed in the list.

integer indicates the user may specify integer values only.

missingokay indicates the user may specify missing (a single period) as a list element.

ascending specifies the user must give the list in ascending order without repeated values. descending specifies the user must give the list in descending order and without repeated values.

sort specifies that the list be sorted before being returned. Distinguish this from modifier ascending. ascending states the user must type the list in ascending order. sort says the user may type the list in any order but it is to be returned in ascending order. ascending states the list may have no repeated elements. sort places no such restriction on the list.

---

option_descriptor optional_varlist:

type	OPname	(capitalization indicates minimal abbreviation)
type	(varlist or (varname	
optionally type	<u>num</u>eric or <u>str</u>ing	
optionally type	min=#	
optionally type	max=#	
optionally type	ts	
type	)	

Examples:
```
syntax ..., ... ROW(varname) ...
syntax ..., ... BY(varlist) ...
syntax ..., ... Counts(varname numeric) ...
syntax ..., ... TItlevar(varname string) ...
syntax ..., ... Sizes(varlist numeric min=2 max=10) ...
```

The result of the option is returned in a macro name formed by the first 31 letters of the option's name.

The macro contains the variables specified by the user, unabbreviated, listed one after the other.

min indicates the minimum number of variables to be specified if the option is given. min=1 is the default.

max indicates the maximum number of variables that may be specified if the option is given. max=800 is the default for varlist (you may set it to be larger) and max=1 is the default for varname.

numeric specifies that the variable list must be comprised entirely of numeric variables; string specifies string variables.

ts indicates the variable list may contain time-series operators.

option_descriptor optional_string:

type	OPname	(capitalization indicates minimal abbreviation)
type	(<u>string</u>	
optionally type	asis	
type	)	

Examples: syntax ..., ... Title(string) ...
            syntax ..., ... XTRAvars(string) ...
            syntax ..., ... SAVing(string asis) ...

The result of the option is returned in a macro name formed by the first 31 letters of the option's name.

The macro contains the string specified by the user or else it contains nothing.

asis is rarely specified; if specified, the option's arguments are returned just as the user typed them, without quotes stripped and with leading and trailing blanks. If you specify this modifier, be sure to use compound double quotes when referring to the macro.

---

option_descriptor optional_passthru:

type	OPname	(capitalization indicates minimal abbreviation)
type	(passthru)	

Examples: syntax ..., ... Title(passthru) ...
            syntax ..., ... SAVing(passthru) ...

The result of the option is returned in a macro name formed by the first 31 letters of the option's name.

The macro contains the full option—unabbreviated option name, parentheses, and argument—as specified by the user or else it contains nothing. For instance, were the user to type ti("My Title") the macro would contain title("My Title").

Remarks

Stata is programmable and that makes it possible to implement new commands. This is done with program define:

```
program define newcmd
      ...
end
```

The first duty of the program is to parse the arguments it receives.

Programmers use positional argument passing for subroutines and for some new commands with exceedingly simple syntax. They do this because it is so easy to program. If program myprog is to receive a variable name (call it varname) and two numeric arguments (call them dof and beta), all they need code is

```
program define myprog
      args varname dof beta
      (the rest of the program would be coded in terms of `varname´, `dof´, and `beta´)
      ...
end
```

The disadvantage of this is from the caller's side: Heaven forbid the caller get the arguments in the wrong order, not spell out the variable name, etc.

The alternative is to use standard Stata syntax. `syntax` makes it easy to make new command `myprog` have syntax

> myprog *varname* $\left[\, , \underline{d}of(\#) \underline{b}eta(\#) \, \right]$

and even to have defaults for `dof()` and `beta()`:

```
program define myprog
        syntax varlist(max=1) [, Dof(integer 50) Beta(real 1.0)]
        (the rest of the program would be coded in terms of `varlist´, `dof´, and `beta´)
        ...
end
```

The args command

`args` splits what the user typed into words and places the first word in the first macro specified, the second in the second macro specified, and so on:

```
program define myprog
        args arg1 arg2 arg3 ...
        do computations using local macros 'arg1', 'arg2', 'arg3', ...
end
```

`args` never produces an error. If the user specified more arguments than macros specified, the extra arguments are ignored. If the user specified fewer arguments than macros specified, the extra macros are set to contain "".

A better version of this program would read

```
program define myprog
        version 7.0                                    ← new
        args arg1 arg2 arg3 ...
        do computations using local macros 'arg1', 'arg2', 'arg3', ...
end
```

Placing `version 7.0` as the first line of the program ensures that the command will continue to work even with future versions of Stata; see [U] **19.1.1 Version** and [P] **version**. We will include the `version` line from now on.

▷ Example

The following command displays the three arguments it receives:

```
. program define argdisp
  1.            version 7.0
  2.            args first second third
  3.            display "1st argument = `first´"
  4.            display "2nd argument = `second´"
  5.            display "3rd argument = `third´"
  6. end
. argdisp cat dog mouse
1st argument = cat
2nd argument = dog
3rd argument = mouse

. argdisp 3.456 2+5-12 X*3+cat
1st argument = 3.456
2nd argument = 2+5-12
3rd argument = X*3+cat
```

Note that arguments are defined by the spaces that separate them. "X*3+cat" is one argument but, had we typed "X*3 + cat", that would have been three arguments.

If the user specifies fewer arguments than expected by **args**, the additional local macros are set as empty. By the same token, if the user specifies too many, they are ignored:

```
. argdisp cat dog
1st argument = cat
2nd argument = dog
3rd argument =

. argdisp cat dog mouse cow
1st argument = cat
2nd argument = dog
3rd argument = mouse
```
◁

❑ Technical Note

When a program is invoked, exactly what the user typed is stored in the macro `` `0´ ``. In addition, the first word of that is also stored in `` `1´ ``, the second in `` `2´ ``, and so on. **args** merely copies the `` `1´ ``, `` `2´ ``, ..., macros. Coding

```
args arg1 arg2 arg3
```

is no different from coding

```
local arg1 `"`1´"´
local arg2 `"`2´"´
local arg3 `"`3´"´
```
❑

The syntax command

syntax is easy to use. **syntax** parses standard Stata syntax, which is

command varlist **if** *exp* **in** *range* [*weight*] **using** *filename*, *options*

The basic idea is that you code a **syntax** command describing which parts of standard Stata syntax you expect to see. For instance, you might code

```
syntax varlist if in, title(string) adjust(real 1)
```

or

```
syntax [varlist] [if] [in] [, title(string) adjust(real 1)]
```

In the first example, you are saying that everything is required. In the second, everything is optional. You can make some elements required and others optional:

```
syntax varlist [if] [in], adjust(real) [title(string)]
```

or

```
syntax varlist [if] [in] [, adjust(real 1) title(string)]
```

or lots of other possibilities. Square brackets denote optional. Put them around what you wish.

Anyway, you code what you expect the user to type. syntax then compares that with what the user actually did type and, if there is a mismatch, syntax issues an error message. Otherwise, syntax processes what the user typed and stores the pieces, broken out into categories, in macros. These macros are named the same as the syntactical piece:

The varlist specified	will go into `` `varlist' ``
The if *exp*	will go into `` `if' ``
The in *range*	will go into `` `in' ``
The adjust() option's contents	will go into `` `adjust' ``
The title() option's contents	will go into `` `title' ``

Go back to the section *Syntax, continued*. Where each element is stored is explicitly stated. When a piece is not specified by the user, the corresponding macro is cleared.

▷ Example

The following program simply displays the pieces:

```
. program define myprog
  1. version 7.0
  2. syntax varlist [if] [in] [, adjust(real 1) title(string)]
  3. display "varlist contains |`varlist'|"
  4. display "     if contains |`if'|"
  5. display "     in contains |`in'|"
  6. display " adjust contains |`adjust'|"
  7. display "  title contains |`title'|"
  8. end
. myprog
varlist required
r(100);
```

Well that should not surprise us; we said the varlist was required in the syntax command, so when we tried myprog without explicitly specifying a varlist, Stata complained.

```
. myprog mpg weight
varlist contains |mpg weight|
     if contains ||
     in contains ||
 adjust contains |1|
  title contains ||
. myprog mpg weight if foreign
varlist contains |mpg weight|
     if contains |if foreign|
     in contains ||
 adjust contains |1|
  title contains ||
. myprog mpg weight in 1/20
varlist contains |mpg weight|
     if contains ||
     in contains |in 1/20|
 adjust contains |1|
  title contains ||
. myprog mpg weight in 1/20 if foreign
varlist contains |mpg weight|
     if contains |if foreign|
     in contains |in 1/20|
 adjust contains |1|
  title contains ||
```

```
. myprog mpg weight in 1/20 if foreign, title("My Results")
varlist contains |mpg weight|
     if contains |if foreign|
     in contains |in 1/20|
 adjust contains |1|
  title contains |My Results|
. myprog mpg weight in 1/20 if foreign, title("My Results") adjust(2.5)
varlist contains |mpg weight|
     if contains |if foreign|
     in contains |in 1/20|
 adjust contains |2.5|
  title contains |My Results|
```

That is all there is to it.

◁

▷ Example

With this in hand, it would not be difficult to actually make myprog do something. For want of a better example, we will change myprog to display the mean of each variable, said mean multiplied by adjust():

```
program define myprog
        version 7.0
        syntax varlist [if] [in] [, adjust(real 1) title(string)]
        display
        if "`title´" ~= "" {
                display "`title´:"
        }
        foreach var of local varlist {
                quietly summarize `var´ `if´ `in´
                display %9s "`var´" "   " %9.0g r(mean)*`adjust´
        }
end

. myprog mpg weight
      mpg    21.2973
   weight   3019.459
. myprog mpg weight if foreign==1
      mpg   24.77273
   weight   2315.909
. myprog mpg weight if foreign==1, title("My title")
My title:
      mpg   24.77273
   weight   2315.909
. myprog mpg weight if foreign==1, title("My title") adjust(2)
My title:
      mpg   49.54545
   weight   4631.818
```

◁

❑ Technical Note

myprog is hardly deserving of any further work given what little it does, but let's illustrate two things using it.

First, learn about the `marksample` command; see [P] **mark**. A common mistake is to use one sample in one part of the program and a different sample in another part. The solution is to create a variable at the outset that contains 1 if the observation is to be used and 0 otherwise. `marksample` will do this and do it correctly because `marksample` knows what `syntax` has just parsed:

```
program define myprog
        version 7.0
        syntax varlist [if] [in] [, adjust(real 1) title(string)]
        marksample touse                              ← new
        display
        if "`title'" ~= "" {
                display "`title':"
        }
        foreach var of local varlist {
                quietly summarize `var' if `touse'        ← changed
                display %9s "`var'" "  " %9.0g r(mean)*`adjust'
        }
end
```

The second thing we will do is modify our program so that what is done with each variable is done by a subroutine. Pretend, in this, that we are doing something more involved than calculating and displaying a mean.

We want to make this modification to show you the right and proper use of the `args` command. Passing arguments by position to subroutines is convenient and there is no chance of error due to arguments being out of order, or at least there is no chance assuming we wrote our program properly:

```
program define myprog
        version 7.0
        syntax varlist [if] [in] [, adjust(real 1) title(string)]
        marksample touse
        display
        if "`title'" ~= "" {
                display "`title':"
        }
        foreach var of local varlist {
                doavar `touse' `var' `adjust'
        }
end
program define doavar
        version 7.0
        args touse name value
        qui summarize `name' if `touse'
        display %9s "`name'" "  " %9.0g r(mean)*`value'
end
```

❑

Also See

Complementary: [P] **mark**, [P] **numlist**, [P] **program**

Related: [P] **gettoken**, [P] **tokenize**, [P] **tsrevar**, [P] **unab**

Background: [U] **14 Language syntax**,
        [U] **19.1.1 Version**,
        [U] **21 Programming Stata**,
        [U] **21.3.1 Local macros**,
        [U] **21.3.5 Double quotes**

Title

sysdir — Set system directories

Syntax

sysdir [list]

sysdir set codeword ["]path["]

adopath

adopath + path_or_codeword

adopath ++ path_or_codeword

adopath - {path_or_codeword | #}

set adosize # $10 \le \# \le 500$

where codeword is { STATA | UPDATES | BASE | SITE | STBPLUS | PERSONAL | OLDPLACE }

Description

sysdir lists and resets the identities of Stata's system directories.

adopath provides a convenient way to examine and manipulate the ado-file path stored in the global macro S_ADO.

set adosize sets the maximum amount of memory in kilobytes that automatically loaded do-files may consume. The default is set adosize 128 for Intercooled Stata and 32 for Small Stata.

These commands have to do with technical aspects of Stata's implementation. With the exception of sysdir list, you should never have to use them.

Remarks

sysdir

Stata expects to find various parts of itself in various directories (folders). Rather than describe these directories as C:\stata\ado\base or /usr/local/stata/ado, these places are referenced by codewords. Here are the definitions of the codewords on a particular Windows computer:

```
. sysdir
    STATA:  C:\STATA\
  UPDATES:  C:\STATA\ado\updates\
     BASE:  C:\STATA\ado\base\
     SITE:  C:\STATA\ado\site\
  STBPLUS:  C:\ado\stbplus\
 PERSONAL:  C:\ado\personal\
 OLDPLACE:  C:\ado\
```

Even if you use Stata for Windows, when you type `sysdir`, you might see different directories listed.

The `sysdir` command allows you to obtain the correspondence between codeword and actual directory and it allows you to change the mapping. Each of the directories serves a particular purpose:

STATA refers to the directory where the Stata executable is to be found.

UPDATES is where the updates to the official ado-files that were shipped with Stata are installed. The `update` command places files in this directory; see [R] **update**.

BASE is where the original official ado-files that were shipped with Stata are installed. This directory was written when Stata was installed and thereafter the contents are never changed.

SITE is relevant only on networked computers. It is where administrators may place ado-files for sitewide use on networked computers. No Stata command writes in this directory, but administrators may move files into the directory or they may obtain ado-files using `net` and choose to install them into this directory; see [R] **net**.

STBPLUS is relevant on all systems. It is where ado-files written by other people that you obtain using the `net` command are installed; by default, `net` installs files to this directory; see [R] **net**.

PERSONAL is where you are to copy ado-files that you write and that you wish to use regardless of your current directory when you use Stata. (The alternative is to put ado-files in your current directory and then they will only be available when you are in that directory.)

OLDPLACE is included for backwards compatibility. Stata 5 users used to put ado-files here, both the personal ones and the ones written by others. Nowadays they are supposed to put their personal files in PERSONAL and the ones written by others in STBPLUS.

Do not change the definitions of UPDATES or BASE, You may want to change the definitions of SITE, PERSONAL, STBPLUS, or especially OLDPLACE. For instance, if you wanted to change the definition of OLDPLACE to `d:\ado`, type

```
. sysdir set OLDPLACE "d:\ado"
```

Resetting a system directory affects only the current session; the next time you enter Stata, the system directories will be set back to being as they originally were. If you want to reset a system directory permanently, place the `sysdir set` command in your `profile.do`; see [GSW] **A.7 Executing commands every time Stata is started**, [GSM] **A.6 Executing commands every time Stata is started**, or [GSU] **A.7 Executing commands every time Stata is started**.

adopath

`adopath` displays and resets the contents of the global macro S_ADO, the path over which Stata searches for ado-files. The default search path is

```
. adopath
  [1]  (UPDATES)   "C:\STATA\ado\updates"
  [2]  (BASE)      "C:\STATA\ado\base"
  [3]  (SITE)      "C:\STATA\ado\site"
  [4]              "."
  [5]  (PERSONAL)  "C:\ado\personal"
  [6]  (STBPLUS)   "C:\ado\stbplus"
  [7]  (OLDPLACE)  "C:\ado"
```

In reading the above, you want to focus on the codewords on the left. `adopath` mentions the actual directories but, were you to change the meaning of a codeword using `sysdir`, that change would affect `adopath`.

The above states that, when Stata looks for an ado-file, first it looks in UPDATES. If the ado-file is found, that copy is used. If it is not found, Stata next looks in BASE and, if it is found there, that copy is used. And so the process continues. Note that at the fourth step, Stata looks in the current directory (for which there is no codeword).

adopath merely presents the information in S_ADO in a more readable form:

```
. macro list S_ADO
S_ADO:     UPDATES;BASE;SITE;.;PERSONAL;STBPLUS;OLDPLACE
```

adopath can also change the contents of the path. In general, you should not do this unless you are sure of what you are doing because many features of Stata will stop working if you change the path incorrectly. At worst, however, you might have to exit and reenter Stata, so you cannot do any permanent damage. Moreover, it is safe to add to the end of the path.

The path may include actual directory names, such as c:\myprogs, or codewords, such as PERSONAL, STBPLUS, and OLDPLACE. To add c:\myprogs to the end of the path, type

```
. adopath + c:\myprogs
  [1]   (UPDATES)    "C:\STATA\ado\updates"
  [2]   (BASE)       "C:\STATA\ado\base"
  [3]   (SITE)       "C:\STATA\ado\site"
  [4]                "."
  [5]   (PERSONAL)   "C:\ado\personal"
  [6]   (STBPLUS)    "C:\ado\stbplus"
  [7]   (OLDPLACE)   "C:\ado"
  [8]                "c:\myprogs"
```

If later you want to remove c:\myprogs from the ado path, you could type adopath - c:\myprogs, but easier is

```
. adopath - 8
  [1]   (UPDATES)    "C:\STATA\ado\updates"
  [2]   (BASE)       "C:\STATA\ado\base"
  [3]   (SITE)       "C:\STATA\ado\site"
  [4]                "."
  [5]   (PERSONAL)   "C:\ado\personal"
  [6]   (STBPLUS)    "C:\ado\stbplus"
  [7]   (OLDPLACE)   "C:\ado"
```

When followed by a number, 'adopath -' removes that element from the path. If you cannot remember what the numbers are, you can first type adopath without arguments.

❑ Technical Note

adopath ++ *path* works like adopath + *path* except that it adds to the beginning rather than to the end of the path. Our recommendation is that you not do this. When looking for *name*.ado, Stata loads the first file it encounters as it searches along the path. If you did not like our implementation of the command ci, for instance, even if you wrote your own and stored it in ci.ado, Stata would continue to use the one in the Stata directory because that is the directory listed earlier in the path. To force Stata to use yours rather than ours, you would have to put at the front of the path the name of the directory where your ado-file resides.

You should not, however, name any of your ado-files the same as we have named ours. If you add to the front of the path, you assume exclusive responsibility for the Stata commands working as documented in this manual.

❑

set adosize

Stata keeps track of the ado-commands you use and discards from memory commands that have not been used recently. Stata discards old commands to keep the amount of memory consumed by such commands below `adosize`. The default value of 128 means the total amount of memory consumed by ado-commands is not to exceed 128K. When an ado-command has been discarded, Stata will have to reload the command the next time you use it.

You can increase `adosize`. Typing `set adosize` 200 would allow up to 200K to be allocated to ado-commands. This would improve performance slightly if you happened to use one of the not-recently-used commands, but at the cost of some memory no longer being available for your dataset. In practice, there is little reason to increase `adosize`.

`adosize` must be between 10 and 500.

Methods and Formulas

`adopath` is implemented as an ado-file.

Also See

Complementary:	[R] **net**, [R] **query**, [R] **update**
Background:	[U] **20.5 Where does Stata look for ado-files?**

Title

---
tabdisp — Display tables

Syntax

tabdisp *rowvar* [*colvar* [*supercolvar*]] [if *exp*] [in *range*], $\underline{c}$ellvar(*varname(s)*)

    [by(*superrowvar(s)*) $\underline{f}$ormat(%*fmt*) $\underline{cen}$ter $\underline{l}$eft $\underline{con}$cise $\underline{m}$issing $\underline{tot}$als

    $\underline{cellw}$idth(#) $\underline{cs}$epwidth(#) $\underline{scs}$epwidth(#) $\underline{stub}$width(#)]

by ... : may be used with tabdisp; see [R] **by**.

Rows, columns, supercolumns, and superrows are defined thus:

row 1	.
row 2	.

	supercol 1		supercol 2	
	col 1	col 2	col 1	col 2
row 1	.	.	.	.
row 2	.	.	.	.

	col 1	col 2
row 1	.	.
row 2	.	.

	supercol 1		supercol 2	
	col 1	col 2	col 1	col 2
superrow 1:				
row 1	.	.	.	.
row 2	.	.	.	.
superrow 2:				
row 1	.	.	.	.
row 2	.	.	.	.

Description

tabdisp displays data in a table. tabdisp calculates no statistics and is intended for use by programmers.

For the corresponding command that calculates statistics and displays them in a table, see [R] **table**.

Although tabdisp is intended for programming applications, it can be used interactively for listing data.

Options

cellvar(*varname(s)*) is not optional; it specifies the numeric or string variables containing the values to be displayed in the table's cells. Up to 5 variable names may be specified.

by(*superrowvar(s)*) specifies numeric or string variables to be treated as superrows. Up to four variables may be specified in *varlist*.

format(%*fmt*) specifies the display format for presenting numbers in the table's cells. format(%9.0g) is the default; format(%9.2f) is a popular alternative. The width of the format you specify does not matter except that %*fmt* must be valid. The width of the cells is chosen by tabdisp to be what it thinks looks best. Option cellwidth() allows you to override tabdisp's choice.

center specifies that results are to be centered in the table's cells. The default is to right align results. For centering to work well, you typically need to specify a display format as well. center format(%9.2f) is popular.

left specifies that column labels are to be left aligned. The default is to right align column labels to distinguish them from supercolumn labels, which are left aligned. If you specify left, both column and supercolumn labels are left aligned.

concise specifies that rows with all missing entries are not to be displayed.

missing specifies that missing cells are to be shown in the table as periods (Stata's missing-value indicator). The default is that missing entries are left blank.

totals specifies that observations where *rowvar*, *colvar*, *supercolvar*, and/or *superrowvar(s)* contain missing are to be interpreted as containing the corresponding totals of cellvar(). Missing is interpreted as numeric missing value or "" depending on variable type. If totals is not specified, missing values in *rowvar*, *colvar*, *supercolvar*, and *superrowvar(s)* are given no special interpretation.

cellwidth(#) specifies the width of the cell in units of digit widths; 10 means the space occupied by 10 digits, which is 1234567890. The default cellwidth() is not a fixed number but a number chosen by tabdisp to spread the table out while presenting a reasonable number of columns across the page.

csepwidth(#) specifies the separation between columns in units of digit widths. The default is not a fixed number but a number chosen by tabdisp according to what it thinks looks best.

scsepwidth(#) specifies the separation between supercolumns in units of digit widths. The default is not a fixed number but a number chosen by tabdisp according to what it thinks looks best.

stubwidth(#) specifies the width, in units of digit widths, to be allocated to the left stub of the table. The default is not a fixed number but a number chosen by tabdisp according to what it thinks looks best.

Limits

Up to 4 variables may be specified in the by(), so with the three row, column, and supercolumn variables, seven-way tables may be displayed.

Up to 5 variables may be displayed in each cell of the table.

The sum of the number of rows, columns, supercolumns, and superrows is called the number of margins. A table may contain up to 3,000 margins. Thus, a one-way table may contain 3,000 rows. A two-way table could contain 2,998 rows and 2 columns, 2,997 rows and 3 columns, ..., 1,500 rows and 1,500 columns, ..., 2 rows and 2,998 columns. A three-way table is similarly limited by the sum of the number of rows, columns, and supercolumns. A $r \times c \times d$ table is feasible if $r + c + d \leq 3,000$. Note that the limit is set in terms of the sum of the rows, columns, supercolumns, and superrows and not, as you might expect, their product.

Remarks

If you have not read [R] **table**, please do so. Then understand that `tabdisp` is what `table` uses to display the tables.

`tabdisp` calculates nothing. `tabdisp` instead displays the data in memory. In this, think of `tabdisp` as an alternative to `list`. Consider the following little dataset:

```
. list

          a      b      c
 1.       0      1     15
 2.       0      2     26
 3.       0      3     11
 4.       1      1     14
 5.       1      2     12
 6.       1      3      7
```

We can use `tabdisp` to list it:

```
. tabdisp a b, cell(c)

          |         b
        a |     1     2     3
   -------+-------------------
        0 |    15    26    11
        1 |    14    12     7
```

`tabdisp` is merely an alternative way to list the data. It is when the data in memory are statistics by category that `tabdisp` becomes really useful. `table` provides one prepackaging of that idea.

Unlike `list`, `tabdisp` is unaffected by the order of the data. Here are the same data in a different order:

```
. list

          a      b      c
 1.       1      3      7
 2.       0      3     11
 3.       1      2     12
 4.       1      1     14
 5.       0      1     15
 6.       0      2     26
```

and yet the output of `tabdisp` is unaffected.

```
. tabdisp a b, cell(c)

          |         b
        a |     1     2     3
   -------+-------------------
        0 |    15    26    11
        1 |    14    12     7
```

Nor does `tabdisp` care if one of the cells is missing in the data.

```
. drop in 6
(1 observation deleted)
```

```
. tabdisp a b, cell(c)
```

	b		
a	1	2	3
0	15		11
1	14	12	7

On the other hand, `tabdisp` assumes that each value combination of the row, column, superrow, and supercolumn variables occurs only once. If that is not so, `tabdisp` displays the earliest occurring value:

```
. input
          a         b         c
6. 0 1 99
7. end
. list
```

	a	b	c
1.	1	3	7
2.	0	3	11
3.	1	2	12
4.	1	1	14
5.	0	1	15
6.	0	1	99

```
. tabdisp a b, cell(c)
```

	b		
a	1	2	3
0	15		11
1	14	12	7

Thus, our previous claim that `tabdisp` was unaffected by sort order has this one exception.

Finally, `tabdisp` uses variable and value labels when they are defined:

```
. label var a "Sex"
. label define sex 0 male 1 female
. label values a sex
. label var b "Treatment Group"
. label def tg 1 "controls" 2 "low dose" 3 "high dose"
. label values b tg
. tabdisp a b, cell(c)
```

Sex	Treatment Group		
	controls	low dose	high dose
male	15		11
female	14	12	7

There are two things you can do with `tabdisp`.

You can use it to list data, but be certain you have a unique identifier. In the automobile dataset, the variable `make` is unique:

```
. list make mpg weight displ rep78
```

```
     make                       mpg   weight  displa~t      rep78
 1. AMC Concord                  22    2,930       121          3
 2. AMC Pacer                    17    3,350       258          3
 3. AMC Spirit                   22    2,640       121          .
  (output omitted )
74. Volvo 260                    17    3,170       163          5
```

. tabdisp make, cell(mpg weight displ rep78)

Make and Model	Mileage (mpg)	Weight (lbs.)	displacement	rep78
AMC Concord	22	2,930	121	3
AMC Pacer	17	3,350	258	3
AMC Spirit	22	2,640	121	
(output omitted)				
Volvo 260	17	3,170	163	5

Mostly, however, `tabdisp` is intended for use when you have a dataset of statistics that you want to display:

. collapse (mean) mpg, by(foreign rep78)

. list

```
     rep78   foreign        mpg
 1.      1  Domestic         21
 2.      2  Domestic     19.125
 3.      3  Domestic         19
 4.      4  Domestic   18.44444
 5.      5  Domestic         32
 6.      .  Domestic      23.25
 7.      3   Foreign   23.33333
 8.      4   Foreign   24.88889
 9.      5   Foreign   26.33333
10.      .   Foreign         14
```

. tabdisp foreign rep78, cell(mpg)

	\multicolumn{6}{c}{Repair Record 1978}					
Car type	1	2	3	4	5	.
Domestic	21	19.125	19	18.4444	32	23.25
Foreign			23.3333	24.8889	26.3333	14

. drop if rep78==.
(2 observations deleted)

. label define repair 1 Poor 2 Fair 3 Average 4 Good 5 Excellent

. label values rep78 repair

. tabdisp foreign rep78, cell(mpg) format(%9.2f) center

	\multicolumn{5}{c}{Repair Record 1978}				
Car type	Poor	Fair	Average	Good	Excellent
Domestic	21.00	19.12	19.00	18.44	32.00
Foreign			23.33	24.89	26.33

Treatment of string variables

The variables specifying the rows, columns, supercolumns, and superrows may be numeric or string. In addition, the variables specified for inclusion in the table may be numeric or string. In the example below, all variables are strings, including `reaction`:

```
. tabdisp agecat sex party, c(reaction) center
```

Age	Party Affiliation and Sex				
	Democrat		Republican	
category	Female	Male	Female	Male
Old	Disfavor	Indifferent	Favor	Strongly Favor
Young	Disfavor	Disfavor	Indifferent	Favor

Treatment of missing values

The `cellvar()` variable(s) specified for inclusion in the table may contain missing values and whether the variable contains a missing value or the observation is missing altogether makes no difference:

```
. list

         sex    response         pop
  1.       0           0          12
  2.       0           1          20
  3.       0           2           .
  4.       1           0          15
  5.       1           1          11
. tabdisp sex response, cell(pop)
```

Sex	Response		
	0	1	2
0	12	20	
1	15	11	

In the above output, the $(1, 3)$ cell is empty because the observation for `sex` $= 0$ and `response` $= 2$ has a missing value for `pop`. The $(2, 3)$ is empty because there is no observation for `sex` $= 1$ and `response` $= 2$.

If you specify the option `missing`, rather than cells being left blank, a period is placed in them:

```
. tabdisp sex response, cell(pop) missing
```

Sex	Response		
	0	1	2
0	12	20	.
1	15	11	.

Missing values of the row, column, superrow, and supercolumn variables are allowed and, by default, are given no special meaning. The output below is from a different dataset.

```
. list
             sex    response         pop
    1.         0           0          15
    2.         0           1          11
    3.         0           .          26
    4.         1           0          20
    5.         1           1          24
    6.         1           .          44
    7.         .           .          70
    8.         .           0          35
    9.         .           1          35
. tabdisp sex response, cell(pop)
```

		response	
sex	0	1	.
0	15	11	26
1	20	24	44
.	35	35	70

If you specify the option `total`, however, the missing values are labeled as reflecting totals:

```
. tabdisp sex response, cell(pop) total
```

		response	
sex	0	1	Total
0	15	11	26
1	20	24	44
Total	35	35	70

It is important to understand that `tabdisp` did not calculate the totals; it merely labeled the results as being totals. The number 70 appears in the lower right because there happens to be an observation in the dataset where both `sex` and `response` contain a missing value and `pop` = 70.

In this example, the row and column variables were numeric. Had they been strings, the option `total` would have given the special interpretation to `sex` = "" and `response` = "".

Also See

Related: [R] **table**, [R] **tabulate**

Title

tokenize — Divide strings into tokens

Syntax

<u>toke</u>nize $\begin{bmatrix}"\end{bmatrix}\begin{bmatrix}string\end{bmatrix}\begin{bmatrix}"\end{bmatrix}$ $\begin{bmatrix}, \underline{pa}rse("pchars")\end{bmatrix}$

Description

tokenize divides *string* into tokens, storing the result in `1´, `2´, ... (the positional local macros). Tokens are determined based on the parsing characters *pchars*, which default to a space if not specified.

Options

parse(*"pchars"*) specifies the parsing characters. If **parse()** is not specified, **parse(" ")** is assumed and *string* is split into words.

Remarks

tokenize may be used as an alternative or supplement to the **syntax** command for parsing command line arguments. Generally, it is used to further process the local macros created by **syntax** as shown below.

```
program define myprog
        version 7.0
        syntax [varlist] [if] [in]
        marksample touse

        tokenize `varlist´
        local first `1´
        macro shift
        local rest `*´
        ...
end
```

▷ Example

We interactively apply **tokenize** and then display several of the numbered macros to illustrate how the command works.

```
. tokenize some words
. di "1=|`1´|, 2=|`2´|, 3=|`3´|"
1=|some|, 2=|words|, 3=||
. tokenize "some more words"
. di "1=|`1´|, 2=|`2´|, 3=|`3´|, 4=|`4´|"
1=|some|, 2=|more|, 3=|words|, 4=||
. local str "A strange++string"
. tokenize `str´
```

315

```
. di "1=|`1´|, 2=|`2´|, 3=|`3´|"
1=|A|, 2=|strange++string|, 3=||
. tokenize `str´, parse(" +")
. di "1=|`1´|, 2=|`2´|, 3=|`3´|, 4=|`4´|, 5=|`5´|, 6=|`6´|"
1=|A|, 2=|strange|, 3=|+|, 4=|+|, 5=|string|, 6=||
. tokenize `str´, parse("+")
. di "1=|`1´|, 2=|`2´|, 3=|`3´|, 4=|`4´|, 5=|`5´|, 6=|`6´|"
1=|A strange|, 2=|+|, 3=|+|, 4=|string|, 5=||, 6=||
. tokenize
. di "1=|`1´|, 2=|`2´|, 3=|`3´|"
1=||, 2=||, 3=||
```

These examples illustrate that the quotes surrounding the string are optional; the space parsing character is not saved in the numbered macros; non-space parsing characters are saved in the numbered macros together with the tokens being parsed; and more than one parsing character may be specified. Also, when called with no string argument, tokenize resets the local numbered macros to empty.

◁

Also See

Complementary: [P] **syntax**

Related: [P] **foreach**, [P] **gettoken**, [P] **macro**

Background: [U] **21 Programming Stata**

Title

| **tsrevar** — Time-series operator programming command |

Syntax

tsrevar [*varlist*] [if *exp*] [in *range*] [, <u>sub</u>stitute <u>l</u>ist]

tsrevar is for use with time-series data. You must tsset your data before using tsrevar; see [R] **tsset**.

Description

tsrevar, substitute takes a variable list that might contain *op.varname* combinations and substitutes real variables that are equivalent for the combinations. For instance, the original *varlist* might be "gnp L.gnp r", and tsrevar, substitute would create *newvar* = L.gnp and create the equivalent varlist "gnp *newvar* r". This new varlist could then be used with commands that do not otherwise support time-series operators or it could be used in a program to make execution faster at the expense of using more memory.

tsrevar, substitute might create no new variables, one new variable, or many new variables, depending on the number of *op.varname* combinations appearing in *varlist*. Any new variables created are temporary variables. The new, equivalent varlist is returned in r(varlist). Note that the new varlist has a one-to-one correspondence with the original *varlist*.

tsrevar, list does something different. It returns in r(varlist) the list of base variable names of *varlist* with the time-series operators removed. tsrevar, list creates no new variables. For instance, if the original *varlist* were "gnp l.gnp l2.gnp r l.cd", then r(varlist) would contain "gnp r cd". This is useful for programmers who might want to create programs to keep just the variables corresponding to *varlist*.

Options

<u>sub</u>stitute specifies that tsrevar is to resolve *op.varname* combinations by creating temporary variables as described above. substitute is the default action taken by tsrevar; you do not need to specify the option.

list specifies that tsrevar is to return a list of base variable names.

▷ Example

```
. tsrevar l.gnp d.gnp r
```

creates two new temporary variables containing the values for l.gnp and d.gnp. The variable r appears in the new variable list, but does not require a temporary variable.

The resulting variable list is

```
. di "`r(varlist)'"
__00014P __00014Q r
```

We can see the results by listing the new variables alongside the original value of gnp.

```
. list gnp `r(varlist)´ in 1/5

         gnp    __00014P    __00014Q         r
 1.      128        .           .          3.2
 2.      135       128           7          3.8
 3.      132       135          -3          2.6
 4.      138       132           6          3.9
 5.      145       138           7          4.2
```

Remember that temporary variables automatically vanish when the program concludes.

If we had needed only the base variable names, we could have specified

```
. tsrevar l.gnp d.gnp r, list
. di "`r(varlist)´"
gnp r
```

The ordering of the list will probably be different from the original list; base variables are listed only once and will be listed in the order in which they appear in the dataset.

◁

❏ Technical Note

tsrevar, substitute is smart and avoids creating duplicate variables. Consider

```
. tsrevar gnp l.gnp r cd l.cd l.gnp
```

Note that l.gnp appears twice in the varlist. tsrevar will create only one new variable for l.gnp and the use that new variable twice in the resulting r(varlist). Moreover, tsrevar will even do this across multiple calls:

```
. tsrevar gnp l.gnp cd l.cd
. tsrevar cpi l.gnp
```

Note that l.gnp appears in two separate calls. At the first call, tsrevar will create a temporary variable corresponding to l.gnp. At the second call, tsrevar will remember what it has done and use that same previously created temporary variable for l.gnp again.

❏

Saved Results

tsrevar saves in r():

Macros
      r(varlist)   the modified variable list or list of base variable names

Also See

Related: [P] **syntax**, [P] **unab**

Background: [U] **14 Language syntax**,
                 [U] **14.4.3 Time-series varlists**,
                 [U] **21 Programming Stata**

Title

unab — Unabbreviate variable list

Syntax

Standard variable lists

> unab *lmacname* : $[varlist]$ $[$, min(#) max(#) name(*string*) $]$

Variable lists that may contain time-series operators

> tsunab *lmacname* : $[varlist]$ $[$, min(#) max(#) name(*string*) $]$

Description

unab expands and unabbreviates a *varlist* (see [U] **14.4 varlists**) of existing variables, placing the result in the local macro *lmacname*. **unab** is a low-level parsing command. The **syntax** command is a high-level parsing command that, among other things, also unabbreviates variable lists; see [P] **syntax**.

The difference between **unab** and **tsunab** is that **tsunab** will allow time-series operators to modify the variables in *varlist*; see [U] **14.4.3 Time-series varlists**.

Options

min(#) specifies the minimum number of variables allowed. The default is min(1).

max(#) specifies the maximum number of variables allowed. The default is max(32000).

name(*string*) provides a label that is used when printing error messages.

Remarks

In most cases, the **syntax** command will automatically handle the unabbreviating of variable lists; see [P] **syntax**. In a few cases, **unab** will be needed to obtain unabbreviated variable lists.

▷ Example

The **separate** command (see [R] **separate**) provides an example of the use of **unab**. Required option **by**(*byvar* | *exp*) takes either a variable name or an expression. This is not handled automatically by the **syntax** command.

In this case, the **syntax** command for **separate** takes the form

```
syntax varname [if] [in], BY(string) [ other options]
```

After **syntax** performs the command line parsing, the local variable by contains what the user entered for the option. We now need to determine if it is an existing variable name or an expression. If it is a variable name, we may need to expand it.

```
capture confirm var `by´
if _rc == 0 {
        unab by: `by´, max(1) name(by())
}
else {
        ( parse `by´ as an expression)
}
```
◁

▷ Example

We interactively demonstrate the unab command with the auto dataset.

```
. unab x : mpg wei for, name(myopt())
. display "`x´"
mpg weight foreign
. unab x : junk
variable junk not found
r(111);
. unab x : mpg wei, max(1) name(myopt())
myopt():  too many variables specified
          1 variable required
r(103);
. unab x : mpg wei, max(1) name(myopt()) min(0)
myopt():  too many variables specified
          0 or 1 variables required
r(103);
. unab x : mpg wei, min(3) name(myopt())
myopt():  too few variables specified
          3 or more variables required
r(102);
. unab x : mpg wei, min(3) name(myopt()) max(10)
myopt():  too few variables specified
          3 - 10 variables required
r(102);
. unab x : mpg wei, min(3) max(10)
mpg weight:
too few variables specified
r(102);
```
◁

▷ Example

If we created a time variable and used tsset to declare the dataset as time series, we can also expand time-series variable lists.

```
. gen time = _n
. tsset time
. tsunab mylist : l(1/3).mpg
. display "`mylist´"
L.mpg L2.mpg L3.mpg
. tsunab mylist : l(1/3).(price turn displ)
. di "`mylist´"
L.price L2.price L3.price L.turn L2.turn L3.turn L.displ L2.displ L3.displ
```
◁

Also See

Related: [P] **syntax**

Background: [U] **14 Language syntax**,
                  [U] **21 Programming Stata**

Title

---
version — Version control

Syntax

version [*#*]

version *#*: *command*

Description

In the first syntax, **version** sets the command interpreter to an internal version number *#* or, if *#* is not specified, shows the current internal version number to which the command interpreter is set.

In the second syntax, **version** executes *command* under version *#* and then resets the version back to what it was before the **version** *#*:... command was given.

For information on external version control, see [R] **which**.

Remarks

version ensures that programs written under an older release of Stata will continue to work under newer releases of Stata. If you do not write programs and if you use only the programs distributed by us, you can ignore **version**. If you do write programs, see [U] **21.11.1 Version** for guidelines to follow to ensure compatibility of your programs across future releases of Stata.

❑ Technical Note

If you have upgraded to the current release (7.0) from a release of Stata prior to Stata 3.0, read this technical note; otherwise, don't bother. With the release of Stata 3.0, changes were introduced to the Stata language, changes serious enough to cause programs written in Stata's language prior to 3.0 not to work. **version** resurrects such programs. If you have old programs or do-files you have written or obtained from the STB (see [U] **2.4 The Stata Technical Bulletin**) prior to the Stata 3.0 release, **version** will make them work. In addition, if you will use the **version** command in all new do- and ado-files you write, you will never again be faced with this incompatibility problem.

To make old do- and ado-files work, edit these files to include the line **version 2.1** immediately after any **program define** command.

❑

❑ Technical Note

The details of how **version** works are as follows. When Stata is invoked, it sets its internal version number to the current version of Stata, which is 7.0 at the time this was written. Typing **version** without arguments shows the current value of the internal version number:

```
. version
version 7.0
```

One way to make old programs work is to set the internal version number interactively to that of a previous release:

```
. version 2.1
. version
version 2.10
```

Now Stata's default interpretation of a program is the same as it was for Stata 2.1. In point of fact, Stata 3.0 is the first instance of an inconsistency in the language being introduced, so setting the version to any number below 3.0 has the same effect—it reestablishes the old interpretation. In the future, however, version 3.0 might differ from version 8.0 and, if it does, setting the version to 3.0 would reestablish the 3.0 interpretation of programs.

You cannot set the version to a number higher than the current version. Since we are using Stata 7.0, we cannot set the version number to 8.0.

```
. version 8.0
version 8.0 not supported
r(9);
```

❑

❑ Technical Note

We strongly recommend that all ado- and do-files begin with a **version** command. In the case of programs (ado-files), the version command should appear immediately following the **program define** command:

```
program define myprog
        version 7.0
        ( etc.)
end
```

❑

Also See

Related: [P] **display**,
                   [R] **which**

Background: [U] **21.11.1 Version**

Title

> **while** — Looping

Syntax

```
while exp {
        stata_commands
}
```

Description

while evaluates *exp* and, if it is true (nonzero), executes the commands enclosed in the braces. It then repeats the process until *exp* evaluates to false (zero). **while**s may be nested within **while**s. If the *exp* refers to any variables, their values in the first observation are used unless explicit subscripts are specified; see [U] **16.7 Explicit subscripting**.

Remarks

while may be used interactively, but it is most frequently used in programs. See [U] **21 Programming Stata** for a complete description of programs.

The *stata_commands* enclosed in the braces may be executed once, many times, or not at all. For instance,

```
program define demo
        local i = `1´
        while `i´>0 {
                display "i is now `i´"
                local i = `i´ - 1
        }
        display "done"
end

. demo 2
i is now 2
i is now 1
done

. demo 0
done
```

The above example is a bit contrived in that the best way to count down to one would be

```
program define demo
        forvalues i = `1´(-1)1 {
                display "i is now `i´"
        }
        display "done"
end
```

while is more usually used in parsing contexts

```
program define ...
        ...
        gettoken tok 0 : 0
        while "`tok´" ~= "" {
```

```
                    . . .
                    gettoken tok 0 : 0
            }
            . . .
    end
```

or in mathematical contexts where we are iterating

```
program define . . .
            . . .
            scalar `curval´  = .
            scalar `lastval´ = .
            while abs(`lastval´ - `curval´) > `epsilon´ {
                    scalar `lastval´ = `curval´
                    scalar `curval´  = . . .
            }
            . . .
    end
```

or in any other context in which loop termination is based on calculation (whether it be numeric or string).

You can also create endless loops using `while`:

```
program define . . .
            . . .
            while 1 {
                    . . .
            }
    end
```

which is not really an endless loop if the code reads

```
program define . . .
            . . .
            while 1 {
                    if . . . { exit }
                    . . .
            }
            /* this line is never reached */
    end
```

Should you make a mistake and really create an endless loop, you can stop program execution by pressing the *Break* key.

Also See

Related:	[P] **foreach**, [P] **forvalues**, [P] **if**,
	[R] **for**
Background:	[U] **16 Functions and expressions**,
	[U] **21 Programming Stata**

Title

> **window** — Programming menus, dialogs, and windows

Description

The `window` commands allow Stata programmers to create menus and dialogs. Below we provide an overview of the commands. In the entries that follow, we fill in the details.

Remarks

The `window` commands are organized as follows:

1. `window menu` creates menu hierarchies; see [P] **window menu**.

2. `window dialog` creates and invokes dialog boxes for obtaining input from the user; see [P] **window dialog**.

   a. `window control` places controls on dialog boxes; see [P] **window control**.

   b. `window fopen` and `window fsave` invoke two standard dialog boxes; see [P] **window fopen**.

3. `window stopbox` displays message boxes; see [P] **window stopbox**.

4. `window manage` minimizes windows, brings them forward, etc.; see [P] **window manage**.

Taken as a whole, this can be an overwhelming amount of material.

Dialog boxes

Dialog boxes—`window dialog` and `window control`—can be understood in isolation. A dialog box is nothing more than a way of obtaining input from the user. A dialog box contains controls, meaning fields where a user might type, buttons that a user might click, or check boxes that a user might check.

Although you may think of dialog boxes and menus together—one pulls down a menu, makes a selection, and a dialog box appears—any Stata program (command) can make use of dialog boxes. One could write a program called `myprog` that, after the user typed

        . myprog

displayed a dialog box to obtain more information and then acted on that information. Here is how the dialog-box process works:

1. Your program defines the fields of a dialog box using `window control`.

2. Your program displays the dialog box using `window dialog`.

3. The user interacts with your dialog box. The user fills in any edit fields, checks any checkboxes, etc., and eventually clicks some button. Each button that the user might click invokes some command, which might be a program or a return (`exit`) statement. You specified how this works when you defined the dialog box.

4. Eventually the user clicks a button that you defined as closing the dialog box and control is returned to the calling program (`myprog`).

Thus, a dialog system might consist of one or more programs. In a one-program system, the program defines the dialog box, setting all the actions to return. In a multiple-program system, one program defines the dialog box and the other programs serve as subroutines to be invoked when the user clicks here or there.

Menus

A menu system is just a logical hierarchy. Think about the pull-downs on the Stata menu bar. Those are called popout menus and Stata, by default, has popout menus called **File**, **Edit**, **Prefs**, etc.

Pull down any of those popout menus and you are presented with a list of more choices. Choose any one and you might (1) be presented with even more choices or (2) cause something to happen (such as the appearance of a dialog box).

That is, menus are lists and each item in the list invokes another list or causes something to happen. The way this happens is that each menu item invokes another menu list or executes a Stata program (command).

`window menu` allows you to

1. create menus, which is to say, create lists of menu entries and associated actions,

   a. set an action to display yet another menu list,

   b. set an action to execute a Stata program (command).

2. specify that a menu list is to be added to Stata's top-level menu bar or to another menu list.

A menu system might involve writing no Stata programs whatsoever. Imagine you wanted to add a pull-down to Stata's top-level menu-bar labeled **Descriptions**. When the user pulled down **Descriptions**, the user would be presented with two choices: **Describe** and **Summarize**. Choose one, and Stata will `describe` the data, choose the other, and Stata will `summarize` the data. Here is how to do that.

You could first create a menu list called **Descriptions** appended to `sysmenu`, Stata's name for its top-level menu bar. Menu list **Descriptions** would contain two entries, one labeled **Describe** and the other labeled **Summarize**. The actions associated with each would be the Stata commands `summarize` and `describe`.

You could do all of that interactively by typing

```
. window menu clear
. window menu append popout "sysmenu" "Descriptions"
. window menu append string "Descriptions" "Describe" "describe"
. window menu append string "Descriptions" "Summarize" "summarize"
. window menu set "sysmenu"
```

It might be easier, however, to put these commands in a program called `addesc` and then just type `addesc`.

Now say that you decide to add another item to **Description**'s list. You wish to add **Other** and, if the user selects that, another menu is to appear with the choices **Letter Value** and **Codebook**, going to Stata's `lv` and `codebook` commands.

You would create another menu hierarchy called **Other** appended to **Descriptions**. **Other** would contain two items: **Letter Value** and **Codebook** with associated actions `lv` and `codebook`. Now when the user pulled down **Descriptions** from the top level, there would be a third choice. Here is the additional code to do that:

```
. window menu append popout "Descriptions" "Other"
. window menu append string "Other" "Letter Value" "lv"
. window menu append string "Other" "Codebook" "codebook"
. window menu set "sysmenu"
```

Putting menus and dialog boxes together

The action associated with a menu item need not be an existing Stata command. It can be a command you write, such as myprog. myprog might invoke a dialog box. The whole thing then appears to the user as if pulling down a menu and making a selection causes a dialog to appear. The user is never aware that he or she is running something called myprog.

Also See

Complementary: [P] **window control**, [P] **window dialog**, [P] **window fopen**,
[P] **window manage**, [P] **window menu**, [P] **window push**,
[P] **window stopbox**

Title

window control — Create dialog-box controls

Syntax

window $\underline{\text{con}}$trol button "*label*" x_{offset} y_{offset} x_{extent} y_{extent} *macroname*

    $\left[\text{default escape help}\right]$

window $\underline{\text{con}}$trol check "*text*" x_{offset} y_{offset} x_{extent} y_{extent} *macroname*

    $\left[\text{left} \mid \text{right}\right]$

window $\underline{\text{con}}$trol edit x_{offset} y_{offset} x_{extent} y_{extent} *macroname*

    $\left[\text{maxlen } \#\right]$ $\left[\text{password}\right]$

window $\underline{\text{con}}$trol static *text_macroname* x_{offset} y_{offset} x_{extent} y_{extent}

    $\left[\{\text{left} \mid \text{right} \mid \text{center}\} \text{ blackframe}\right]$

window $\underline{\text{con}}$trol radbegin "*text*" x_{offset} y_{offset} x_{extent} y_{extent} *macroname*

window $\underline{\text{con}}$trol radio   "*text*" x_{offset} y_{offset} x_{extent} y_{extent} *macroname*

window $\underline{\text{con}}$trol radend   "*text*" x_{offset} y_{offset} x_{extent} y_{extent} *macroname*

window $\underline{\text{con}}$trol ssimple *list_macroname* x_{offset} y_{offset} x_{extent} y_{extent} *macroname*

    $\left[\text{parse}(parse\_character)\right]$

window $\underline{\text{con}}$trol msimple *list_macroname* x_{offset} y_{offset} x_{extent} y_{extent} *macroname*

    $\left[\text{parse}(parse\_character)\right]$

window $\underline{\text{con}}$trol scombo *list_macroname* x_{offset} y_{offset} x_{extent} y_{extent} *macroname*

    $\left[\text{parse}(parse\_character)\right]$

window $\underline{\text{con}}$trol mcombo *list_macroname* x_{offset} y_{offset} x_{extent} y_{extent} *macroname*

    $\left[\text{parse}(parse\_character)\right]$

window $\underline{\text{con}}$trol clear

where x_{offset}, y_{offset}, x_{extent}, and y_{extent} are literal numbers (#).

$(x_{\text{offset}}, y_{\text{offset}})$ specifies the upper-left corner of the control relative to the upper-left corner of the dialog box. $(x_{\text{extent}}, y_{\text{extent}})$ specifies the control's size. Units of measurement are approximately one-fifth the width of a character horizontally and one-eighth the height of a character vertically.

Description

window control defines controls on dialog boxes. Controls include, for example, buttons, check boxes, and the like. When the user accesses a control (presses a button or checks a box), a command is executed or a global macro is defined.

Remarks

Remarks are presented under the headings

> *The command button control*
> *The check box control*
> *The edit control*
> *The static control*
> *The radio-button control group*
> *List box controls*
> *Combo box controls*
> *Clearing old controls*
> *Putting it all together*
> *Defining global macros*

The command button control

<u>win</u>dow <u>c</u>ontrol button "*label*" x_{offset} y_{offset} x_{extent} y_{extent} *macroname*

$\left[\text{default escape help}\right]$

Command buttons are used to perform an action and are typically labeled OK or Cancel.

macroname is a global macro that contains the command to be executed when the user clicks the button.

default marks this button as the default button for the dialog; if users press *Enter* it will be as if they clicked this button. escape marks this button as associated with the *Escape* key on the keyboard; if users press *Escape*, it will be as if they clicked this button. help marks this button as associated with the *F1* key on the keyboard; if users press *F1*, it will be as if they clicked this button. The specifications default, escape, and help may be included in any combination. An obvious command to assign a button with the help specification is the whelp *topic* command; see [R] **help**.

For example,

```
window control button "OK" 10 10 30 10 DB_ok
```

defines a button labeled OK and executes $DB_ok when the user clicks the button.

The check box control

<u>win</u>dow <u>c</u>ontrol check "*text*" x_{offset} y_{offset} x_{extent} y_{extent} *macroname*

$\left[\text{left right}\right]$

Check boxes are used to obtain input concerning Boolean options, those with just two possibilities.

macroname is a global macro. If, at the outset, *macroname* is undefined or contains 0, the box is unchecked; otherwise it is checked. Later, *macroname* contains 0 if the box is unchecked and 1 if it is checked.

left and right specify whether the text labeling the check box is to be to the left or right of the box. right is the default and left is allowed under Windows only. For portability reasons, we caution against specifying left.

For example,

```
window control check "Robust" 10 10 35 10 DB_chk
```

defines global macro DB_chk to contain 1 if the user checks the box and a 0 otherwise.

The edit control

> window control edit x_{offset} y_{offset} x_{extent} y_{extent} *macroname*
>
> $\left[\text{maxlen } \#\right]$ $\left[\text{password}\right]$

Edit controls are used to obtain text input.

macroname is a global macro. At the outset, *macroname* contains what is to be preloaded into the edit field; *macroname* may be undefined. Later, *macroname* contains what the user typed.

password replaces the characters that the user types with * characters in the edit field. maxlen # prevents the user from typing more than # characters.

For example,

```
window control edit 10 10 100 10 DB_edit
```

defines global macro DB_edit to contain the input from the user.

The static control

> window control static *text_macroname* x_{offset} y_{offset} x_{extent} y_{extent}
>
> $\left[\text{left right center blackframe}\right]$

Static controls are used to display text information or draw frames. They differ from edit controls in that the user may not change the static text.

text_macroname is a global macro that contains the text to be displayed.

blackframe draws a frame (rectangle) defined by the (x_{offset}, y_{offset}) and (x_{extent}, y_{extent}). When the blackframe specification is used, the contents of *text_macroname* are ignored. left specifies that the text should be left-justified, right that it be right-justified, and center that it be centered. left is the default.

For example,

```
window control static DB_stat 10 10 100 10
```

displays the contents of global macro DB_stat on the dialog.

Much later, when the dialog box is displayed by window dialog you can change the contents of global macro DB_stat and those changes will be reflected in the open dialog box, but sometimes with a lag. To make the changes appear instantly, use window dialog update; see [P] **window dialog**.

The radio-button control group

window control radbegin "*text*" x_offset y_offset x_extent y_extent *macroname*

window control radio   "*text*" x_offset y_offset x_extent y_extent *macroname*

window control radend   "*text*" x_offset y_offset x_extent y_extent *macroname*

A radio-button control group allows the user to choose one of several alternatives.

You must specify the same global macro *macroname* for all commands in a group. At the outset, *macroname* contains which button is selected (1, 2, 3, . . .). If *macroname* is undefined, button 1 is selected. Later, *macroname* is redefined to contain the button number actually selected.

A radio-button control group has at least two choices that are defined using the **radbegin** and **radend** commands. Additional choices are defined by the **radio** commands that appear in between.

Example:

```
window control radbegin "Unpaired and unequal" 10 10 90 10 DB_rad
window control radio    "Unpaired and equal"   10 20 90 10 DB_rad
window control radend   "Paired"               10 30 90 10 DB_rad
```

defines macro DB_rad to contain 1, 2, or 3 depending on which button the user selects.

List box controls

window control ssimple *list_macroname* x_offset y_offset x_extent y_extent *macroname*

$\big[$**parse**(*parse_character*)$\big]$

window control msimple *list_macroname* x_offset y_offset x_extent y_extent *macroname*

$\big[$**parse**(*parse_character*)$\big]$

A list box presents an edit field on top of a list. The user may type in the edit field and/or choose one or more items from the list. The list box will automatically include a scroll bar if the number of choices is large. When users click on an item in the list, that item is copied to the edit field. If users then click on a second item, **ssimple** list boxes replace the contents of the edit field with the new selection. **msimple** list boxes append the second choice to the first with a space in between.

macroname is a global macro. As with an edit control, at the outset *macroname* contains the initial contents of the edit field (*macroname* may be undefined) and is redefined to contain what the user types.

At the outset, *list_macroname* (a global macro) contains the choices to be filled into the list. The choices are the words recorded in *list_macroname*, each word being a choice. That is convenient for most purposes but will not work if individual choices contain multiple words. In such cases, you may use any choice-separation character you wish and then include the **parse**(*parse_character*) specification.

For example,

```
window control ssimple DB_list 10 10 30 100 DB_sl
window control msimple DB_list 60 20 30 100 DB_ml
```

uses the contents of DB_list to fill in two different list boxes. The choices will then be accessible to the programmer as $DB_sl and $DB_ml.

Combo box controls

> window control scombo *list_macroname* x_{offset} y_{offset} x_{extent} y_{extent} *macroname*
>
> [parse(*parse_character*)]
>
> window control mcombo *list_macroname* x_{offset} y_{offset} x_{extent} y_{extent} *macroname*
>
> [parse(*parse_character*)]

A combo box is like a list box—an edit field in which the user may type with an associated list from which the user may choose. The difference is that the list does not show. Instead, the edit field has a down-arrow button and, if the user clicks that, the list pops down. The list box will automatically include a scroll bar if there is a large number of choices.

When users click on an item in the list, that item is copied to the edit field. If users then click on a second item, scombo list boxes replace the contents of the edit field with the new selection. mcombo list boxes append the second choice to the first with a blank in between.

macroname is a global macro. As with a list box, *macroname* contains the initial text (if any) and is redefined to contain what the user types.

list_macroname (a global macro) works in the same way as it does for a list box.

Note that even though combo box controls display only the edit box, you define y_{extent} to include the space you want for the drop-down list box.

Example:

```
window control scombo DB_list 10 10 30 100 DB_sc
window control mcombo DB_list 60 20 30 100 DB_mc
```

will use the contents of DB_list to fill in two different list boxes. The choices will then be accessible to the programmer as $DB_sc and $DB_mc.

Clearing old controls

window control clear erases from Stata's memory any previously defined dialog controls. Controls are automatically cleared from memory when the dialog box is closed.

The window control clear command is useful when you are programming a dialog box in Stata. If a do-file has defined several controls but then exits due to an error, you should correct the error in the do-file. Type window control clear to clear the controls the do-file defined, and then re-execute the do-file. Better would be to make window control clear appear before any other window control commands in your do-file.

Putting it all together

Here we present a sample dialog that contains all the previously mentioned controls. You may need to resize the Stata window to see all of the controls on the dialog box.

(*Continued on next page*)

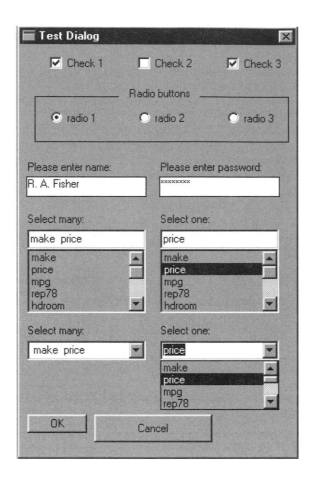

To run the example, run the do-file below and then type `mycmd` to the Stata prompt. In the figure above, we had `auto.dta` loaded when we ran `mycmd`.

─── top of dialog.do ─────────────

```
macro drop DB*
capture program drop mycmd
program define mycmd
        version 7.0
        * Check boxes
        global DB_chk1 = 0
        global DB_chk2 = 0
        global DB_chk3 = 0
        window control check "Check 1"  20 5 50 10 DB_chk1
        window control check "Check 2"  80 5 50 10 DB_chk2
        window control check "Check 3" 140 5 50 10 DB_chk3

        * Frame with title
        global DB_rad "Radio buttons"
        window control static DB_rad 10 28 172 25 blackframe
        window control static DB_rad 65 25  55 12 center

        * Radio button group defaults to option 1
        global DB_rval = 1
        window control radbegin "radio 1"  20 35 35 10 DB_rval
```

```
                window control radio    "radio 2"  80 35 35 10 DB_rval
                window control radend   "radio 3" 140 35 35 10 DB_rval

                global DB_nval ""
                global DB_eval ""
                global DB_pval ""

                global DB_name "Please enter name:"
                window control static DB_name 5 60 80  9
                window control edit           5 70 80 10 DB_nval

                global DB_pass "Please enter password:"
                window control static DB_pass 95 60 80  9
                window control edit           95 70 80 10 DB_pval password maxlen 8

                global DB_many "Select many:"
                global DB_one  "Select one:"

                window control static  DB_many 5  90 80  9
                window control msimple DB_var  5 100 80 50 DB_ms

                window control static  DB_one 95  90 80  9
                window control ssimple DB_var 95 100 80 50 DB_ss

                window control static  DB_many 5 150 80  9
                window control mcombo  DB_var  5 160 80 40 DB_mc

                window control static  DB_one 95 150 80  9
                window control scombo  DB_var 95 160 80 40 DB_sc

                window control button "OK"     5 200 40 10 DB_ok default
                window control button "Cancel" 50 200 80 15 DB_ca

                global DB_ok "showvals"
                global DB_ca "exit 3000"

                syntax [varlist]
                global DB_var "`varlist'"
                wdlg "Test Dialog" 10 10 190 235
        end
        capture program drop showvals
        program define showvals
                display
                if $DB_chk1 {
                        display "You checked check box 1"
                }
                else { display "You did not check check box 1" }
                if $DB_chk2 {
                        display "You checked check box 2"
                }
                else { display "You did not check check box 2" }
                if $DB_chk3 {
                        display "You checked check box 3"
                }
                else { display "You did not check check box 3" }
                display "You selected choice $DB_rval from the radio buttons"
                display "You entered the name $DB_nval"
                display "You entered the password $DB_pval"
                display "You selected $DB_ms from the select many list box"
                display "You selected $DB_ss from the select one list box"
                display "You selected $DB_mc from the select many combo box"
                display "You selected $DB_sc from the select one combo box"
        end
```

———————————————————————————————— end of dialog.do ————————

Defining global macros

When you write code for defining the controls on a dialog box, note that the global macros that are used as input for the controls do not have to be defined when the control is defined. You can define them before you use the `window dialog` command, or you can define them after the dialog is running and then refresh the controls using the `window dialog update` command.

References

Newton, H. J. 1997. ip16: Using dialog boxes to vary program parameters. *Stata Technical Bulletin* 36: 11–14. Reprinted in *Stata Technical Bulletin Reprints*, vol. 6, pp. 77–81.

Also See

Complementary: [P] **window dialog**, [P] **window menu**

Background: [P] **window**

Title

window dialog — Create dialog box

Syntax

<u>win</u>dow <u>d</u>ialog *"description"* $\left\{ x_{\text{offset}}\ y_{\text{offset}} \mid\ \cdot\ \cdot\ \right\}$ x_{extent} y_{extent}

<u>win</u>dow <u>d</u>ialog update

where *description* is the words that will appear as the title of the dialog and $(x_{\text{offset}}, y_{\text{offset}})$ specifies the upper-left corner of the dialog box relative to the Stata window. x_{offset} may be specified as . as may be y_{offset}, meaning the default location for dialog boxes. $(x_{\text{extent}}, y_{\text{extent}})$ specifies the size of dialog box. Units of measurement are approximately one-fifth the width of a character horizontally and one-eighth the height of a character vertically.

Description

window dialog displays a dialog box with the controls that have previously been defined by window control.

window dialog update redraws the controls.

Remarks

window dialog is the second step in programming a dialog box. First, you define the dialog box's controls using window control. Then you display it—open it—using window dialog.

Remarks are presented under the headings

> *Opening (displaying) a dialog box*
> *Working with an open dialog box*
> *Closing the dialog box*
> *User-preferred positioning of dialog boxes*
> *Updating information on the open dialog box*

Opening (displaying) a dialog box

Once the controls of the dialog box have been defined by window control statements, you can use window dialog to open it. For example, a program might contain the statements

```
window control button "OK" 10 10 30 18 DB_ok
window control button "Cancel" 50 10 30 18 DB_ca
global DB_ok ...
global DB_ca ...
window dialog "Sample dialog" . . 100 55
```

The example above is over-simplified because it does not deal with handling the dialog's requests. That is covered below.

337

Working with an open dialog box

Consider the following dialog-box program:

```
program define ex1
      version 7.0
      window control button "Sum" 10 10 30 18 DB_sum
      window control button "Error" 50 10 30 18 DB_er
      window control button "Cancel" 90 10 30 18 DB_ca
      global DB_sum "summarize mpg"
      global DB_er "exit 111"
      global DB_ca "exit 3000"
      window dialog "Sample dialog" . . 140 55
end
```

Type ex1 at the Stata prompt to display a dialog box with three buttons, labeled **Sum**, **Error**, and **Cancel**. Clicking **Sum** executes the command 'summarize mpg'. Clicking **Cancel** executes 'exit 3000', which will cause the window dialog command to exit with return code 3000 and cause ex1 to terminate with the same return code. We will explain the **Error** button momentarily.

You should try this example. When you click **Sum**, Stata will summarize mpg and the dialog box will remain open. Click **Sum** again and Stata will summarize mpg again. Click **Sum** with no dataset in memory and summarize will produce an error message but the dialog box will still remain open. Only when you click **Cancel** will the dialog box go away.

Dialog boxes, evidently, do not vanish easily. Errors in the commands they execute, such as summarize mpg when there is no mpg, do not cause them to close. If you think carefully about this, you will be surprised. summarize mpg when there is no mpg, for instance, produces a return code of 111. Note that our **Error** button also returns 111. Try the button. Nothing happens! The dialog stays open. Yet clicking **Cancel** causes the dialog to exit (with return code 3000).

One button executes exit 111 and the other exit 3000 and yet they have very different outcomes.

Dialog boxes close only when the return code is between 3000 and 3099. Nothing else will cause them to close (except clicking on the Close box, which is just like exit 3000).

Why do dialog boxes do this? Because there will be occasions where you want a dialog box to remain open while commands are executing and those commands might fail. If you really want a dialog box to exit, the command must issue a return code in the range 3000 to 3099.

Closing the dialog box

When you want a dialog box to close, the action invoked must issue a return code in the range 3000 to 3099.

Any dialog box that you design should contain at least two command buttons, one that does something (often labeled **OK**) and another labeled **Cancel** which calls the whole thing off. Here is a program that only does something after the dialog box closes:

```
program define ex2
        version 7.0
        window control button "OK" 10 10 30 18 DB_ok
        window control button "Cancel" 50 10 30 18 DB_ca
        global DB_ok "exit 3001"
        global DB_ca "exit 3000"
        capture noisily window dialog "Sample dialog" . . 100 55
        if _rc==3001 {              /* user clicked okay */
                display "user clicked OK"
        }
        /* Just exit if the user clicked cancel */
end
```

This is a very common dialog-box control program and it differs importantly, if subtly, from ex1. ex1 did something while the dialog box was up. This one waits until the dialog box closes. You can use either style or even combine them.

For most applications, the ex2 style is preferable. You should use the ex1 style only when the result is truly interactive. For instance, perhaps you have a histogram up and, as the user clicks a button, the number of bins is incremented or decremented by 1. That would be coded using the ex1 style. If instead the dialog box is just gathering information to execute some request, the ex2 style is preferable.

Note that a dialog box could have more than one action:

```
program define ex2v2
        version 7.0
        window control button "Sum" 10 10 30 18 DB_sum
        window control button "Describe" 50 10 30 18 DB_des
        window control button "Cancel" 90 10 30 18 DB_ca
        global DB_ca "exit 3000"
        global DB_sum "exit 3001"
        global DB_des "exit 3002"
        capture noisily window dialog "Sample dialog" . . 140 55
        if _rc==3001 {
                summarize
        }
        else if _rc==3002 {
                describe
        }
        /* Just exit if the user clicked cancel */
end
```

Just remember, the return codes 3000 to 3099 are special. No other Stata command returns them. They are reserved for dialog-box communication.

User-preferred positioning of dialog boxes

Users often move dialog boxes after they are displayed. You should honor this preference. The easiest way to do that is to use '. .' to represent the x_{offset} and y_{offset}. In the examples above, you have seen us code statements like

```
window dialog "Sample dialog" . . 140 55
```

This means the dialog box is to appear wherever the user likes (based on where he or she last moved the previous dialog) and that its size is 140×55.

Alternatively, if you want to force the position of a dialog box, you can code statements like

```
window dialog "Sample dialog" 30 40 140 55
```

window dialog saves the final position of the dialog box in r(x) and r(y).

Updating information on the open dialog box

As dialog box controls are manipulated, the associated global macros are automatically updated.

If a dialog box stays open and calls a Stata program, however, and if that program wishes to change the contents of the macros and have those changes immediately reflected on the screen, you code 'window dialog update'. You only need code this if you want the change immediately reflected in the dialog box. The dialog box will be automatically updated when the subprogram returns.

Saved Results

window dialog (not window dialog update) saves in r():

Scalars
$r(x)$ x offset of dialog box
$r(y)$ y offset of dialog box

References

Schmidt, T. J. 1997. ip15: A dialog box layout manager for Stata. *Stata Technical Bulletin* 35: 16–20. Reprinted in *Stata Technical Bulletin Reprints*, vol. 6, pp. 71–77.

Also See

Complementary: [P] **window control**, [P] **window menu**, [P] **window push**,
[P] **window stopbox**

Background: [P] **window**

Title

---
window fopen — Display open/save dialog box

Syntax

<u>win</u>dow {<u>fo</u>pen | <u>fs</u>ave} *macroname* "*title*" "*filter*" [*extension*]

Description

`window fopen` and `window fsave` allow Stata programmers to use standard **File-Open** and **File-Save** dialog boxes in their programs.

Remarks

`window fopen` and `window fsave` call forth the operating system's standard **File-Open** and **File-Save** dialog boxes. The commands do not themselves open or save any files; they merely obtain from the user the name of the file to be opened or saved and return it to you. The filename returned is guaranteed to be valid and includes the full path.

The filename is returned in the global macro *macroname*. In addition, if *macroname* is defined at the outset, its contents will be used to fill in the default filename selection.

title is displayed as the title of the file-open or file-save dialog.

filter is relevant only with Windows; it is ignored by Stata for Macintosh and Stata for Unix but it still must be specified. One possible specification is "", meaning no filter. Alternatively, *filter* consists of pairs of descriptions and wildcard file selection strings separated by '|', such as

```
"Stata Graphs|*.gph|All Files|*.*"
```

Stata for Windows uses the filter to restrict the files the user sees. The above example allows the user either to see Stata graph files or to see all files. Windows will display a drop-down list from which the user can select a file type (extension). The first item of each pair (`Stata Graphs` and `All Files`) will be listed as the choices in the drop-down list. The second item of each pair restricts the files displayed in the dialog box to those that match the wildcard description. For instance, if the user selects `Stata Graphs` from the list box, only files with extension `.gph` will be displayed in the file dialog box.

Finally, *extension* is optional. It may contain a string of characters to be added to the end of filenames by default. For example, if the *extension* were specified as `xyz`, and the user typed a filename of `abc` in the file dialog box, `abc.xyz` would be returned in *macroname*.

In Windows, the default *extension* is ignored if a *filter* other than `*.*` is in effect. For example, if the user's current filter is `*.gph`, the default extension will be `.gph` regardless of what *extension* was specified.

❑ Technical Note

Since Windows allows long filenames, *extension* can lead to unexpected results. For example, if *extension* were specified as `xyz` and the user typed a filename of `abc.def`, Windows would append `.xyz` before returning the filename to Stata, so the resulting filename is `abc.def.xyz`. Windows users should be aware that if they want to specify an extension different from the default, then they must enter a filename in the file dialog box enclosed in double quotes: `"abc.def"`. This applies to all programs, not just Stata. ❑

If the user presses the **Cancel** button on the file dialog, `window fopen` and `window fsave` set *macroname* to be empty and exit with a return code of 601. Programmers should use the `capture` command to prevent the 601 return code from appearing to the user.

▷ Example

```
                                                    ── top of gphview.ado ──────
program define gphview
        version 7.0
        capture window fopen D_gph "Select a graph to view:" /*
            */ "Stata Graphs (*.gph)|*.gph|All Files (*.*)|*.*" gph ;
        if _rc==0 {
                display "User chose $D_gph as the filename."
                graph using "$D_gph"
        }
end
                                                    ── end of gphview.ado ──────
```

. gphview

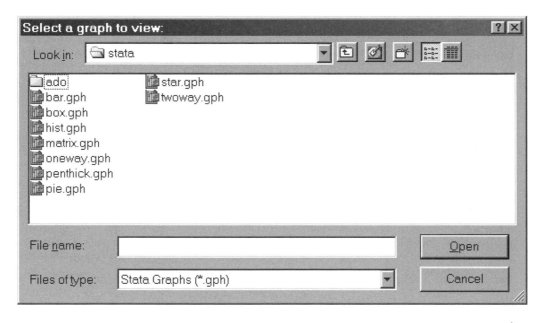

◁

Also See

Complementary:	[P] **window control**, [P] **window dialog**, [P] **window menu**, [P] **window stopbox**
Background:	[P] **window**

Title

---
window manage — Manage window characteristics

Syntax

<u>win</u>dow <u>man</u>age minimize   (*Windows and Macintosh only*)

<u>win</u>dow <u>man</u>age restore

<u>win</u>dow <u>man</u>age prefs {load | save | default}

<u>win</u>dow <u>man</u>age update variable

<u>win</u>dow <u>man</u>age print {graph | log}

<u>win</u>dow <u>man</u>age associate   (*Windows only*)

<u>win</u>dow <u>man</u>age forward *window-name*

where *window-name* can be command, dialog, doeditor, graph, help, log, results, review, or variables.

Description

window manage gives Stata programs the ability to invoke features from Stata's main menu.

Remarks

window manage accesses various parts of Stata's windowed interface that would otherwise be available only interactively. For instance, say a programmer wanted to ensure that the graph window was brought to the front. An interactive user would do that by pulling down **Window** and choosing **Graph**. A Stata program could be made to do the same thing by coding 'window manage forward graph'.

Remarks are presented under the headings

> *Minimizing the main Stata window (Windows and Macintosh only)*
> *Restoring the main Stata window (Windows only)*
> *Windowing preferences*
> *Refreshing the Variables window*
> *Printing Graphs and Logs*
> *Restoring file associations (Windows only)*
> *Bringing windows forward*

Minimizing the main Stata window (Windows and Macintosh only)

window manage minimize minimizes (hides) the Stata window. With Stata for Windows, this has the same effect as clicking on the minimize button on Stata's title bar. With Stata for Macintosh, this has the same effect as pulling down the Application menu (the little Stata icon in the upper-right corner) and choosing **Hide Stata**.

Example:

```
window manage minimize
```

minimizes the overall Stata window if you are using Stata for Windows and hides Stata's windows if you are using Stata for Macintosh.

Restoring the main Stata window (Windows only)

window manage restore restores the Stata window if necessary. This command is allowed only with Stata for Windows.

With Stata for Windows, this command has the same effect as clicking the Stata button on the taskbar.

Example:

```
window manage restore
```

restores Stata's overall window to its normal, nonminimized state.

Windowing preferences

window manage prefs { load | save | default } loads, saves, and restores windowing preferences.

Stata for Macintosh and Stata for Unix allow only window manage prefs default, which is equivalent to **Prefs–Restore Defaults**.

Stata for Windows allows load, save, or default. window manage prefs save is equivalent to pulling down **Prefs–Save Windowing Preferences**. window manage prefs load is equivalent to pulling down **Prefs–Load Windowing Preferences**. window manage prefs default is equivalent to pulling down **Prefs–Default Windowing**.

Example:

```
window manage prefs default
```

restores Stata's windows to their "factory" appearance.

Refreshing the Variables window

window manage update variable forces an update of Stata's Variables window, the window that displays the currently loaded variable names and their labels. Stata normally updates this window between interactive commands only. If you run a long do- or ado-file which changes the data in a way which would affect the Variables window, the change will not be visible until the do- or ado-file completes.

window manage update variable allows a do- or ado-file to force an early update of the Variables window to reflect any changes.

Example:

── top of vars.do ──────────

```
use auto
drop make
window manage update variable
drop price
window manage update variable
drop mpg
window manage update variable
label variable weight "Weight of car"
window manage update variable
```

── end of vars.do ──────────

If you were to run the above do-file and there were no `window manage update variable` commands in it, you would not see the changes made to the variables until after the do-file completed.

Printing Graphs and Logs

`window manage print { graph | log }` invokes the actions of the **File–Print Graph** and **File–Print Log** menu items. If there is no current graph or log, `window manage print` does nothing; it does not return an error.

Example:

```
window manage print graph
```

displays the print dialog box just as if you pulled down **File–Print Graph**.

Restoring file associations (Windows only)

In Stata for Windows, `window manage associate` restores the default actions for Stata file types. For example, another application could take over the `.dta` extension so that double-clicking on a Stata dataset would no longer launch Stata. `window manage associate` restores the association between all Stata file extensions (such as `.dta`) and Stata. This is equivalent to pulling down **Prefs** and selecting **Restore File Associations**.

Bringing windows forward

`window manage forward` *window-name* brings the specified window to the top of all other Stata windows. This command is equivalent to pulling down **Window** and choosing one of the available windows. The following table lists the *window-name*s which `window manage forward` understands:

window-name	Stata window
`command`	Command window
`dialog`	Dialog window
`doeditor`	Do-file editor window
`graph`	Graph window
`help`	Help/search window
`log`	Log window
`results`	Results window
`review`	Review window
`variables`	Variables window

If a window would not have been available on Stata's **Window** menu (if it would have been grayed out), specifying that *window-name* after `window manage forward` will do nothing. For example, if there is no current log, `window manage forward log` will do nothing; it is not an error.

Example:

```
window manage forward results
```

brings the Results window to the top of the other Stata windows.

Under Stata for Unix, specifying the Command, Results, Review, or Variables Windows will bring the main Stata window forward since these Windows are all contained within one window.

Also See

Background: [P] **window**

Title

> **window menu** — Create menus

Syntax

<u>win</u>dow <u>men</u>u clear

<u>win</u>dow <u>men</u>u append popout *"defined_menuname"* *"appending_menuname"*

<u>win</u>dow <u>men</u>u append string *"defined_menuname"* *"entry_text"* *"command_to_execute"*

<u>win</u>dow <u>men</u>u append separator *"defined_menuname"*

<u>win</u>dow <u>men</u>u popout *"new_menuname"*

<u>win</u>dow <u>men</u>u set *"defined_menuname"*

Note: the quotation marks above are required.

"defined_menuname" is the name of a previously defined menu or one of the system menus *"sysmenu"*, *"sFile"*, *"Edit"*, *"Prefs"*, or *"Window"*. The Macintosh also allows *"defined_menuname"* to be *"Search"* or *"Tools"*.

Description

window menu allows you to add new menu hierarchies.

Remarks

Remarks are presented under the headings

> *Overview*
> *Clearing previously defined menu additions*
> *Defining menu items which invoke other menus*
> *Defining menu items which invoke actions*
> *Defining separator bars*
> *Declaring an orphan menu*
> *Activating a menu system*
> *Keyboard shortcuts (Windows only)*
> *Examples*
> *Advanced features: built-in actions*
> *Advanced features: Creating checked menu items*
> *Advanced features: Adding to other Stata menus*
> *Advanced features: Adding Stata's menus to yours*
> *Putting it all together*

Overview

A menu is a list of choices. Here are two menus:

The bar along the top is called the top-level menu. There is only one of these in all of Stata, but you can add to it or even replace it. The three choices below **Regression** form another menu—a submenu—called a popout.

A menu item is a word or phrase that appears in a menu that, when selected, causes something to happen. That something can be the popping out of yet another menu or the invocation of a Stata command or program. **Regression** is a menu item that invoked another menu. **Simple** is a menu item and we would guess that choosing it would cause something other than another menu to be displayed.

A menu hierarchy is the collection of menus and how they relate.

window menu allows you to create menu hierarchies, set the text that appears in each menu, and set the actions associated with each menu item.

Everything revolves around menu items. A menu is a collection of menu items. What happens when a menu item is chosen is defined by the menu item. There are three types of menu items,

1. Popouts, which is jargon for a menu item whose associated action is to display yet another menu.

2. Strings, which is jargon for a menu item whose associated action is to invoke a Stata command or program.

3. Separators, which are not exactly menu items at all. They are instead horizontal lines that separate items within a menu.

A menu is formally defined as an ordered list of menu items. The action of adding a new member to the end of the list is called appending a menu item. New menu hierarchies are defined from the top down, not the bottom up. Here is how you create a new menu hierarchy:

1. You append to some existing Stata menu a new popout item using window menu append popout. That the new item is itself an empty menu is of no consequence.

2. You append to the new popout item other items, which might be more popouts or strings or separators, all done with window menu append. In this way, you fill in the new popout menu you already appended in step 1.

3. If you appended popout items to the menu you defined in step 2, you append to each of them so that they are fully defined. This requires even more window menu append commands.

4. You keep going like this until all the popout items are defined. Then you tell Stata's menu manager that you are done using window menu set.

Everything you do up to step 4 is merely definitional. It is at step 4 that what you have done takes effect.

You can add menus to Stata. Then you can add more menus. Later, you can add even more menus. What you cannot do, however, is ever delete a little bit of what you have added. You can add some menus and window menu set, then add some more and window menu set, but you cannot go back and remove part of what you added earlier. What you can do is remove all the menus you have added, restoring Stata to its original configuration. window menu clear does this.

So, in our opening example, how did the **Regression** menu-item ever get defined? By typing

```
. window menu append popout "sysmenu" "Regression"
```

```
. window menu append string "Regression" "Simple" ...
. window menu append string "Regression" "Multiple" ...
. window menu append string "Regression" "Multivariate" ...
. window menu set "sysmenu"
```

sysmenu is the special name for Stata's top-level menu. The first command appended a popout menu item to sysmenu called **Regression**. At this point, **Regression** is an empty popout menu.

The next three commands filled in **Regression** by appending to it. All three items are strings, meaning items that when chosen, invoke some Stata command or program. (We have not shown you what the Stata commands are; we just put '...'.)

Finally, window menu set sysmenu told Stata we were done and to make our new additions available.

Clearing previously defined menu additions

```
window menu clear
```

clears any additions that have been made to Stata's menu system.

Defining menu items which invoke other menus

```
window menu append popout "defined_menuname" "appending_menuname"
```

defines items that appear in the top-level menu or which invoke other menus. This command creates a menu item with the text *appending_menuname* (the double-quote characters do not appear in the menu item when displayed) attached to the "*defined_menuname*" item. It also declares that the "*appending_menuname*" will invoke further menu items—that *appending_menuname* is a popout menu. Menus may be appended to Stata's top level menu using the command

```
window menu append popout "sysmenu" " appending_menuname"
```

For example,

```
window menu append popout "sysmenu" "New Menu"
```

appends **New Menu** to Stata's top-level menu.

Defining menu items which invoke actions

```
window menu append string "defined_menuname" "entry_text" "command_to_execute"
```

defines items that invoke actions. This command creates a menu item with the text "*entry_text*" which is attached to the "*defined_menuname*"

For example,

```
window menu append string "New Menu" "Describe" "describe"
```

appends the menu item **Describe** to the **New Menu** item defined previously and specifies that if the user selects **Describe** the describe command is to be executed.

Defining separator bars

> `window menu append separator "defined_menuname"`

defines a separator bar. The separator bar will appear in the position in which it is declared and is attached to an existing popout menu. You may not add separator bars to the top level menu.

For example,

> `window append separator "New Menu"`

adds a separator bar to **New Menu**.

Declaring an orphan menu

> `window menu popout "new_menuname"`

declares an empty, orphan menu. By orphan we mean only that it has not been attached anywhere in the menu hierarchy yet. Typing

> `window menu append popout existing-menu new-menu`

is equivalent to typing

> `window menu popout new-menu`
> `window menu append popout existing-menu new-menu`

That is, `window menu append` declares the menu for you if it does not exist and attaches it somewhere in the hierarchy. When the menu does exist, it merely attaches it in the hierarchy.

As such, `window menu popout` does not look very useful. However, if you plan on replacing Stata's top-level menu in its entirety, you need to create a menu hierarchy that is in no way a part of the existing menu hierarchy and then use another command. You do that by starting with a `window menu popout`. Once you have the new hierarchy, you use `window menu set` to replace Stata's top-level menu.

For example,

> `window menu popout "Top Level"`

defines a new menu named **Top Level**.

Activating a menu system

> `window menu set "defined_menuname"`

activates a menu system.

There are two cases. Consider first the case where you have added to Stata's existing menu structure. Thus, `sysmenu` will continue to be the top-level menu. `window menu set "sysmenu"` reactivates the `sysmenu` and picks up all your additions.

Now consider the case where you wish to replace Stata's top-level menu. Then you previously created an orphan menu, say **Top Level**, and appended a hierarchy to it. `window menu set "Top Level"` puts the new menu system in place.

These are actually both the same case from Stata's point of view. `window menu set name` sets the existing menu structure *name* to be the top level.

For example,

> `window menu set "sysmenu"`

will activate all the defined menus that were appended to the `"sysmenu"`. If instead we were replacing Stata's top-level menu, we might code

```
window menu set "Top Level"
```

Keyboard shortcuts (Windows only)

When you define a menu item, you may assign a keyboard shortcut. A shortcut (or keyboard accelerator) is a key that allows a menu item to be selected via the keyboard in addition to the usual point-and-click method.

By placing an ampersand (**&**) immediately preceding a character, you define that character to be the shortcut. The ampersand will not appear in the menu item. Rather the character following the ampersand will be underlined to alert the user of the shortcut. The user may then choose the menu item by either clicking with the mouse or holding down *Alt* and pressing the shortcut key. Actually, you only have to hold down *Alt* for the top-level menu. For the submenus, once they are pulled down, holding down *Alt* is optional.

If you need to include an ampersand as part of the "*entry_text*", place two ampersands in a row.

It is your responsibility to avoid creating conflicting keyboard shortcuts. When the user types in a keyboard shortcut, Stata finds the first item with the defined shortcut.

Example:

```
window menu append popout "sysmenu" "&Regression"
```

defines a new popout menu named **Regression** that will appear on the top-level menu bar and that users may access by pressing *Alt-R*.

Examples

▷ Example

Below we use the `window menu` commands to add to Stata's existing top-level menu. The following may be typed interactively:

```
window menu clear
window menu append popout "sysmenu" "&Data"
window menu append string "Data" "&Describe data" "describe"
window menu set "sysmenu"
```

`window menu clear`
Clears any user-defined menu items and restores the menu system to the default.

`window menu append popout "sysmenu" "Data"`
Appends to the system menu a new menu called `Data`. Note that you may name this new menu anything you like. You can capitalize its name or not. The new menu appears to the right of all the existing menu items since this is at the top level of the menu system.

`window menu append string "Data" "&Describe data" "describe"`
Defines the name to be displayed (including a keyboard shortcut). This name is what the user will actually see. It also specifies the command to execute when the user selects the menu item. In this case we will run the `describe` command.

```
window menu set "sysmenu"
```
Causes all the menu items that have been defined and appended to the default system menu to become active and to be displayed.

◁

▷ Example

Instead of simply adding to Stata's existing menu system, you may replace it from the top-level on down. In the following, we define one menu item; you would presumably define more. This may be typed interactively.

```
window menu clear
window menu popout "MyTopLevel"
window menu append popout "MyTopLevel" "Commands"
window menu append string "Commands" "&Describe" "describe"
window menu set "MyTopLevel"
```

If we wanted to define the C of the "Commands" to act as a keyboard shortcut, we could instead specify the third command as

```
window menu append popout "MyTopLevel" "&Commands"
```

The reference name would remain Commands so that even with the keyboard shortcut, we do not alter the fourth command to include the & character.

◁

Advanced features: built-in actions

Recall that menu items can have associated actions:

window menu append string "*defined_menuname*" "*entry_text*" "*command_to_execute*"

Actions other than Stata commands and programs can be added to menus. In the course of designing a menu system, you may include menu items that will open a Stata dataset, save a Stata graph, or perform some other common Stata menu command.

You can specify "*command_to_execute*" as one of the following

"XEQ about"
displays Stata's About dialog box. The About dialog box is accessible from the default system menu by pulling down **File** and selecting **About**.

"XEQ save"
displays Stata's File Save dialog box in order to save the dataset in memory. This dialog box is accessed from the default system menu by pulling down **File** and selecting **Save**.

"XEQ saveas"
displays Stata's File Save As dialog box in order to save the dataset in memory. This dialog box is accessible from the default system menu by pulling down **File** and selecting **Save As...**.

"XEQ savegr"
displays the Save Stata Graph File dialog box that saves the currently displayed graph. This dialog box is accessible from the default system menu by pulling down **File** and selecting **Save Graph**.

"XEQ printgr"
prints the graph displayed in the graph window. This is available in the default menu system by pulling down the **File** menu and selecting **Print Graph**. Also see [P] **window manage**.

"XEQ use"
:   displays Stata's File Open dialog box that loads a Stata dataset. This is available in the default menu system by pulling down the **File** menu and selecting **Open...**.

"XEQ exit"
:   exits Stata. This is available from the default menu system by pulling down the **File** menu and selecting **Exit**.

"XEQ printlog"
:   prints the currently opened log to the default printer. This is available in the default menu system by pulling down the **File** menu and selecting **Print Log**.

"XEQ conhelp"
:   opens the Stata help system to the default welcome topic. This is available by clicking on the **Help!** button in the help system.

Advanced features: Creating checked menu items

command_to_execute in

> <u>win</u>dow <u>m</u>enu append string "*defined_menuname*" "*entry_text*" "*command_to_execute*"

may also be specified as CHECK *macroname*.

Another detail that serious menu designers will want is the ability to create checked menu items. A checked menu item is one that appears in the menu system as either checked (includes a small check mark to the right) or not.

"CHECK *macroname*" specifies that the global macro *macroname* should contain the value as to whether or not the item is checked. If the global macro is not defined at the time that the menu item is created, Stata defines the macro to contain zero and the item is not checked. If the user selects the menu item in order to toggle the status of the item, Stata will place a check mark next to the item on the menu system and redefine the global macro to contain one. In this way, you may write programs that access information that you gather via the menu system.

Note that you should treat the contents of the global macro associated with the checked menu item as "read only". Changing the contents of the macro will not be reflected in the menu system.

Advanced features: Adding to other Stata menus

You can add items to menus other than the top-level menu.

You may window menu append to **File** (specify "sFile"), **Edit** (specify "Edit"), **Prefs** (specify "Prefs"), and **Window** (specify "Window"). The Macintosh also allows appending to **Search** (specify "Search") and **Tools** (specify "Tools").

Advanced features: Adding Stata's menus to yours

You may window menu append popout to your menu name "sFile", "Edit", "Prefs", and "Window"; the Macintosh also allows "Search" and "Tools". When you append one of Stata's menus to yours, you obtain the full subhierarchy. For instance, if you append Stata's **File** menu by typing

```
. window menu append popout "mymenu" "sFile"
```

you obtain all the items and submenus of Stata's **File** menu.

Putting it all together

In the following example, we create a larger menu system. Note that each of the items in the menu is defined using the `window menu append popout` if there are further items below it in the hierarchy. Other items are defined with `window menu append string` if the item does not have further items below it.

```
────────────────────────────────────────────────── top of lgmenu.do ──────────
capture program drop mylgmenu
program define mylgmenu
        version 7.0
        win m clear
        win m append popout "sysmenu" "&Regression"
        win m append popout "sysmenu" "&Graphics"
        win m append popout "sysmenu" "&Tests"

        win m append string "Regression" "&Simple" "choose simple"
        win m append string "Regression" "&Multiple" "choose multiple"
        win m append string "Regression" "Multi&variate" "choose multivariate"

        win m append string "Graphics" "&Scatterplot" "choose scatterplot"
        win m append string "Graphics" "&Histogram" "myprog1"
        win m append string "Graphics" "Scatterplot &Matrix" "choose matrix"
        win m append string "Graphics" "&Pie chart" "choose pie"

        win m append popout "Tests" "Test of &mean"
        win m append string "Tests" "Test of &variance" "choose variance"

        win m append string "Test of mean" "&Unequal variances" "CHECK DB_uv"
        win m append separator "Test of mean"
        win m append string "Test of mean" "t-test &by variable" "choose by"
        win m append string "Test of mean" "t-test two &variables" "choose 2var"

        win m set "sysmenu"
end
capture program drop choose
program define choose
        version 7.0
        if "`1'" == "by" | "`1'" == "2var" {
                display as result "`1'" as text " from the menu system"
                if $DB_uv {
                        display as text "  use unequal variances"
                }
                else {
                        display as text "  use equal variances"
                }
        }
        else {
                display as result "`1'" as text " from the menu system"
        }
end
capture program drop myprog1
program define myprog1
        version 7.0
        display as result "myprog1" as text " from the menu system"
end
──────────────────────────────────────────────────── end of lgmenu.do ──────────
```

Running this do-file will define a program `mylgmenu` that we may use to set the menus. Note that the menu items will not run any interesting commands as the focus of the example is in the design of the menu interface only. To see the results, type `mylgmenu` in the Command window after you run the do-file. Below is an explanation of the example.

The command

```
win m append popout "sysmenu" "&Regression"
```

is a popout type menu because it has entries below it. If the user clicks on **Regression**, we will display another menu with items defined by

```
win m append string "Regression" "&Simple" "choose simple"
win m append string "Regression" "&Multiple" "choose multiple"
win m append string "Regression" "Multi&variate" "choose multivariate"
```

Since none of these entries open further menus, they use the `string` version instead of the `popout` version of the `window menu append` command. This part of the menu system appears as

Similarly, the **Graphics** popout menu system is built by first declaring that the **Graphics** menu item should be part of the system menu and that there will be items beneath it. In order to declare that there are further choices, we use the `popout` version of the command

```
win m append popout "sysmenu" "&Graphics"
```

and then populate the menu items below **Graphics** using the `string` version of the `window menu append` command.

```
win m append string "Graphics" "&Scatterplot" "choose scatterplot"
win m append string "Graphics" "&Histogram" "myprog1"
win m append string "Graphics" "Scatterplot &Matrix" "choose matrix"
win m append string "Graphics" "&Pie chart" "choose pie"
```

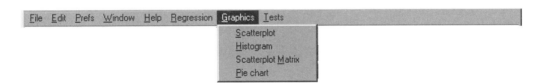

For the **Tests** menu, we decided to have one of the entries be another popout menu for illustration. First we declared the **Tests** menu to be a popout menu from the system menu using

```
win m append popout "sysmenu" "&Tests"
```

We then defined the entries that were to appear below the **Tests** menu. There are two items: one of them is another popout menu and the other is not. For the popout menu, we then defined the entries that are below it.

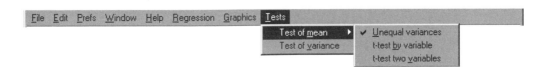

Finally, note how the commands that are run when the user makes a selection from the menu system are defined. For most cases, we simply call the same program and pass an argument that identifies the menu item that was selected. Each menu item may call a different program if you prefer. Also note how the global macro that was associated with the checked menu item is accessed in the programs that are run. When the item is checked the global macro will contain a 1. Otherwise it contains zero. Our program merely has to check the contents of the global macro to see if the item is checked or not.

Also See

Complementary:	[P] **window control**, [P] **window dialog**, [P] **window manage**
Background:	[P] **window**

Title

window push — Copy command into Review window

Syntax

<u>win</u>dow push *command-line*

Description

window push copies the specified *command-line* onto the end of the command history. *command-line* will appear as the most recent command in the #review list, and will appear as the last command in the Review window.

Remarks

window push is useful when one Stata command creates another Stata command and executes it. Normally, commands inside ado-files are not added to the command history. But an ado-file such as a dialog interface to a Stata command might exist solely to create and execute another Stata command.

window push allows the interface to add the created command to the command history (and therefore to the Review window) after executing the command.

▷ Example

```
―――――――――――――――――――――――――――――――― top of example.ado ――――――――
program define example
        version 7.0
        display "This display command is not added to the command history"
        display "This display command is added to the command history"
        window push display "This display command is added to the command history"
end
―――――――――――――――――――――――――――――――― end of example.ado ――――――――
. example
This display command is not added to the command history
This display command is added to the command history

. #review
3
2 example
1 display "This display command is added to the command history"

.
```

◁

Also See

Complementary: [P] **window dialog**,
[R] **#review**

Background: [P] **window**

357

Title

window stopbox — Display message box

Syntax

window <u>stopbox</u> { stop | note | rusure } [*"line 1"* [*"line 2"* [*"line 3"* [*"line 4"*]]]]

Description

window stopbox allows Stata programs to display message boxes. Up to four lines of text may be displayed on a message box.

Remarks

There are three types of message boxes available to Stata programmers. The first is the stop message box. window stopbox stop displays a message box intended for error messages. This type of message box always exits with a return code of 1.

▷ Example

```
. window stopbox stop "You must type a variable name."  "Please try again."
```

```
--Break--
r(1);
```

◁

(Continued on next page)

The second message box is the `note` box. `window stopbox note` displays a message box intended for information messages, or notes. This type of message box always exits with a return code of 0.

▷ Example

```
. window stopbox note "You answered 3 of 4 questions correctly."  "Press OK to continue."
```

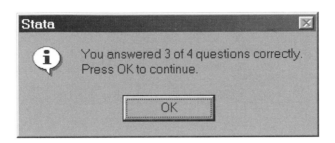

◁

The only way to close the first two types of message boxes is to click the **OK** button displayed at the bottom of the box.

The third message box is the `rusure` (say, "Are you sure?") box. This message box lets a Stata program ask the user a question. The user can close the box by clicking either **OK** or **Cancel**. The message box exits with a return code of 0 if the user clicks **OK** or exits with a return code of 1 if the user clicks **Cancel**.

A Stata program should use the `capture` command to determine whether the user clicked **OK** or Cancel.

▷ Example

```
. capture window stopbox rusure "Do you want to clear the current dataset from memory?"
"Press OK to clear or Cancel to abort."
```

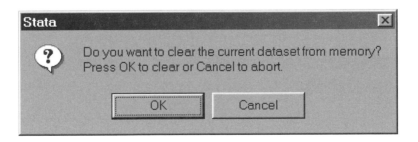

```
. if _rc == 0 { clear }
```

◁

Using the stopbox to warn of illegal input

If you program dialog boxes and wish to validate the user input collected by the dialog, you may warn of invalid input with a stopbox. Here we use `window stopbox` to display an error message if the information collected in the dialog box is not valid.

```
                                                  ─────── top of sampdlg.do ───────
capture program drop sampdlg
program define sampdlg
        version 7.0
        window control static "Please input a number between 0 and 1:" 10 10 40 10
        window control edit 55 10 15 10 DB_num
        window control button "OK" 20 20 10 15 DB_ok
        window control button "Cancel" 40 20 10 15 DB_ca
        global DB_ok "checknum"
        global DB_ca "exit 3000"
        capture noisily window dialog "Sample input check" 10 10 60 40
        if _rc>3000 {
                di "input was ok - can run program based on input"
        }
end

capture program drop checknum
program define checknum
        version 7.0
        capture confirm number $DB_num
        if _rc {
                window stopbox stop "Please input a number"
                exit    /* Do not close dialog */
        }
        if $DB_num < 0 | $DB_num > 1 {
                window stopbox stop "Number not between zero and one"
                exit    /* Do not close dialog */
        }
        exit 3001      /* Input OK, so close dialog */
end
                                                  ─────── end of sampdlg.do ───────
```

Run the `sampdlg.do` file and then type `sampdlg`. Try entering invalid data. If you click on the **Cancel** button, the program will exit, but if you click on the **OK** button, the program will verify that the information is correct. If it is not correct, a stopbox appears and you may try again.

Also See

Complementary: [P] **capture**, [P] **window dialog**

Background: [P] **window**

Author Index

This is the author index for the *Stata Programming Manual*.

Subject Index

This is the subject index for the *Stata Programming Manual*. Readers interested in other topics should see the index in Volume 4 of the *Stata Reference Manual*, or in the *User's Guide*. If interested in graphics, see the index in the *Stata Graphics Manual*.

Semicolons set off the most important entries from the rest. Sometimes no entry will be set off with semicolons; this means all entries are equally important.

W

while command, [P] **while**

White/Huber/sandwich estimator of variance, *see* robust

window control command, [P] **window control**;
    [P] **window**

window dialog command, [P] **window dialog**;
    [P] **window**

window fopen command, [P] **window fopen**;
    [P] **window**

window manage command, [P] **window manage**;
    [P] **window**

window menu command, [P] **window menu**;
    [P] **window**

window push command, [P] **window push**; [P] **window**

window stopbox command, [P] **window stopbox**;
    [P] **window**

Z

zero matrix, [P] **matrix define**